COLONIALISM AND UNDERDEVELOPMENT IN EAST AFRICA

The Politics of Economic Change 1919–1939

Colonialism and Underdevelopment in East Africa

THE POLITICS OF ECONOMIC CHANGE
1919–1939

E. A. BRETT

Lecturer in Political Science
University of Sussex

NOK Publishers, Ltd. · New York

First published
in the United States of America
by NOK Publishers, Ltd.
150 Fifth Avenue
New York, New York 10011

Library of Congress Catalog Card Number 72-97704
International Standard Book Number 0-88357-000-9 (cased)
International Standard Book Number 0-88357-001-7 (paper)

Printed in the United States of America

STUDIES IN EAST AFRICAN SOCIETY AND HISTORY

GENERAL EDITOR:
Professor G. N. Uzoigwe
Department of History, University of Michigan, Ann Arbor

The interrelatedness of the various aspects of African Studies is not always emphasized. This unique series—the first to have an inter-disciplinary orientation—covers a wide range of materials for students of East African society and history. As it encompasses works in history, politics, anthropology, sociology, economics, religion, law, education and literature, it affords a welcome outlet for the growing and diversified researches being carried out in East Africa by scholars of different persuasions. . .Each book is independent; together they will comprise the richest literature in East African Studies.

G. N. Uzoigwe

NOK Publishers, Ltd. · New York

For Amelia

Preface

This work is an attempt to explore the nature of the connection between colonialism and underdevelopment. Colonialism is a system of rule which assumes the right of one people to impose their will upon another. This must inevitably lead to a situation of dominance and dependency which will systematically subordinate those governed by it to the imported culture in social, economic and political life. By the end of the nineteenth century Europe and Africa confronted each other in respective states of development and undevelopment, the latter term being defined by Europeans in relation to the lack of African progress in the techniques required to sustain an advanced materialistic culture. Whatever one's feelings about the relative philosophical merits of the two styles of life, there is no doubt that the apparatus of Western culture was infinitely superior to that of Africa in subjecting others to its will. Its control over the scientific revolution and its products in the fields of warfare, administration and economic production enabled it to 'discover' the world beyond its own, to conquer this and divide it up between the leading European nations. In the face of such odds African opposition was quickly overcome and unequal relations between the two forces were regularized through the creation of the colonial system, which rapidly transformed the undevelopment of African society into the underdevelopment of colonial society.

These two terms are used extensively in the current literature, though often without any very precise indication of what they mean. An attempt will be made to outline my own assumptions in the Introduction; here it is only necessary to say that the work as a whole attempts to use the data drawn from a particular historical case as the empirical basis for an examination of the connections between metropolis and colony in the twentieth century and of their impact upon the change process in the underdeveloped world. The work makes none of the usual distinctions between political and economic variables, but is concerned to look at the total process of change in the structures of production in Africa as these were mediated by the dominant institutions of the metropolis. I am well aware of the scale of this task, and of my own limitations with respect to its resolution. But I am utterly convinced of the necessity of this mode of proceeding in the social sciences and therefore present the results as at least a preliminary attempt to come to terms with the theoretical and practical difficulties involved. The end-result can be seen as part history, part economics and part political science; I prefer to regard it as an untutored contribution to the old tradition of political economy and more especially to its Marxist variant.

This work has been with me now for more than ten years. The original research was completed in 1965 and presented as a Ph.D. dissertation to London University in 1966.[1] At that stage documentation was confined to private correspondence, personal interviews with some of the actors involved, and the public record. My debt to all those who allowed me the use of either their papers or their time is very considerable since the exercise would have been impossible without them. My revision of the original manuscript – which has produced a wholly new Introduction and conclusions, extensively modified overall structure, and a revision of all the substantive chapters – was undertaken from about 1968. During this time I was able to look at the Cabinet Papers from 1919 to 1927, but not to make any use of the Colonial Office Papers themselves. This omission, is, of course, the major weakness of the work and all my judgements must be considered in the light of my inability to test them against the full official record. The extensiveness of this revision was only partially imposed upon me by access to additional information. The Cabinet Papers for the early years of my period did not require any changes in my overall emphasis or interpretation, they only clarified and dated more accurately the origins of the evolution of British aid policy. The published record had made it clear that this had begun with the unemployment induced by the depression of the early twenties; the private record showed how direct the relationship was between these two things, and made it possible to trace in some detail the steps taken to modify colonial policy in the light of the demands created by British unemployment. Chapter 4 was extensively modified in the light of this information: the subsequent alterations stemmed from the changed perspectives induced by the evolution of the theoretical debate relating to the whole issue of the relationships between development and colonial dominance over the last five years.

The original trajectory of my research was derived from certain very vaguely formulated assumptions about the necessary connection between colonial economic development and public policy. It was, perhaps, an attempt to test Hobson's thesis of the economic origins of this policy in the light of the then (late fifties, early sixties) British Government's evident willingness to transfer formal political control to the African nationalist movements throughout the continent. I was concerned to examine the earlier development of economic policy in colonial Africa in order to arrive at some sort of understanding of how this related to the necessity for and the nature of political control. This orientation involved a detailed examination of the political debate over colonial economic policy in the inter-war period and required an attempt to assess the concrete impact of these policies, since this in turn determined the context for subsequent stages of the debate up to and including the final decision that formal control could be transferred.

The results of this work produced the substantive chapters of my thesis, and the lapse of time has only led me to change their emphasis and not their focus or content since the original orientation still seems to hold.

But this empirical work was set into a very limited and, in some ways, a very conservative general theoretical context. In London I worked in the general ethos of the Institute of Commonwealth Studies where the tendency in Colonial History was towards a thorough empiricism in a framework which did not question the overall validity of Britain's colonial contribution to African development except where extensive settlement had been allowed. This environment certainly encouraged me to take at face value a great deal in the material which I was given and did not lead me to make any serious attempt to relate it to the broader questions of colonialism and underdevelopment which have now forced themselves into the centre of all serious work in this general field. This conservative tendency was, if anything, strengthened by my years in Uganda, when the dominance of the colonial history tradition à la Hancock was replaced by that of the then dominant behavioural tradition in Political Science; a tradition to which I had originally been exposed in South Africa, where I had come to the conclusion that the main methodological problems could be resolved through the use of pressure-group analysis in the style of

Arthur Bentley and David Truman. The cumulative impact of these tendencies can be seen in the general assessment of the over-all impact of the colonial experience of the local society presented in the original thesis.

But the end of 1966 introduced a more radical perspective into the work going on in East Africa, notably through the contributions of Richard Sklar and John Saul. In England it was quickly evident that the behavioural tendency in modernization theory was coming under heavy attack from the Left, both because of the emergence of a new generation of intellectuals and more especially because of a growing awareness of the deepening crisis in the Third World, as the earlier optimistic assumptions about rapid progress were disappointed by events. Discussions with colleagues and especially with graduate students intensified my earlier reservations and led to an attempt at a re-evaluation of my earlier assumptions about developmental theory, which produced the new Introduction to this book – recently published in *Cahiers d'Etudes Africaines*,[2] and slightly modified yet again here – and to a general reassessment of the overall conclusions of the original work. The evidence derived from Britain in East Africa is, obviously, only a particular case of the operation of the colonial system and does not provide a basis for all-encompassing generalizations; but if this approach is a valid one it should provide the basis for comparison with other areas and ultimately for an attempt to formulate a general theory which will be far more widely applicable.

NOTES

1. *Development Policy in East Africa Between the Wars: a study of the Political Influences involved in the Making of British Policy – 1919–1939.*
2. 'Dependency and Development: some problems involved in the analysis of change in Colonial Africa' *Cahiers*, Vol. XI. (44), 4ᵉ Cahier, MCMLXXI.

*　　*　　*

Over the years more people have made a major contribution to this enterprise than can possibly be acknowledged here. The list of private papers found in the bibliography is the outcome of the generosity of the individuals concerned or of their trustees; perhaps a special word of thanks should go to the Joint East Africa Board, where Mr Philip Broadbent and Lord Colyton gave me access to what constitutes a primary source for any examination of Britian's role in Eastern and Central Africa. My work was greatly assisted by the intellectual and financial resources of several institutions over this period – the London School of Economics, the Institute of Commonwealth Studies, London, Makerere University in Uganda, and Sussex University. Finally, I am especially indebted to Kenneth Robinson, my supervisor, to John Lonsdale and Ralph Austen for access to their own notes, and to a wide variety of people for comments on the text at various stages, in particular Cyril Ehrlich, Geoffrey Engholm, Morris Jones, Lucy Mair, Michael McWilliam, John Ballard, Raymond Apthorpe, Martin Legassick, Andrea Hopkinson and Theo Mars.

E. A. Brett
Sussex 1972

Contents

Tables

Introduction

Development and Dependency in Colonial Africa

Control over advanced mechanical and social technology[1] enabled the West to extend an empire over most of the world by the end of the nineteenth century. Its demands broke open old societies. Soldiers and administrators had to be paid, commerce to make profits, railways to carry produce, and missionaries provided with converts to literate religions. As capital, administration and Church followed the explorers and soldiers, functioning colonies emerged controlled by light-skinned people with an absolute faith in the superiority of their culture and of their corresponding right to rule the dark-skinned inhabitants.

This process initiated a continuing revolution of many phases, many styles and many implications. External dominance and internal dependence created a situation which inevitably 'transformed the entire social fabric of the people whose countries are now underdeveloped.'[2] Export-oriented economies had to be created,[3] traditional social structures modified and existing political authorities made to accept their subordination to the foreign invader. This occurred as surely under systems of indirect rule as under direct rule. In the latter no real attempt was made to reduce the impact of the new forces upon existing structures; in the former they generally conflicted with, and undermined, traditional practice. 'To the extent that chiefs were able to assimilate the bureaucratic norms established by the central government, they became alienated from their subjects.'[4] Equally significant, these changes in social, economic and political structures meant the emergence of new social forces in indigenous society whose interests could be expected to conflict on many levels with those of both the colonial and traditional élites. Although it may have dragged 'individuals and peoples through blood and dirt, through misery and degradation'[5] in the process, imperialism in Africa as in Asia began to fulfil a 'double mission . . . one destructive, the other regenerating – the annihilation of old Asiatic society, and the laying of the material foundations of Western society in Asia.'[6]

The revolution is everywhere incomplete. Few would argue with any confidence that many parts of the Third World have entirely escaped the condition of underdevelopment which Marx observed in India more than a century ago. Change is inevitable and the possibility of emancipation now exists. But there is no guarantee that change will take progressive forms, or that it will benefit all people equally when it occurs. Social scientists have tended to take an optimistic view and assume that change must take positive forms (hence the general use of terms like 'development' and 'modernization'), but there is no special reason for this and many to lead us to the opposite conclusion. For some countries and for some groups within all countries, the conditions in which they find themselves will admit of nothing but stagnation or regression. Countries unable to establish an autonomous control over their own developmental resources, and groups whose economic base must be undermined by technological innovation, can expect no coming advantage and cannot therefore be expected to participate positively in the change process. In the West we expect politics to be characterized by conflict in the metropolitan centres, but we know that this will be mitigated by our wealth and by the degree to which our institutions have been adapted to meet the needs of advanced technological society. In Africa and Asia we can make no such assumptions:

> The age of technology makes questionable what we live by; it uproots us, and it does so all around the globe. And to the great Asian cultures it does so more violently, since they lack the transitional period in which the West was producing the technological world – a world that now, finished and overpowering, engulfs people whom their past culture has neither prepared for nor disposed towards it.[7]

During the early period of Western industrialization social conflict was intense and brutal. Nothing else can be expected in the Third World. Favourable circumstances might mitigate the level of dislocation but it would be unreal to assume that change will occur without it. But it should be noted that while conflict is an inescapable condition of change, all conflict will not necessarily lead to progressive change. It would be as mistaken to hope for change that did not threaten existing beliefs, interests and institutions, as to assume that any attack on them will invariably lead to real social improvement. To improve reality we must understand it, we must understand in particular the way in which the action of actual social institutions impinges on a social situation and tends to advance or retard the development of the society concerned.

This study starts from the assumption that these processes must be studied historically, since present opportunities are determined by past decisions and man's capacity to act must be assessed in relation to real rather than experimentally created conditions.[8] We must therefore seek in our historical experience the variables which influenced particular processes of development or regression in order to understand both the situation of present generations and the way in which past generations handled problems in the same sphere. To do this we require a definition or 'type concept'[9] of sufficient precision to ensure that we are talking about the same thing when we move from different stages of the past to the present and on into projections of the future.

Traditional political science has been largely concerned with problems associated with some more or less precisely defined notion of 'democracy', but 'development' (or 'modernization', its equivalent) relates to much wider issues about which it is far more difficult to speak precisely. In isolation the word implies change and progress; it tells us nothing about how we are to recognize change or what is to constitute progress. It is an essentially evaluative term and is widely used as such to justify the actions of virtually everyone working in the Third World. We are all developers now. But the presence or absence of the terms does not, of course, tell us anything about the presence or absence of the phenomenon. Many 'developers' do little more than develop their family fortunes; many illiterates who have never heard the term in fact work almost continuously for development. To provide a basis for comparison, evaluation and prediction, our definition must provide objective criteria against which intentions and actions can be measured quite independently of the perceptions of the actors concerned.

Development or modernization is seen in much of the contemporary Western academic literature as 'the process of change towards those types of social, economic and political systems that have developed in Western Europe and North America from the seventeenth century to the nineteenth and have then spread to other European countries and in the nineteenth and twentieth centuries to the South American, Asian and African continents.'[10] Knowledge of 'Western complex systems'[11] is thus said to provide a basis from which a model or ideal type of developed society can be derived, and this is then juxtaposed against one of traditional or underdeveloped society drawn from anthropological accounts of small-scale and isolated non-Western communities. The resulting image of developed society is characterized by structures which are, for example, highly differentiated, organically integrated and very productive, and by behaviour conditioned by universalistic, achievement and specific norms. Traditional societies on the other hand have undifferentiated, mechanically integrated and unproductive structures and behaviour conditioned by particularistic, ascriptive and diffuse norms.[12] Particular societies can then be located on this continuum between traditional and modern through the formulation of social and economic indicators such as urbanization, industrialization and literacy, which enable apparently precise measurements to be made. This procedure has been most effectively developed in economics, where national income accounting, which equates growth in G.N.P. with development, now has some place in the activities of virtually every central bureaucracy in the world. The assumptions which this model makes about any developmental process are necessarily accompanied by others about the way in which it is most likely to occur. These may include elaborate stage models like that developed by W. W. Rostow,[13] they may also assume that modernity will be transferred from developed to developing countries in some preordained and inevitable way.[14] These questions relating to processes are, of course, critical to any analysis of the relationship between advanced colonial powers and backward colonial territories, and must be examined in some detail here. Before doing this, however, it is necessary to look more closely at the philosophical implications of the terms which define the continuum between the two polar types.

This continuum must first be recognized as being predominantly normative in its derivation and use. Although it is argued that these constructs are 'empirical generalizations'[15] derived directly from observations of reality rather than from the observers' subjective value system, this claim does not hold up under examination. They are not (and could not be) derived from the observation of all advanced or traditional societies or of all aspects of behaviour in the societies which are so chosen, but are deliberately and systematically selective. The image of 'Western complex society' tends to be based upon experience in the functioning democracies, notably in their Anglo-American version. On the other hand the image leaves out or treats as aberrations societies like Nazi Germany, which were undoubtedly Western and complex but hardly conformed to supposedly universal modern norms in much of their public and private behaviour. Again, it can be shown that behaviour even in the most 'advanced' democracies is as much governed by 'traditional' as by 'modern' norms. The ideal types represent dominant beliefs (held both by actors in the society and by academic observers) about how people ought to behave, or are used as myths to rationalize behaviour after the event.[16] The critics assess actual behaviour in these societies very differently from the Parsonian school. While Talcott Parsons might see the technique and style of Europe in terms of a universalistic ethic and achieved status, Fanon finds in it 'only a succession of negations of man and an avalanche of murders',[17] and no one can deny that Western complex systems number Auschwitz, Hiroshima and Vietnam among their achievements. This means that the ideal type of developed society is not derived from any simple observation of the facts (or 'empirical reality') of Anglo-American society, but that the characteristics taken to indicate advancement are derived from a logically prior value-system which determines what the observer is to see and count and what he is to ignore. The same considerations apply to the characteristics allocated by the model to traditional society. Such societies also manifest a much wider range of structural characteristics than could ever be included in a single theoretical construct, while those assigned to 'traditional man' often appear to have been derived from little more than the desire by colonial administrators and their academic advisers to explain failures to 'adapt to modernity'.[18] In fact where the structure of opportunity has permitted it, supposedly traditional people have often adapted very quickly and struck observers with the 'modernity' of their characteristics.

The argument can be taken even further. Similar difficulties would arise even if the model of developed society could be shown to be derived from purely empirical observation of behaviour in such societies, and if no similar forms of behaviour could be observed in traditional society. The use of ideal types derived from 'Western complex systems' as a measuring-rod against which to determine progress (another equivalent for 'development') in other systems is to imply a normative preference for the kind of existence found in such societies. Other societies have existed which have considered themselves to be highly advanced, and have measured their own advancement and other peoples' backwardness against quite other qualities and achievements than we use now – for example in relation to religious purity, military excellence, artistic refinement, and so on. The decision to use the Western model of development in preference to any of these is easily understandable, but must be recognized for what it is – a normative, not an empirical, judgement. But since I believe that all social scientific models are normatively based, this fact alone does not necessarily detract in any important way from the use of the Western model of development as the basis for an analysis. An effective critique of such models should not confine itself to an exposure of unstated normative assumptions, but must also show that these are inappropriate or contradictory, or that implementation is impossible because of the nature of existing circumstances. Equally important, any critique of this kind must be followed by the development of alternatives which are theoretically tenable and empirically valid in the sense that they suggest policies which can be effectively implemented. The nature of the relationship between values and empirical observation is one of the most confused areas in the present confusion which characterizes the social sciences in the development field. In order to make at least my own position clear it is therefore essential to outline it very briefly before examining the methodology which has determined my approach to the material.

Analysis presupposes normative assumptions which determine the choice of subject, the selection of evidence and the criteria against which outcomes are assessed. Ideal types or models embody these assumptions and at the same time relate them to the social facts under observation. They are hypothetical statements about processes;[20] idealized descriptions of the 'forms of action'[21] involved in the functioning of particular institutions. Social science is not concerned with abstract systems of normative assumptions for their own sake, but with their relation to the concrete activities in which they are manifested as an integral part of social life. Although values cannot be derived from facts they can only be meaningfully considered in relation to facts; that is in relation to social action. Thus the ideal type is not an arbitrary or purely subjective construct, but is based upon a critical evaluation of reality; it is a statement not of how an institution operates, but of how it ought to operate to achieve the full potentiality intimated by its structures and objectives. Adam Smith, Max Weber and J. S. Mill had no experience of a 'free competitive market', an 'impersonal bureaucracy' or a 'representative democracy' before they formulated these concepts. But their constructs were not simply invented but derived from the observation of actual economies, bureaucracies or democracies, which, while they did not conform to the ideal in every respect, did do so in part and seemed to derive their efficacy from the extent to which they did so. The value of the model thus lies in its ability to demonstrate the difference between the actual and potential achievements inherent in the operation of a given institution.

But the fact that our view of reality is conditioned by normative assumptions does not imply that there can be no distinction between facts and values, or that perceptions are simply a function of 'subjective valuations'.[22] Although this ability varies, everyone distinguishes on some level between evaluations and perceptions of reality. For social scientists the problem is more complex since they:

> . . . in fact concern themselves with three different kinds or levels of data; (i) 'what actually happens', (ii) what people think happens, (iii) what they think ought to happen, their legal and moral values.[23]

Although there is no doubt that valuations (and, indeed, the whole structure of the personality) strongly influence perception, it is equally true that individuals with very different values can be made to agree on some of the facts in a given situation, although they will differ with regard to their moral implications. And this is also true for the social scientist who is attempting to understand the whole situation, but he must also take into account the fact that his perspective will differ from that of any of the actors concerned. Beattie cites Lévi-Strauss in asserting that 'what actually happens' is itself a 'construct of the analyst' and 'not necessarily that of the people studied.'[24] And this construct, too, will have a factual and an evaluative component, both of which will be related to those of the actors but not directly derived from them. The observer will therefore need to be able to separate four components in his mind – his own values and his perceptions of reality, and the values and the perceptions of the actors he is observing. His ability to deal 'objectively' with his subject-matter will be derived from an ability on the one hand to avoid bias[25] in his use of evidence, and on the other to identify and understand the implications of his own values, to 'bring them out in the open and put them in order.'[26]

The desire to create a 'value-free social science' derives from the misleading assumption that 'there are no values in the objective sense, only subjective valuations';[27] that while it is possible to talk objectively about facts, values are 'merely subjective' and not amenable to rational discussion. But this view is both theoretically untenable and likely to produce its own particular form of bias. Social science is a 'science of persons' and therefore concerned with qualitatively different problems from those of natural science, which is a 'science of things'.[28] The study of persons must differ from the study of things because social scientists are people and not things. To attempt to be objective by attempting to depersonalize social relations (for example by considering them simply as interacting sets of roles) must lead to reificiation and 'false knowledge'. As Laing says:

> It is unfortunate that personal and subjective are words so abused as to have no power to convey a genuine act of seeing the other as person [sic] . . . but imply immediately that one is merging one's own failings and attitudes into one's study of the other in such a way as to distort our perception of him. In contrast to the reputable 'objective' or 'scientific', we have the disreputable 'subjective', 'intuitive', or, worst of all, 'mystical'. It is interesting, for example, that one frequently encounters 'merely' before subjective, whereas it is almost inconceivable to speak of anyone being 'merely' objective.[29]

The social scientist derives his understanding of man from the fact that he is a man:

> And though by men's actions we do discover their designe sometimes: yet to do it without comparing them with our own, and distinguishing all circumstances, by which the case may come to be altered, is to decypher without a key, and be for the most part deceived, by too much trust, or by too much diffidence; as he that reads, is himself a good or evil man.[30]

But beyond this, the assumption that values are merely subjective is derived from an untenable distinction between the individual and his social situation. Values are not invented by individuals (social scientists or otherwise) but derived from their position in a historically determined social structure; by their relationship to the traditions of activity evolved in that society, and more especially to those relating to the activity of people of their status and function.[31] The important thing about the social scientist in our society is that he is expected to distinguish his own position from that of the actors he observes. He is supposed to be free to hold any opinions he chooses, he has access to a developed historical tradition of knowledge in his subject and to comparative evidence from a variety of cultures; his economic interests should not depend on the outcome of the conflicts which he is studying in the same way as those of the actors concerned. He is neither capitalist nor worker, politician nor voter, chief nor peasant, and should therefore be able to see their situation more objectively than they. But he, like each of them, is a member of society and concerned ultimately with some notion of the 'public interest' against which everyone must ultimately attempt to measure his actions.

While the observer's model may not be understood by the actors because 'actual action goes on in a state of inarticulate half-consciousness or actual unconsciousness of its subjective meaning',[32] it should not include knowledge which differs in kind from theirs. What it should do is incorporate all their knowledge and raise this to a higher level of generality. In doing so it should expand their level of consciousness and enable them to see the world anew, 'as if suddenly awakened in a house with which they had only supposed themselves to be familiar.'[33] In fact it will usually be found that the observer tends to identify the public interest with that of particular groups or strata in society, and to derive his evaluative assumptions from theirs. Adam Smith spoke for the rising bourgeoisie, Marx for the proletariat; many developmentalists accept the objectives and perspectives of the new political and technological élites. If we accept this, then there is no point in rejecting particular models simply because they have a normative component; their value will depend upon their content, the social interest with which they tend to identify, their ability to explain observed phenomena, and the implication of their use for the course of future social action.

All this suggests that our models of society must ultimately have prescriptive and hence political implications. They are to be seen as arguments in favour of particular courses of action based upon assumptions about the ultimate nature of human needs and empirical observation of the effects of past actions upon subsequent situations. Taken together theory and experience make it possible for us to increase our ability to predict outcomes of changes in behaviour. The objective value of such formulations will be determined by the ease with which significant social groups are able to identify with their objectives, accept their explanations and implement their recommendations. The objective importance of the model of the free market system was derived not from some overriding system of natural law, as Smith assumed, but from the political power of the social strata which identified with it. Once they had achieved predominance, MacPherson argues, 'no individual in it could escape from it, and hence all rational men had to accept the market concept of justice as the only one'.[34] The Third World is still searching for a model of development which will provide the intellectual basis for the mobilization of their populations for an effective programme of national development.

Before ending this digression one further point must be made. The great theoretical models which have served to expand man's consciousness and direct social action were normatively based and produced action which tended to strengthen the position of some classes and undermine that of others. Yet these models characteristically attempt to make universalistic and evolutionary claims for themselves. They are presented in terms of some absolute system of values and often assume that the action which they recommend must invariably take place because of the conditions inherent in the state of society. Thus Veblen shows how Smith assumed 'a wholesome trend in the natural course of things', which would lead inevitably to a situation which approximated to his ideal;[35] while Marxism assumes the inevitable victory of the proletariat. But of course the actual creation of the free market system depended on the decisions of men, and MacPherson probably overstates the degree to which the assumptions which it incorporated were generally accepted even in the eighteenth and nineteenth centuries. The achievement of this kind of society depended upon the political predominance of the classes which believed in it, and was not attained in the many areas where this predominance could not be established.[36] Thus great care must be taken not to attribute too much to the model; the mere fact that it provides criteria against which rationality can be measured does not in any way presuppose the 'actual predominance of rational elements in human life',[37] for that will depend upon the conjunction of political and social forces in the community concerned. These optimistic evolutionary assumptions have exerted a powerful influence over development studies (we talk incessantly of growth rates, for example, but never of 'regression rates') and should be resisted. The fact that we know what development is, does not mean that we will be able to persuade the politically powerful to agree with us, or that they will be able to take the recommended action if we do.

This suggests that the formulation of models is not merely an academic exercise but critical to the way we see the world and directly relevant to any political action we might take to change it.

And the most inclusive model is that of development, which must provide images that can be used to interpret the results of any specific process of historical change and to provide alternative programmes and policies, which can be put into effect and will then 'terminate with social change'.[38] We must now ask whether the Third World can be expected to use models of development derived from knowledge of 'Western complex systems' for this purpose, and are immediately faced by an intense contradiction. Can the Western ideal be used like this by peoples whose contact with the West has taken the form of conquest, enslavement and subjection to various forms of social, economic and political subordination for four hundred years or more? Europe created the enlightenment at home while its subjects extracted the wealth of the tropics by murder, torture and deceit. As a result Europe is often seen as the builder of underdevelopment, not development,[39] the imitation of European models an invitation to 'mortifying setbacks', not the key to progress.[40] And these facts cannot be isolated from the work of academic model-builders because the achievements of Western social thought have been as potent an instrument of control as its military and industrial technology. Western culture, dominated by the scientific approach in this sphere as in many others, has claimed and enforced a general superiority 'to any and all other systems of civilised life'.[41] Whatever his past achievements, colonized man was made to learn the colonial culture, to study the histories of Europe and not his own because he was told that there was 'no African history to teach . . . only the history of Europeans in Africa'.[42] And there can be little doubt that these assumptions were widely accepted; this cultural dominance created a 'dependency complex'[43] which led many colonial peoples to accept the 'characteristics assigned to them by the dominant group'.[44] To the extent that they did so they denied themselves the possibility of liberation; instead of resisting they manned the armies and carried the guns which maintained the colonial system.[45] If the acceptance of Western assumptions and of the associated political and economic linkages with the West was the source of their powerlessness, how can a theory based upon the need to imitate Western achievements serve to free them from their underdevelopment?

The contradiction can be clarified by looking at the contrasting positions being advanced in the contemporary intellectual debate. The Parsonian tradition, which essentially identified with the interests of Western capitalism and hence with the dominant elements in the power structures of the Third World, takes an essentially optimistic view of the nature of the relationship between the developed and the underdeveloped world. Since the Western model is the goal, and since capitalism is not seen as an essentially exploitative system, they see progress or development coming from any increase in contact which will tend to diffuse 'knowledge, skills, organisation, values, technology and capital to a poor nation, until over time, its society, culture and personnel become variants of that which made the Atlantic community economically successful.'[46] At the other extreme, Frank sees the relationship as a form of latter-day imperialism in which developed metropolis and underdeveloped satellite exist in a single system of purely exploitative political and economic control. This single system of capitalistic relationships has its headquarters in the leading metropolitan capitals of Europe and the United States and these are linked to the underdeveloped periphery through a series of satellites, each one of which serves to extract the economic surplus from those below it and to transmit some part thereof to those above it in the international hierarchy. Contact with the metropolis does not diffuse advanced techniques but serves to intensify underdevelopment and increase the size of the surplus removed:

> In the metropolis–periphery relationship of each of these levels, as in that of the international one which engulfs them all, the metropolis sucks capital out of the periphery and uses its power to maintain the economic, political, social and cultural structure of the periphery and its peripheral metropoles and therewith to maintain as long as possible the capitalist imperialist system which permits this exploitation. The essential internal contradiction of the capitalist system as a whole, while permitting the relative development of some, thus produces and maintains the underdevelopment of others on the international, national, regional, sectorial, and local levels.[47]

This, then, means that development can only occur, not by increasing the intensity of the contact with the developed centres through trade, aid, etc., but by an escape out of the whole capitalist system itself, a 'socialist escape from the capitalist structure which necessarily produces and maintains that underdevelopment'.[48]

Between these two positions lies the view of Marx himself set out in his articles on India already quoted, and that of Mao Tse-tung, whose assessment of the ambiguity of the impact of imperialism is strikingly similar:

. . . by penetrating into China the imperialist powers have on the one hand accelerated the disintegration of China's feudal society, caused factors of capitalism to emerge in China and transformed the feudal society into a semi-feudal one, and on the other hand imposed their ruthless rule on China and reduced an independent China into a semi-colonial and colonial China.[49]

Capitalism is seen in this analysis as a force with two faces. On the one hand it ruthlessly destroys the independence and self-sufficiency of non-Western societies in the search for profits; on the other, by doing so it acts as the 'unconscious tool of history' by introducing them to the most advanced social and material culture in the world, which the dominance of feudal institutions had previously excluded from them. They would essentially agree with Jaspers that the European heritage:

. . . is valid of itself, independently of its origin. It is not a unique culture but the property of man as such, of man as a rational being. It is identically transferable. Where it has once been acquired, it can, with more or less talent, be cultivated – whether for mere use, for participation in further scientific research, or for technical inventions. The necessary talent is no basic trait or permanent condition of nations.[50]

Given these assumptions, those who take the middle position must accept that development cannot occur without some degree of contact with the metropolitan centres (which now, of course, also include the non-Western regions of Japan and China); on the other hand they must also argue that autonomous and hence continuous development will only occur when the periphery can establish exchange relations with these centres, which do not tie it into a system of dependency likely to perpetuate the under-development created by complete subordination to the dominant institutions of international capitalism.

If one accepts this basic position, as I do, it becomes clear that there is no easy solution to the contradiction between the negative impact of Western dominance upon progress of the Third World, and that world's need to make at least some use of the social and mechanical technology developed in the advanced centres to overcome its existing condition of underdevelopment. Much of the contemporary pessimism about the future of the Third World derives from the recognition of the obstacles to the establishment of the political and the intellectual base for a developmental strategy capable of both sustaining the independence of indigenous economic and political structures and maintaining the links with the developed world required to sustain the technological advance needed to liberate the mass of the world's population from poverty, dependence and disease. Yet this will only occur when a way has been found to acquire what is valuable in the Western tradition without sacrificing the ability to resist foreign dominance in the political, economic and cultural spheres.[51] Indeed, the ability to resist dominance will depend upon the ability of Third World countries to gain control of at least some of the techniques which could otherwise be used to control them.[52] But the ability to do this will result not simply from the wish but from the nature of the particular configurations of political, economic and social forces which control policy at the national and international levels. Many Third World countries are dominated by indigenous and external forces whose interests are opposed to modernization – until their power is broken no change will take place.[53] But even where positive change is politically possible it will only occur when certain intellectual conditions are met. Good intentions are not sufficient; they must be backed by an adequate 'critical theory of society'[54] which takes full account of the productive potential created for the world by Western experience, which relates this to the contemporary conditions of Third World societies, and which can make an effective appeal to social groups in those societies capable of using it to take control of the dominant institutions and use them to promote development.

Theoretical adequacy must be achieved on two levels. Firstly, it must involve a genuine understanding of the Western tradition, and more especially, of the critical or negative elements in that tradition. This tradition is no monolithic structure, but had developed through its ability to maintain 'the power of negative thinking – the critical power of Reason'.[55] We can broadly distinguish two general tendencies in modern social thought. One is the behavioural school, which makes use of structural–functional categories, with Parsons as a key modern source and Almond and Easton its leading exponents in Political Science. This school is primarily concerned with problems relating to the stability, persistence or maintenance of given systems,[56] and it uses the concept of a 'stable equilibrium' as 'a defining characteristic of structure'.[57] With this starting-point 'all categories terminate in the existing order',[58] since systems must be evaluated in relation to their ability to adjust or adapt, rather than to change in any revolutionary way. The best that can be hoped for is a consideration of the possibility of a 'moving equilibrium', a dubious concept when one considers the need for radical transformation facing the countries of the Third World. The acceptance of this equilibrium model tends to reduce the ability to criticize the structure of power which has determined both the present and the past relationship between the colonial and colonized peoples; it serves to perpetuate their dependence and subordination. Its theoretical inadequacy and dangerous practical implication are clearly exposed in Frank's article already cited.[59] But while it is relatively easy to reject these formulations, it is less easy to produce a coherent alternative which will lead to an effective programme of action. The basis for such an alternative must be sought in the intellectual traditions which start from conflict assumptions, and which are committed to the need to restructure rather than maintain the existing order. It is no accident that the theories which have most readily been taken over from the West by Third World theorists derive from this radical tradition, for example the Marxism of Lenin and Mao Tse-tung and the revolutionary humanism of Fanon. These theories incorporate an understanding of the Western achievement, but start from the assumption that Western dominance must be destroyed before true liberation can occur; both of these elements must be present in some form before effective action can be taken.

Secondly, Western models can only provide a point of reference, they cannot be transplanted unmodified from one society to another. Therefore societies wishing to make use of Western experience and technology will only be able to do so if they themselves have an adequate theoretical grasp of their own situation – of their needs and resources, and the possibilities for the mobilization of their own populations. The mere existence of a body of advanced technical knowledge in the outside world does not provide any basis for advancement even where the foreign exchange is available to acquire the physical assets required to set it up locally. The new technology will make a positive contribution only where it is relevant to local needs and can be adapted to suit local conditions. This is as true of welfare-oriented institutions like modern hospitals[60] as it is of economic and political arrangements. The technical knowledge which creates the ability to run machines or heal diseases must be accompanied by 'practical knowledge'[61] of the circumstances of time and place which will enable them to be utilized with greatest benefit. This means that the understanding of Western modes must be backed by an equally profound understanding of the nature of developing societies – unless this occurs the result will be the creation of expensive but useless monuments to Western technology. Carried out in this way the adoption of Western models is not an imitative and dependent activity; it is a creative process which must ultimately result in the evolution of new social forms and autonomous modes of thought. When this is achieved the West in turn will come to the Third World for models, witness even now the influence of Gandhi, Mao and Guevara on contemporary European thinking.

Any colonial history, if it is to transcend 'the horizon of the existing social order',[62] should start from a theoretical position which refuses to accept the actions of the dominant colonial classes at their own evaluation, but does not induce an uncritical rejection of the achievements of the period, since these, however inadequate, must provide the foundations for the next generation. Bearing this in mind, it is now possible to examine the normative assumptions which together serve to define the way in which the term 'development' is to be used in the rest of this work in relation to the analysis of the general process of social change. In this regard I am primarily concerned with three aspects of change – those relating to the structure and size of economic production, the nature of the distribution of the social product, and the location of control over social processes. These concerns embody a set of related normative assumptions – that production be maximized, distribution equalized, and control decentralized. The issues raised by these assumptions can be discussed in relation to the corresponding analytical categories – growth, equity and autonomy.

'Growth', however difficult to measure,[63] will be used in the sense familiar in the literature on economic development. It will be taken to relate primarily to growth in the monetary economy and therefore to the introduction of modern technology and the expansion of production for the market. The structure of the subsistence sector, important as it is, will be neglected on the assumption that this did not constitute a major dynamic factor in the change process. Most economic analysis has tended to focus exclusively upon the analysis of growth, and to ask few questions about the distribution of its benefits. But such questions are critical for an analysis which does not see development purely in economic terms. Ethically it is possible to argue that economic growth is of little value where its benefits are appropriated by a small minority. This means that distribution must be judged in relation to its equity – its tendency to equate performance with reward. It appears to be necessary to accept quite large inequalities in rewards, especially during periods of rapid growth (even Marx accepted that 'the cry for an *equality of wages* rests . . . upon an absurd mistake')[64] but it should be possible, however roughly, to determine whether particular inequalities are in fact 'necessitated by genuine social needs, technical requirements, and the physical and mental differences among . . . individuals.'[65] Structurally the nature of the distribution of the social product is critical because it exerts a fundamental influence upon the process of social and political change. A process of cumulative causation can be shown to operate in these matters;[66] those classes which are able to appropriate the bulk of the surplus will, by so doing, increase their ability to influence the future structure of production and the institutions of social and political control; those who cannot will find their influence progressively reduced. These processes of upward and downward mobility, resulting in class formation and social control, operate in all societies, but are very visible and of critical importance in societies undergoing radical transformation of the kind induced by colonial penetration.

'Autonomy' is used here to incorporate the wide range of assumptions implied by words such as independence, freedom and participation.[67] It defines a particular kind of exchange relationship, one in which complete equality prevails; in an autonomous situation neither party can impose its will upon the other. Its polar opposite is one of dependency, in which one party determines the situation for the other – in this case the pure colonial situation. The use of this term raises a wide range of implications. Firstly, it must be positively defined; it does not simply imply the absence of 'overwhelming concentrations of power'[68] of the liberal tradition, but suggests the ability of any individual, group or state to act independently in a given situation because of an ability to control the techniques which structure that situation. An illiterate has no autonomy with regard to a trained bureaucrat or trader because he cannot understand their environments, yet depends upon the services they provide. This means that autonomy must be related to a given level of social and mechanical technology.[69] Colonial populations were autonomous with regard to their pre-colonial structures but dependent upon colonial structures which were imposed upon them and which depended upon skills which they had not acquired. This condition will only end when they have assimilated enough of these skills to become 'truly masters of all the material means which make possible the radical transformation of society'.[70] Secondly, autonomy must depend upon the ability to innovate at the level of the most advanced technology. At present innovation is virtually monopolized by the West. Since many of the benefits of growth industries 'can be virtually monopolized by the first country to innovate',[71] dependence will finally disappear only when the Third World, like Japan, has acquired the ability to produce new forms on equal terms with the developed world. This, of course, implies that colonial dependency relationships do not end with the termination of formal legal control, but continue for as long as the situation of substantive inequality persists.

The term 'development' is therefore used in this work to denote a change process characterized by increased productivity, equalization in the distribution of the social product, and the emergence of indigenous institutions whose relations with the outside world, and particularly with the developed centres of the international economy, are characterized by equality rather than by dependence or subordination. Against this notion will be contrasted '*un*development' and '*under*development'. Frank uses these terms extensively, but without adequate explanation. In my view the former relates to situations isolated from the system of international exchange – in East Africa a condition which probably existed in a pure form only before the slave trade hundreds of years ago. 'Underdevelopment', on the other hand, will be used here to relate to a condition of dependence – one in which the activities of a given society are subjected to the overriding control of an external power over which it can exert little direct influence. Used in this sense it it possible to come to terms with Frank's claim that underdevelopment is not an original condition of Third World society, but is the product of its relationship with the West. Colonialism can be accused of 'the development of underdevelopment' if it can be shown that its impact upon local society was such that it created a situation in which the latter could only continue to function by continuing to accept dependence on the dominant external powers. Much of this work will be devoted to an examination of the extent to which this accusation can or cannot be substantiated by a close analysis of the way in which a particular African region was incorporated into the world economy by the old colonial system.

The difficulties involved in the use of these three concepts are considerable. They each present major problems of measurement and are even more difficult to use together since they can come into direct conflict with each other. In the short term it might be necessary to sacrifice equality for growth by centralizing power in order to enforce maximum rates of saving and investment; alternatively it might be necessary to forgo some measure of growth to maintain independence from external sources. But in the long term they can be shown to be functionally interrelated – autonomy must depend upon continued economic growth; this in turn will depend upon the ability to resist the dominance of external or internal groups whose interests are opposed to the changes which growth must bring. Both are only likely to continue to be achieved where broad strata of the society can participate effectively in political, social and economic development on terms which they accept as equitable. This degree of complexity makes simple definitions and refined measurement impossible – all we hope for are rough approximations and broad generalizations. But this seems preferable to the alternative of 'sacrificing the relevance of subject-matter to the elegance of analytical method; it is better to deal imperfectly with what is important than to attain virtuoso skill in the treatment of what does not matter'.[72]

It is necessary now to consider the kinds of structures involved in the colonial situation, the way they related to each other and the dynamic factors which caused movement in one direction or another.

Interaction in the early stages of colonial administration was determined by the dominance which the agencies of foreign control were able to assert over the indigenous structures which they overran. The latter exhibited a wide range of social forms, but from the European point of view were all in relative terms small-scale, isolated and technically backward. And their internal differences were of limited importance when compared with their general subordination to the dominant structures introduced in virtually every sphere of life by the new rulers. New administrative, economic, religious and educational institutions were extended and consolidated, establishing new centres from which radical change in rural society was bound to flow. These centres were controlled by a new class of expatriate whose ends and methods were determined with reference to the European metropolitan centre; these, in turn, imposed new demands upon local society and established the limits within which the now dependent indigenous structures of social control would be free to operate. These pre-colonial formations were not entirely incorporated by the new colonial system – they were required to change in favour

of new demands only up to the point required for the purposes of
the colonial political economy but no further than that.[73] The
dependent structures – the chiefs, Native Councils and Courts –
were expected to provide for the maintenance of law and order,
the production of cash crops, the collection of taxes, and the un-
skilled labour required by the new economic and administrative
system. Beyond this the new authorities encouraged the perpetu-
ation of 'traditional' values, these being seen as fundamental to
the maintenance of the 'traditional' or 'tribal' social order. The
maintenance of this order, in some attenuated form, was fundamental to a system which did not have the desire or the resources
to modernize the whole of its new domain in any basic way.[74]
But the continued survival of these dependent structures should
not be taken as proof of the continued existence of some earlier
'traditional' society. The changes imposed by colonialism were
partial but fundamental – they undermined the old structures at
their most vulnerable points. The chief might still command his
people, but he now deferred to the District Commissioner. When
faced with a threat to his authority his ultimate recourse lay with
the colonial state, not the pre-colonial social and political sanctions. The old closed economy was broken open, the old verities
challenged, and new demands created by the authority of Western
religion, education and medical services. These dependent structures drew such independent authority as they had from the past,
but they survived in the present only because the colonial power
did not choose to destroy them. But their hold on the future was
wholly problematical in the face of the changes introduced by the
new institutions. For the future the critical question was not the
nature of traditional values but access to the modern resources
embodied in the dominant colonial structures. These were distributed very unevenly; their impact upon dependent society varied
very sharply as a result. Their presence or absence in the form of
roads, schools, etc. initiated chains of cumulative causation which
led some individuals and groups to move forward very rapidly,
others to stagnate or even regress in relation to the changes taking
place in society as a whole. These movements were fundamental to
the development process on all levels; it is only possible to come to
terms with the contemporary structure of social, economic and
political stratification when they are properly understood.

This suggests that colonialism began by creating a dualistic
situation based upon the juxtaposition of dominant colonial and
dependent indigenous structures, the former introducing the

dynamic element into the situation and deriving their objectives from the metropolitan centre, the latter serving the former and exercising an independent authority derived from pre-colonial systems of social organization only within the limits set by the requirements of the metropolitan centre. Up to the Second World War this system gave every appearance of stability in most parts of tropical Africa. In its most enlightened guise it was characterized by the paternalism of the colonial agent on the one hand, and the apparently willing deference of the African subject on the other. Because of its apparent stability it lent itself to analysis in equilibrium terms and was so studied by anthropologists and other more or less academic advisers to the colonial authority. But this harmony was more apparent than real; the appearance of colonial law and order overlaid a deep-seated contradiction. And it is now clear that the original relationship can only be understood in relation to this contradiction, and that the forces which it released were to create the need for 'the suppression of the old society by the new one'.[75] This, once again, requires some methodological explanation.

While much social analysis starts from assumptions of equilibrium, I would argue with Leach that 'real societies can never be in equilibrium',[76] and further that the degree of conflict involved in colonial society was of a particularly intense kind. The relations between colonial and dependent structures were characterized by great inequality, however cordial the day-to-day interactions of the parties concerned. The expatriates might have been happy to exercise their paternalism indefinitely, but the African population could not be expected to accept their dependence in the same spirit. During the initial stages of penetration the indigenous populations were in no position to challenge this situation short of suicidal wars or rebellions, like that forced upon the Zulu in Natal at the end of the nineteenth century. But the new situation was a dynamic one; the interaction between colonial and dependent structures gave rise to new structures and new forces in the colonized society which were bound ultimately to challenge the dominant political order. The colonial power was forced, in its own interests, to transfer certain skills and resources to the indigenous population; they built railways, roads and schools, introduced new crops and revolutionized the system of economic exchange.[77] This meant that for the coming generation reality was not always totally dominated by a system of monolithic and exploitative control, but gave a small minority the opportunity to acquire the skills required to exploit the new situation 'as a means of social advancement'.[78] The process of doing this created new resources, new classes and new demands, and so altered 'the structure of society itself'.[79]

But this process took place within a general framework of grievance derived from perceived exploitation. The emergent classes were given access to opportunities on very unequal terms; where their interests conflicted with those of the colonial authorities the latter could be expected to use their power to ensure their own preponderance.[80] The emerging indigenous classes perceived reality in terms of inherited inequality, blocked economic opportunities and social discrimination. This was bound to create a desire to resist and replace the colonial structure; the new skills gave them some of the resources with which to attempt this. Thus the broad historical process must be seen in dialectical terms – during the first stage, colonial and dependent structures were juxtaposed in conditions of intense but, after the period of initial conquest, for the most part unexpressed conflict; this relationship and the creation of the new colonial economic system subsequently gave rise to new social forces, which were ultimately to stand in opposition to both. Thus the first stage of colonialism, when the conflict was latent, terminated in a second during which the battle was to come out into the open and be fought on different terms. Originally the District Commissioner and Chief divided the territory between them; once this situation had matured through the introduction of a cash economy, an educational system, and so on, both, from their different perspectives, faced the nationalist politician and the new forces which he represented. But it should again be noted that the process was not one of pure conflict, but an interaction in which 'convergent and divergent currents . . . [were] inseparably interwoven'.[81] The emergent forces were themselves the product of the resources made available by the colonial state; their opposition to that state stemmed from the limits which it sought to impose upon their ability to acquire more of the resources. It was the conjunction between these positive and negative elements in the experience of some sections of colonial society that introduced the dynamic elements into the colonial situation.

This study is primarily concerned with the first stage of this process – with the period during which colonial control was consolidated and the new administrative and economic structure created, and African society maintained in a state of virtually unmitigated dependence. But this stage must be considered in relation to its implications for the future, and especially to its tendency to restructure African society and hence produce the emergent indigenous classes capable of replacing colonial control by creating fully autonomous structures in the sense of that term set out earlier. The foundations for these new structures were created during this period. The distribution of modern resources determined the life chances of the rising African generation; the emergence of a new political, economic and social élite depended upon their allocation. The configuration of forces during the second stage of colonial control, when nationalist movements had emerged (and, indeed, after independence) depended upon the nature of this allocation and can therefore only be understood in relation to it.

Again it is important to note that this approach does not imply the existence of some inevitable 'law of historical development'. Western dominance was bound to induce conflict and change, but the scale, content and direction of change depended upon particular circumstances – the nature of the colonial presence on the one hand and of the pre-colonial formations it confronted on the other. It would be reassuring but excessively optimistic to anticipate 'the inevitablity of emancipation through social conflict'.[82] Emancipation occurs only where the circumstances are favourable: in many places the lack of physical resources, the dominance of reactionary classes, or the weakness of the colonial presence, seems likely to hold up progress for as far ahead as anyone cares to look. Our problem is to identify both the positive and negative factors in given situations and thus improve our ability to make realistic assessments about future courses of action.

This leads into the consideration of the last of my methodological problems. I have suggested a model through which we can identify the fundamental interactions and the historical stages of any developmental process in a colonial situation. To take the analysis a step further it is necessary to identify and abstract the dynamic factors in the situation, the variables which will influence the actual outcomes of particular interactions in particular situations and produce movement in one direction or another.

At any point in time most social action will take place in relation to an established and unequal distribution of resources, regulated through a complex system of social control.[83] The bulk of these resources will be devoted to the maintenance of this existing structure, to 'simple reproduction' in the Marxist sense,[84] and will take the form of immobile capital assets, goods required to meet existing levels of consumption or values 'embedded in fixed, ascriptive, relations and groups'.[85] But in every society there will at some time at least be a margin between actual consumption and actual production; there will also be some possibility of moving existing resources from one use to another. The control, sources and scale of these 'free-floating resources'[86] will determine the nature of the change process: allocated to particular purposes they will set cumulative growth processes in motion, taken from existing uses they will induce cumulative processes of decline. These positive and negative processes taken together will over a shorter or longer period revolutionize the whole structure of social relations. The critical factor in social change, therefore, is not so much the absolute level of production as the composition of the surplus which can be appropriated and put to new uses. Its size, source and allocation will determine the speed and direction of change and must therefore provide the primary focus for analytical attention.

The size of the actual surplus at any point in time will be determined by the difference between actual consumption and actual production. But it would be misleading to confine attention to the actual surplus as though this constituted an absolute social category. Any surplus, economic or otherwise, is not absolute but relative to the social situation. Its size will depend upon the prevailing interaction between values, power and technological capacity, and will change with any of them. A surplus can only come into existence where a new opportunity has been identified, it will actually be made available only where the relevant group has sufficient social control[87] to appropriate it, and it will produce new assets only where the technological capacity exists to exploit it. The interaction between the consciousness of new objectives, social control and technical capacity will determine 'what things and how much a given society produces, who is responsible for production, how much is consumed and in what proportion by the various groups in the society [and] how much is saved or diverted from consumption and for what purposes . . .'[88] The identification of new needs, changes in institutional control or technological innovation will alter the size of the surplus and its implications for future development. Thus the actual surplus appropriated at any time will constitute only a small part of the potential surplus available if under-utilized resources were brought into use, productivity increased without a corresponding increase in consumption, or vice versa.[89] The existence of a potential surplus is a critical factor in the competition between groups at any point in time – this will take the form of an effort to obtain control over the institutions through which these additional resources can be captured and redirected.

Changes in the movement of resources must therefore be understood in relation to both sacrifice and appropriation, that is, to the transfer of assets from one part of society to another. Identification of the source of supply will suggest areas of likely relative downward mobility. Where one social category constantly gives up a larger relative percentage of its assets than it obtains in return its relative position in the social structure will deteriorate. This will be true even where its absolute level of income is rising, but more slowly than that of other sections of the community:

> A house may be large or small; as long as the surrounding houses are equally small it satisfies all social demands for a dwelling. But let a palace arrive beside the little house and it shrinks from a little house to a hut. . . . Our desires and pleasures spring from society; we measure them, therefore, by society and not by the objects which serve for their satisfaction. Because they are of a social nature they are of a relative nature.[90]

The analysis must also take account of the fact that a surplus can be derived from internal or external sources; assets can be transferred from the metropolis to the colony and vice versa. New resources can therefore be created at the periphery without any internal sacrifices; on the other hand internal resources can be sacrificed without creating any corresponding growth in local assets.

If the source of free-floating resources indicates areas of downward mobility, their allocation determines potentialities for growth. Particular groups in society will appropriate some portion of the surplus and convert it into new productive resources in the form of 'additional capital'.[91] This ability will depend upon control over any or all of a wide range of factors – for example, access to military technology, religious sanctions or socially necessary skills. Its effects will be to expand cumulatively the ability to control resources and hence to advance their relative social position.

This very bald statement requires some further development. Firstly, it is clear that concentration upon control over the surplus enables us to give concrete empirical content to the conflict-model outlined earlier. Change occurs because certain groups are able to utilize the surplus and advance their position relative to that of others in the society. To understand this process we must be able to isolate the factors which provide them with this ability, the constraints within which they are able to operate it and the scale and productivity of the resources to which it gives them access. This requires that we both identify the critical groups which are competing for resources within any given political system (in this case the colonial, dependent and emergent structures outlined earlier) and also that we establish the terms on which the leading groups are able to extract them from the rest.[92] Any surplus will be derived from an exchange relationship – for example that between the tax-collector and the peasant, the trader and his customer – to which both parties will make some sort of contribution. The critical question relates to the terms on which this takes place – what profit or loss does each party derive from the relationship? While it can be assumed that each is attempting to maximize his own interest, the degree of reciprocity involved can vary from a situation in which benefits are completely equalized to one in which one party is totally subordinated to the other.

Secondly, a concern with control and the ability of some groups to grow at the expense of others should not lead to unrealistic assumptions about their ability to determine all the outcomes of particular decisions and therefore their own future social position. Control is always partial; even the governors of a totalitarian state cannot determine all the consequences of every decision in advance and have therefore to contend with some measure of uncertainty.[93] Dominant groups have to provide subordinate groups with some form of payment for their services, and this can, over time, alter their relative positions. Decisions will always have 'unanticipated consequences',[94] which may again direct resources towards groups for which they were not originally intended. If this were not the case revolutions would never succeed, because they depend upon a change in the distribution of social control which is necessarily against the interests of the ruling class. It is possible here to use the concept of indirect influence to take account of the ability of subordinate groups to benefit from decisions taken either without any reference to their interests (as where they can make use of a road built essentially for some other group) or from those taken on their behalf by other groups whose interests coincide partially with theirs. The broader the issues and the longer the time-scales involved, the lower is the ability to predict and control outcomes. This is especially true in the general field of economic development, where the ability to shape the future consciously is still exceedingly low.

Thirdly, when assessing the ability of particular groups to to control resources it is necessary to take into account factors built into the structure of the situation which are rarely questioned but which do in fact exert a decisive influence over the life chances of the groups involved. The fundamental assumptions which determine the relationships in any society are rarely brought to the surface; they lie 'hidden in the dim depths'[95] and produce unquestioning habits of deference and command. This is the area in which outcomes are determined by 'non-decisions';[96] however difficult, it is the task of the social scientist to bring them to the surface and make their implications explicit.

In conclusion it is perhaps worth trying to relate this discussion of change factors to the methodological considerations outlined earlier. I have argued that change occurs where groups are able to extract surpluses from society and apply them to new uses, and that the primary groups competing in the colonial situation are those which constitute the colonial, dependent and emergent structures which make up the colonial political economy. Thus the nature of the change process will be determined by the relative ability of each of these to get control over free-floating resources; more precisely, it will depend on the terms under which they enter into exchange relationships with each other. Growth will depend upon the relative productivity of the resources transferred from one use to another. It has a general aspect, where it relates to the increase in total social product it also has a particular aspect in relation to the expansion of one group in relation to the rest of society. This latter aspect leads to the consideration of questions relating to distribution, equity and changes in social structure, since these can be quantified in relation to the scale and productivity of (or rate of return on) the transferred assets. It should be noted here that the level of conflict in the total situation will be heavily influenced by the tendency for total resources to expand or contract. Where total resources are expanding it will be possible for subordinate groups to be provided with an increase in absolute levels of consumption despite an increase in their relative deprivation. This will not eliminate conflict, as Marx points out in the passage cited earlier, but may make it easier to contain. But it is important here not to allow the existence of high living standards in absolute terms to blind us to changes in relative deprivation.

This is likely to be highest among relatively well-placed groups whose position is either deteriorating or cannot improve fast enough because of the opposition of entrenched competitors. Finally, it will be possible to determine the tendency for autonomous structures to evolve within the colonial situation by determining the ability of the emergent structures to establish favourable exchange relationships with the other structures in society and continuously increase their span of social control. Their ability to obtain the resources which determine the ability to modernize – access to capital, skills and political structures – will determine the point at which they are able to eliminate the influence of both the dominant colonial structures and their indigenous subordinates.

It remains to consider the nature of the actual institutions and events to be considered in relation to this framework. In this study an attempt will be made to consider the relationship between the imperial decision-making process and the evolution of modern economic structures in East Africa between the two world wars. The major concern will be with the origins and effects of policy; with the nature of the group pressures which initiated it, and with its impact upon the structure of economic and, ultimately, political and social life. The constitutional position and recruitment patterns of political institutions during the period will be taken as given, and attention will be confined to the way in which they carried out their functions. This approach must leave many important questions unanswered, but it should show very clearly the way in which political decisions were arrived at, and how they actually affected critical aspects of the change process.

Policy areas were chosen for consideration in relation to their importance for the development of the modern economy, the amount of political controversy which they aroused, and the amount of information readily available about them. They include the debate about the whole ideology of colonial development, and decisions relating to the provision of capital, the regulation of transport and tariffs, the growth of secondary industry, the development and structure of agricultural production for the market and the marketing and processing of commodities. There will be some discussion of education, but virtually nothing relating to banking and commerce. Material has been drawn from Kenya, Uganda and Tanganyika, although no attempt was made to cover the same policy areas for each of them.

Three levels of political activity have to be distinguished in

East Africa during this period: British, territorial and regional. The territories were legally subordinated to Britain, and depended on her for the provision of capital, skills, markets and manufactured products. East African interests had therefore to compete for resources within the British political system as one set of groups among many. But the territories were soon able to raise a growing percentage of their economic needs locally, and were allowed to administer these through an increasingly differentiated and autonomous set of local institutions. These were originally created by, and subordinated to, the British presence; they were, and remained, dependent on the metropolis in that they were staffed at the decision-making level by the British colonial service; and they operated within a framework of assumptions and regulations largely created by the traditions of the British colonial system. But there was, none the less, a sense in which these institutions constituted distinct political entities almost from the beginning. Most of their staff spent long periods in 'their' colony and identified themselves with some of its interests; their institutions raised an increasing percentage of their economic resources locally, they operated within a separate (though not independent) system of pressure-group activity at the local level, and they were expected to adapt the wider colonial tradition to the specific conditions prevailing in the particular colony. On the third level, the existence of close economic contact between the three territories led to the establishment of a regularized pattern of inter-territorial economic relations, and to the emergence of a rudimentary set of inter-territorial political institutions. These were subordinated both to the British and to the local institutions, but nevertheless did have their own sphere of action, and were able to exert some influence on the passage of events. The main, though not the exclusive, interest in this study will be with the functioning of the British institutions. This is primarily because of the availability of sources, but it can also be justified by the dominance of British political and economic interests in East African development during the earlier colonial period which will be considered here. Every effort will be made, however, to consider the relationship between the three levels of activity, since it is clear that they can only be understood as part of a single whole.

East Africa as a region provides a useful focus for comparative research because its constituent parts were very similar in some ways, yet very different in others. The three territories were controlled by the same colonial power during this period, they displayed roughly the same levels of development, and they contained roughly the same amounts of cultivable land and population, although they differed in physical size and in the accessibility of these resources. Yet they were to develop along rather different lines, especially with regard to the role of expatriate enterprise in the agricultural sector, and in political life. In Kenya this role was to be predominant, and the actual passage of events was to be heavily influenced by the ethic which conditioned the pattern of change in South Africa and Southern Rhodesia. In Tanganyika expatriate enterprise was to be very important in the rural sector, but was never to dominate it as it did in Kenya, while the territory was also administered under a League of Nations Mandate. In Uganda agriculture was dominated by African peasant production, and the ethic on which it was governed was derived more from West African than South African models. Each of these patterns produced different social, economic and political results, so the region provides access to a wide range of the kinds of forms taken by colonial development in Africa. In addition, their proximity and unified control produced the attempt at inter-territorial co-ordination which is in itself an interesting and important area for analysis. Co-ordination involved the region in attempts to reconcile actually and potentially conflicting interests within a framework which did not contain a single political body able to exercise a clearly overriding authority. The problems involved in this sort of activity are of continuing interest in Africa, where the importance of regional economic unity is widely accepted, but the political machinery for bringing it into being hardly exists.

NOTES

1. Cf. K. Mannheim, *Freedom, power and democratic planning*, London, Routledge, 1951, p. 6, for a discussion of 'Social Techniques' and 'Social Inventions'.
2. A. G. Frank, 'The Sociology of Development', in *Catalyst*, no. 3, Summer 1967, p. 39.
3. R. Pares, 'The economic factors in the history of the Empire', in *Econ. Hist. Review*, 2nd ser., VII, 3 May 1937.
4. R. A. Austen, *Northwestern Tanzania under German and British rule*, New Haven, Yale U.P., 1968, p. 255, and cf. also L. A. Fallers, *Bantu Bureaucracy*, Chicago, Univ. of Chicago Press, 1965.
5. Karl Marx, 'Future results of British rule in India', in *Selected Works*, vol. I, Moscow, Foreign Languages Publishing House, 1962, p. 356.
6. *Ibid.*, p. 353.

7. K. Jaspers, *The future of mankind*, Chicago, Univ. of Chicago Press, 1963, p. 72.
8. My view here, as in many other places, is best expressed by G. Lukacs, *History and class consciousness*, London, Merlin Press, 1971.
9. Max Weber, *The Theory of Social and Economic Organisation*, Glencoe, Free Press, 1964, p. 109.
10. S. Eisenstadt, *Modernisation, Protest and Change*, Englewood-Cliffs, Prentice-Hall, 1966, p. 1.
11. G. Almond and J. S. Coleman, *The politics of the developing areas*, Princeton, U.P., 1961, p. 16.
12. This is a very crude over-simplification of a wide range of literature among which the work of Durkheim, Weber, Parsons, Redfield and Almond is clearly of critical importance.
13. W. W. Rostow, *The Stages of Economic Growth*, London, C.U.P., 1960.
14. Some of the literature involved is unsympathetically reviewed in Frank, *op. cit.* (note 2).
15. T. Parsons, 'A functional theory of change', in A. and E. Etzioni, *Social Change*, New York, Basic Books, 1964, p. 84.
16. Frank, *op. cit.*, illustrates this point very effectively.
17. F. Fanon, *The wretched of the earth*, Harmondsworth, Penguin Books, 1967, p. 256.
18. For example Boeke's assumptions about the 'backward-sloping supply curves of effort and risk-taking' in traditional society (cf. G. M. Meier, *Leading issues in development economics*, New York, O.U.P., 1964, pp. 55 ff.). For a general discussion cf. R. Apthorpe, 'Two planning theories of social change', in E. A. Brett, ed., *Public Policy and Agricultural Development in East Africa*, Nairobi, East African Publishing House, forthcoming.
19. For example P. Hill, *Migrant Cocoa-farmers of Southern Ghana*, London, C.U.P., 1963; and material by Feldman, Rigby, and others, in Brett, *op. cit.*
20. Cf. T. Veblen, 'The preconceptions of economic science', in *The place of science in modern civilisation*, New York, Russell, 1961, p. 164.
21. Weber, *op. cit.*, p. 110.
22. The phrase is from G. Myrdal, *The political element in the development of economic theory*, London, Routledge, 1953, p. 13.
23. J. M. H. Beattie, 'Understanding and Explanation in Social Anthropology', in *Brit. Journal of Sociology*, vol. 10, 1959, p. 47.
24. *Ibid.*, p. 57; cf. also Weber, *op. cit.*, pp. 111–12.
25. By exhibiting 'a wide sympathy for all the persons and interests engaged in a situation'. M. Oakeshott, 'The activity of being an historian', in *Rationalism in Politics*, London, Methuen, 1962, p. 161.
26. Oakeshott, 'The political economy of freedom', *op. cit.*, p. 37.
27. Myrdal, *op. cit.*, p. 13.
28. R. D. Laing, *The divided self*, Harmondsworth, Penguin Books, 1965, p. 24.
29. *Ibid.*, pp. 24–5.
30. T. Hobbes, *Leviathan*, London, Collins, 1962, p. 60; cf. also Weber, *op. cit.*, pp. 91–2.
31. Two views of this position from opposite ends of the political spectrum can be found in Oakeshott, *Rationalism in Politics, op. cit.*, and in Lukacs, *History and class consciousness, op. cit.* (note 8).

32. Weber, *op. cit.* (note 9), p. 111.

33. C. Wright Mills, *The sociological imagination*, New York, O.U.P., 1959, p. 8.

34. C. B. MacPherson, *The political theory of possessive individualism*, Oxford, O.U.P., 1962, p. 86. He presumably means no rational *bourgeois* man, since many very rational men from other classes were less than convinced.

35. Veblen, *op. cit.* (note 20), pp. 114 ff.

36. Cf. Barrington Moore, *Social origins of dictatorship and democracy*, Boston, Beacon Press, 1966.

37. Weber, *op. cit.*, p. 92.

38. H. Marcuse, *One-dimensional man*, London, Sphere Books, 1968.

39. A. G. Frank, *Capitalism and underdevelopment in Latin America*, New York, Monthly Review, 1967, W. Rodney, *How Europe underdeveloped Africa*, Dar es Salaam, Tanzania Publishing House, 1972.

40. Fanon, *op. cit.* (note 17), p. 252.

41. Veblen, *op. cit.* (note 20), p. 1.

42. Hugh Trevor-Roper, cited in A. A. Mazrui, *Ancient Greece in African Political Thought*, Nairobi, East African Publishing House, 1967, pp. 23-4.

43. Jean-Paul Sartre, 'Introduction', in Fanon, *op. cit.*, p. 19.

44. E. A. Brett, *African attitudes*, Johannesburg, South African Institute of Race Relations, 1963, p. 33.

45. For example, read R. Robinson and J. Gallagher, *Africa and the Victorians*, London, Macmillan, 1961, on the role of the Indian army in the British system of control.

46. Manning Nash, 'Introduction, Approaches to the Study of Economic Growth', in *Journal of Social Issues*, vol. 29, no. 1 (January 1963).

47. A. G. Frank, 'Dialectic, not Dual Society', in *Latin America, Underdevelopment or Revolution*, New York, Monthly Review, 1969, pp. 227-8; cf. also 'The Development of Underdevelopment', in *ibid.*

48. *Ibid.*

49. 'The Chinese Revolution and the Chinese Communist Party', in *Selected Works*, New York, International Publishers, 1954, vol. 3, p. 80.

50. Jaspers, *op. cit.* (note 7), p. 72.

51. Cf. P. A. Baran, *The political economy of growth*, New York, Monthly Review, 1962, p. 158 for a description of the particular circumstances which enabled Japan to do this.

52. F. Riggs, *Thailand, the modernisation of a bureaucratic policy*, Honolulu, East-West Center Press, 1966, discusses this question with regard to Thailand's ability to escape colonization in the nineteenth century.

53. Fanon (*op. cit.*, esp. Ch. 3) and Frank (*op. cit.* note 2 and *op. cit.* note 39) both reject the national bourgeoisie as a basis for an alternative strategy, feeling that they have allowed themselves to be completely incorporated into the international power structure.

54. Marcuse's phrase, *op. cit.*, p. 10.

55. *Ibid.*, p. 26.

56. Cf. G. Almond and J. S. Coleman, *op. cit.* (note 11), and G. Almond and G. Powell, *Comparative politics*, Boston, Little Brown, 1966, where the tendency is less noticeable; D. Easton, *A framework for political analysis*, Englewood-Cliffs, Prentice-Hall, 1965, Ch. VI, and *A systems analysis of political life*, New York, Wiley, 1965, esp. pp. 14-15.

57. Parsons, *op. cit.* (note 15), p. 84.
58. H. Marcuse, describing Hegel's system, *Reason and revolution*, New York, Humanities Press, 2nd ed., 1954, p. 258.
59. 'The Sociology of Development', *op. cit.* (note 2).
60. Cf. for example M. King, 'Aspects of Medical Care in Developing Countries' (mimeo), Paper presented to Institute of Development Studies Conference in Social Planning, University of Sussex, April 1968.
61. Oakeshott draws a useful distinction between practical and technical knowledge in *Rationalism in Politics, op. cit.* (note 25), pp. 7 ff.
62. Baran, *op. cit.* (note 51), p. 24.
63. P. J. D. Wiles, *The political economy of Communism*, Oxford, Blackwell, 1962, Ch. 12, on problems of measurement.
64. Marx, 'Wages, Prices and Profit', in *Selected Works*, vol. 1, *op. cit.* (note 5), p. 426.
65. Marcuse, *op. cit.* (note 58), p. 49.
66. On this point cf. Veblen, *op. cit.* (note 58); G. Myrdal, *et al.*, '*The Principle of Cumulation*', in Etzioni, *op. cit.* (note 15); and especially K. Marx, *Capital*, vol. 1, London, Allen & Unwin, 1958.
67. It is used in this way with regard to personality types by G. Jahoda, *White man*, London, O.U.P., 1961, pp. 107 ff.
68. Oakeshott, 'The political economy of freedom', *op. cit.* (note 31), p. 40.
69. For an excellent discussion cf. J. McDermott, 'Technology: the opiate of the intellectuals', in *New York Review of Books*, 31 July 1969. What he says about the anti-democratic implications of advanced technology applies with particular force to the Third World.
70. Fanon, *op. cit.* (note 17), p. 250.
71. R. Williams, ed., *May-Day Manifesto*, Harmondsworth, Penguin Books, 1968, p. 61.
72. Baran, *op. cit.* (note 51), p. 22.
73. Cf. Apthorpe, *op. cit.* (note 18).
74. S. Eisenstadt, *The political systems of Empires*, New York, Glencoe, Free Press, 1962, pp. 24–5 and pp. 300 ff. for a discussion of the need to maintain traditional institutions in the change process.
75. Mao Tse-Tung, 'On Contradiction', *Selected Works*, vol. 2, San Francisco, China Books, 1965, p. 16.
76. E. R. Leach, *Political systems of Highland Burmah*, London, Athlone Press, 1970 Reprint, p. 4.
77. Cf. for example Marx, *op. cit.* (note 5), pp. 354–6; Mao Tse-Tung, 'The Chinese Revolution and the Chinese Communist Party', *op. cit.*, pp. 74–82.
78. Leach, *op. cit.*, p. 8.
79. *Ibid.*
80. Cf. G. Balandier, 'The Colonial Situation', I. Wallerstein, ed., *Social change*, New York, Wiley, 1966, pp. 36 ff.
81. G. Simmel, *Conflict*, Glencoe, Free Press, 1955, p. 26. For a more extended version of my own position, cf. E. A. Brett, 'Politics, Economics and Rationality', in *Social Science Information*, VIII, 2 April, 1969, pp. 52 ff.
82. R. Sklar, 'Political Science and National Integration', *Journal of Modern African Studies*, vol. 5, no. 1 (1967), p. 1.
83. This discussion is drawn from my 'Politics, Economics and Rationality', *op. cit.*, pp. 59 ff.

84. Cf. P. M. Sweezy, *The theory of capitalist development*, New York, O.U.P., 1942, p. 76; Marx, *Capital*, vol. 1, Ch. 23.

85. Eisenstadt, *op. cit.* (note 74), p. 25.

86. *Ibid.*, especially pp. 27 ff.

87. E. A. Ross, 'Social Control', in R. Bierstedt, *The making of society*, New York, Random House, 1959.

88. H. Pearson, 'The economy has no surplus', in K. Polanyi, *et al.*, *Trade and market in the early Empires*, Glencoe, Free Press, 1957, p. 339.

89. Cf. Baran, *op. cit.* (note 51), chapter 2 on the notion of 'potential surplus'.

90. Marx, 'Wage, Labour and Capital', *op. cit.* (note 84), pp. 93–4.

91. Cf. Sweezy, *op. cit.* (note 84), pp. 79 ff., and Marx, *Capital*, vol. 1, part VII, on the process of capitalist accumulation.

92. A very successful example of this kind of analysis is to be found in Barrington Moore, *op. cit.* (note 36); the group theories in Political Science will also prove helpful.

93. Cf. Brett, *op. cit.* (note 81), p. 59.

94. A. Kaplan, 'Some Limits on Rationality', C. J. Friedrich (ed.), *Rational decisions*, New York, Atherton Press, 1964, p. 60.

95. Ross, *op. cit.*, p. 341.

96. Cf. P. Bachrach and M. S. Baratz, 'Decisions and Nondecisions', in *American Political Science Review*, 57, no. 3, September 1963.

PART I

The Ideological and Institutional Context

I

The Social Theory of Colonialism

The British, we are told, govern without benefit of theory. They claim a 'genius for empiricism' and a 'reluctance to conceive and much less define any end or ultimate goal'.[1] For the Empire this commitment to empiricism was complemented by one to devolution – by a belief that decisions should be taken by 'those on the spot who have first-hand acquaintance with the facts'.[2] The latter assumption depended on the former – the absence of an overriding programme for colonial development made it possible for local officials to be given considerable freedom of action and for subsequent deviations in practice to be justified as the inevitable outcome of differences in local circumstances and traditions. The resulting myth of the practical official responding to facts rather than theories could then serve in this area (as in many others) as an effective defence against those fundamentally out of sympathy with the general assumptions on which the colonial system rested. Since they, unlike the local official, trader or planter, could have no first-hand access to the 'facts', their criticisms could be set aside without difficulty as 'doctrinaire' or 'impractical'.

But these assumptions of the colonial governing class should not, of course, be taken at face value. Political decisions in the British Empire were as dependent on ideology as those taken in any other political system. Any difference was one of style rather than substance; it lay in the manner in which the fundamental assumptions of colonial rule were articulated, sustained and transmitted. Some systems have attempted to systematize and codify their ultimate conception of the basis of the social order and of social purpose; the British governing class has preferred to keep its fundamental assumptions unstated and incoherent. The class, despite its own protestations to the contrary, does carry with it a general framework of assumptions which condition its actions in its political roles; assumptions which are probably the more powerful and inclusive for being left undefined. The British ruling class has operated within a very stable and homogeneous culture which

exists in its political, as in its other forms, as a structure of reciprocal expectations operationalized through an old and highly
developed set of institutions. The lack of articulation in dogma is
compensated for by the high degree of articulation in the institutions. Since individuals know what is expected of them as members
of Parliament, the Bank of England, the Stock Exchange, or the
Colonial Service, and since all of these and the other institutions of
political control have over time and by trial and error established
a fairly clear knowledge of what they can and cannot do if the
system is to survive in its present form, the individuals who run
them do not need to bother themselves with general questions of
political theory. Ideology exists instead in the form of established
habits of behaviour, in the knowledge which each individual in a
position of authority has of what is expected of him when he deals
with particular problems. He does indeed respond to the 'facts',
but he does not act empirically if by that is understood action
which is not conditioned by a set of general normative assumptions
about the basis of social authority and the nature of social goals.
In the British system this kind of knowledge is not taught directly
by reference to established ideological texts but is acquired indirectly by potential recruits to positions of authority through the
'observation and imitation of the behaviour of [their] elders'[3] in
that remarkably coherent set of socializing agencies – the upper-
middle-class family, the public schools and the ancient univer-
sities. The dominance of these institutions has been so complete
that upward mobile individuals from further down the social
hierarchy have had to adapt their behaviour to the norms which
they have established. The modern ruling class acquired its
general training in social attitudes and managerial skills in the
family, school and university; particular skills and attitudes were
then acquired when individuals moved into specialized institutions
and were trained by those already there.

The colonial ruling class in its various manifestations formed a
specialized sub-culture of this kind and one very much in the
mainstream of this wider culture. This group, taken as a whole,
shared a very broad view of the nature of the colonial situation and
of proper behaviour within it, and it in turn was divided into
specialist sub-groups – primarily administrators, traders, planters,
and educationalists either secular or sacred – which developed a
specialized set of assumptions relating to their particular role within this general framework of overriding ideas and values. Their
coherence as a group and their commitment to the colonial ethic

was secured by a careful process of selection and socialization. They were largely drawn (and this is especially true of the administrative class, their leading sector) from 'the class which has made and maintained the British Empire'; a class which considered itself to be endowed with 'an almost passionate conception of fair play, of protection of the weak and of "playing the game"'; one which had learnt 'personal initiative and resource, and how to command and to obey'; and finally one which because of the special quality of its preparation was assumed to be 'in no danger . . . of falling prey to that subtle moral deterioration which the exercise of power over inferior races produces in men of a different type'.[4] Once selected the colonial agent entered service in conditions which were especially conducive to the maintenance of an exclusive and very narrow view of the Imperial mission and of his own obligations within it. The new recruit would probably begin work upon some remote country station where he would spend many years subordinated to the will of an existing hierarchy with the power to decide all future prospects of promotion. He would be encouraged to develop and display qualities of personal initiative, and direct surveillance would be very limited on isolated outposts, but his actions and attitudes would nevertheless develop within the broad limits of the established ethic. For while his isolation would protect him from direct surveillance from above, it would also cut him off from new currents in the intellectual life of the metropolis and reinforce his dependence on the dominant values of the colonial environment. His social context would consist on the one side of colleagues and associates – the world of the District Headquarters and the Club, which was confined exclusively to expatriates and which imposed, through its rituals and activities, a powerfully developed code of behaviour and sense of group solidarity. The consequences of deviation have been clearly shown in the work of Graham Greene and Somerset Maugham; the phenomenon was still clearly visible during my own visits to the South African Protectorates in the fifties and to East Africa in the sixties. His other world, which he came out to direct and control, consisted of peoples which, if they were not actually considered inferior, were necessarily considered immature and therefore perhaps to be studied and understood in the manner of the sympathetic anthropologist (and many British district officials made capable amateurs in this field), but not to be treated as equals and allowed a decisive say in determining the long-term future of their country. Given this fundamental inequality built into the colonial situation, effective contact between expatriate and even the most prominent members of the indigenous society was precluded. Thus the only social contacts which would not be contaminated by these contradictions and inequalities were those with his own race and class living in the extreme cultural isolation of the African bush. These people therefore inhabited a community with the dimensions of a medieval village – they knew each other's business, they shared each other's certainties, and, because they depended so heavily on each other in an otherwise alien world, they could enforce their collective norms through a variety of direct and indirect social pressures.

Looked at from a contemporary perspective the group presents itself as a kind of collective caricature; it is difficult to take them seriously because their view of the world and their mission was stripped so completely of its social and intellectual base during and after the Second World War. Because all of them were implicated in the same system it is now easy to find in the picture only the unity of outlook – the fact that all of them took so many institutions for granted which we can now see to have been built upon sand. The actors of the time (and the contemporary tradition of Imperial historiography) overlooked the uniformities and the underlying theoretical consensus and saw only the disagreements between different elements in the colonial ruling class which they mistook for a debate about the fundamentals. On the other hand the current tendency is to recognize only the general orientation of the kind of colonialism which they represented and to overlook the significance of the conflict which was continuously evident within the broader consensus. To avoid either form of over-simplification we must be able to relate the general and the particular aspects of the ideology to each other – to understand the basis of the consensus, to identify the points and sources of conflict within it and to relate each element to the others. The high degree of agreement over fundamentals made it possible for the system to sustain a considerable degree of conflict over detail; it ensured, to use Schurman's terminology, that the contradictions which existed between the interests of the various sections of the ruling class would take on essentially non-antagonistic forms and be resolvable 'by peaceful means'.[5] These conflicts then tended over time to produce changes in the consensus as the various groups responded to the opportunities and the contingencies created by the situation. The end result was a remarkably peaceful process of incremental change which appeared to do very little to alter the nature of the international socio-economic substructure upon which the whole colonial system was based. But this peace and the continuation of processes of incremental rather than revolutionary change depended upon the stability of this sub-structure. Once Britain's position in the world, or the relationship between colonial society and the colonizing élite changed in any fundamental way, all the assumptions would collapse and bring the system down with them. This being so the primary objective of the colonial ruling class was to ensure that their actions and policies would serve to maintain this sub-structure so that it would continue to exhibit the features which supported their social theory and the right to rule which they based on it. Our problem here is therefore to attempt to explicate the elements in this theory which served to maintain their system of control and condition the decisions which they took in order to enforce it; it is equally important for us to consider the conflicts which the nature of the colonial situation tended to produce within that theory and the forces which tended to undermine its ability to sustain itself in the long run.

The colonial ruling class were united through the homogeneity of their social background and through their collective belief in Britain's pre-eminence in the world and in the validity of the institutions which had created this. More particularly they shared almost without exception the twin assumptions of virtually any form of colonial system – that the colonized peoples were not capable of governing themselves 'under the strenuous conditions of the modern world',[6] and that the relationship between the interests of colonized and colonizer was an essentially reciprocal and creative rather than an exploitative and contradictory one. 'The African Negro,' in Lugard's view, 'lacks power of organization and is conspicuously deficient in the management and control alike of men or of business.'[7] Further, they took for granted that Britain's presence in Africa was a prerequisite for the promotion of 'progress in civilization and justice'.[8] The established structure of political and economic relationships was generally considered to be the only possible basis for progress, and it was widely assumed that any new aspirations which might develop within the indigenous population could be taken care of through the gradual modification of existing institutions in the manner of the old Dominions. 'Our goal in the administration of the Dependencies . . .' said Leopold Amery, Under-Secretary of State for the Colonies, in 1920, is to 'enable every part of the Empire to obtain, in the fulness of time, and when conditions make it possible, full power of controlling its own affairs and developing its own destinies.'[9] This view was shared by most people involved in the colonial system (though Kipling, and no doubt others like him, believed that even the Indians would 'never stand alone'[10]) but was at that time invariably complemented by the conviction that the period of tutelage must stretch well beyond the foreseeable future.

The men who attempted to implement these assumptions were by no means the most rapacious colonial ruling class which the world has seen. Coming from an established upper-class stratum with strongly developed traditions of honesty and service they did not, for the most part, go out to the colonies to make fortunes or to assert their racial superiority. They expected and received a generous standard of living, they marked off their social status with fancy uniforms for ceremonial occasions, and expected outward and visible marks of respect from their subjects. But they did not take bribes, they attempted to administer the law impartially, many of them went out with a very sincere commitment to the advancement of the territories under their command and developed a strong commitment to what they considered to be the best interests of their subjects. The tradition was thus one of paternalism rather than exploitation, assuming as it did the moral superiority of the governors, the cultural immaturity of the governed, and the organic unity of the community within which they interacted. This complex of assumptions conditioned the exercise of all forms of political, economic and social control in the colonial world. They served to legitimize a political system in which authority was monopolized by a European élite, an economic system which confined African participation to a limited range of subordinate tasks,[11] and a social system stratified by race which assumed the inherent superiority of the imported culture over all indigenous forms.

These general assumptions operated both at the British centre and at the colonial periphery. Although the commitment to devolution allowed the local élite to get on with day-to-day administration unencumbered by close supervision, the strength and pervasiveness of the overriding ethic ensured that their actions would tend to reinforce rather than undermine the Imperial connection. But these ideological commitments were not the only constraints within which they had to operate. The colonial ruling class had also to come to terms with the demands imposed upon them by the need to establish and maintain an authoritative system of social control over a community which shared none of the assumptions or the historical experience of the subordinate classes in the metropolis. To do this they had to create a new set of institutions which would serve to maintain their authority in the political, economic and social spheres – in each area this required the importation of an appropriate set of justificatory myths which would serve to convince the élite of their right to assert social discipline and the indigenous population of the need to obey. In the political sphere they had to devise three kinds of structures – they required an administrative structure which could maintain law and order, collect taxes and service the economy: they needed a political structure capable of regulating conflict within the African population and with regard to their relations with expatriates; and they had also to find some means of dealing with the often conflicting demands made upon the system by the expatriate interests which operated inside the Colonies and which were expressed politically both at the local level and in the metropolitan country itself. In the economic sphere they had to create a productive capacity which would be sufficient to maintain the minimal administrative and military presence required to sustain foreign control; once this had been achieved they were expected to encourage rapid growth of those forms of local economic activity – notably the production of primary products – which were likely to make the most direct contribution to the expansion of the metropolitan economy. In the social sphere they had to regulate interaction between expatriates and the indigenous community, and within both of these communities; and they had also to create a system of education which would equip selected members of the indigenous community with the value and skills required for the honest and efficient performance of the subordinate tasks which the colonial system created. The institutions and assumptions evolved to establish British control in these areas will be considered in the next two chapters; here it remains to distinguish between the two major forms which British penetration assumed in the African context.

I have argued thus far that colonial ideology had to develop within two major sets of constraints – those imposed by the ideological presuppositions introduced into the situation by the new governing class, and those originating in the exigencies of the local social situation which they had to bring under their own control. Within these limits there can be discerned two broad types of social theory whose relative dominance depended upon the nature of the structure of production created in the export sector. The distinction here was between those in which agriculture came to be based upon an expatriate farming class, and those in which African peasant producers were dominant. The former lay in areas of temperate climate – South Africa, Southern Rhodesia, Algeria and the regions of Northern Rhodesia, Nyasaland, Tanganyika and Kenya which lay along what General Smuts called 'the broad backbone of Eastern Africa'.[12] The latter were dominant in the remainder of the continent where, with some marginal exceptions like the Belgian Congo, Liberia and the Ivory Coast, it was generally assumed that cash-crop production would be predominantly in the hands of African peasant producers.

Large-scale settler agriculture required access to a cheap labour force which could only be supplied by the indigenous African population. The fact that Africans would have to enter the labour market in this way rather than cultivate their own holdings produced a fundamental difference in the social structure of the two kinds of system, which served to influence every other aspect of economic and political organization. These differences led to the emergence of two competing ideologies which served to rationalize the resulting sets of relationships. Each of these was dominant in particular regions – the settler view in Southern Africa, the peasant view in West Africa. In areas like Eastern Africa where neither system was able to establish an early predominance the two views co-existed in often intense conflict. The outcome of the struggle depended on a wide range of political and economic eventualities both at the metropolitan and the local level, and the analysis of these will constitute one of the primary preoccupations of this work. But to understand how these concrete events were viewed by the major protagonists one has first to attempt to set out the major assumptions implicit in each view.

Since the settler view originated and existed in its most highly developed form in the south it is as well to take a South African formulation as a starting-point, more especially since the East African settlers looked very consciously to the south for both ideological and political support. In November 1929 General Smuts delivered the Rhodes Memorial Lectures at Oxford in which he dealt at length with the general questions of settlement and native policy. At this time the whole question of the future of settlement in East Africa was being discussed in relation to proposals for closer union between the three territories, and the lectures were given with this controversy very much in mind. They consciously attempted to systematize the case for settlement, and became an important influence in that controversy. Both the settler and the peasant views began from the notion of the African's essential immaturity with reference to the problems created by modern industrial society, and both assumed that Africa could be led into the modern world only through agencies imported from European society. But the settler view argued that Africans could only be inducted into 'civilization' through close and continuous contact with an established European community, whereas the peasant view was that the process could be led by small groups of essentially expatriate administrators, missionaries and traders. According to Smuts 'the easiest, most natural and obvious way to civilize the African native is to give him decent white employment',[13] and, further:

> . . . without large-scale permanent European settlement on this continent the African mass will not be moved, the sporadic attempts at civilization will pass, Africa may relapse to her historic and pre-historic slumbers, and once more only mining holes and ruined forts may ultimately remain to bear testimony to future ages of what once was.[14]

This being so it was argued that there was no inherent contradiction between the interests of Africans and settlers, rather a natural reciprocity of interest:

> From the native point of view, therefore, just as much as from the white . . . point of view, nay even more from the native point of view, the policy of African settlement is imperatively necessary.[15]

Since Africans could only benefit from what Europeans brought with them no special guarantees were required to ensure that their interests were safeguarded; instead the Europeans could be exclusively entrusted with running of the country in accordance with their superior scale of civilized values. All that was required was 'an awakened public conscience among the whites' which would 'not silently tolerate injustice or abuses', and which would ultimately 'come to form an efficient safeguard for native interests'.[16] In deference no doubt to liberal opinion there was a commitment to training Africans 'to stand by themselves', to develop a 'sense of responsibility' and 'a sense of pride in their own system'.[17] This, however, had to be achieved through segregated institutions responsible for local government work; on no account were Africans and Europeans to share the same institutions or even living space or else the most dire consequences must necessarily follow:

> This separation is imperative, not only in the interests of a native culture, and to prevent native traditions and institutions from being swamped by the more powerful organisation of the whites, but also for other important purposes, such as public health, racial purity, and public good order. The mixing up of two such alien elements as white and black leads to unhappy social results – racial miscegenation, moral deterioration of both, racial antipathy and clashes, and to many other forms of social evil. In these great matters of race, colour and culture, residential separation and parallel institutions alone can do justice to the ideals of both sections of the population.[18]

Further, this necessity was not derived from social considerations alone; it also depended upon the necessity of maintaining the traditional authority structures in order to relieve the central authority of a large part of the load involved in maintaining social discipline among the African population.

> From time immemorial the natives of Africa have been subject to a stern, even ruthless discipline, and their social system has rested on the despotic authority of their chiefs. If this system breaks down and tribal discipline disappears, native society will be resolved into its human atoms, with possibilities of universal Bolshevism and chaos which no friend of the natives, or of the orderly civilization of the continent, could contemplate with equanimity.[19]

Smuts recognized the very powerful pressures drawing Africans into the 'white' sector and the strong tendency of such contact to break down these traditional values and structures. But he felt that it was not 'white employment' that created the problem, 'but the abandonment of the native tribal home by the women and children'.[20] This he felt should be prevented by the law which should 'only allow the residence of adult males for limited periods and for purposes of employment among the whites'.[21]

The concern in all of this was to meet the humanitarian opposition to white settlement on its own ground, to argue not merely that African and European interests did not conflict, but that they were directly dependent upon each other. But this was only half the case; the other half rested upon the assumption that only an active settlement policy could open up Africa's 'vast resources' to the world. For Smuts (and in this he was using exactly the same language as the Imperialist movement in the Conservative Party led by Joseph Chamberlain, Milner and Leo Amery) Africa constituted Britain's great 'undeveloped estate'[22] whose empty highland land should be filled with active British settlers, thus relieving population pressure and unemployment in Britain, expanding British control over raw materials and increasing the market for British exports. This view denied the ability of a European presence based primarily upon missionaries and civil servants to achieve this – Christianity alone was too ineffectual and in any event could not hope to make as strong an appeal 'to the native mind' as Mohammedanism,[23] while civil servants were necessarily too cautious and unadventurous to be entrusted with the responsibility for stimulating development.[24] Thus the need both to bring Africans to civilization and to bring African resources into the British sphere could be seen to depend upon the establishment of a new South Africa in the north. It required a purposeful policy designed to put the present colonies in Eastern Africa 'in the way of becoming in time another important self-governing unit of the Empire',[25] and thus to lay 'the foundations for a great future Dominion'.[26] For those who accepted his fundamental assumptions about the nature of traditional society and the nature of the relationship between capital and labour in the colonial situation the case for settlement could be shown to have a universal importance which far transcended the narrow interests of the white community in Africa itself. In their development was to be found 'something of far-reaching importance for Africa, for the Empire and for the world'.[27] Nothing short of this would suffice:

> No flash in the pan of exploitation will really help the course of African civilization . . . only an ever-present, settled European order can achieve that high end. The call of Africa for civilization, the call of the world for tropical products, and the call of these islands for migration and employment combine to give very real force to the case which I am making today.[28]

This general view served to legitimate the claims being put forward both in London and East Africa on behalf of the settler minority. It was opposed, however, both in metropolis and colony, by a range of interests which denied some of its fundamental postulates and argued that the task of colonial development could be achieved more efficiently and more justly in a system based upon peasant rather than settler production. Both views shared a stereotype of the African as a 'traditional man' – happy-go-lucky, irresponsible and indolent (displaying low 'need-achievement', to use contemporary terminology), though the later supporters of the peasant tradition were far more open than their opponents to evidence of the ability of Africans to assimilate European skills and values through education.[29] But a critical difference existed with regard to their attitude to the necessary implications of the relationship between settler and African interests in the economic sector. Whereas the settler view argued that these interests were necessarily reciprocal, the peasant view asserted that there was a strong tendency for them to come into direct conflict. Smuts's argument depended upon the assumption that there was an abundance of empty and fertile land in the African highlands so that the establishment of a large settler community would not limit the ability of the African population to support itself.[30] Its opponents, however, argued that the existence of European enterprise in such areas necessarily depended upon the importation of African labour either through 'some organized system of immigration', or 'some form of more or less open compulsion'.[31] Further it was argued that this supply was likely to be very unstable and, more importantly, that the high costs of maintaining white managers ('the most expensive of God's creatures') in the tropics, and of maintaining the minimum level of services for operations of the required scale made the large plantation a very uneconomic means of exploiting most tropical products.[32] By comparison the small-scale peasant producer was relatively efficient not so much in the technical sense (his methods were inevitably inferior to the planter's) but in relation to costs. He had no fixed capital costs, almost all his labour was supplied by his family, and he was exceedingly resistant to price fluctuations.[33] Indeed proponents of the then very popular theories of the backward-sloping supply curve of effort and risk-taking among traditional producers argued that a fall in price tended to produce an increase in effort and production;[34] to this could be compared the inevitable tendency for plantation producers either to be forced out of business in these circumstances or to be forced back on to the State for direct assistance. Thus on the one hand it was argued that peasant producers could be the primary agency for development, since they were capable of producing 'a progressive increase in output that [would] beggar every record of the past, and [would be] altogether unparalleled in all the long history of European agricultural enterprises in the tropics.'[35] On the other it was argued that the impact of a large European sector on African society must inevitably be considerable and highly disruptive both in social and political terms. Thus they claimed that the presence of a European community in a country must inevitably give rise to demands for political participation and control (which the settler case, of course, did not deny) and must thus create a situation in which African rights would become entirely dependent on the goodwill of the white community. Addressing himself to the Tanganyika settlers Cameron said:

> you . . . press insistently for the development of the political side so far as it affects not the natives but the Europeans. You want that side strengthened as soon as possible so that you may go from strength to strength and become so securely entrenched that there will be no place left for the native in the political structure *unless you please to give it to him*. You desire to create here an ultimate complete dominance for the white man based on what you call 'responsible government'.[36]

And Cameron and his supporters at least felt that to allow this would inevitably mean that their obligations to the African population would 'go by default'.[37] This theory, too, argued that the development of African traditional institutions was essential 'to prevent the natives from "going under" and becoming a servile people', that it provided the 'only way of keeping his society together; the only way in which he can be trained in public affairs'.[38] But unlike Smuts they felt that it would be impossible to maintain viable African institutions in a system politically and economically dominated by settler institutions. Cameron, for example, based his opposition to proposals for closer union in East Africa on the fact that the increase in settler control which these implied would lead to the rapid termination 'of the work I was doing in Tanganyika in the field of local native government',[39] while the Clifford case assumed that:

> if half of the male population . . . should be obliged to go and come intermittently from plantations to their homes, it would be a matter of only a few years before native administrations would be destroyed or at least their development retarded.[40]

Stated in its extreme form the peasant view denied the necessity or the desirability of promoting any forms of expatriate enterprise because of their necessarily deleterious impact upon African institutions. In fact, however, most of its protagonists did not take their opposition this far. Lugard felt that plantations 'of limited area, owned by Europeans, are useful as object-lessons in improved methods',[41] and Cameron that there were 'certain agricultural processes' which European enterprise could manage but which were 'beyond the capacity of the African tribesman'.[42] But their view was based on the recognition of the necessity for keeping such developments within very limited bounds: of treating them as an adjunct to the primary task of building up peasant production and local African institutions, rather than of using them as the primary lever in the whole developmental process like the proponents of the settler position. Most especially, this view was strongly opposed to the case of the small settler, or to the development of a class of European 'mechanics and artisans'.[43] Small farmers 'without an independent income' would have to come to terms with Tanganyika's 'cruel climate for the agriculturist' and 'their disillusionment would be tragic'.[44] European artisans would be forced to compete with Africans and Indians, and they too would find it hard to survive. Now both these categories were critical to the evolution of the fully-fledged settler-dominated communities of the south. Without them the European political base depended upon the efforts of a largely expatriate class which was often not even the owner of its own capital. Managers on six-year contracts looking to England for retirement were not the stuff of which great white Dominions were to be made. What was wanted was small men settled in a new country for life, committed to imposing their control on it for the sake of their children and grandchildren. It was for this reason that men like Grigg, a key governor of Kenya, who understood the political realities, called for a rapid expansion in small-scale settlement. For men like Cameron and Clifford, such people were merely parasites who depended on the subventions which the colonial system could exact from the African population; for men like Lord Delamere in Kenya, Smuts, and Sir Edward Grigg, Governor of Kenya from 1925–30, they were the 'real root of our civilisation in Africa'.[45] In subsequent chapters some attempt will be made to examine the validity of these competing claims; at this point it is only necessary to note the very different long-term implications of the two views.

All this is to suggest that British policy in Africa developed within an ideological framework which took as its starting-point the assumption that only the Western world could bring civilization and progress to Africa and that the British Empire was in fact the most advanced Western agency for this purpose. In this respect it is important to understand that the colonial system was seen by its agents as essentially a moral force; as an agency whose primary purpose was to bring Africans to civilization and, by bringing Africa into the mainstream of Western trade and intellectual life, to bring the benefits of African resources to the rest of the world. 'Under no other rule' than that of the British Empire, Lugard believed, 'does the African enjoy such a measure of freedom and impartial justice, or a more sympathetic treatment.'[46] Whatever we now conclude to have been the actual objective impact of that rule on the development of the countries concerned (and this is very likely to differ sharply from the colonialists' own view of what they were achieving) it is necessary to understand that their motivation was largely derived from this image of their role as the advance guard of a civilization with a universal message equally applicable to the whole of the underdeveloped world. But this message could only be promoted through the establishment of concrete institutions capable of performing the tasks which the new kind of life demanded. Political order had to be maintained, production of new kinds encouraged, educational structures created and social relations managed. Each of these systems of control required both ideology and organization; a set of justificatory assumptions and a concrete institutional structure. It is impossible to discuss the ideological and organizational aspects of particular structures separately. The next two chapters will therefore attempt to look at the most important of them in a general way before moving on to a discussion of their actual performance in the period under consideration.

NOTES

1. W. G. M. Ormsby-Gore (later Lord Harlech), *Developments and opportunities in the Colonial Empire*, London, no pub., 1929, p. xi.
2. *Report of the Commission on Closer Union of the Dependencies in Eastern and Central Africa*, Cmd. 3234 of 1929, p. 87.
3. M. Oakeshott, 'Political education', in *Rationalism in Politics*, London, Methuen, 1962, p. 129; perhaps the most concise statement on this process can be found in A. Gramsci, *The modern prince and other writings*, New York, International Publishers, 1957.
4. Sir F. D. Lugard, *The dual mandate in British tropical Africa*, Edinburgh, Blackwood, 1922, p. 132. A good deal more to the same effect will be found in Sir R. Furse, *Aucupqrius; recollections of a recruiting officer*, London, O.U.P., 1962, with a general and not very rewarding survey of recruiting practices and their implications in R. Heussler, *Yesterday's rulers*, Syracuse, U.P., 1963.
5. F. Schurman, *Ideology and organisation in Communist China*, Berkeley, Univ. of Calif. Press, 1968, p. 53.
6. Article 22 of the Covenant of the League of Nations.
7. Lugard, *op. cit.*, pp. 69–70.
8. *Ibid.*, p. 95.

9. House of Commons, *Debates*, 11 viii 20, v. 133, c. 490.
10. From *Soldiers Three*, cited in D. Daiches, *Some late Victorian attitudes*, London, Deutsch, 1969, p. 21.
11. Some of the economic aspects are dealt with in C. Ehrlich, 'Some social and economic aspects of paternalism in Uganda', *Journal of African History*, vol. IV, part 2 (1963).
12. J. C. Smuts, 'African settlement', in *Africa and some world problems*, Oxford, Clarendon Press, 1930, p. 56.
13. *Ibid.*, p. 48.
14. *Ibid.*, pp. 50–1.
15. *Ibid.*, p. 49.
16. *Ibid.*, p. 60.
17. 'Native policy in Africa', in *op. cit.*, p. 91.
18. *Ibid.*, p. 93.
19. *Ibid.*, p. 87.
20. *Ibid.*, p. 100.
21. *Ibid.*
22. 'African settlement', in *op. cit.*, p. 63.
23. *Ibid.*, p. 53.
24. *Ibid.*, p. 54–5.
25. *Ibid.*, p. 64.
26. *Ibid.*, p. 66.
27. *Ibid.*, p. 64.
28. *Ibid.*, p. 66.
29. See, for example, Sir Donald Cameron's confidential evidence to the Joint Select Committee on Closer Union in East Africa in the Passfield Papers.
30. Smuts, *op. cit.*, pp. 55–60.
31. Sir Hugh Clifford, cited in R. L. Buell, *The native problem in Africa*, vol. 1, New York, Macmillan, 1928, p. 772.
32. *Ibid.*, p. 773.
33. *Ibid.*
34. On the theory cf. G. M. Meier, *Leading issues in development economics*, New York, O.U.P., 1964, p. 56; note also Ormsby-Gore's statement confirming it in Buell, *op. cit.*, p. 775.
35. *Ibid.*, p. 774.
36. Tanganyika, Native administration memoranda, No. 1, *Principles of native administration and their application*, 2nd ed., 1930, p. 2. Emphasis in original.
37. *Ibid.*
38. *Ibid.*, p. 3.
39. Sir D. Cameron, *My Tanganyika service*, London, Allen & Unwin, 1939, p. 225.
40. Buell, *op. cit.*, p. 774.
41. Lugard, *op. cit.*, p. 295.
42. Cameron, *op. cit.*, p. 39.
43. *Ibid.*, p. 40.
44. *Ibid.*
45. Sir Edward Grigg, House of Commons, *Debates*, 25 vii 1935, v. 304, c. 2082. Cf. also his speeches: 14 vii 33, v. 280, c. 1482; 9 vii 36, v. 314, c. 1484; 7 vi 39, v. 348, c. 483. Note also Elspeth Huxley, *White man's country*, 2nd ed., London, Macmillan, 1953, p. v.
46. Lugard, *op. cit.*, p. 5.

2

The Political Structures

A colonial power must control populations with very different social systems from its own, which are distributed at great distances from the metropolitan and territorial capitals and which in the African case often manifested very low levels of social and economic differentiation. It has to overcome problems of authority, distance and cost – to persuade subject peoples to accept both its version of law and order and its control over their dominant social institutions; to create an organizational capacity capable of transmitting orders from the centre and enforcing them on the periphery; and to do all this without incurring costs which are so high that they render the whole exercise valueless. The scale of these problems depends upon the extent of the Empire in relation to the resources at the disposal of the metropolis and equally upon the intensity of the social change which the metropolitan power wishes to induce at the local level.

These problems existed in an exceedingly intense form for the British Empire in the twentieth century. Its span of control, at its highest point after the First World War, was immense; its own resources heavily over-extended. Britain as the preponderant world power of 1860 had been reduced to one which found it increasingly difficult to maintain its parity with the United States, Germany and Japan by 1919.[1] And although Britain attempted to contain within a very narrow compass the degree of social change which its presence produced at the local level, this was an intrinsically impossible task because of the dynamic nature of the economic structure which it was forced to introduce.[2] As a result the British colonial system tended to operate from a position of weakness during the period under review, and this conditioned many of the attitudes which dominated policy-making. Again, the contradiction between the need to limit social change and the need to create a new export-oriented colonial economy made it very difficult for viable institutions of political control to be set up and sustained over the long term. In the rest of this chapter an attempt will be made to look at the development of these institutions within this general context of international weakness and internal contradiction.

Whatever the importance of strategic or philanthropic concerns among those who originally took Britain into Africa at the end of the nineteenth century,[3] those who kept her there in the twentieth were obsessed with the need to create an export economy which would draw her directly and profitably into the British system of international trade. By the end of the First World War a powerful faction in public life saw the colonies as areas of immense economic potential. 'Give them the ordinary scientific apparatus they require,' said Churchill to the Liverpool Chamber of Commerce, 'and they will return you a plentiful reward for every pound that is invested in them.'[4] The actual level of such investment never corresponded to the hopes of the imperialists like Chamberlain, Milner and Amery, but it was to be much greater in the twenties than tends now to be realized. The establishment and maintenance of this economic infrastructure demanded an extensive and positive role for the colonial state, the establishment of a sizeable expatriate community at the local level, and sufficient restructuring of indigenous African political institutions to make it possible for them to supervise the move from production for purely local needs into production for the international market.

The smooth functioning of the colonial political system depended upon the successful resolution of four distinct problems. Firstly, an administrative system had to be created at the local level capable of maintaining law and order, collecting taxes and managing the economy. Secondly, machinery had to be evolved to deal with the demands and the conflicts arising out of the needs of the expatriate communities imported to man the new colonial institutions. Thirdly, demands and conflicts arising out of colonial policy had to be integrated into the machinery of British government since this was the point where ultimate political authority was vested. Finally, relations with the indigenous population had to be regularized through the establishment of institutions capable of settling internal disputes, maintaining social order and regulating their contacts with the expatriate world. Four sets of institutions were set up to meet these needs. The Colonial Service was created to provide the administrative apparatus. Local Legislative and Executive Councils were set up to represent the interests of the expatriate communities. In Britain colonial affairs were integrated into the wider system of government through the evolution of the Colonial Office as a Ministry in its own right. And finally the system of indirect rule institutionalized through the chieftaincies and Native Councils was used to regulate the affairs of the indigenous community. Before looking more closely at these structures, it is necessary to consider in more detail a general assumption of colonial political theory which has already been mentioned.

British theory in this area constantly assumed that the contradiction between the need for change and the very limited availability of metropolitan resources to initiate and manage that change could be resolved through the devolution of power to effectively decentralized political and administrative structures. It was widely believed that colonies could be quickly equipped with the basic administrative and economic infrastructure and thereafter meet their own costs from internal sources. Local structures – administrators, Legislative Councils and even Chiefs – were expected to carry out their duties with only minimal recourse to the centre. Ormsby-Gore, then Under-Secretary of State for the Colonies, told the Commons that 'the attempt always to govern from here with an official majority, without regard to the sentiment, often very narrow and inexperienced, of pioneers, of the men who are living on the spot, and to disregard them would be one of the worst failures of British Colonial History.'[5] And Lugard considered that the first principle of native administration was that 'liberty and self-development can best be secured to the native population by leaving them free to manage their own affairs through their own rulers, proportionately to their degree of advancement, under the guidance of British staff, and subject to the law and policy of the administration.'[6] Every effort was made also to devolve responsibility for social organization away from the hands of government in the fields of social and economic services. Despite the significant role played by the State in the economic sphere, primary responsibility for production and distribution remained in the hands of private entrepreneurs, while education was left largely to the missions, and social welfare services were provided through the traditional authorities or not at all.

When practice conformed to this theory London could virtually ignore the day-to-day financial and administrative problems of vast portions of the colonial Empire, and the drain upon British resources became negligible. But successful praxis of this kind depended upon a number of considerations. On the ideological level it required the continued effectiveness of the socialization of the colonial ruling class into the basic assumptions of the colonial ideology, and the willing acceptance of subordination on the part of the indigenous population, and especially the class within it which manned the local political institutions. Equally important, it depended upon an ability to manage economic and political affairs in a manner which made it possible to avoid the emergence of unreconcilable conflicts between any of the main social formations involved in the whole process. During periods of quiescence when such conflicts were at a low level the whole operation took on the appearance of a self-regulating mechanism which travelled along a preordained path without direction or assistance from the outside. But the nature of the colonial situation and of the capitalistic relations of production which it created made such conflict inevitable. In the short term this could be managed through the political institutions to be described below; in the long term it was to require a fundamental modification of the whole system. In the rest of this chapter I shall deal with the state machinery, in the next with the organization of services provided privately.

The administrative backbone of colonial control stretched from the Secretary of State in London through the local Governor and thence down to the village headman or chief via the Secretariat and the Provincial and District Administration. As more resources became available this structure of general administration was complemented by specialized services provided on a departmental basis, with field officers – in agriculture, public works, health, etc. – responsible to a Permanent Secretary in the Secretariat who would in turn be responsible to the Governor. However strong the informal commitment to devolution, the formal authority structure was very hierarchical and centralized. Lines of command and communication could not be broken, making each subordinate heavily dependent upon his superior and giving the Governor a great deal of power since all information (and all recommendations for promotion) had to be channelled through him. In London the Colonial Office was originally organized on an essentially geographic basis. Its role was seen as advisory to the Secretary of State and it was never allocated any functions which might involve it in direct administration. During the late twenties it began to develop specialist services in fields like economic and educational policy and to set up advisory committees mainly composed of individuals with colonial experience, or directly involved in colonial affairs. A great deal has been written about the nature of this system so it need detain us no further.[7]

During the inter-war period a considerable expansion took place in the economic services, which were organized on an East Africa-wide basis. During the twenties a strong attempt was made to federate the three territories, but this failed because of local and British opposition to the likely extension of Kenyan settler influences which it appeared to presage. A loose regional authority was set up in 1926 to co-ordinate policy. Decisions were taken by the three Governors sitting in conference, although the central authority had no final authority and no power to 'affect in any way the equal responsibility of each Governor for his own territory to the Secretary of State.'[8] Decisions had to be reached unanimously and unresolved conflicts of interest were ultimately decided by the Secretary of State. The first meeting was in 1926, the second in London in 1927, and the conference met annually or more often from 1930. It was provided with a secretariat consisting of one senior official with only clerical assistance. During this period it was principally concerned with regulating transport and customs policy, but it also discussed a wide range of questions of general interest like industrialization or commodity restriction schemes. At this level decision-making was therefore heavily centralized in the person of the three Governors, and the interests involved had to operate through them.

Expatriate interests were represented at the local level on Legislative Councils which were set up in Kenya before the War, in Uganda in 1922 and in Tanganyika in 1926.[9] Although the proportions differed, each contained representatives of the main interest-groups which existed in the local community – essentially of agriculture, commerce and the missions – together with the heads of the governmental departments, who constituted a majority. African interests were indirectly represented, if at all, through Europeans, usually missionaries. Only in Kenya were unofficial members elected, and of these Europeans were allocated eleven seats (eight of these to agricultural interests despite the fact that farmers constituted less than half the white population), Asians five and Arabs one. Here unofficial members also sat on the Executive Council, the highest decision-making body. In Kenya the European agricultural interests were probably the most important single influence upon policy, for reasons which have been considered in an extensive literature.[10] In Tanganyika and Uganda unofficial members were nominated, not elected, with more Europeans than Asians. But because of the much smaller role of expatriate enterprise in the agricultural sector their influence on the general evolution of policy, although considerable, as Engholm's thorough study of Uganda shows, was never as decisive as it was in Kenya. These expatriate interests were constantly involved in the political process both through these formal institutions and through an extensively developed system of informal links with local officials. Where they were able to obtain what they wanted without difficulty through these formal and informal links British politics were not involved, but as soon as any irreconcilable conflict arose which could not be settled locally this was immediately taken up in Britain, where all the major local expatriate groups had strong connections with groups directly involved in the British political system. Once this had occurred the issue would be fought out within the British sphere, which thus became of paramount importance. Since a great many resources for local development were also dispensed directly by the British authorities in response to pressures emanating from British interests involved in colonial affairs, it is clear that the structure of the colonial political system at the metropolitan level was of crucial importance and must therefore be considered in some detail.

In Britain the Secretary of State's legal authority included the power to legislate for the colonies without consulting Parliament at all. This power became less important once local legislative structures had been developed since they produced the great bulk of legislation, although in a context where the Governor could control the votes of the official majority and the Secretary of State had the power of veto.

The Secretary of State was responsible for his actions to the Cabinet and ultimately to Parliament, but neither of these bodies appear to have been able to exert an influence which was either continuous or direct. This was especially true of Parliament, which was even denied the right to discuss contentious colonial legislation directly. Amery refused to put the Kenya Native Lands Trust Bill before Parliament on the ground that it could 'only be a body supervising and controlling through the Secretary of State the administration of the Colonies', but never 'in detail a legislative body for the Colonies'.[11] The only regular debates on colonial questions were held during the annual presentation of the Colonial Office estimates and rarely lasted more than an afternoon. Where the British Government was asked to provide money directly for colonial purposes debates could and did occur; otherwise it was left to private members to raise particular issues through questions or motions. Again, the wide range of colonial problems, and their general remoteness from the centre of British politics, appears to have limited even the Cabinet's role in controlling the actions of the Secretary of State. Cabinet minutes for the first few years after the War contain discussions of only a few very large issues of colonial policy, more especially those where British interests appeared to have been directly involved or where major conflicts of interest at the local level had occurred. And even in such cases the Cabinet was not always directly consulted. Churchill, for example, did not consult it before a major speech on Kenyan policy in 1922, saying afterwards:

> An enormous mass of business has to proceed, and decisions have to be taken in every sphere of the administration of the Colonial Office, and cannot be in every case, specifically referred to the Cabinet.[12]

The interests of British groups involved in colonial and especially East African affairs could be brought to bear through the Colonial Office, the political parties, the Cabinet or, in some cases, the colonial administration itself. Success or failure depended on so wide a range of factors and contingencies that it is impossible to attempt to specify them in advance; it is simply necessary to give some indication of the nature of the more important linkages involved.

Interest in the Colonies was generally confined to a very limited range of groups specifically involved in one or more aspects of local affairs. The general public took almost no interest in them, so that decisions could make virtually no impact on either party's electoral standing. As an active Labour member on these issues put it:

> This question of the Colonies, important as it is, has not much electoral value in the constituencies . . . but it is a vital question in the House of Commons.

Colonial issues did have to be taken seriously by Parliament and the parties, and they were often of 'vital' importance to the limited numbers of individuals actually affected by them. The two major parties both set up specialized groups concerned with colonial affairs and these were directly linked to the major interests involved through overlapping membership and constant social interaction. These linkages were necessary for both parties and groups, since they guaranteed the parties access to the information required for policy-making and debate and the groups access to decision-making structures. In the Conservative Party the Imperial Affairs Committee was seemingly established in 1924 and usually contained at least one member of the Joint East Africa Board, the leading business group at that time.[14] On the Labour side a committee of the same name was made up of a group of M.P.s and of outsiders who had taken a prominent part in the colonial debate. Leonard Woolf was its secretary, and Norman Leys and MacGregor Ross, former Kenyan officials, were important members. Both the latter had written important works criticizing the Kenyan administration, and it seems probable that their position on the committee made it possible for them to exert a very direct influence on debate in Parliament. Ormsby-Gore, in fact, attributed the fact that 'left wing' opinion in England had 'always been more worried over the treatment of natives in Kenya than anywhere else' to the 'activities of Norman Leys and MacGregor Ross'.[15] A number of important debates also occurred in the Lords, where the interest and position derived more directly from personal involvement and experience – the Archbishop of Canterbury, for example, drew his interest in Africa from the role of the Church, Lord Lugard had been an African Governor, Lord Chelmsford Viceroy of India, and Lord Cranworth owned sisal estates in Kenya.

In the Commons the major contribution to debate was made by a small and stable group of M.P.s, mainly located on the Labour and Liberal side. Between 1925 and 1929, 258 of the 325 questions asked on Kenya were put by only six members, and 103 of these by Josiah Wedgwood alone. Yet it is also true that 170 M.P.s contributed to the debate on East African or general colonial questions during the same period, even if this only took the form of a single question. A fairly clear difference in attitude is visible between the two parties. The Conservatives were mainly concerned with the promotion of economic development in the Colonies and they tended to support the settler view. Labour, at least until the late thirties, took little positive interest in the development debate except with regard to the protection of African labour. The activists in the party devoted almost their whole attention to the Kenya question and were principally concerned with the protection of Africans from settler pressures. The Liberals appear to have identified with them in this. These differences show fairly clearly when the questions asked by the twenty most frequent contributors in the Commons are analysed in relation to party, subject and attitude:

TABLE I[16]

Parliamentary Questions 1925–9 by Party, Subject and Attitude

Subject		Economic Development			Kenyan Administration		
Attitude		Support	Neutral	Hostile	Support	Neutral	Hostile
Numbers	M.Ps.	Questions			Questions		
Conservative	9	78	33	3	2	3	0
Liberal	2	9	14	0	2	11	55
Labour	9	19	15	6	1	14	206

Source: House of Commons Debates, 1925–9.

These differences of attitude largely conditioned the channels through which extra-Parliamentary groups sought access to debate. Business interests operated almost exclusively through the Conservative Party; religious and humanitarian groups tended to find their major spokesmen on the Liberal and Labour side. But the latter tendency was not in any way complete, since such groups do appear to have been able to get some support on some issues from the Conservatives.

Too much should not, however, be made of these differences, since very powerful pressures tended to drive the system towards consensus when policy decisions had to be made and implemented. Firstly, policy had to be put into effect in a situation where, even by 1919, there already existed a coherent set of economic and administrative interests which necessarily served as the agents for central policies. These policies had therefore to operate within the limits of tolerance determined by what these groups could be persuaded to accept. A major change in policy would necessarily have involved a crisis in confidence among groups adversely affected and this in turn would have involved serious administrative and economic problems. Thus such changes would only be made under the pressure of very strong ideological commitment, and there are few signs that Labour dissatisfaction with the Conservatives' Kenyan and economic policies ever amounted to anything more than a concern about details. The party had certainly not formulated an alternative developmental strategy and, in the absence of this, was never in a position to do more than modify these details, since anything more would have demanded

an attempt to evolve new structures of administrative and economic control. Secondly, of course, the period was dominated by the
Conservative Party, and Labour was in office only briefly and then
without an overall majority. But there is in any event little
evidence that the Party would have taken a stronger line even if it
had had a majority.

It is in fact very easy to document the strenous efforts made on
both sides to ensure continuity and consensus. Major Commissions, when not manned by non-politicians, tended to be
politically balanced.[17] On the Kenya issue, the 1923 White Paper
which declared the paramountcy of African interests was issued by
a Conservative Colonial Secretary;[18] in the politics of the next
decade Conservatives were to concern themselves with modifying
it in the favour of settlers, the Left with reaffirming its commitment to African interests. In the economic field both Labour
Ministries were to introduce and implement development schemes
formulated by their predecessors – the 1924 railway loan for
Uganda and the 1929 Colonial Development Act, both of which
will be discussed later. The Conservatives, on the other hand,
were willing to accept Labour demands with reference to fair
employment, Amery, for example, accepting an amendment to
the 1926 East African Transport Loan Bill stating that 'fair
conditions of labour [should be] observed in the execution of all
works carried out under any loan raised in pursuance of this
Act'.[19] Again, Ramsay MacDonald also appears to have avoided
any direct confrontation with the settler lobby by passing over
the group which had been active in the anti-Kenyan debate when
allocating the colonial portfolios in the Cabinet.

Three kinds of interests had direct access to these British
institutions – humanitarian groups, the Asian community and
business interests of one kind and another. The first were primarily
concerned with questions of African welfare, and were most effectively located in the various missionary organizations with East
African commitments, but they also operated through more secular
organizations like the Anti-Slavery and Aborigines Protection
Society, which took a general interest in African conditions. The
work of the missionaries has been discussed elsewhere,[20] and,
although something will be said about this influence, my primary
concern will be with the business interests. The Asian community
was less directly represented in Britain but could, on major issues
like the question of the franchise in Kenya, bring pressure to
bear along a route which took in the Congress Party in India, the

Viceroy, the India Office in London and the Cabinet itself. These pressures were to be of considerable importance on a number of issues, though on the whole they also are not central to this study.

The most pervasive and effective influence on economic policy was almost certainly exerted by the representatives of British capital directly or indirectly involved in East Africa. One can distinguish here between two kinds of interests – those continuously and actively involved and organized to ensure continuous contact with the authorities, and those whose interests merely involved intervention when particular issues arose. The London Chamber of Commerce was probably the first to establish a permanent organization of the former kind, this being in operation by 1919 with Sir Humphrey Leggett of the British East Africa Corporation as its Chairman.[21] The Manchester Chamber of Commerce set up an East African sub-committee in 1919,[22] while the Liverpool Chamber had a small East African sub-committee in operation by 1922 and a full section by June 1925.[23] These bodies tended, after 1923, to confine themselves to the narrower commercial questions, and in that year the Joint East Africa Board (J.E.A.B.) was set up in London to represent 'those sections of the British community which are actively interested in the agricultural, commercial, financial and industrial development of East Africa'.[24]

The Board was established during a period of great political tension in Kenya: it was conceived as a means of linking British interests in East Africa with their British counterparts, and in particular of modifying the conflict which had emerged between settler and commercial interests at this time. During the years immediately after the War Leggett of the London Chamber had evidently wielded 'great influence . . . with the officials at the Colonial Office',[25] and both he and other members of the commercial community in Kenya at that time were dubious about the value of the economic contribution made by the settlers to the Kenyan economy.[26] Sydney Henn, an M.P. who had had coffee interests in Uganda immediately after the War, and whose son was to farm coffee in Kenya during the inter-war period, had visited East Africa in 1922, and in 1923 collaborated with Ormsby-Gore, then Under-Secretary of State, to bring together the main East African interests into a single organization on the lines of the Joint West Africa Board. The Board was functioning by June 1923, and in July Ormsby-Gore announced that it would be 'able to confer from time to time with the Colonial Office [on any matter] that will help forward the development and prosperity of the East African Dependency.'[27] Both Leggett and the settlers were apparently afraid that the Board would undermine their independence. In correspondence with C. K. Archer, then Chairman of the leading settler organization, the Convention of Associations, Henn felt constrained to stress their desire to strengthen rather than weaken local interests, saying:

> So far from wishing to run East Africa from this end, the main aim of the Board (so far as I am concerned) is to strengthen local interests out there by fighting their battles with the Colonial Office on the one hand and the public on the other, until they are able to achieve complete independence, which can only come when the country is sufficiently developed to yield a revenue proportionate to its needs.[28]

Archer replied that there was no feeling of antagonism to the Board, only one of apprehension at the powers it might assume.[29] The Convention then accepted its existence and was given three members, the largest single group on it, who were nominally drawn from the Associated Producers of East Africa, a loose British grouping of people with agricultural interests in East Africa.[30] Leggett apparently attempted to defend his independence by setting up a Joint East Africa Committee of the three main Chambers of Commerce, which claimed the right to regular meetings with the Colonial Office on 'purely commercial questions' but accepted that the Board should be concerned with 'broad questions, political in character'.[31] This was rejected by Ormsby-Gore who, while recognizing the London Chamber's continued right of access, was not willing to see a group established which would overlap with the Board.[32] Ormsby-Gore used his influence to persuade the Manchester and Liverpool Chambers to join the Board,[33] and by September 1925 Manchester and Liverpool had officially accepted a seat apiece and London was to be 'unofficially represented by one of their members [i.e. Leggett]'.[34] This, according to Henn, brought 'to an end the duel with Leggett who will be reduced to his right proportion at this end in East African affairs'.[35]

During the inter-war period the Board represented the major British firms with African interests, though it does not appear to have represented the banks which presumably dealt with the Colonial Office direct. It always contained one or more M.P.s prepared to interest themselves in East Africa though not necessarily with direct East African interests of their own. The Chairman was an M.P. for all but one year between 1923 and 1939.[36] Local bodies like the various Chambers of Commerce and the

Uganda Planters' Association were represented on it through British-based individuals with interests in the relevant colonies. It quite consciously represented 'British' interests and had no connection with African or Asian organizations.[37] The Colonial Office decided that relations would be confined to issues raised by the Board, and that it would not 'consult the [Board] on any point . . . or initiate discussion.'[38] Formal correspondence with the Colonial Office appears to have been limited, and contact confined to conferences attended by senior officials and usually the Under-Secretary of State. There were twelve of these between 1923 and 1932, one in 1936, and another in 1937. The Board gave evidence to all the major Commissions of Enquiry of the period and had frequent discussions with Governors and other senior local officials when the latter visited England. These official contacts were strongly reinforced by informal relationships with senior politicians, and with British and East African officials, as the Henn Papers show. In this, as in other areas of British politics, a broad network of contacts within the élite was crucial to the decision-making process. Formal discussions and formal organizations appear to have been of importance only in the final resolution of issues after a long process of informal discussion and negotiation. J.E.A.B. Members were not frequent contributors to Parliamentary debate; they spoke only when wider support was needed to give impetus to official policy or on the relatively rare occasions when they had been unable to achieve a satisfactory solution in private. The organization concerned itself with virtually all the large questions of public policy discussed in the period with the exception of the problem of representation on the local Legislative Councils. Its influence appears to have been greatest in the twenties and to have declined in the thirties.

British economic interests were not exclusively represented through the Board. Specific interests were always able to take up particular questions with the Colonial Office, where the more important of them were assured of a sympathetic hearing. The Colonial Office made full use of business interests when solving specialized problems. A panel of such men was usually appointed to advise the Colonial Secretary at Imperial Conferences, and Sir Philip Cunliffe-Lister used the City in formulating his case for the Ottawa Conference,[39] and businessmen made up the greater part of the special bodies set up to organize aid programmes – the Colonial Development Advisory Committee, the Empire Marketing Board, and the Empire Cotton Growing Corporation.

To end this account of the British institutions it is necessary to mention official British Commissions of Enquiry; to overcome the dependence of the British authorities upon East African counterparts for information, appropriately selected individuals or groups would be sent out to conduct on-the-spot enquiries. These were especially popular when considerable controversy had been aroused on major issues of policy; an attempt would then be made to find a 'neutral' and if possible technically respectable individual to go out and produce recommendations which would resolve the disagreement. About ten of these went out during the period, and their reports exerted a pervasive influence on the whole colonial debate of the time.[40]

As long as the African population could be persuaded not to question the basic assumptions of the colonial political economy, expatriate politics could operate as a virtually self-contained system with its primary focus located in the metropolitan and territorial capitals. This deference to the colonial authority also made it possible for African affairs to be regulated through a completely separate set of structures which confined African political activity to the local level, and connected local structures to the centre through an essentially administrative apparatus. During this period it was generally assumed that the 'tribal' nature of the African consciousness ruled out the possibility of their representing their own interests at the centre of colonial politics. They were to be represented, if at all, on local councils whose boundaries would be coterminous with the limits of the pre-colonial tribal political authorities. Where local issues had to be related to the centre this became the responsibility of the District and Provincial Administration, which it was assumed would be able to sound out local opinion both formally through the chieftaincy and the Councils, and informally through contacts with the local populations. And within the limits of their general acceptance of the British colonial ethic, there is no doubt that many District Officers were able to build up strong commitments to their District and a considerable understanding of local social and political structure.

The ideology and organization of African administration constituted the Indirect Rule system. This assumed that authority should, as far as possible, be vested in existing traditional structures and notably in the Chiefs; that these should be provided with an independent source of finance and that they should be responsible for social discipline and the provision of local services – roads, health, education, and so on. In the more developed areas Native

Councils were set up which advised the Chief, but in all areas the District Commissioner, despite his supposedly advisory role, exercised the final authority. A great deal has been written about this system, and little needs to be added here to these descriptions.[41] It is sufficient to note at this point that its effectiveness varied considerably, depending on the nature of the pre-colonial situation and on the nature of the developmental strategy being followed in particular times and places. Where existing political structures were well articulated (as in the case of the Baganda) very considerable authority could be devolved to them. Where, on the other hand, they were small and undifferentiated, 'tribes' had virtually to be invented. Thus in parts of Tanganyika 'hitherto unknown clan elders, village tribunals, and even entire new tribes were discovered, regrouped, and duly gazetted as collective or joint Native Authorities'.[42] Further, despite the belief of men like Smuts and Sir Edward Grigg, Governor of Kenya,[43] that the maintenance of traditional authority was essential in areas of settlement, the Indirect Rule system could never function as it was intended where expatriates acquired a dominant position in the agricultural sector. This was essentially because the development of settlement required the net transfer of resources from the African to the expatriate sector and hence very repressive economic policies, as will be shown in the examination of the Kenyan case. Since the Native Authorities would have to identify at least in part with the colonial state, their authority with the African populations would be inevitably undermined. On the other hand, where peasant production provided the economic base far more resources could go directly into the African sector and the authority structure was brought under far less pressure.

Any discussion of the Indirect Rule system inevitably raises the larger question of its long-term stability in relation to its connection with the rise of African nationalism and the influences of 'tribal' or 'traditional' values on African political life. I have already argued that the viability of the colonial system depended upon the maintenance of these traditional values, that the system could survive, like Eisenstadt's Historical Empires:

> . . . only in so far as its rulers could maintain, within the framework of the same political institutions, simultaneously and continuously, both [modern and traditional] levels of legitimation, support and political organisation.[44]

This meant that far from being something to be overcome through the extension of modern techniques into the rural sector, traditionalism had to be maintained as a primary source of control for the régime. This fact was to be of the most central importance to the evolution of the colonial political economy, and a great deal of attention will be devoted to it in subsequent chapters.

Overall the colonial power structure represented the interests of those who were rich and white far more completely than those who were poor and black. Access did not depend on the size of the group, but upon its economic indispensability. Those groups which provided services that were essential to the future of the colonial economy could expect some consideration from the authorities; those who were articulate and aware of the long-term consequences of policy decisions (something from which Africans were almost entirely excluded) were most likely to be able to take advantage of situations of confusion or difficulty (which were very common) to maximize their interests at the expense of the rest. Groups strongly represented both in Britain and locally could usually be victorious over groups represented only in one place or the other. Despite the very considerable advantages which accrued to British interests in this structure (the existence, in effect, of a 'Power Elite'), power was not completely monolithic, nor were Africans totally excluded. Although British interests were in general agreement about the basic assumptions and objectives of colonial policy, many conflicts did exist between various sectors of the class – between missionaries and settlers, settlers and commerce, processors and middlemen and so on. These conflicts almost always arose in relation to issues which directly affected the interests of the African population, and it was therefore possible that one party to an issue might also attempt to advance African interests as a partial legitimation for his own case. Again, where Africans played a significant role in production, primarily in the centres of peasant cash-cropping, their tacit support for policy was required, since it was always possible for them to cut production and hence to threaten the financial viability of the administration. This was not a very powerful sanction since Africans soon came to depend upon their cash incomes for far more than simple tax payment, and it by no means compensated for the directness of the representation of the leading capitalist interests, but it did mean that they could not be totally ignored.

At the same time, to say that Africans had little representation and expatriates a great deal, is not to say that the latter were able to control the developmental process in any total way – the long-term failure of colonialism in its classical form shows very clearly the limits of British power in this regard. The consequences of policy could never be fully anticipated, the contradictions inside the ruling class limited their ability to formulate completely coherent strategies, and the impact of the new system upon the subject population soon produced new interests there which could not be effectively managed in the traditional way. It is now necessary to look at the assumptions and structures which conditioned the exercise of power in the sphere of production, before turning to a more detailed examination of this relationship between the political superstructure and the economic base as it worked itself out in the events of the period under review.

NOTES

1. Cf. esp. E. J. Hobsbawm, *Industry and Empire*, Harmondsworth, Penguin Books, 1969, pp. 178 ff.
2. Cf. C. Meillasoux, 'From reproduction to production', in *Economy and society*, vol. 1, no. 1, February 1972.
3. Cf. R. Robinson and J. Gallagher, *Africa and the Victorians*, London, Macmillan, 1961.
4. Liverpool Chamber of Commerce, *Monthly Journal*, June 1921, p. 132; for the intellectual origins cf. especially the pre-war writings of Lord Milner and Joseph Chamberlain.
5. House of Commons, *Debates*, 20 ii 28, v. 213, c. 1310.
6. Sir F. D. Lugard, *The dual mandate in British tropical Africa*, Edinburgh, Blackwood, 1922, p. 94.
7. Notably, Lord Hailey, *An African survey*, Revised 1956, London, O.U.P., 1957; C. Parkinson, *The Colonial Office from within*, London, Faber, 1947.
8. Amery to Grigg, 20 viii 26 (Walker Papers).
9. Cf. G. Bennett, *Kenya, a political history*, London, O.U.P., 1964; M. Bates, *Tanganyika under British administration*, Oxford D.Phil., 1957; G. Engholm, *Immigrant influences on the development of policy in the Protectorate of Uganda*, London Ph.D., 1967.
10. Notably Bennett, *op. cit.*; M. R. Dilley, *British policy in Kenya colony*, New York, Nelson, 1937; E. Huxley, *White man's country*, London, Macmillan, 1935.
11. House of Commons, *Debates*, 13 vii 28, v. 219, c. 2712.
12. House of Commons, *Debates*, 14 ii 22, v. 150, c. 798.
13. House of Commons, *Debates*, 12 vii 34, v. 292, c. 581.
14. Sir Sydney Henn, Chairman of the Joint East Africa Board, wrote to Sir Robert Coryndon (Governor of Kenya) 3 iii 24 mentioning its establishment (Henn Papers). Henn and Sir John Sandeman Allen, both Chairmen of the Joint East Africa Board, were members. (Cf. also J.E.A.B. Minute Book, 5 iii 30.)
15. Ormsby-Gore to Grigg, 24 viii 30 (Altrincham Papers).
16. Questions on development could either relate generally to the whole of the Colonial Empire or specifically to East Africa. I have classified them in

accordance with what seemed to be the intention of the speaker; this was particularly easy for the Kenyan questions where they appeared to have been part of a concerted campaign.

17. In particular the East Africa Commission (the 'Ormsby-Gore Commission') of 1924, and the *Joint Select Committee on Closer Union in East Africa* (House of Lords, 184) of 1931. For Labour criticism of the failure to include a Labour representative on the Hilton Young Commission, cf. House of Commons, *Debates*, 14 xi 27, v. 210, c. 608–9; 20 ii 28, v. 213, c. 1281–1312.

18. This was *Indians in Kenya*, Cmd. 1922 of 1923.

19. House of Commons, *Debates*, 10 xii 26, v. 200, c. 2437.

20. Especially in R. Oliver, *The missionary factor in East Africa*, London, Longmans, 1952.

21. London Chamber of Commerce, *Annual Reports*, 1919 ff.

22. Manchester Chamber of Commerce, *Monthly Record*, December 1919, p. 348.

23. Liverpool Chamber of Commerce, *Monthly Record*, July 1922, p. 152; June 1925, p. 119.

24. Chairman's statement to the first meeting of the Board, Minutes, 24 vi 23.

25. Henn to Archer, 10 ii 25 (Henn Papers).

26. Cf. Leggett's memo. to the Joint Select Committee on East Africa; also Henn's *Notebook of a trip to East Africa*, 1922–3 (Henn Papers).

27. House of Commons, *Debates*, 25 vii 23, v. 167, c. 506.

28. Henn to Archer, 16 i 24 (Henn Papers).

29. Archer to Henn, 29 ii 24 (Henn Papers).

30. For details of its activities cf. *Joint Select Committee on Closer Union in East Africa, op. cit.* (note 17), vol. II for evidence from its representatives.

31. London Chamber to Colonial Office, 1 v 25 (this and other correspondence in the J.E.A.B. files).

32. Ormsby-Gore to London Chamber, 8 v 25 (J.E.A.B. files).

33. *Ibid.*, 7 ix 25.

34. Henn to Archer, 7 ix 25 (Henn Papers).

35. *Ibid.*

36. Henn, 1923–9; Sir John Sandeman Allen, 1929–34; Sir Geoffrey Peto, 1935; Sir Charles Ponsonby 1935–. Peto was not an M.P. in 1935, but had been one previously.

37. Cf. their *Annual Report*, 1930, p. 8.

38. Unsigned letter headed 'Downing Street' 13 viii 23 (J.E.A.B. files).

39. Lord Swinton, *I remember*, London, Hutchinson, 1948, p. 65.

40. The major commissions are listed in M. Perham, *Lugard*, vol. II, London, Collins, 1960, p. 675.

41. Hailey, *op. cit.* (note 7); L. Mair, *Native policies in Africa*, London, Routledge, 1936; R. L. Buell, *The native problem in Africa*, New York, Macmillan, 1928; R. A. Austen, *Northwestern Tanzania under German and British rule*, New Haven, Yale U.P., 1968.

42. *Ibid.*, p. 155.

43. Grigg's views, with strong acknowledgements to Smuts, are set out in *Kenya's opportunity*, London, Faber, 1955.

44. S. Eisenstadt, *The political systems of Empires*, New York, Free Press of Glencoe, 1962, p. 25.

3

The Economic Structures

A. COMPLEMENTARITY AND PRIMARY PRODUCTION

British attitudes to colonial development were decisively conditioned by her needs as a major manufacturing and capital-exporting country. The resulting demand for external markets and cheap sources of raw materials had always influenced policy; these demands were greatly intensified by the effects of the War, which suddenly exposed her competitive weakness and heightened the importance of the markets which could be directly controlled through the colonial system. Britain's international decline had begun many years before – in the 1860s according to Hobsbawm[1] – but the slow process of decline up to 1914 was immensely quickened between the wars when 'the Victorian economy of Britain crashed in ruins'.[2] This collapse manifested itself in several important ways. There was to be almost continuous underemployment in traditional export industries – especially cotton textiles, coal mining, shipbuilding and steel. European markets were disrupted by the War and, once reorganized, were to produce modernized industry capable of driving Britain out of their own and other markets. The liquidation of external assets and the acceptance of large American loans during the War increased the need to export and highlighted the growing economic and political predominance of the United States in areas once dominated from London. Said the Chancellor of the Duchy of Lancaster:

> Remember that by the service of our debt to America we have to find many millions a year, and at the same time we have to purchase raw material from America amounting to many millions a year. Every single £ that we can take off the American exchange so much the better for us, especially if it is spent within the British Empire. The development of cotton, sugar and tobacco – all these are matters of the most vital importance, not only in providing our own people here with employment, but they are especially essential because if it is essential to purchase these commodities they should be purchased if possible from our own people.[3]

Finally, the period also saw the rise of governments throughout the non-colonial world committed to protection and direct subsidies to displace British exports from their own markets and those under their colonial control. And even the British Commonwealth behaved in the same way. A representative of the Association of British Chambers of Commerce attributed lack of overseas demand to 'the great development of manufacturing in our customer countries . . . What is going on in Brazil is going on to a greater or lesser extent in almost every other country and very largely in our own Colonies.'[4]

Only the dependent colonial empire appeared to be blessedly free from this tendency towards economic nationalism. The Colonies had almost no indigenous capital, narrow internal markets and technically backward populations; they were thought to lack the raw materials required for heavy industry and since they had only recently been drawn into the world economy could be expected to remain at the simplest levels of economic production for the foreseeable future. Perhaps more important, though rarely mentioned, all their economies were controlled by Britain with British interests very much in mind. As a result their governments could be relied on not to introduce the protective policies which were being utilized with such uncomfortable effects in other parts of the world formerly dominated by British commerce. They could therefore be seen from Britain as areas capable of producing tropical and semi-tropical raw materials required for home industry and as soft markets for even the simplest British commodities. This basic view was put simply and forcefully at the meeting in 1923 of the Empire Cotton Growing Corporation:

> I believe we shall in the future see the whole of our cotton coming from our own Dominions [i.e. Empire]. I believe that we shall thus secure cheaper cotton, cheaper raw materials for the use of our British manufacturers. I also believe that in doing that we will be supplying a market for our own people beyond the seas, and that the money that they obtain for their cotton may to a great extent be spent in making purchases from the mother country. It is an ideal for which we all ought to work, that the money obtained from us should in a different form come back to this country. When we are able to do that we are really, though separated by thousands of miles, an Empire united and strong.[5]

This view assumed a natural harmony of economic interests between metropolis and colony – British capital invested in colonial infrastructure would make possible rapid increases in the production of colonial primary products; their sale, preferably to metropolitan manufacturers, would in turn create the markets for manufactured exports. Since the interests of both parties were reciprocal and not competitive no question of exploitation could arise; both parties benefited equally from the exchange, and colonial welfare depended on and made possible the success of British industry. As the leading economic imperialist of the period, L. S. Amery, never tired of extolling the multiple virtues of the system:

> I think we have never realised sufficiently the immense economic possibilities of those Colonies, and the immense wealth that could be created by science, energy, and organization in those parts of the world. The prime object, of course, of that development must be the welfare of the inhabitants of those regions. Our first duty is to them; our object is not to exploit them, but to enable them materially, as well as in every other respect, to rise to a high plane of living and civilization. But I am as sure as I stand here that we cannot develop them and help them without an overspill of wealth and prosperity that would be an immense help to this country in the difficult times that lie ahead.[6]

At the colonial end this system required that each territory find one or more primary products in demand on world markets to provide the basis for this 'legitimate trade' which, as Hancock shows, was considered to be the necessary prerequisite for the ending of the slave trade.[7] At the British end it required export-oriented industry capable of taking advantage of the opportunities created by new colonial markets. Britain's economic predominance had ensured that the latter condition could be met in the nineteenth century. Indeed this predominance had been so considerable that important sectors of establishment opinion had come to believe that imperial control was an irrelevance and that free trade would automatically draw backward societies into 'a set of economies dependent on and complementary to the British, each exchanging the primary products for which its geographical situation fitted it . . . for the manufactures of the world's workshop.'[8] And although the advance of manufacturing in former customer countries behind protective walls had broken down the conditions which made these larger assumptions possible, Britain in the early twenties was still a strong enough industrial and commercial power to be able to assume that colonial markets would always tend to prefer British goods. The problem was therefore clearly one of creating demand by expanding colonial primary production since, with production in the developed economies relatively buoyant for most of the years from 1919 to 1929, the demand for primary products was fairly reliable. In this situation the optimistic picture painted by Amery and his associates could be accepted without much criticism, at least among the political and economic establishment.

But by the end of the decade competitors were not only driving Britain out of their own markets but out of imperial markets as well. Low-cost producers in India, Hong Kong, and most especially in Japan, virtually eliminated British manufacturers from the cheaper end of the cotton textile market and were also threatening to make inroads into other sectors. Further, this coincided with the sharp down-turn in international economic activity induced by the Depression, which had a particularly dramatic impact on the price of raw materials and hence on the buying power of colonial producers. Since British exports were dear in relation to those of her competitors it no longer seemed so natural for African and Asian peasants to exchange their products for those of Manchester and Birmingham; it therefore became necessary for the British to call up their political power to try to force them to buy British or not at all. Thus in the 1930s Britain imposed limits upon Japanese exports to most of the colonial empire despite strong opposition from local interests. At this point it became clear that the welfare of colonial populations was perhaps less important than that of populations living a little closer to Westminster. As the Manchester Chamber of Commerce put it:

> . . . no reasonable person can doubt that the pace of decline in textile imports [into the colonies] from this country was being accelerated by reason of Japanese competition to a degree which gravely threatened Lancashire's principal export trade. In view of the vast population which directly or indirectly depends upon the Lancashire textile industry, this vital question became a national and imperial one as opposed to a merely local or sectional interest, and undoubtedly the quota policy was therefore as fully justified in the interests of the Colonies as of that of Lancashire.[9]

And in the much rougher conditions of the thirties Amery's commitment to the civilization of colonial peoples turned into Cunliffe-Lister's refusal to consult local interests on trade policy[10] because:

> Whatever decision will give the most trade is the decision which this country ought to take and I do not think it ought to be deflected

from that decision by any consideration of principle or whatever it may be. Let us get the best decision in the interests of British trade and take that decision and carry it through.[11]

Thus the economic ideology of the period required both that colonial development be confined to forms of production which would not compete with British manufactures and that colonial consumers prefer British commodities however uncompetitive.

In the short term this commitment to the evolution of a primary producing sector could no doubt be justified in terms of the interests of the local economy since it gave them access to the world market and hence to the advanced technology of the time.[12] But the tendency to look at colonial problems from a British perspective of course precluded any serious attempt to promote the secondary and tertiary economic activities which a long-term process of structural change towards full industrialization would have required. Thus it was generally assumed that all such activities, when they did have to be set up locally, should be given over to British firms if there was any real chance of these performing them effectively – the special privileges and favours given to them were myriad and will be documented in some detail in later sections. Perhaps more important, the commitment to complementarity induced policies and attitudes which were likely actively to inhibit progress beyond the level of simple primary production. According to Ormsby-Gore:

I do not think there are many industrial developments, either immediately taking place or likely to take place in the vast bulk of our Colonial Empire. Looking to the future, practically nowhere is there any coal or iron to be found within the Colonial Empire, and you are dealing with peoples and with financial conditions which are not likely to lend themselves to factory production. The whole emphasis is likely to be upon forest, animal and agricultural development.[13]

These attitudes were no doubt common among manufacturing interests opposed to colonial industrialization because of potential competition, they were also common in both humanitarian and Labour circles. Among the former the attitude stemmed from a powerful rejection of the worst features of British industrialization, an idealization of the 'traditional' African way of life and a similar idealization of rural England. According to Margaret Bondfield, a Labour M.P.:

We want to prevent these colonies having to go through the dreary process of the ordinary industrial countries, of a period of economic slavery, a period of sweated conditions of labour, a period which has the terrible effect of blighting whole generations of people.[14]

This view was particularly strong in the Colonial Service, recruited as it was from those educated in the public schools and Oxbridge, with their idealization of rural England, and their accompanying belief in the traditional systems of deference and hierarchy.[15] It was also, of course, very functional in relation to the need to maintain traditional African systems of rule and authority, discussed in the previous chapter. This view was also held very strongly in Labour circles where it contributed directly to their anti-Imperialist line. But in these circles it was probably less disinterested than appeared on the surface since British workers were as worried as their masters by the threat to their living standards posed by the development of competitive industry in low-wage economies. C. R. Buxton, leading humanitarian and Labour M.P., said of colonial populations:

> This great reservoir of low-priced labour may have a deleterious effect on the position of the white labourer wherever he may be found.[16]

Thus the Labour Party in the period under review showed almost no positive interest in stimulating colonial development, but confined its attention to securing fair conditions of labour for colonial workers which, while they would no doubt improve the conditions of those who found work, were also likely to preclude the emergence of colonial industry based upon labour-intensive techniques. Indeed, the Labour Party went so far as to vote against the use of British money to bridge the Zambesi unless an undertaking was given that it would not be used for the export of coal from the Tete coalfield in Portuguese territory.[17]

Thus Tory manufacturers, Liberal and Labour humanitarians, and paternalist administrators could all, from somewhat different perspectives, support policies based upon the assumption that colonial economic development meant the evolution of primary export production complementary to Britain's manufacturing production. In the short term the development of primary exports was no doubt important for the areas concerned, and access to British resources to develop their infrastructure a major advantage. But in the long term this complex of attitudes was deeply inimical to structural economic change. It will be shown in later sections how industrialization was inhibited because of pressures from

British manufacturers and from local administrators concerned to 'preserve the agricultural population',[18] and how the interests of expatriate companies led to policies which confined African participation to 'the comparatively menial and unremunerative task of cultivation' and excluded him from 'the more attractive fields of primary marketing, ginning and the trade'.[19] More generally it led to educational policies which attempted to perpetuate existing hierarchies in traditional life by providing sons of chiefs with a superior education so that they might 'take their proper places as leaders of thought, morals, society and government';[20] limited the poor to village schools concerned to ensure that they 'should not be educated above their station in life';[21] and assumed that the general purpose of the exercise should be to train lower-level personnel for an essentially agrarian and dependent economic system:

> On the educational side this means that primary schools must have a rural background and atmosphere, and that secondary and higher institutions must be conducted in such a way that men and women whom they produce will be fitted to take their part, whether on the land or in offices or professions in a community which is mainly agricultural and entirely dependent on the soil.[22]

Serious government support for education only began in the 1920s and by 1937 expenditure on education was £70,000 in Tanganyika (3·3% of total budget), £88,000 in Kenya (3·3%) and £90,000 in Uganda (5·2%). By then only one school in East Africa had reached full secondary standard, catering for 210 students from Uganda, 44 from Kenya, 17 from Tanganyika and 4 from Zanzibar.[23] For the rest provision depended upon the missionaries, whose primary concern was with literacy and evangelism: hardly a basis for a long-term process of radical economic change.

Although these views were pervasive and always predominant they did not go entirely unquestioned during the period. They depended for their hegemony, of course, upon the domination of external groups in economic decision-making, groups more concerned with the furtherance of their own than local interests when economic policies were being decided. But there was at least one significant if partial exception to the above rule – the Kenyan settlers, though in most respects opposed to the advancement of African interests, were in a very real sense economic nationalists when conflicts arose between broader Kenyan and

British interests. They were willing and able to press for policies committed to building up internal rather than export markets, and even for protection for industrialization despite what they saw to be the opposition of British manufacturing interests.[24] Further, by the end of the 1930s British manufacturers had largely lost the East African market despite efforts made on their behalf by the British Government; at this point British commercial interests, responding to a suggestion from a Kenyan farming group, were prepared to accept the development of local secondary industry if this did not provide 'for cheap native labour in East Africa to compete with British labour', but directed 'its products to those markets where the Japanese were cutting out British goods'.[25] And this, of course, 'provided such industries could be organized in conjunction with industry in this country.'[26]

Within this broad framework of attitudes local administrators were expected to evolve specialized economic institutions capable of transforming largely subsistence-based economies into exporters of raw materials and importers of British manufacturers. More will be said of the structures created for the organization of this exchange, but before doing so it is necessary to set out what appear to be important aspects of the Imperial experience which conditioned local responses to the problem of establishing viable export economies.

Britain was, by the end of the nineteenth century, the world's most experienced Imperial power. This experience had probably taught her that the worst excesses of colonial exploitation did not pay in the long term – the American revolt had demonstrated the costs of trying to hold down a politically-conscious colonial population; Indian experience showed that an effective administrative structure and extensive economic infrastructure was required if exploitation was not to destroy totally the basis of social and political order. More specifically, the Empire provided a range of models or 'possible politico-economic set-ups'[27] which could be adopted by those looking round for the means of getting the African economies going. Two such models have already been discussed with respect to the peasant or settler views of development, the first based on West African, the second on Southern African experience. To these should be added the plantation view, differing in important respects from the others and to make an important contribution to East Africa. Plantation development was perhaps the preponderant mode in much of Asia and the Caribbean. It shared with settlement the commitment to large-scale economic units managed by expatriates and introducing the local population to the monetary economy as wage labourers rather than as peasant proprietors. The critical difference lay in the location of ownership and control; plantations were financed from Britain and managed by expatriates who did not intend to settle. They also tended to be larger (although some of the larger Kenyan settlers like Lords Delamere and Scott operated on the same scale) and better financed since many settlers came out with little capital. The distinction will be discussed in more detail in the chapters on Kenya and Tanganyika. What must be stressed here is the fact that the commitment to settlement necessarily made a more radical impact upon the local political economy because settlers, with the long-term horizons of people preparing the way for their children, necessarily demanded political control and special rights to land, social services, etc.; while planters were less demanding since they only required security for their capital. In East Africa the commitment to peasant production was never raised to the level of dogma as it appears to have been in West Africa, where the large companies were prohibited from opening up large estates,[28] and plantations did develop in all three territories. But in the event settlement was to become the predominant form in Kenya, plantations were significant among expatriates in Tanganyika, though not more important than peasant development, and peasant production was to become dominant in Uganda. Finally it is perhaps worth mentioning the Imperial commitment to railways – while the first stage of the British industrial revolution was based on the export of textiles, much of the second was based upon railway building both at home and abroad.[29] This commitment was continued into the development of the African empire and much official activity devoted to financing and building railways into the African interior, often with disappointing results.

B. THE STATE AND PRIVATE ENTERPRISE

The British were as committed to capitalism in Africa as they were at home, but they recognized that its relationship to the State must take into account sharp differences in circumstances. Most important, especially in East Africa, was the poverty of both human and material resources in the area. There were no obvious accumulations of local capital or extensive markets to be taken over; in fact the Government in the nineteenth century had been quite unable to persuade serious businessmen to take an interest in the area and had been forced to take on itself the expensive business of opening up the interior in the 1890s for strategic reasons connected with the security of the Suez Canal.[30] The Uganda railway, the prerequisite for the development of any form of 'legitimate trade', had to be financed by the British Government, which received neither interest nor capital repayment of the original grant, which was written off under the Colonial Development Act in 1940.[31] Far from private enterprise opening up the country, it was the Government which 'had to pave the way, by extensive public works and administrative services, not only for European settlement, but also for all modern economic activity'.[32] In these circumstances private interests wishing to obtain the advantages resulting from these efforts on their behalf did not attempt to enforce the commitment to *laissez-faire* which characterized their activities at home. Indeed, in 1937 the Joint East Africa Board went so far as to argue that it was now incumbent on 'the Imperial and local Governments to accelerate development – or to put it another way – to plan to make things happen rather than let them happen.'[33] And Ormsby-Gore, discussing the Colonial Development Act in 1929, claimed that they were 'not in the least interested as to whether any particular expenditure under this proposal is socialism or not.'[34] Thus from the beginning both administrators and private interests accepted a commitment to a managed economy which presupposed that government must take 'a responsibility for general guidance of the economy as a whole'[35] which Beer claims only emerged effectively in England itself with the national Government in 1931.[35]

The managed economy was based upon a fairly consistent division of labour. This allocated to the State the provision of infrastructure services, agricultural extension and research, and control over the legal framework of marketing and production; it gave private enterprise the right to develop production, processing and marketing through either expatriate capital or African peasant production. This was the general rule; it was not, however, adhered to rigidly since private interests did provide services when they could be made to pay, while the State involved itself in direct production when this seemed to be useful and not likely to originate through unaided private enterprise. In 1923 Ormsby-Gore could say:

Apart from transport services, model stock farms, and experimental plantations, state trading is not carried on in the Colonies to any great extent. The only definite instances which I have been able to find are the Government colliery in Nigeria, a saltern in Ceylon, a Government flax mill in St. Helena, and a few cotton ginneries in various West Indian islands. The importation of sheep was undertaken by the Government of the Straits Settlements in accordance with the recommendation of a local Commission on profiteering with a view to breaking a monopoly and covering the price of mutton.[37]

In East Africa, Kenya was to attempt to finance flax mills in the late thirties,[38] while Tanganyika participated with private industry in setting up a local salt industry and a meat-canning factory.[39] This pattern of co-operation has been greatly extended in the post-war period, but the process did not involve any fundamental changes in ideology.

Although characterized by general agreement, the relationship between private enterprise and the State involved considerable conflict in those areas where the interests of the two sides overlapped. Private interests were, of course, always concerned about the Government's regulatory activities in any sector of the economy, and those affected always attempted to have their positions represented before changes were made. These questions will be dealt with at greater length in the relevant chapters; here we will be more concerned with questions which arose directly related to the allocation of spheres of influence between one side and the other. On the most general level the private sector was very well aware of the importance of the Government's contribution to development through the expansion of infrastructure, and used its influence to increase this whenever possible. Less frequently the interests of particular enterprises came into conflict with those of an administrative agency. In such cases the latter would attempt to use *laissez-faire* ideology to advance its claims despite the wider commitment to economic management. Two cases of this kind raised particularly large issues and were debated at both the local and the metropolitan level, both concerning the extension and management of the Kenya–Uganda railway. Being located in so critical an area they were of considerable importance in themselves; equally important is the light which their progress throws upon the nature of the decision-making process and the balance of power between administrative and private interests in the period. The first case concerns the construction of the extensions to the railway in the 1920s, most especially whether this was to be controlled by a private British contractor, or managed by the railway administration itself; the second concerns the control and extension of unloading facilities in Mombasa harbour.

Between 1919 and 1930 the original railway from Mombasa to Lake Victoria was extended into Uganda and a number of branch lines were built into the Kenyan Highlands; this, together with the deep-water wharves built in Mombasa harbour, constituted by far the largest single developmental investment made in the country during the period. As a first step in this programme the Uasin Gishu line was built, 146 miles long and intended to open a new area of settlement and to provide the first stage of the direct line to Uganda.[40] The contract for the line was negotiated by the Crown Agents for the Colonies with a British firm, which was given full control over the whole operation and a guaranteed profit of 5% over and above all administrative expenses. No public tenders were called for though offers were apparently obtained from three firms.[41] This procedure provided the Colony with a system which involved divided control between the Government-controlled railway administration and the company, duplication of supervisory staffs, and a company whose work was to prove inefficient, behind schedule and very expensive. This line was to cost £16,731 per mile to build; the rest of the Uganda extension £6,900 and the branch lines very much less.[42] Christian Felling, a new manager recruited from South Africa, arrived in the country in 1923 with instructions to improve the railway's finances. It was then decided that the second of the two lines already planned, and all subsequent lines, should be built under the direct control of the Department. This decision did not, in fact, eliminate all private enterprise since the railway tendered the work out to 'local private enterprise', on a competitive basis.[43] As a result:

> The prices are lower than those paid to similar sectional sub-contractors for the Uasin Gishu line, the profits of the [British] intermediary between the Government engineers and sub-contractors being eliminated, and heavy administrative expenditures consequent upon duplication of staff and other features of the Uasin Gishu contract is avoided.[44]

It should also be noted when considering the controversy which this decision produced that no question arose of private enterprise taking any part in the actual administration of the railway itself. In his own account later Felling said:

> There is no objection in this country to a private company building any railway line to connect with the main line, but we have had no

application from private companies to be permitted to do so, for the simple reason that in a young, developing colony a private Railway Company cannot exist without special conditions in the matter of land and the like, special protection in the matter of rates, and probably subsidies.[45]

Felling's decision aroused strong opposition in Conservative circles in the House of Commons, which included Sir John Norton Griffiths, Governing Director of the firm involved in the Uasin Gishu project. He chose to remain discreetly silent in the debate which followed though he did give evidence to the Committee of Enquiry set up to go into it. In June 1923 the Under-Secretary was asked why it had been decided to build the East and West African railways departmentally rather than by private enterprise.[46] After an admission that the Secretary of State had decided in May that all Kenyan railways in the existing programme would be departmentally built[47] it was announced that a committee would be set up forthwith to examine the whole question of the relationship between State and private enterprise in colonial development.[48] This decision was followed by a barrage of hostile questions from no less than fifteen Tory luminaries, not previously identified with colonial issues, attacking the departure from the principle of private tendering in the name of 'private enterprise' and increased efficiency [sic].[49] 'Business men and men of enterprise' were asked to give their suggestions to the Commission,[50] and in the same debate Henn of the J.E.A.B. complained of a general feeling in East Africa that private enterprise was being discouraged by excessive governmental intervention, especially in Tanganyika.[51] In the latter stages of this campaign, which appears to have originated in the very localized conflict between the railways and Norton Griffiths & Co., every effort was being made to legitimate these claims by dressing them up in the otherwise not especially fashionable guise of free enterprise. According to Felling:

> When I was in London in 1924, fighting in the interests of the Colony for better principles in connection with railway construction, the impression was deliberately fostered by interested parties that my intention was to eliminate private enterprise ...
>
> It should be unnecessary for me to say that I have never supported government control over work where private enterprise is likely to be effective and economical. My record and all the opinions I have expressed here should bear witness to that; but apparently the facts are ignored because of a desire in interested quarters not so much to

establish competitive private enterprise as to maintain monopolistic private enterprise. One point I am firm on. If there is to be a monopoly in a public utility service it must be a government or municipal monopoly.[52]

This desire to 'maintain monopolistic private enterprise' was to be characteristic of most of the political efforts of particular vested interests in colonial policy-making, but was to be less successful in this case than in many others.

The Ronaldshay Committee sat at the end of 1923 and reported early in 1924; it was composed of senior Tory politicians, officials (including Lord Lugard) and business representatives. On the general question of overall state control they recognized that 'no wholly private company' would be willing to build 'a developmental railway in tropical Africa . . . without special inducements . . . which would render construction by the State itself a more economic alternative.'[53] Only Sir Edwin Stockton, M.P., a Manchester businessman, felt that they should be run on 'purely business lines' and that government in East Africa should now provide the inducements required to gain the participation of private enterprise.[54] The Committee was less specific on the more relevant issue of private contracting. They recognized the virtues of the departmental method, especially for a long-term building programme, but saw advantages in private contracting, especially for small territories and harbour building. Being unable to arrive at a unanimous conclusion they could make 'no recommendations in favour of one system or the other',[55] and could do no more than suggest that a more flexible approach to the private sector 'would result in exciting a more widespread interest in that part of the Empire'.[56]

These recommendations constituted a clear victory for the Kenya railway administration and ensured that the very large programme of construction still to be undertaken be controlled locally rather than by Norton Griffiths or its equivalent. Felling's satisfaction, expressed in his 1925 report,[57] was not shared in the Commons, where rumblings from the private enterprise lobby continued to be heard into 1925.[58] On the face of it this represented an important victory for administrative and local interests over private British pressures and evidence of Britain's impartial commitment to Imperial trusteeship. A more realistic interpretation emerges from a consideration of the broader context of capitalist relationships in East Africa. The predominant interests in this larger context were not the contracting interests but settlers, planters and the banking interests which financed them, together with the import–export firms. These groups were totally dependent upon the railway and threatened with extinction if it was unable to provide them with services at a price which provided them with a reasonable margin of profit. They could not afford to subsidize incompetent and high-cost contractors and therefore put their weight behind the evident efficiency of the administration. The London Chamber of Commerce put their views to the Committee, arguing that since the State would usually be able to raise capital on more favourable terms and would be satisfied with a 'moderate' return upon its capital it would thereby enable 'lower rates to be charged', thus 'stimulating production, i.e. the real basis of development and of all auxiliary private enterprise'. And although they too felt that construction should 'as far as possible be made the subject of public tender', they accepted that circumstances varied greatly and that they could not lay down any binding rules.[59]

Similar issues were raised by the need to expand the facilities in Mombasa harbour during the 1920s. Cargo was moved from ship to shore by two privately-owned lighterage companies which paid a small fee to the Government for cranage facilities. One was controlled jointly by the Union Castle Co. and the British India Steam Navigation Co., the other by a South African family firm, while the shipping companies, organized through the Conference Lines, had been given full control of all landing and delivery at the port through an agreement with the Government operative from January 1921. In that year work began on two deep-water berths which would have eliminated much of the need for lighters. The first berth was opened in 1926. Traffic was increasing very rapidly, being in 1925 195 % more than the 1922 figure, and early that year Felling recommended that two further wharves should be built.[60] This brought into the open the conflict between the shipping 'ring' as Felling called it,[61] with an interest in a monopolistic service which Grigg claimed caused 'shippers . . . to be fleeced by excessive lighterage charges',[62] and the interests of the local administration and producers who were forced to use the service. The shipping companies, concerned to maintain the very high returns from lighterage and about the possibility of State control over the whole port, opposed the building of the new wharves altogether, claiming that the new berths would cost more than 'the provision of lighterage facilities of similar capacity.'[63] In July Grigg was in England where he put the case to the J.E.A.B.[64]

and presumably to the Colonial Office, and the Board, though internally divided, pressed for 'immediate construction' at the end of the month.[65] The local commission sat in Kenya at the end of the year and early in 1926 presented its report, which recommended construction of the berths and the elimination of competition between lighters and berths by letting out all the work to a single contractor, who was to work 'in the name of the Harbour Department'.[66]

But in England the shipping interests were busy and Amery was persuaded not to accept this decision but to refer the question to the Imperial Shipping Committee on which these interests were strongly represented. This Committee's report was apparently available by July and published in September; it rejected both local recommendations; suggesting instead that the lighters should be left uncontrolled and that future building be held up until the 'comparative cost, all things considered, of the two systems' had been decided by the free play of competition.[67] Grigg was given an illuminating impression of the inner working of the system by Ormsby-Gore:

> Inchape and Kylsant [the shipping owners] are of course very active. The position as I see it is that Amery can only refuse to accept the views of so authoritative body as the Imperial Shipping Committee, with the backing of all the big shipping lines, if you put up a really strongly argued case against it. It will be no use saying the local shipping representatives on the local commission agreed. So everything depends upon what you and Felling can put up against this embarrassing report. . . . I am anticipating that Inchape and Kylsant will try and press Amery to accept the Shipping Committee's report, and he will have a very difficult time in persuading them to change their view.[68]

Local officials reacted strongly against this report,[69] both on the grounds that economy demanded that most of the traffic pass across the berths, and that 'free competition' would be illusory because of the linkages between lighters and shipping interests. Again the true conflict was not between administration and private interests, but between two competing sets of private interests – the shipping companies on the one hand and the producers and traders on the other. Conrad Walsh, Kenya's Commissioner for Customs, noted that the port should be maintained in the interest of the latter and, since they also would have to carry its costs, 'Government is responsible as trustees to the taxpayers and not to the Steamship Companies.'[70] In England

Leggett of the London Chamber supported the local recommendations and, after some dispute the J.E.A.B. also strongly supported this position and regretted that they 'had not taken a sufficiently firm stand against the influence of interested parties in this country' before the Imperial Committee.[71]

Presented with strong financial arguments by the Kenyan administration backed up by the majority of the British trading and producing interests, Amery, after first supporting the Imperial Committee,[72] accepted the local recommendations, giving permission to build the new berths late in 1926. In the following year all handling and lightering of cargo was taken over by a contractor on a ten-year basis with effective control vested in the hands of the railways.[73] Again the administration backed by producers and exporters had defeated a powerful group of London interests who had attempted to use private-enterprise norms to back up a case primarily motivated by the desire for monopolistic profit margins.

These cases would seem to illuminate very clearly the nature of the relationship between colonial, state and private interests. Commitment to the 'managed economy' did not involve any ideological doubts about the right of private interests to exploit resources when they could do so profitably without excessively raising the costs of everyone else. One can also set against the evidence presented here the fact that Major Grogan was paid no less than £350,000 in 1925 for rights to land and broken-down wharfage facilities in the Mombasa port area, which could not have cost him £50,000.[74] What does emerge is the congruence between the interests of a bureaucracy committed to large-scale centralized administrative structures for reasons of simplicity of management and economy and those of private producing and trading groups that needed to have services provided at the cheapest possible rate. Particular private interests used traditional 'free enterprise' arguments based upon the need for competition only when they felt their semi-monopolistic positions threatened by encroachments from the State, but these arguments bore no relation to the issues involved in the actual conflict, which was really about the relative advantages to different private interests of a state versus a private monopoly for the provision of essential services. In the cases detailed here the State solution was accepted because the most important of the capitalist groups were not prepared to pay subsidies to the incompetence or greed of others of their number. It was thus possible for the latter – railway contractors or shipping companies – to be isolated despite their evident success in marshalling support in Britain, and defeated to the evident benefit of the local interests and, in all probability, of the local economy in general. The result of these tendencies was the emergence of a general commitment to a strong state, and acceptance of the right of established large-scale organizations, public and private, to be allowed to exist in an essentially uncompetitive environment. Whereas in these cases state power was to be used to create large governmentally-controlled units, in many others it was to be brought into play by well-represented private groups to eliminate competition and thereby to rescue themselves from extinction. This, however, will be matter for the final section; it remains here to look at the organization of common economic structures and services in the region as a whole.

C. ECONOMIC CO-ORDINATION IN EAST AFRICA

Although geographically contiguous and part of the same colonial empire, the East African territories were administered as separate administrative and political units. This in turn has produced the boundaries of the contemporary nation states in the region and thus determined their scale as units of political-economic control. The resulting units, although large by pre-colonial African standards, are very small in relation to the needs of modern economic organization, most especially with regard to the size and accessibility of markets. This has led to the suggestion that long-term economic growth will only be possible if economic boundaries are widened,[75] a belief which provided the Pan-African movement with much of its momentum in the terminal colonial and early independence periods. These arguments and movements took their origin from the decisions taken during the colonial period, which determined both the scale of the original units and the disposition of economic decision-making power as between local and regional authorities. Although the main outlines of colonial administrative jurisdictions were established very early, the distribution of control between territorial and regional authorities was a matter of continuous negotiation and reorganization in East Africa right up to the 1940s, with the establishment of the East African High Commission.[76] The allocation of functions to the regional and territorial authorities has always been of the greatest importance to the various interests involved in the local political economy; shifts in this allocation invariably altered their relative influence over policy. This meant that changes in allocation were always the subject of considerable political conflict; an analysis of this conflict sheds a great deal of light on the location of economic power in the area as well as providing us with an understanding of the nature of the services which were to be provided on a central-ized basis. The material should also provide some insights into the general nature of the political problems involved in attempts to change the scale of any economic unit; these problems would seem to have been seriously neglected in much of the recent debate about the need for African integration, despite the fact that the issue has been an important one in inter-territorial relations since the beginnings of colonial administration.

The lines of administrative command in East Africa converged on the territorial capitals and extended through these capitals to the metropolis. This fact determined the location of most state-controlled developmental resources since the territory was also the unit of financial administration – territorial resources therefore determined the size of the tax base and the level of expenditure on economic services, which were so central to the evolution of the cash economy. These facts also made the territory the prime focus for the political forces which had achieved some level of conscious-ness and organization during the period; these were primarily concerned with representation on the Legislative Council and with access to the local bureaucracy. But the local economies were not in any sense self-contained; the monetary sector was heavily directed to the world market and many of the most important institutions involved in servicing the exchanges which this required were organized for the purpose on regional rather than territorial lines. This is particularly true of the private sector where many of the larger, and especially British, firms – predominant in banking and trade, but also important in processing and plantations – tended to operate inter-territorially, generally from headquarters in Kenya. On the other hand many of the smaller and usually Asian firms – especially in retailing, but also in processing and planting – tended to be primarily located in one territory although they would often have connections in others through business and/ or family ties. And peasant production, of course, was heavily territorially oriented since few Africans were able to develop links across territorial boundaries. This division of administrative and economic labour was bound to cause problems where the interests of inter-territorial firms conflicted with those of terri-torially-oriented bureaucracies. But these problems could have been resolved through London were it not for the fact that a number of important economic services were actually organized on an inter-territorial basis. For our purposes the most important of these were inter-territorial transport (including railways), customs, posts and telegraphs, and currency. Currency was administered by the East African Currency Board from London. This was established in 1920 and was to be responsible for maintaining a unified currency for the region until the end of colonial rule.[77] Although monetary policy in the period clearly had a considerable impact on the nature of the developmental process I was unable to gain access to relevant sources and will therefore not be dealing with the issue here. Posts and Telegraphs were to be centrally organized but occasioned no serious conflict and can therefore also be left to one side. During the period, in fact, the politics of railways and customs was to dominate inter-territorial exchanges, and the resulting decisions were to have a clear and very significant impact upon the location of economic activity and the relative advantages of key economic interests. It is in these two areas that the crucial battles were fought. Their management did require the development of local machinery for the evolution of inter-territorial policy, and it is with this that the rest of this section must be concerned.

The 1920s witnessed a major political debate in British and East African politics, deriving from attempts to bring the three territories into a single administrative union. This issue was finally settled only in 1931 with the report of the Joint Select Committee on Closer Union in East Africa,[78] which concluded that unification should not be considered and that common services should be regulated through the machinery of the Governors' Conference, already discussed, which did not have any authority to impose decisions on unwilling territories. In the absence of a local authority with unified decision-making powers, matters in dispute had either to be settled through negotiation or referred to London for final solution. During the twenties several issues which could not be settled locally had arisen, and the controversy which they aroused had a significant effect upon the progress of the negotiations then in process with respect to closer union. The ultimate failure to produce any unified authority meant, however, that they had also to be resolved in the same way as the less controversial issues which predominated in the thirties. This being so it therefore would seem perfectly justifiable to ignore this wider political debate over closer union and consider the questions of policy that were resolved under the existing machinery.

i. *Railway Policy*

Railway zones bore little relation to territorial boundaries in East Africa. The northern system from Mombasa, originally extending to Kisumu on Lake Victoria and subsequently to Kampala, served both Kenya and Uganda and was the only economic outlet for both territories' produce until the advent of lorries in the late twenties. The southern system, consisting of the Central (Dar es Salaam to Kigoma on Lake Tanganyika) and Northern (Tanga to Arusha) Lines served only Tanganyika and parts of the Congo. However, this system had to compete for traffic with the Kenya–Uganda railway, which served much of Tanganyika's Lake Region across Lake Victoria, and also Kilimanjaro Region by a branch line (the Voi-Taveta or Voi-Kahe Line) which joined the Northern Line with the Kenya–Uganda Line. This overlapping between railway and territorial jurisdictions produced two distinct sets of conflicts – those between Kenyan and Ugandan interests with regard to the disposal of resources on the Kenya–Uganda system; and those between the northern and southern railway systems over competition for traffic in the two areas served by both. These conflicts were manifested in continuous disagreements over policy, which were also to lead to demands for the establishment of inter-territorial machinery for railway administration which would represent a wider range of the interests involved. This machinery had been brought into existence by 1931 and was to remain in effect until the further reorganization occasioned by the Second World War.

With regard to the relationship between Kenyan and Ugandan interests on the northern system, the main conflicts originated in the dominance which Kenyan settlers were able to establish over railway policy before the War and maintain, although with increasing difficulty, into the twenties and thirties. Between 1903 and 1921 the railway was run as a part of the Kenyan adminis-tration, and its surplus, a large percentage of which derived from the Ugandan trade, was used to subsidize Kenya's revenues. Partly as a result of Ugandan objections to this procedure it was separated from the general administration and turned into a self-contained service after 1921. The General Manager worked in Nairobi, was an official member of the Kenyan legislature and was also entitled · to speak in the Ugandan one on railway matters. Policy issues were considered by the Kenya and Uganda Railway Advisory Council, which consisted of two official and two unofficial representatives of each of the two territories and which was advised by the General

Manager. Both Manager and Council were responsible to the Governor of Kenya in his capacity as High Commissioner for Transport, who was in turn subjected to the overriding jurisdiction of the Secretary of State. Ugandan pressure led to the creation of a 'Joint High Commissionership' to include both Governors in 1935, but considerable power was delegated to the Governor of Kenya and the change does not appear to have made any real difference.[79]

The predominance of settler interests in railway policy-making was an expression of their dominance in internal Kenyan politics and of the dominance of the Kenyan administration in railway administration. Ugandan pressure for the broadening of this control was thus essentially directed against a system which made it possible for a disproportionate share of transport resources to be put into the development of the settler economy in Kenya. This struggle worked itself out in conflicts over rating policy on the one hand and branch-line building on the other, to which it is now necessary to turn.

Railway rates were the primary source of dispute. Public policy in Kenya was based upon the assumption that all communities should be made responsible for the well-being of the settler sector, and the railway was used as a primary means of operationalizing this commitment. The use of the railway for this purpose had the additional advantage of distributing the load across territorial boundaries since it could be used to extract a surplus from Ugandan and Tanganyikan producers, which could then be reallocated to those in Kenya. By 1921 the railway had established that rating policy could be used differentially to encourage particular groups of producers, and had used this principle to provide special privileges to Kenyan producers of temperate-climate foodstuffs, who were, by 1919, predominantly of settler origin. These privileges took two forms. Firstly, low rates on exports, most especially on maize and wheat, which did not cover costs and hence had to be subsidized by other traffic. In fact the deficit was largely recovered from the very high rates charged on cheap imported textiles – largely for African consumers – and on exports of raw cotton and coffee. Cotton was almost exclusively produced by Africans in Uganda and Tanganyika; Kenyan settlers and planters produced a great deal of coffee, but rather more originated in Tanganyika and in Uganda. Although it has not been possible to work out the balance sheet with any exactitude, there is little doubt that this process made it feasible for the railways to keep the rate on maize and wheat down to levels which enabled their producers to compete effectively with South African and Argentinian competitors and hence remain in business.[80] Secondly, the railway was also used to increase the protection given to Kenyan producers through the so-called 'Country Produce Rates', which imposed very low export and very high import rates on locally-produced articles like wheat, butter and sugar. This again imposed a tax on all consumers served by the railway for the benefit of a group of producers who, with the exception of Ugandan sugar producers, were almost exclusively located in the Kenyan highlands.

It is clear that this rating structure in fact ensured that African consumers and producers paid rates which served to subsidize particular groups of expatriate producers – even Ugandan expatriate sugar producers who became effective in the late 1920s fell into this category. Opposition to them, however, did not arise directly out of African representations since they were not effectively mobilized until very much later. Instead it derived from other expatriate groups which served as intermediaries between Africans and the world economy, notably the traders whose turnover depended upon the scale of African export production and the corresponding purchasing power which this produced. High export rates on African produce reduced the surplus available for expenditure on imported manufactures, and high rates on the import of these also cut volume and margins for both wholesalers and retailers. Further, Kenyan protective policies also raised costs of basic foodstuffs (the items covered by the Country Produce Rates) and hence the costs of the whole trading and administrative sector. Thus the conflict was not exclusively territorial, since Kenyan trading interests, especially those centred upon Mombasa, also tended to support the Ugandan view, although their strength of purpose appears to have been considerably weakened by the persuasiveness of their settler neighbours.

Ugandan opposition to these differential rating systems was continuous into the thirties but of little effect. Despite this opposition the maize rate was actually reduced at the start of the Depression, and even Grigg admitted that it was 'carried at a loss now, and a very heavy loss I should think'.[81] But in the 1930s Uganda began to wish to export increasing amounts of cotton seed (as opposed to the higher-valued lint cotton, which could bear the higher rate) and was able to secure the low export rate for this. But even this decision was moderated in Kenya's favour since the railway allocated a disproportionate share of available wagon space to maize rather than cotton seed even after the recommendation of the Gibb report in 1932.[82] The Country Produce Rates and the high rates on imported textiles were strongly attacked into the late 1920s, and the Railway Advisory Council was even persuaded to reject them in 1929, when the Kenyan unofficial representative of Mombasa voted with the Ugandan representatives against them.[83] But this decision was not put into effect and the issue was discussed at the Governors' Conference in 1930 when Grigg, ably supported by Lord Delamere and his settler associates, who were given free access to its deliberations, was able to persuade Sir William Gowers, the Governor of Uganda, that they should be maintained despite the fact that the latter had been sent with a strong brief to eliminate them. In his support for this, as well as other elements of the Kenyan case, Grigg was at one point prepared to claim:

> The security of the Empire in East Africa was not inseparable from the success of white settlement. White settlement had gone so far that a really serious setback which endangered confidence in its future would endanger at the same time our whole civilization in East Africa.[84]

The Ugandan representatives raised the matter with the Joint Select Committee in London, criticizing the rates on textiles and the Country Produce Rates.[85] The Committee passed responsibility for assessing these matters to two Commissioners, Moyne, who was to look into the equity of rating policy in Kenya with reference to African and European shares, and Gibb, who had to consider railway policy in East Africa as a whole. Moyne considered the cotton textile rate to be inequitable,[86] but Gibb, looking at it in terms of what the traffic would bear, disagreed.[87] It was maintained, though reduced slightly in 1936 when growing surpluses permitted this. Gibb found opinion in Uganda and Tanganyika and even the majority of those who gave evidence to him in Kenya opposed to the Country Produce Rates, and he advocated a system designed to maximize revenue by cutting some of the highest and raising some of the lowest rates.[88] He even proposed a railway board responsible for policy in London, which would be free from the local pressures which he felt had introduced 'political' factors into policy to the detriment of sound railway finance.[89] The latter proposal was also at least partially motivated by the fact that African interests were not represented at all. To justify the need for 'absentee control' he claimed in private: 'Unless the railway steadily aims at paying its way there will rapidly arise very unfair treatment of the native on account of the railways.'[90] This proposal was strongly rejected, as was his opposition to the Country Produce Rates. These continued to operate, and the combination of Ugandan commitment to the low rate on seed cotton, together with the settlers' increased ability to produce the protected commodities in adequate quantity, tended to reduce the general opposition to them. In this, as in many other areas to be explored, the value to minority economic interests of strong commitments, good social contacts, and effectively placed representation, was clearly demonstrated.

A similar tale can be told with respect to building policy. A general balance between the interests of the two territories with regard to the actual location of new work was maintained, since the Kenya Government financed and controlled the expansion of its own branch-line system, while British cotton interests were responsible for ensuring adequate finance to extend the main line into Uganda in 1924.[91] But the Kenyan branch lines were built largely into settler areas which were as yet sparsely populated and which in any case specialized in low-rated products and therefore operated according to the rather odd principle that 'the more traffic the branch carries, the greater the loss'.[92] The losses on the first branches led to sharp protests from Ugandan interests and as a result it was decided, after the railways were reorganized in 1926, that the Government concerned should meet the losses on any branch line built against the advice of the High Commissioner and the Railway Council.[93] But three lines had been built before this decision came into effect and the system had to carry their losses thereafter.[94] In any event the basis for calculation of losses on subsequent lines was exceedingly generous – interest and sinking fund payments on the capital were not even included in calculating costs.[95]

This policy provoked very strong pressures from the Uganda Chamber of Commerce and the Uganda Cotton Association in the early thirties, when the Depression produced a sharp drop in railway revenue and led to heavy losses.[96] The pressure took the form of an attempt to have the formula in accordance with which the losses were calculated altered, but this again was successfully resisted by the Kenyans. It finally abated in the second half of the thirties when rising revenues made it possible for rates to be reduced although nothing was done about the differential benefits which the service bestowed.

The disputes between the Kenya–Uganda and Tanganyika systems raised many of the same kinds of issues, but in this case separate administrative structures were maintained and relations had to be conducted either *ad hoc* or through the Governors' Conference. Competition for traffic between the two systems was located in the two most productive areas of Tanganyika – the Lake Region, which produced the bulk of the Territory's cotton and low-grade Robusta coffee, and Kilimanjaro Region, which produced most of the high-grade Arabica coffee crop. Both crops had a high value-to-weight ratio and could thus, unlike maize and wheat, sustain railway rates sufficiently high to provide a surplus for the railway. Access to them was therefore an important factor in maintaining the financial viability of the railway system and the contribution it could make to particular agricultural communities.

The first issue to take concrete form concerned the Kilimanjaro Region. The northern section of the Tanganyikan system consisted of a line from the port of Tanga to Moshi, which was subsequently extended to Arusha. During the War a connection was built between the Kenya–Uganda Line and the Northern Line between Voi and Kahe, thus providing the area with two outlets. Since it did not produce sufficient traffic to justify both, its retention made the upper half of the Northern Line virtually redundant. This fact led the Tanganyikan administration to attempt to close the connection after the War, with strong support from commercial interests in Tanga, although against the opposition of unofficial interests both in Kenya and among the small Tanganyikan settler community on Kilimanjaro. Both Kenyan and Tanganyikan settlers wished to maintain their links because of their commitment to the larger ideal of settler unity, while the latter also benefited from access to the better-developed facilities in Mombasa.

In 1920 F. D. Hammond, a British expert then surveying the East African railways prior to their reorganization, recommended the use of the Mombasa route because of the value of the port, and the uprooting of the upper part of the Northern Line. The Tanganyikan Government continued its opposition and the British Government supported them, stressing the opposition of the Tanga Chamber of Commerce to the alternative.[97] In July Delamere raised the matter in the Lords, and the official reply made it clear that the decision had been at least partially conditioned by Tanganyika's mandated status.[98] The Joint East Africa Board also took up the issue and put its weight behind the

Kenyan position,[99] and by January 1924 had learned that the British Government had agreed that Kenya should take the line over and work it at its own expense.[100] But in deference to Tanganyikan pressures the Northern Line was not touched and both outlets continued to be used.

This solution gave Tanganyika the worst of both worlds. The bulk of the higher-rated traffic took the more attractive Kenya route and the Northern Line ran at a loss conservatively estimated at £500,000 between 1919 and 1931.[101] Since the Tanganyika system was always far weaker than the Kenya–Ugandan the situation produced continuous local discontent. Visiting British Commissions recognized the problem and recommended that the Northern Line be handed over to Kenya to run.[102] The local governments were unable to reach agreement, however, and the drain continued till the Second World War. It seems clear that the connection would have been severed but for the fact that the Kenyan interests were able to mobilize effective support in London in the critical months in 1923; no equivalent support could be found for a solution which would have divided the costs and benefits in a more equitable manner.

The second problem related to railway building and the allocation of traffic in the Lake Region. This area was serviced exclusively by the Kenya–Uganda system by steamer during the German period and the opening years of the twenties. In 1924 the Tanganyika Government suggested building a branch from Tabora on the Central Line to Shinyanga, a point about half-way to the lake, a recommendation which could expect sympathetic treatment in London because of the general commitment to colonial railways and cotton growing. In 1925 Sir Donald Cameron, the new Governor, pressed for an extension of this branch to the lake itself, where it would have been in a position to compete for traffic with the existing Kenya–Uganda service.[103] His view was supported by the Empire Cotton Growing Corporation,[104] the Joint East Africa Board[105] and the East Africa Commission, and was also apparently strengthened by Tanganyika's mandated status and the fact that Germany might be able to 'make out a case at Geneva' if Britain could be accused of subordinating 'the interests of the Mandated Territory to those of our own possessions in the neighbourhood'.[106] It was strongly opposed by the Kenyan administration because of the likely loss of Tanganyikan traffic and even the fear that Uganda might be able to force 'competition through Mwanza'.[107] This possibility meant that Uganda might be able to challenge the whole settler-dominated rating system already discussed,[108] although there is no evidence that Cameron ever contemplated this, since they did not have the facilities to handle the Uganda trade.[109]

The issue was discussed by the Governors in November 1925[110] when Grigg and Gowers jointly cabled London to oppose the line without consulting Cameron. Cameron strongly attacked this action and rejected the possibility of 'Tanganyika placing herself in the same position as Uganda in the matter of railway communications',[111] and was informed by Amery that the line could go through.[112] Grigg continued to oppose it at the Governors' Conference in January, and it was included in the terms of reference of the East African Railway Committee, which accepted it in March 1926.[113] The connection was completed in 1928 and the rates on the two railway systems were unified to avoid competition. Tanganyika did not develop independent lake-steamer services so the new line only served the area due south of the lake; the Kenya system continued to carry more than two-thirds of Tanganyika's Lake Province exports.[114]

This situation in turn raised local opposition when the Central Line lost its access to traffic from the Congo in 1931 at the same time as it was being badly affected by the Depression. This produced heavy losses and the railway had to be subsidized from tax and loan funds and to cut its operating costs by almost half in five years to eliminate its current deficits. The matter was raised at the Governors' Conference in 1933, when Symes of Tanganyika claimed that strong local dissatisfaction existed and asked for some action to 'meet the susceptibilities' of the interested groups.[115] But the other Governors stressed the losses to them resulting from the building of the Mwanza Line and were only willing to consider compensating Tanganyika when the traffic from Tanganyika had reached 'the amount carried in the year preceding the opening of the Mwanza line'.[116] In 1937 an agreement was reached with regard to the pooling of traffic, but the situation still strongly favoured the Kenya system – in 1939 the administration estimated that their traffic paid the latter £93,200 after covering out-of-pocket costs.[117] After making losses in the first two years of the Depression the Kenya system moved back into continuous surplus and remained there, having acquired large betterment funds and reserves and a traffic density eight times higher than the Tanganyikan by the end of the decade.[118] When these leakages are added to those resulting from competition on the Northern

Line, it is clear that Tanganyika lost to the Kenya system potential traffic and profits which would have completely eliminated its financial difficulties and put it into a much stronger position to expand its services during this period.

ii. The Customs Union

Tariffs, like railways, can make a decisive difference to the opportunities of particular groups in a developmental process; in many situations they can make the difference between survival as a social and economic entity and total disappearance. This fact was clearly understood by the settler communities in East Africa, though not so well by the less carefully informed indigenous population. Again, the pressures on policy derived from this knowledge were to dominate the debate around this question, which also took place in a regional context. In this case two principal interests favoured the predominant commitment to a customs union, the protection of certain local products and the free movement of all commodities across internal boundaries. The settlers, who were principally responsible for persuading the Kenyan administration to accept a policy of protection for locally-produced temperate-climate foodstuffs in 1922,[119] saw the common market as another means of extracting a surplus from their neighbours; the British trading interests had no especial commitment to protection, but were strongly in favour of anything which made it possible for them to run their businesses in a unified manner across the whole region and thus keep down their costs. Opposition came mainly from small traders centred upon a single territory who wished to escape the competition of their larger multi-territorial rivals; it also derived from the expatriate community outside agriculture, who resented paying high prices for supplies of butter, cheese, bacon, wheat, etc., which were both poor in quality and uncertain in quantity until the 1930s. Once established, of course, the existence of the common market made it impossible for individual territories to follow independent tariff policies and to provide unilateral protection for particular producers or relief for particular categories of consumer. The issue has been a very real and divisive one in post-war East African politics, so this material should again illuminate some of the fundamental political problems involved in obtaining and maintaining agreement in areas of economic policy characterized by sharp conflicts of interest.

Kenya and Uganda formed part of the same customs administration from the start of colonial administration; indeed, Kenya
appropriated all the revenue on Ugandan imports until 1909,
when the latter was given a fixed percentage of the revenue. In the
early twenties two critical changes had to be incorporated into the
system – the tariff revision of 1922 in Kenya and the integration of
Tanganyika into the union. The 1922 change involved both an
increase in the tax on certain commodities of mainly European
consumption to replace revenue lost because the latter had refused to pay income tax, and the introduction of protective levels
of duty on temperate-climate foodstuffs for the benefit of settler
producers.

Both these changes resulted from purely Kenyan needs and
conditions, but the maintenance of the customs union meant that
they would have to be accepted by consumers in the other territories as well. Uganda was induced to accept the protective duties
despite opposition, although a new tariff was introduced at a
Customs Conference in 1922.[120] In 1923, again despite local
opposition, Tanganyika was made to equalize external tariffs with
the north and permit the 'free exchange of local produce',[121] thus
effectively opening up her market to Kenyan high-cost production. Ormsby-Gore claimed that this was 'the only thing to do in
three contiguous territories'.[122] These decisions were strongly supported by British interests – the London and Manchester Chambers of Commerce refused to support the Uganda Chamber's
opposition to the duties,[123] while the Joint East Africa Board
consistently supported the creation of a full customs union.[124] In
1924 Tanganyika took authority to vary tariffs unilaterally and
ended protection on butter and cheese (then virtually unobtain-
able) in 1925.[125] At the same time it still limited the free movement
of imported goods, which assisted local traders in competition
with distributors in Mombasa and Nairobi. These limits were
strongly opposed by all the main British groups – in 1926 the
London, Manchester and Liverpool Chambers pressed for a full
union at a meeting with the Colonial Office,[126] as did the Joint
East Africa Board.[127] The East Africa Commission, in characteristically ambiguous terms, went so far as to claim that: 'Tanganyika . . . has everything to gain and little to lose by a union which
is giving every satisfaction so far as Uganda is concerned.'[128] So
despite the British Government's original reservations, because
of the need to protect Tanganyikan 'interests at the ports . . .
whose trade might suffer under a customs union',[129] a final

agreement setting up a full union was signed with effect from August 1927.

This settlement, again effectively extending the subsidy to Kenyan settler agriculture across the whole region, was subjected to close scrutiny in 1929/30 when the whole issue of regional economic co-ordination was being considered in relation to the question of closer union. The Commission on Closer Union (the Hilton Young Commission), which reported early in 1929, considered that the amount of conflict raised by these economic issues made some sort of central authority necessary, though they made no judgements on the equity of existing arrangements.[130] A Kenya Tariff Committee, with unofficial interests strongly represented, supported the customs union and protection, though it was prepared to see the protective duties lowered to 30%; a Uganda Committee which followed it opposed protection and called for a heavy reduction in duties as well as an end to the Country Produce Rates already discussed. The Tanganyika Legislative Council also favoured a reduction in the level of duty.[131] The issue was discussed in detail at the Governors' Conference in 1930, at which Grigg strongly supported the Kenyan case and was heavily backed up in his demand by the access granted to the settlers. Their presence was especially important since the Tanganyikan community was also represented and had been persuaded by Delamere to accept the Kenyan position.[132] This tended to undermine Cameron, who showed the clearest understanding of the issues involved and might otherwise have pressed his opposition further. Despite their presence, however, they were forced to give some ground. In exchange for the decision to maintain the Country Produce Rates on the railway the general duty on the protected items was reduced to 30%, and in addition the principle of suspended duties was introduced, which allowed individual territories to reduce the duty on most items by 10%.

The matter was discussed again in 1932/3 with respect to Tanganyika when Sir Sydney Armitage-Smith, a British Treasury official sent out to discover means of reducing her expenditure and increasing revenue, concluded that protection 'has injured both the consumer and the revenue of Tanganyika',[133] and therefore that the territory 'should cease to deplete her revenue and impoverish her citizens by protecting the products of her neighbours'.[134] This report was strengthened by a request from the Permanent Mandates Commission asking for information about the effects of the customs union on the territory. In December

1932 Cunliffe-Lister, Secretary of State, told the J.E.A.B. that the effect of the report was to force him 'to take action to secure equitable arrangements in a mandated territory', and that this should occur before the next annual meeting of the Commission 'when otherwise this preferential trade would undoubtedly be challenged'.[135] The next months were spent producing a case which would convince the Permanent Mandates Commission, who do not, in any case, ever appear to have exercised any close watch on the affairs of their ward. In January the Dar es Salaam Chamber called for immediate steps to restore the Territory's balance of trade and revenue, and to protect consumers 'and the existing and potential industries of this Territory',[136] though the Association of Chambers of Commerce of Eastern Africa, dominated by Kenya, attacked the Armitage-Smith Report as 'subversive' of their policy.[137] The main item in Tanganyika's adverse balance of trade was sugar, and the Governors' Conference, concerned to assist Symes of Tanganyika in his desire 'to make a satisfactory report on the sugar position in Geneva', agreed in February 1933 to reduce the import duty and impose a local consumption tax on all the sugar imported into the territory. In exchange Symes agreed to take 'remedial action' if overseas imports increased.[138] In March the J.E.A.B. resolved that a weakening of the customs union would be 'disastrous to economic development' and a retrograde step for 'the settlers in those territories and the business interests there and at home connected with them',[139] and they passed this to the Colonial Office together with some figures on East African trade provided for them by the East Africa Office in London. The latter had been requested by Cunliffe-Lister to assist him in his forthcoming discussions with Symes, but did not correspond to those published by the territory itself.[140] The Tanganyika case was published shortly afterwards and stressed the value to Tanganyika of access to northern 'manufacturing processes', distribution networks, and protected markets; it argued that losses on customs revenue had to be offset by losses to Kenya and Uganda on exports from Tanganyika, and claimed that the sugar concession would bring a revenue of £10,000 p.a., force a reduction of prices and serve as 'an inducement to the local establishment of a sugar factory in Tanganyika itself'.[141] The Permanent Mandates Commission was apparently satisfied, and in August the J.E.A.B. recorded a decision approving 'the continuance of the existing customs union'.[142] This decision ended conflict which threatened the principle of the customs union as such; this was to be maintained intact until independence, and dispute confined to detail.

The effects of this decision, however, were to contradict the J.E.A.B.'s bland assumption that the advantages of the union would even themselves out over time.[143] The central question to be resolved concerned control over the internal market for both imports and local products. This was small and could not therefore be divided too many ways before economies of scale were lost; those enterprises which captured predominant positions in the early stages of development could expect to maintain them and to eliminate future competitors, thus producing a tendency to concentration rather than an equitable distribution of available surpluses. This tendency was clearly demonstrated in the latter years of the thirties, when the economic centre of gravity in the region shifted decisively in favour of Kenya, which became the primary distribution, manufacturing and temperate-climate foodstuff-producing area for the region as a whole. Figures in this area are uncertain, but the Tanganyika Government did publish some regularly from 1935; they demonstrate very clearly the growing tendency for the more advanced and profitable activity to gravitate to Kenya, with Uganda being able to maintain some advantages, but for Tanganyika to lose. This tendency can be documented by looking at the figures for distribution, internal trade, trade in protected goods, and trade in locally processed goods.

In the 1930s some 20–25% of Tanganyika's imports were being handled from Kenya, the percentage being larger at the end than the beginning of the decade:

TABLE II

Percentage of Tanganyikan Imports Distributed from Kenya

1930	17	1933	24	1936	22
1931	17·5	1934	24	1937	25
1932	22	1935	20	1938	24

Source: 1930–7 calculated from amount of total customs revenue credited to Tanganyika in relation to total receipts (*Annual Report*, 1934, p. 144; 1937, p. 69); 1938 from figures of trade coming through Kenya and total trade (*Annual Report*, 1938, p. 208).

With regard to local production the initial beneficiaries of the union were the Kenyan foodstuff producers, but by the thirties Uganda had become a large exporter of sugar, cigarettes and manufactured tobacco. But Tanganyika generally maintained an adverse balance of trade with the other two, and this tended to increase.

TABLE III

Tanganyika: Trade with Kenya and Uganda, 1926–38 (£000s)

	Imports from	Exports to	Balance
1926	135	145	+10
1927	179	146	−33
1928	140	140	0
1929	195	122	−73
1930	178	119	−57
1931	173	89	−84
1932	164	104	−60
1933*	154	143	−11
1934	251	205	−46
1935	258	181	−77
1936	226	179	−46
1937	300	216	−84
1938	320	227	−94

Source: Annual Report, 1932, pp. 130, 131, 133; 1935, pp. 179–80; 1936, pp. 203–4; 1938, pp. 205–6.
* Figures for 1933 not strictly comparable, drawn from Governors' Conference Memorandum, *Review of position regarding customs tariffs, suspended duties, etc.*, May 1934. This probably underestimates the deficit, since the figures it gives for 1931 and 1932 are lower than those given above.

Further, the main beneficiaries of the union were the producers of protected products, since they were being paid a subsidy by consumers in neighbouring territories, and here again Tanganyika was consistently disadvantaged:

TABLE IV

Tanganyika: Trade with Kenya and Uganda in Protected Goods, 1934–8 (£000s)

	Imports	Exports	Balance
1934	165	174	+9
1935	178	137	−41
1936	149	129	−20
1937	190	158	−32
1938	202	166	−36

Source: Annual Reports, 1935–8.

Finally, the common market expanded the openings for manufactured products, and here again the advantages appear to have
been predominantly exploited by the northern territories, which
became increasingly dominant in the Tanganyikan market as the
decade progressed:

TABLE V

*Tanganyika: Trade with Kenya and Uganda in
Locally Processed Goods, 1934–8 (£000s)*

	Imports	Exports	Balance
1934	86	82	−4
1935	91	42	−49
1936	111	20	−91
1937	141	14	−127
1938	143	10	−133

Source: Annual Reports, 1935–8.

The major factor in this progressive worsening was the diversion of
Tanganyikan cigarettes from the export to the local market,
coupled with a rapid growth in the import of both from Uganda.
Further, Kenyan processed exports grew very rapidly, especially
cement, flour and aluminium hollow ware. By the end of the
decade a clear pattern favouring the northern territories appears
to have been established, and this was to be maintained and
accentuated until independence.

This is not of course to suggest that Tanganyika would have been
willing to encourage the production of the commodities involved
given the right to independent control over tariff policy. In fact
the willingness to maintain a policy which did at the very least
cost the local taxpayer a great deal in lost customs revenue for the
benefit of high-cost producers in neighbouring territories merely
accentuated the general weakness of the economic policies followed
by a leadership which, after the departure of Cameron (who at
least understood the problem and opposed some of the worst of the
effects), allowed the territory to be exploited in the most direct
and damaging way by the more advanced economic groups in
the other territories. The widely held view that Britain 'neglected'
Tanganyika's economic needs during the colonial period can in
fact be directly attributed to the working out of the effects of
a common transport and customs policy: Britain tended in fact to

provide the territory with as much in the way of general developmental resources as the other two,[144] but in these areas Tanganyika suffered direct and measurable losses of income which were enormous in relation to the size of the contemporary economic base, while the indirect losses accruing from forgone economic opportunities through her resulting dependence on northern services, producers and suppliers is incalculable. The whole system was based upon the fact that the dominant expatriate interests involved in the East African economy were committed to protectionism and a common market, and worked from bases predominantly concentrated in Kenya. Their views were allowed to prevail despite the presence of the Permanent Mandates Commission, which appears to have given Tanganyikan interests a very small amount of leverage in Britain but at no point to have exerted any decisive influence over events.[145] The Tanganyika administration itself showed some resistance in the 1920s, but this collapsed in the thirties: Symes's role in the Governors' Conferences in particular was almost wholly capitulationist, while the commercial and settler groups involved were too small and too dependent on Kenya to exert any effective influence in their own defence. This was also an area in which the issues, although directly affecting welfare of African consumers and producers throughout the region, were too complex and technical to be understood by the humanitarian groups that were supposed to defend their interests in London. As a result, directly exploitative policies which extracted surpluses from the poorest of the farming communities for the benefit of the wealthiest went entirely unnoticed and could be discussed in London as 'economic' issues of interest only to the commercial and producing groups directly involved.

This account should have exposed some of the basic assumptions which characterized policy-making in this area, the kinds of conflicts which had to be resolved, and the institutional structure which emerged from the whole process. Looking at the interaction of policy and economic forces in this way makes it clear that superficial distinctions between 'political' and 'economic' spheres merely obscure the fundamental unity of a situation where particular interests were competing for resources and, more especially, attempting to create institutionalized structures which would guarantee them privileged access to surpluses which could be derived from local productivity. In this case the resources at stake were the traffic available for competing transportation systems, and the limited markets for locally produced commodities. The political nature of the issues at stake was obscured by their technical complexity and the fact that the arena within which they were contested was not controlled by a single authoritative decision-making structure, but by a confederal authority which derived its ability to take unified decisions from common subordination to a single outside authority. This latter fact made it possible for the resulting system to survive despite the manifestly inequitable way in which costs and benefits were divided both between and within different territories. Once the external authority withdrew the system could be expected to collapse unless a more equitable division could be arranged – something which the independent governments have been unable to achieve, at least with respect to tariffs and currency, though not with respect to transport.

NOTES

1. E. J. Hobsbawm, *Industry and Empire*, Harmondsworth, Penguin Books, 1969, p. 178.
2. *Ibid.*, p. 207.
3. House of Commons, *Debates*, 25 vii 23, v. 167, c. 589. Sir George Schuster, closely associated with the Gezira scheme in the Sudan at that time, also stressed this point very strongly in an interview.
4. *Committee on industry and trade* [*The Balfour Committee*], Cmd. 3282 of 1929, Minutes of evidence, p. 1.
5. Empire Cotton Growing Corporation, *Report of the Second Annual General Meeting*, 1923, p. 8.
6. House of Commons, *Debates*, 30 vii 19, v. 118, c. 2182.
7. W. K. Hancock, *Survey of British Commonwealth affairs*, vol. II, *Problems of economic policy*, London, O.U.P., 1940.
8. Hobsbawm, *op. cit.*, p. 136; cf. also R. Robinson and I. Gallagher, *Africa and the Victorians*, London, Macmillan, 1961, ch. 1.
9. Manchester Chamber of Commerce, *Annual Report*, 1934, p. ix.
10. House of Commons, *Debates*, 14 ii 33, v. 274, c. 830.
11. House of Commons, *Debates*, 1 vii 32, v. 267, c. 2211.
12. This is, of course, the basis on which leading academic apologists for the colonial system justified its activities, notably Hancock (see Bibliography).
13. House of Commons, *Debates*, 30 iv 29, v. 227, c. 1498–9.
14. House of Commons, *Debates*, 30 iv 29, v. 227, c. 1459.
15. This view is implicit in Sir R. Furse, *Aucuparius; recollections of a recruiting officer*, London, O.U.P., 1962.
16. House of Commons, *Debates*, 11 xii 29, v. 233, c. 591.
17. House of Commons, *Debates*, 11 xii 29, v. 233, c. 591.
18. The Governor of Uganda, *Proceedings of the Conference of East African Governors*, April 1935, p. 6.
19. C. Ehrlich, *The marketing of cotton in Uganda*, London Ph.D., 1958, p. 32.
20. F. V. Carter, *Education in Uganda*, London Ph.D., 1967, p. 46.

21. *Ibid.*, p. 49.
22. *Commission on higher education in East Africa*, col. 142, 1937, p. 14.
23. *Ibid.*, p. 35.
24. Their views were forcefully stated to the Governor's Conference in 1930 – cf. *Proceedings of the Conference of East African Governors*.
25. J.E.A.B., Minutes, 2 iv 36.
26. *Ibid.*, 5 vi 36.
27. Peter Wiles's phrase, *The political economy of communism*, Oxford, Blackwell, 1962, p. 2.
28. Cf. W. K. Hancock, *op. cit.* (note 7), p. 173 ff.
29. Hobsbawm, *op. cit.* (note 1), p. 115.
30. Cf. Robinson and Gallagher, *op. cit.* (note 8).
31. K. Robinson, *The dilemmas of trusteeship*, London, O.U.P., 1965, p. 32.
32. S. H. Frankel, *Capital investment in Africa*, London, O.U.P., 1938, pp. 256–7.
33. J.E.A.B., *Memorandum on East African Development*, 1937.
34. House of Commons, *Debates*, 12 vii 29, v. 229, c. 1295.
35. S. H. Beer, *Modern British politics*, London, Faber, 1969, p. 278.
36. *Ibid.*
37. House of Commons, *Debates*, 11 vii 23, v. 166, c. 1357.
38. Colonial Development Advisory Committee, *Annual Report*, 1938–9, p. 11.
39. Tanganyika, *Annual Report*, 1925, 1926.
40. Cf. W. McGregor Ross, *Kenya from within*, London, Allen & Unwin, 1927, pp. 238–55; M. F. Hill, *Permanent way*, vol. I, Nairobi, East African Railways and Harbours, 1949, p. 410.
41. House of Commons, *Debates*, 18 v 20, v. 129, c. 1257–8; 16 vi 20, v. 130, c. 1276.
42. Kenya, *Annual Report*, 1926, 1928; *Railway Report*, 1924.
43. *Ibid.*, 1923, p. 8.
44. *Ibid.*, 1923, p. 8.
45. Felling to Walker, 14 i 27 (Walker Papers).
46. House of Commons, *Debates*, 18 vi 23, v. 165, c. 977.
47. House of Commons, *Debates*, 25 vi 23, v. 165, c. 1912.
48. House of Commons, *Debates*, 2 vii 23, v. 166, c. 15–16.
49. Cf. House of Commons, *Debates*, July 1923, vols. 165–7.
50. House of Commons, *Debates*, 25 vii 23, v. 167, c. 497–8.
51. *Ibid.*, c. 530–1. He was probably mainly concerned with the conflict in progress then between the Governor and plantation interests. Cf. Ch. 7 below.
52. Felling to Walker, 14 i 27 (Walker Papers).
53. *Private enterprise in British tropical Africa*, Cmd. 2016, 1924, p. 18.
54. *Ibid.*, pp. 23–4.
55. *Ibid.*, p. 12.
56. *Ibid.*, p. 11.
57. *Railway Report*, 1925, p. 10.
58. Cf. esp. House of Commons, *Debates*, 25 ii 24, v. 170, c. 187–202.
59. London Chamber of Commerce, *Memorandum adopted at a joint meeting of members of the West African Section and the East African Section of the London Chamber of Commerce . . . for submission to the Private Enterprise Committee*, in *Annual Report*, 1923, p. 3.
60. Details from Kenya, *Port Commission of Enquiry*, 1926; Hill, *op. cit.*; *Railway Reports*, 1920/1–1925.

61. Felling to Dutton, 17 viii 26 (Altrincham Papers).
62. Grigg to Amery, 11 xi 26 (Altrincham Papers).
63. J.E.A.B., Minutes, 1 iv 25.
64. J.E.A.B., Minutes, 29 vii 25.
65. Minutes of Colonial Office Conference, 31 vii 25.
66. *Op. cit.*, p. 24.
67. *Report on . . . Mombasa (Kilindini) Harbour . . .* Cmd. 2713, pp. 12–14.
68. Ormsby-Gore to Grigg, 23 vii 26 (Altrincham Papers).
69. Relevant memos. mainly September 1926 in Altrincham Papers.
70. Memo. on Imperial Shipping Committee Report, 8 ix 26 (Altrincham Papers).
71. J.E.A.B., Minutes, 4 viii 26.
72. Amery to Grigg, 22 ix 26 (Altrincham Papers).
73. Cf. *Railway Report*, 1927.
74. Cf. McGregor Ross, *op. cit.* (note 40), pp. 162–3.
75. Cf. R. Green and A. Seidman, *Africa, unity or poverty*, Harmondsworth, Penguin Books, 1968.
76. For a brief account cf. E. A. Brett, 'Closer union in East Africa', in D. Austin and H. N. Weiler, *Inter-state relations in Africa*, London, Institute of Commonwealth Studies, 1965.
77. Cf. W. Newlyn and Rowan, *Money and Banking in British Colonial Africa*, Oxford, Clarendon Press, 1954.
78. Three vols., House of Lords, 29 of 1930 and 184 of 1931.
79. *Proceedings of the Governors' Conference*, May 1934, pp. 2–3; January 1935, p. 8. For a general account of the organization of railway administration cf. G. F. Engholm, *Immigrant influences on the development of policy in . . . Uganda . . .* Ph.D., London, 1967.
80. Most of the key figures are given in Engholm, *op. cit.*, pp. 252–9. An indication of the nature of the situation can be gathered from the fact that the railway estimated that it required a rate of 5·5 cents per ton mile to break even, while maize was carried at roughly 3 cents and cotton at 10 cents per ton mile.
81. Confidential evidence to the Joint Select Committee, Webb Papers.
82. *Report . . . on railway rates . . . in Kenya, Uganda and Tanganyika*, Cmd. 4235, p. 24, cf. Engholm, *op. cit.*, pp. 255–9.
83. Engholm, *op. cit.*, p. 141.
84. *Proceedings of the Governors Conference*, 1930, p. 9.
85. Vol. II, qu. 2790–2, 3057–60; vol. III, p. 33.
86. *Report . . . on certain questions in Kenya*, Cmd. 4093, pp. 19–20.
87. *Op. cit.*, p. 23.
88. *Ibid.*, p. 20.
89. *Ibid.*, p. 13.
90. Gibb to Walker, 16 iv 33 (Walker Papers).
91. Discussed in Ch. 4 below.
92. Kenya, *Railway Report*, 1929, p. 10.
93. *Ibid.*, 1926, p. 9.
94. Cf. *ibid.*, 1928, p. 9 for figures.
95. *Ibid.*, 1929, p. 10.
96. Engholm, *op. cit.*, pp. 260–2.
97. House of Commons, *Debates*, 27 iii 23, v. 162, c. 261.

98. House of Lords, *Debates*, 5 vii 23, v. 54, c. 833–4.
99. House of Commons, *Debates*, 31 vii 23, v. 167, c. 1367; J.E.A.B., Minutes, 1 viii 23 and 5 ix 23, citing correspondence with the Colonial Office.
100. J.E.A.B., Minutes, 9 i 24.
101. Gibb Report, *op. cit.*, p. 49.
102. *East Africa Commission; East Africa Guaranteed Loan Commission*, Cmd. 2701 of 1926; Gibb Report.
103. D. Cameron, *My Tanganyika service*, pp. 69–71; Cameron to Henn, 4 xii 25 (Henn Papers).
104. E.C.G.C., *Report of the Advisory Council*, 1924, p. 14.
105. J.E.A.B., Minutes, 4 xi 25.
106. Ormsby-Gore to Grigg, 23 vii 26 (Altrincham Papers).
107. E. Grigg, *Imperial policy in East Africa* (Memo. to 1927 Governors' Conference in London), p. 17.
108. *Ibid.*, p. 15.
109. Cameron, *op. cit.*, pp. 236–7.
110. Cf. *ibid.*, pp. 124–5; Altrincham (Sir E. Grigg), *Kenya's opportunity*, pp. 193–5.
111. Cameron to Grigg, 20 viii 26 (Altrincham Papers).
112. Cited in Amery to Grigg, 20 viii 26 (Altrincham Papers).
113. *Report of the East African Guaranteed Loan Committee*, Cmd. 2701 of 1926, p. 45.
114. *Proceedings of the Governors' Conference*, October 1933, p. 18.
115. *Ibid.*, pp. 19–20.
116. *Ibid.*, p. 21.
117. M. F. Hill, *Permanent way*, vol. II, p. 248.
118. *Ibid.*, p. 251.
119. *Report of the Commission . . . on the financial position and system of taxation of Kenya* (Pim Report), col. 116 of 1936, pp. 29–30.
120. *Ibid.*
121. *Annual Report*, 1923, pp. 30–1.
122. House of Commons, *Debates*, 25 vii 23, v. 167, c. 506.
123. Cf. Engholm, *op. cit.* (note 79), pp. 170–1.
124. J.E.A.B., Minutes, 1 viii 23, 9 i 24.
125. Tanganyika, *Annual Report*, 1925, pp. 43–4; Sir Robert Coryndon to Henn, 5 v 24 (Henn Papers).
126. J.E.A.B., Minutes, 7 iv 26.
127. *Ibid.*
128. *Op. cit.*, p. 128.
129. Colonial Office reply to J.E.A.B. request for end of duties, J.E.A.B.–C.O. Conference, Minutes, 17 vi 24.
130. *Commission on Closer Union . . .* , pp. 131–2.
131. *Proceedings of the Governors' Conference*, January 1930, 3rd meeting, p. 6.
132. Walker to Wilson, 13 i 30 (Walker Papers).
133. *Report . . . on a financial mission to Tanganyika*, Cmd. 4128, pp. 22–3.
134. *Ibid.*, p. 25.
135. C.O.–J.E.A.B. Conference, Minutes, 8 xii 32.
136. Resolution 25 i 33, letter to J.E.A.B. 11 iii 33 (J.E.A.B. files).
137. Memorandum, January 1933, J.E.A.B. files.
138. *Proceedings of the Governors' Conference*, February 1933, pp. 21–2.

139. J.E.A.B., Minutes, 2 iii 33; J.E.A.B., *Annual Report*, 1933, p. 14.
140. Colonial Office to J.E.A.B., 14 iii 33; East Africa Office to J.E.A.B., 30 iii 33.
141. Tanganyika, *Annual Report*, 1932, pp. 127–33; The 1933 *Annual Report* anticipated that the tax would raise £12,000 (p. 46).
142. J.E.A.B., Minutes, 3 viii 33.
143. J.E.A.B. to Colonial Office, 6 iii 33 (J.E.A.B. files).
144. Cf. Chapter 4 below.
145. This is my general feeling about their role, which therefore leads me to dispute the more positive assessment in B. T. Chidzero, *Tanganyika and international trusteeship*, London, O.U.P., 1961.

PART II

The International Context: Britain's Economic Crises and Colonial Development

4

British Unemployment
and Colonial Aid

The major factors which conditioned Britain's attitude to the problem of colonial development were set out very generally at the start of the previous chapter. In this section an attempt will be made to document the British response to these pressures, a response which was concretely manifested in policies designed to create an infrastructure which would encourage the development of primary export production, and to manage a trading system which would ensure British producers favoured access to colonial markets. The impetus behind the main programmes which emerged derived essentially from the conditions which prevailed during the two great economic crises that marked the inter-war period – the strains created by reconstruction of the international economy immediately after the end of the War, and those produced by the international collapse during the Depression. It is now necessary to look at the effects produced by these events in more detail, and to show more precisely how the most important policy initiatives stemmed from them.

The colonial and metropolitan economies were not separate, but complementary parts of a single system. Colonial prosperity depended directly upon the prosperity of metropolitan industry, since this both created the market for their raw materials and supplied them in turn with finished products. But the reciprocal nature of this relationship also linked the prosperity of metropolitan manufacturers to the success of colonial production, since they required markets for surplus production and plentiful (and therefore cheap) supplies of raw materials to ensure their competitiveness and profitability. The relationship was, of course, very unequal. The metropolitan sector quite clearly played the leading role; each colony depended very heavily on the metropolis but the metropolis depended very little upon any one colony or group of colonies. Indeed, British trade with the developed world and the older Dominions was always of much greater importance to her than trade with the whole colonial Empire – in 1924 the latter made up 6·8% of her exports, in 1931 10%.[1] During the whole of this period Britain also obtained large amounts of primary production from the developed world – for example cotton and tobacco from the U.S.A. and temperate-climate foodstuffs from Canada and Australasia. But the question of colonial development nevertheless featured heavily in British policy-making for two main reasons: firstly, however small its present output, the colonial Empire promised massive expansion if only its under-utilized resources could be brought into use; secondly, this development could be controlled from Britain in accordance with the principles set out in the first part of the previous chapter and thus contribute maximum advantage to British interests in the process. Further, although the colonial trade was not of primary importance to the British economy as a whole, it could be of great importance to particular groups of manufacturers with a special interest in colonial markets – this was particularly true for the Lancashire cotton textile industry and for parts of the steel industry as well. Thus colonial development was treated as a central problem of British economic policy during these years, a problem whose solution could be expected to contribute materially and directly to ending the crisis which the ruling class faced in one form or another for the whole period. Stated in its most general terms, their problem was to stimulate colonial development in directions which would provide British industry with the largest possible returns – to maximize consumption of British products and export of British requirements. In this way the Colonies could be made to contribute directly to the success of British industry – to keeping the workforce employed, and the profits high. Equally important, by doing this the Colonies could also contribute directly to political stability; they could moderate the danger of social disruption and political upheaval, which constituted a very real threat to established society, especially in the years immediately after the First World War.

The initial impetus behind the emergence of a conscious British programme of colonial aid and development can be located in the economic crisis which began at the end of the War and was only moderated towards the end of 1922 as the first post-war depression began to lift. The crisis was generalized across the face of European capitalism: its symptoms were stagnating trade, unemployment and inflation in the economic sphere; social dislocation, mounting discontent and unrest in the political. At the end of the War European governments had to come to terms with these problems and attempt to rescue their countries from threatened socialist revolutions. England was no exception. In 1919 the War Cabinet conducted a series of meetings concerned with 'Unemployment and the State of Trade'; at one of these in particular many of the key issues were considered. It is worth looking at some of its assumptions since these show very clearly how the statesmen saw the problem and how they believed it might be solved.

Far from being committed to a policy of *laissez-faire*, the meeting took as its starting-point the fact that government was primarily responsible for solving the problem by strong action to improve welfare, and more especially to create the conditions in which trade could flourish. The alternative was revolution. According to Lloyd George, talking of the need to 'quieten labour':

> It is [the workers'] conviction that they have come in vain to the doors of Parliament, and that promises made by one party or another have only produced measures that did nothing. The Town Planning Bill has not produced three houses; the Small Holdings and Allotments Bill has not produced anything substantial – they have not made a real change. That is the kind of thing that has made them feel 'Well, it is no good going to Parliament, we must trust to our own power,' and they strike, and a strike may end in revolution.[2]

This possibility was the primary motivating force behind policy during these years; the problem was to ensure employment and hence stave off the worst forms of social disruption which might finally undermine general support for the capitalist system. As he said again later in the same discussion, 'you must give the people a horizon, or they will look at their wretched surroundings, and once they lose hope there is nothing but revolution and trouble'.[3] But although Government assumed this responsibility, prevailing free-enterprise ideology allowed it only a limited range of strategies for dealing with the problems involved. Direct intervention was limited by the very small size of the public sector, while deficit financing was not yet fashionable. The Cabinet did consider in detail the possibilities of an expanded programme of capital investment in social services, especially in housing, mainly prompted by Lloyd George, who could not understand why a nation which had expected to raise £2,000,000,000 for another year of war should find it difficult to raise £71,000,000 for public works.[4] But the conservative element in the Cabinet showed considerable resistance to heavy reliance on this kind of programme, not least because of the likelihood that it might destroy 'the basis of private enterprise in such an industry as the building industry'.[5] Thus it was generally assumed that the job of the Government was to create conditions which would 'give confidence to Capital' by re-establishing trade. In Austen Chamberlain's words:

> The really important thing for the safety of our position is to get our trade going, and, above all, to get our export trade going, and it is no real compensation for that if we are spending an enormous amount of money on housing or anything like that.[6]

But the problems facing British industry in overseas markets were clearly understood; it was generally recognized that protectionism abroad and high costs at home had transformed former economic superiority into a weakness which could only be concealed by exploiting special access to the Empire in order to maintain former standards of living. Amery captured this diminished sense of competence very exactly when he said:

> We are in fact no longer the sort of country that can compete industrially in the open market except in certain industries. . . . It really comes to this, that we can both carry out our social reform and develop an immense trade, but mainly if not almost entirely within the Empire.[7]

And the meeting was even told (although how far it accepted the implications of the information is not so certain) that the lack of competitiveness did not derive from excessively high wages, since Lloyd George pointed out that he had obtained information on comparative wage rates:

> . . . and in fact I was going to use it the other way, in order to show how much better the wages were here. I dropped it like a hot coal, because I found they were not much better than in Germany.[8]

Since the Government could not intervene directly to do very much to relieve this incompetence in British industry they had to find ways and means of subsidizing it, of finding soft markets and other outlets to keep factories open and men employed. During the next few years they were to undertake a number of programmes of public works in Britain and to contribute directly to unemployment relief. But these were not given central importance; the critical changes would have to take place in the Empire.

These policies, pressed most consistently by Leo Amery through the Empire Industries Association, the Empire Economic Union and a multitude of books and pamphlets,[9] were given concrete form in the twenties in the programmes of settlement for the

Dominions, and, of particular importance for our purposes, of development for the Colonies.

The impetus behind colonial development was at its most intense in the years immediately after the War when the threat to political stability in particular was at its height. But the same factors continued to operate during the rest of the twenties, culminating in the passage in 1929 of the Colonial Development Act, a much misunderstood and underestimated piece of legislation. The Depression of the thirties changed the situation by reducing the apparent potentialities for colonial trade and development, but was succeeded in turn by a period of rising prosperity, a return to earlier optimism, and an attempt to rectify the limitations of the 1929 legislation in the 1940 Colonial Development and Welfare Act, which in turn served as the basis for the aid effort of the forties and fifties. The rest of this chapter will therefore look at the development of policy as it was affected by these wider circumstances, concentrating in particular upon the earlier period when most of the creative thinking in this field really took place – the years between 1919 and 1923, which provided the initial impetus to the policies, and those leading up to the 1929 Act when increasingly ambitious programmes were initiated and the attempt was finally made to set up machinery which would give continuity to the aid effort and fairly extensive resources for it.

Those committed to colonial development had to overcome two major sources of opposition. Firstly, despite the acceptance in the Colonies of the necessity for active state intervention in the economy, the prevailing assumption in Britain was that such matters should normally be settled on commercial terms. This meant that investments, even where made by the State, should be capable of showing a commercial return within a relatively limited period. But the African territories in particular possessed almost no infrastructure – communications were almost non-existent, the indigenous population had little training or experience, and administrative control was unevenly distributed and superficial in its impact. This meant that an enormous amount had to be invested before any return could be expected, so that very little could be done if purely commercial criteria were applied. The imperialist school saw this very clearly, as Milner demonstrated in 1910:

> I suppose [colonial development] is a question of money, and though we are so much more liberal than we used to be, I do not think we are as yet anything like liberal enough in the conception of

what is needed for the equipment of an undeveloped country, and in
realising how much you must spend without immediate return if you
are going to make a success of it in the long run.[10]

This meant that capital had to be found from sources which did
not apply normal commercial criteria and this, in the context of
the time, necessarily required the support of the British Government. Large-scale capital investments could be raised on the
London capital market, but the lack of commercial viability
meant that governmental backing of some kind was essential if
most colonies were to be able to take any advantage of its facilities.
In some cases no more than a guarantee would suffice; more
often, however, it became clear that direct assistance from the
Treasury for the payment of interest was essential as well. It was
thus clear to imperialists like Milner and Amery that colonial
development required official British aid, that is, grants or loans
which were provided on non-commercial terms and which therefore imposed some demands on British taxpayers. Such policies
could expect to meet opposition from domestic interests concerned
to raise money for other services, opposition which took concrete
form in the need to convince the Treasury of the justification for a
high priority for colonial spending. And this need then raised the
second major source of opposition, since the Treasury had traditionally applied very rigid limits on any British spending in the
Colonies, which were all expected to become financially self-
sufficient as soon as possible. All the African territories had had to
receive grants in aid during the first years of British control: these
grants were administered very stringently by the Treasury and
severe limits imposed upon the independence of the local administration until they had balanced their budgets.[11] This meant that
policies which involved direct financial assistance to the colonial
Empire were likely to meet strongly-entrenched opposition from
the Treasury itself, and could only expect to succeed if they
achieved considerable momentum through weighty support from
well-positioned political groups.

The unemployment crisis has already been identified as one of
the major sources of this momentum; another, especially important immediately after the War, was the desire to achieve
economic self-sufficiency for strategic reasons. Guaranteed access
to markets and materials became more important than comparative costs in this analysis, and Empire self-sufficiency became
a goal of policy as a result. The Committee on Commercial and
Industrial Policy argued as the war ended:

The war has directed public attention to the extent to which the United Kingdom and the British Empire as a whole are dependent upon foreign countries, not only for certain manufactured commodities of great importance . . . but also for a large number of raw materials which are not produced at all, or are produced on a scale altogether incommensurate with our requirements within the British Empire. . . . The main conditions in regard to these various commodities, and especially as to the extent of our dependence upon foreign sources of supply, were of course familiar before the war to those directly concerned with each particular article, but it is doubtful if they were at all widely known or if their significance for the industrial position of this country, especially in times of international disturbance, was generally appreciated.[12]

Further, the short boom immediately after the War produced high raw materials prices, making it possible for the Colonies to envisage expanded programmes of capital expenditure. This also led British manufacturers to accept the need for colonial development, which would increase their sources of supply and hence reduce raw material prices and their own costs, thus creating a political and economic context in which aid programmes could expect a very sympathetic hearing. No one, of course, appears to have noticed the fact that an expansion in supply would reduce raw material prices and thereby also reduce both colonial capacity to repay loans and to import finished products. This contradiction was to manifest itself in recurrent budgetary and commercial crises in the history of colonial development, but the fact does not seem ever to have dampened the optimism which re-emerged during upswings in the developmental cycle.

While the demand for self-sufficiency and the need to increase exports because of unemployment tended to produce a generalized commitment to programmes of colonial development, that for raw materials tended to take specific forms derived from the needs of particular classes of manufacturer in difficulties. By far the most important of these for our purposes were the textile industrialists who, because of disease in the American cotton fields, were forced to pay what they regarded as unreasonable prices for raw cotton from the end of the War until about 1926. Their needs were to be of prime importance in determining both the nature of the aid programme ultimately evolved in East Africa and the areas in which it was to be spent. The conjunction of pressures which emerged between 1919 and 1922 produced both a number of specific initiatives designed to meet particular developmental needs and the first discussion of the general relationship between colonial development and British unemployment and of the need to begin a larger and more general programme.

The Committee on Commercial and Industrial Policy had stressed the need for more scientific research in the Colonies to discover and utilize new raw material sources, and also the shortage of an adequate Empire cotton supply. From this kind of preoccupation emerged the Colonial Research Committee initiated by Lord Long, Milner's predecessor at the Colonial Office, the Imperial College of Tropical Agriculture in Trinidad in 1921, and the Empire Cotton Growing Corporation in 1923. The Research Committee was originally allocated £100,000 to be spent over five years, but had its grant cut to £2,000 per annum in the Depression of 1921/2.[13] The Imperial College opened in 1922, was financed by contributions from the Colonies, private enterprise and an Imperial grant, and it served as a centre for research and training for the whole colonial Empire.[14]

The Empire Cotton Growing Corporation (E.C.G.C.) was set up in response to the insecurity of the American cotton supply, and worked on the assumption that the primary need was for research and the provision of trained manpower that could put this into practice through colonial Agricultural Departments.[15] Pressure of this kind had originated during the War, but it was greatly intensified by the difficulties experienced by the textile industry, especially as the activities of the boll weevil greatly reduced American crops and pushed prices to record levels in 1919 and 1920.[16] The Manchester Chamber of Commerce pressed the issue actively from 1920 till about 1925, when the problem receded, and the formation of the E.C.G.C. was only one of the outcomes of this activity. The Corporation was given a capital grant of £979,000 by the Government and the revenue from a levy of 6d. per bale of raw cotton consumed by participating firms. The levy was originally voluntary, but was made binding through the Cotton Industry Act in 1923; it was reduced to 3d. in 1928 and 1d. in 1933 on the grounds that nothing more was required. The grant, representing the Government's share in the profits from the Egyptian Cotton Control Scheme of 1918–19, was made over in perpetuity and the Corporation managed by a Board of Management representing the British and Empire Governments and the Lancashire trade. Its functions were primarily scientific and educational, the more commercial aspects of cotton promotion being left to the British Cotton Growing Association, which had been set up by the Lancashire trade before the War. In action it subsidized local research, helped to finance training at the Imperial College of Tropical Agriculture, made direct grants to local agricultural departments, published a quarterly review,[17] and pressed in Britain for funds for better transport facilities into cotton-growing areas. Its major areas of involvement were in Uganda and the Sudan, with Tanganyika becoming important in the thirties.

Finally, to complete this account of the minor agencies for colonial development created in the twenties, it is worth mentioning the Empire Marketing Board. The Baldwin government agreed at the Imperial Conference to impose a number of preferential duties in favour of certain Empire products. These agreements were repudiated by Labour in 1924 and not restored by Baldwin. Instead an annual grant of £1 million was allocated to the E.M.B., the approximate cash value of the preferences in question.[18] The Board spent its money on advertising campaigns for Empire products in Britain and also spent a good deal on research overseas, which their secretary claimed they regarded 'as of quite as much importance as the advertising side'.[19] It was wound up in 1933, on the ground that the acceptance of Imperial Preference by Britain absolved the Government from the original obligation to finance it.

It is now possible to turn to the larger debate which linked British unemployment with colonial development and more particularly with colonial railway building. It was this connection between unemployment in the British engineering industry and the possibilities of stimulating colonial primary production through railways which created the impetus for a debate that was to lead to a general acceptance of the validity of aid programmes where these could be shown to make a recognizable contribution to the British economy. The general strategy was intensively discussed at Cabinet level in the second half of 1921; this led to experiments in the use of governmental resources to stimulate development which became increasingly complex as the decade progressed, until the principle, still very ineffectually developed, but significant nevertheless, of the need for a general colonial aid programme had been accepted and put into effect in 1929.

The fears of social dislocation expressed at the War Cabinet discussion already cited were modified by the boom which developed in 1919 and lasted into the latter part of 1920.

Unemployment fluctuated around 400,000 (about 2 %) during these months, being as low as 1·6% in August 1920 according to Lloyd George.[20] But the boom was succeeded by a recession which took the figure to 1·6 million in April 1921 and to 2·2 million by July.[21] Almost a million were on short time and growing numbers were likely to exhaust their right to unemployment benefit under the Unemployment Insurance Act. Numbers declined into September, reaching about 1·5 million, but 290,000 had exhausted their rights and this figure had increased to 613,000 by October. Unemployment had become a critical political issue, and the threat of social dislocation was again a very real one. It had become particularly explosive in London, where the Mayors of the working-class boroughs were becoming increasingly radical in their demands. The situation was expected to worsen again in the winter, and the Cabinet was under increasing pressure to produce new policies before Parliament opened on 18 October.

A special Cabinet Committee on Unemployment comprising the Chancellor of the Exchequer, the Secretary for Scotland and the Ministers of Labour and Health, was appointed early in September and met regularly during the following weeks. Lloyd George was meanwhile suffering from a tooth infection at Gairloch near Inverness and was only well enough on 22 September to meet a deputation of London Mayors who made the journey to press for urgent action; this was followed by a statement of a very general kind promising a programme of public works and assistance.[22] Members of his Cabinet then also made the pilgrimage to discuss all this, and the Committee was enlarged to include Agriculture, Overseas Trade and also Churchill for the Colonies. Finally Lloyd George called a select week-end Conference organized by Hilton Young, Financial Secretary to the Treasury, which included a couple of 'experts', and representatives of banking, engineering, and iron and steel manufacturing. The Gairloch Conference met on 1 and 2 October. At it the Prime Minister was able to impress those present with his practical grasp of affairs, and they for their part were able to agree on the need to cut retail costs and prices and hence to make it possible to reduce nominal wages, on reduction in national expenditure, and on steps to make the international demand for British goods effective through an officially-backed export credit scheme.[23] The last of these recommendations was to be critical for our purposes, since the Cabinet quickly recognized that colonial projects could make a very concrete contribution to increasing demand in this way.

The Cabinet discussions which followed Lloyd George's return to London now included careful consideration of the scale of proposed colonial public works, and of the possibilities of increasing these and the corresponding orders for British firms through official assistance of some sort. On the 6th they discussed a paper by the President of the Board of Trade, and proposals submitted by Hilton Young to the final Gairloch Conference. The former stressed the urgency of the situation resulting from the bitterness developing among the unemployed and the fact that these men who had 'fought in the war' would not be 'prepared to see their families endure misery and want without a serious struggle and even disorder'. But more to the point, it also noted that conversations with bankers suggested:

> . . . that a guarantee by the Government of the interest on loans required to finance new works and expenditure on railways and similar undertakings in India and in the Colonies and South America, would lead to the immediate placing of large orders in this country.[24]

The Hilton Young proposals suggested that the same line of argument had been pressed at Gairloch since they envisaged government assistance which would 'in all cases . . . take the form of a guarantee', and would be used to promote capital works at home and such works in 'the British Empire and foreign countries' as would lead to orders being placed with British firms.[25] They subsequently discussed a report dated 10 October prepared by the Colonial Office and written by Sir James Stevenson,* which set out the details of colonial projects already planned and considered the amounts which might be spent, given assistance which made it possible for particular colonies to raise the capital. The document is in many respects a blueprint for the 1929 Act and is therefore worth considering in some detail.[26] It claimed that immediate orders worth £8 million were being held up 'owing to the financial position of the Colonies and the depression of trade'; that telegrams had been sent out to ten colonies informing them that the Cabinet was anxious to see orders placed as soon as possible and that this was a good time to act since interest rates were low; and asking them to estimate the amounts which they felt could be spent. It stated that everything possible was being done to ensure that the Colonies '*make a substantial contribution towards the*

---

* Commercial Advisor to the Colonial Office, 1921 (created 1st Baron Stevenson of Holmbury, 1917).

immediate problem of placing orders in this country' (emphasis in the original). It then went on to classify capital projects into A – those planned, B – those which could be initiated if capital could be raised through a loan at the expense of the colony, and C – those which would require a Treasury guarantee, free grant or other form of assistance. Potential expenditure was estimated at A – £25 million, B – £21 million, and C – £17 million, and it was thus argued that £40 to £50 million could be absorbed. It was felt that each colony would be able to bear a share of the loan charges with a revival in trade although in some cases two or three years' grace would be necessary. Perhaps most important for the future, it argued that relatively few projects had been put up under C, though many desirable schemes did exist which could not be financed in present circumstances. It therefore recommended that £2 million be set aside over two years to assist certain colonies to meet loan charges for at least one to two years, and for grants 'to some of the poorer colonies offering good prospects of development which are not in a position to issue loans on their own account'.

These proposals now merged with the Gairloch proposals for guarantees to prospective borrowers likely to use British manufactures; the final recommendation envisaged the Government's guaranteeing capital works at home or abroad up to a maximum value of £25 million, applications to be considered 'by a strong committee representing business and financial experience'.[27] The Treasury was initially opposed to the principle of a government guarantee to any body which might be able to raise the money without it, since this might create liabilities which would lead to a 'consequent depreciation of government credit',[27] although it did accept the scheme while initially pressing for an outside limit of only £15 million.[27] The Cabinet Unemployment Committee considered the £15 million limit 'entirely inadequate',[28] and on 14 October Churchill told the Cabinet that he was already negotiating loans worth £20–25 million, of which 65% was to be spent in the United Kingdom, and that he was now limited by colonial credit, which 'could be substantially increased if the Imperial Government would make further credit available'.[29] On 17 October he produced an additional memorandum extending the earlier Colonial Office arguments by pointing out that various overseas structures – less-developed colonies, protectorates, municipalities and some independent and unofficial bodies – were not in a position to raise loans on the open market. He produced a schedule of almost £8 million worth of work which had had to be cancelled, involving £4 million worth of British orders, and suggested that these could be begun with British assistance in the form of interest-free advances, an undertaking to meet loan charges, or a direct grant towards some part of the cost.[30] At this point the Cabinet, presumably at the insistence of the Treasury, was not prepared to accept the more radical of these proposals, pointing out that '*grants* to the poorer colonies' (emphasis in original) would go beyond the Gairloch proposals:

> . . . and would be putting the Colonies into a better position than public utility undertakings at home. Schemes of this kind should be submitted to the Gairloch Scheme Committee in the normal way. Any proposal to enable the Colonies to borrow cheaply at the expense of the British Treasury involved a further depreciation of Government stocks and consequential outcry from Banks and other large holders of these stocks.[31]

The meeting finally concluded:

> That there are certain Imperial development schemes which will provide substantial employment at home and which in present circumstances can be adequately financed without assistance from the Imperial Government. There are also other similar schemes of a highly promising nature which are held up or very seriously retarded by reason of financial difficulties.
>
> The Government are prepared to assent to the proposition that schemes in this latter category (which would not in present circumstances be brought forward in the ordinary way) may be submitted to the Gairloch Committee for consideration whether they come from India, the Dominions, the Crown Colonies or the Protectorates.[31]

Out of all this emerged the Trade Facilities Act, 1921, which was introduced to Parliament on 20 October[32] and provided for government guarantees for interest and sinking fund payments for capital works in Britain and abroad, to make possible work which would lead to orders for British goods. Preference was to go to the Empire, and both Lloyd George in a general statement about unemployment,[33] and the Chancellor of the Exchequer when he introduced the Bill, stressed the contribution likely to be made by colonial development to the alleviation of 'unemployment in this country'.[34] A limit of £25 million was imposed on spending, the committee of business and financial interests was appointed to consider applications, and a limit of twelve months was imposed on their operation.

The Act itself appears to have been of negligible importance in actually stimulating new colonial projects. The programme of colonial works referred to in the Colonial Office memoranda had been initiated without special assistance, through access to the London capital market during the buoyant months which terminated towards the end of 1920. Capital was readily available and colonial administrations willing to borrow because their own financial position appeared to be strong during a period of high commodity prices and correspondingly high revenue. The rather extravagant financing for the Uasin Gishu Line in Kenya and accompanying harbour works discussed in the previous chapter were one part of this scene. But the Depression of 1921/2 exposed this strategy by reducing prices, precipitating financial crises in all but the strongest territories, and hence leading to an immediate reduction in all developmental work likely to involve any increases in expenditure. The position merely exposed the contradiction involved in an economic strategy which attempted to combine a reduction in government spending on current account with an expansion in government aid to capital projects, since neither private enterprise nor colonial or for that matter local government agencies in Britain were likely to be prepared to invest in new works when demand was visibly declining. The Treasury, in relation both to Britain and to any colony likely to get into financial difficulties, made up for its willingness to give way on the principle of state guarantees for capital projects by a savage programme of retrenchment, to which a business community already suffering from a lack of effective demand gave every encouragement. The Geddes Committee was set up in 1922 to carry out this work once the Depression was under way, and was able to recapture all the ground won by the expansionists in the previous year. It very firmly reasserted the old principle of colonial self-sufficiency:

> At the present time the provision of Public Funds must necessarily be limited to urgent requirements, and the development of [the East African] countries, ought, in our opinion, to be regulated mainly by the ability of the local Governments and private undertakings to raise funds independently.[35]

But the proposals stimulated by the 1921 crisis remained in circulation, to be revived each time circumstances arose which allowed political weight to be brought to bear behind them. Most especially, the commitment to railways continued and was to be given a decisive impetus by the cotton famine and the demands from Manchester for alternative and cheaper sources of supply.

The Trade Facilities Act continued to be renewed and extended. This had guaranteed £46 million by June 1924 and had to meet only one call for the guarantee, involving a sum of less than £4,000.[36] The Cabinet continued to discuss colonial development in 1922 and 1923. By February of the latter year it was able to consider a joint memorandum by the Colonial Secretary and President of the Board of Trade which advanced a detailed case for colonial development to reduce unemployment benefit, create a 'complementary trade' and assure Empire rather than American sources of raw materials. They therefore suggested:

> . . . that a Bill should be introduced giving the Secretary of State power to subsidise schemes of Imperial development subject to a financial limit that the annual cost to the Imperial Exchequer should not exceed £2 million a year.[37]

And although the formulation of the Colonial Development Act was to wait a further six years, the Cabinet nevertheless agreed:

> . . . while measures of relief and extensions of uncovenanted benefit are being proposed as palliatives in the present serious crisis, the main policy of the Government lies in the direction of the development of trade and industry in all their branches, and more particularly of Empire Development and Empire Settlement.[38]

And by the latter part of the year it is clear that it was to a combination of protection and the Empire that the Government was looking for a long-term strategy to deal with the country's economic weakness. At a meeting in October concerned with the likely effects of unemployment, the need for a protective tariff was agreed together with a programme of Empire Development through the production of cotton, sugar and tobacco designed to bring the pound up to parity with the dollar in New York.[39] The meeting also accepted the need for an election within six months, and this, of course, produced the first Labour Government early in 1924.

The central element in this strategy on the colonial side was railway development. The pressures from Britain in 1921 and 1922 led to extensive investigations in various colonies as to the feasability of new lines, and by 1923 the Cabinet was aware of a number of possibilities. In April Cunliffe-Lister (then Lloyd-Graeme) for the Board of Trade could describe this as a 'programme of development' of the Colonies, involving the use of

British credit to ensure the initiation of works which would place 'immediate orders in this country', and lead to 'the creation of wealth and the production of raw materials in these Colonies', which must create 'mutual trade for generations to come'.[40] Numerous schemes were being considered, the most important for our purposes being a loan of £3·5 million to extend the Kenya–Uganda Line to Kampala. Its primary purpose was to open up the rapidly-growing cotton industry, and it was agreed that the Treasury would meet interest charges for the first five years. The project was evolved during 1923 and introduced by Labour in February 1924. Ormsby-Gore, the former Conservative Under-Secretary of State for the Colonies, was virtually allowed to introduce the Bill, and advanced it with the hope that it constituted 'a precedent, and a very useful precedent' to be applied to other 'Colonies and Protectorates'.[41]

The next stage in this process again involved East African railways and more especially cotton development. In 1924 Ormsby-Gore had gone with a small commission to look at various aspects of East African policy, and, hardly surprisingly, claimed that 'the further economic development of both native and non-native production in East Africa is dependent on the early provision of increased transport facilities, and in particular, on new railway construction'. They therefore recommended an expenditure of no less than £10 million, with interest to be met for the first five years by the Treasury.[42] This recommendation received strong support from financial interests. As early as October 1923 Henn of the Joint East Africa Board had suggested the need for 'very large' expenditure on African railway development,[43] while the Manchester Chamber of Commerce's obsessive concern with the raw material problem dated from the latter part of 1922. Once the Commission had reported and the project was under consideration strong pressure was brought to bear by cotton interests, pressure strong enough to warrant a special interim report from the Balfour Committee on Industry and Trade setting out the evidence submitted to it on behalf of these interests.[44] The value of colonial railways and the need for heavy expenditure on them was an important item in the Chairman of the Manchester Chamber's half-yearly address in July 1925,[45] while the actual loan was strongly supported by the J.E.A.B. throughout. In the event, again because of Treasury opposition, Amery was unable to get an exemption from interest and had to remain satisfied with an Imperial guarantee. But the loan was nevertheless an important departure, since the commitment to spend £10 million on railways, roads and scientific research made it possible for those involved to construe the Act as a general attack on the whole problem of colonial development. The main Labour spokesman on the Bill made this clear when he said:

> . . . no section of the House disputed the very great importance of the principle which is before us, and very few will deny that in all probability at the moment we are laying the foundations of a financial programme which may operate on a large scale in the development of the British Empire.[46]

A high-level committee, headed by Sir George Schuster, was sent out to East Africa to consider alternative schemes, and this, pointing out the disadvantages of providing a fixed sum for which a group of territories would then have to compete, called for 'machinery which would provide for the continuous study of new developments and afford to the various dependencies an assurance that they would have a fair chance at all times to raise money for really sound and carefully prepared projects.'[47] For those committed to colonial development the 1926 Loan Act had another defect also, in that it made only the most limited contribution to the territories' ability to raise funds. It did nothing at all for the range of poorer territories discussed in the Colonial Office memorandum outlined above, which could initiate nothing without grants of one sort or another. Even the work of the Schuster Committee on the 1926 Act was affected by the unwillingness of the Treasury to allow an interest-free period, since this made it impossible for them to recommend a proposal to connect the Tanganyikan and Northern Rhodesian railway systems, which was strongly supported both by local administrations and by the Joint East Africa Board.[48]

The continuing commitment to colonial works as a part of a strategy to deal with the high levels of unemployment which persisted in certain sectors of British industry, notably in heavy industry, combined with the experience of the previous ten years, finally produced the Colonial Development Act of 1929. The Gairloch scheme, the Colonial Office recommendations, and the experience of railway building in the 1920s which was extended across much of the colonial Empire and manifested in East Africa in the 1924 and 1926 Loan Acts, created the basis for a forward policy. In addition, two very large projects – the connection between the Tanganyika and Northern Rhodesian railway systems, and a railway bridge across the Zambesi – had been projected for the 1926 loan but could not be completed because of its financial limitations. Both would produce large orders for British steel and engineering firms, and both required the sort of financial assistance which the 1929 Act was designed to give. The Act was put forward by the Conservatives as a central element in their campaign for the 1929 election. Opening the campaign Baldwin said:

If you sum up what our ideal is – to find permanent employment – you may sum it up in this way, I think: that it is the modernization of industry at home and the multiplication of markets overseas. And that has caused us to look once more at the development of our Colonies. I do not use the phrase 'development of the Empire', because the self-governing Dominions are self-governing, and our great contribution to them can be made by giving them the best of our people. . . . Overseas, and particularly in Africa, we have territories of vast potentiality, and we want to help them to develop. We have done something; we have done something through the Palestine and East African Loans; and it is our policy, and it has been to see that further capital is forthcoming in the most convenient form as the need arises from time to time for colonies which obviously cannot finance their own development. . . . The interest charges which fall on a colony while works are under construction, or while they are still unfruitful, are often too heavy for the Colony in its present state to bear. That militates against early development, and so we shall provide out of Imperial funds for such sums as are required – within a maximum to be attuned to our needs, but it will be substantial in the way of giving the help of which I have spoken – to pay the interest in initial years of unfruitful schemes which otherwise must be postponed, and in any other way to assist them to mature. We propose to establish an independent Commission to watch over this matter and to advise the Government on the most profitable use of these new resources for the development of our Colonial territories. (Cheers)[49]

Both Labour and Liberal leaders stressed colonial development as part of the attack on British unemployment, but neither were as specific in their recommendations.[50] In the event it was in fact Labour which formed the Government and which again showed itself willing to implement legislation already evolved for it. J. H. Thomas was given general responsibility for dealing with unemployment and introduced the Bill on 12 July, ten days after the reassembling of Parliament. It was given high priority, accepted by all parties, and passed through the Commons in a week.[51] It was debated in the Lords the following week,[52] and the Colonial

Development Advisory Committee had been appointed to consider schemes by 26 July.[53]

The Act clearly grew out of the concern with British unemployment rather than with the problem of colonial underdevelopment, although the prevailing belief in the natural harmony of economic interests between metropolis and dependency ensured that those who promoted it could very genuinely believe that it would also 'promote [the Colonies'] welfare and the welfare of millions of people in them'.[54] An amendment was added requiring fair conditions of labour on all schemes financed through it, and the Colonial Office at least attempted to assert that the commitment to increase British employment should be liberally rather than narrowly interpreted. At this point it was still possible to assume that any increase in local economic activity would tend to promote colonial trade and that the predominant part of this would be provided by the British economy. Lord Passfield attempted to make this clear to the Governors through his Permanent Secretary:

> Lord Passfield wishes to make it clear that the attitude of the Advisory Committee towards applications is not governed by a narrow view of the unemployment problem here. The Committee is ready to entertain applications which involve little actual purchase of material in this country, or even none, if the object to which it is proposed to devote the money is one which may be expected to promote the development of the Colonial Dependency in question, and thus indirectly to add to its wealth and consequent purchasing power, to the general benefit of the trade of the Empire.[55]

The Act could not be used to assist education, but it could be used for health because of the 'consequent improvement . . . in the productive capacity of the populations affected, resulting in increased purchasing power.'[56]

The Act allowed for an annual expenditure of only £1 million, with all unspent balances being returned to the Treasury. The small size of the grant is generally taken as evidence that little importance was attached to colonial development at the time, but this is to misunderstand the nature of the assumptions and conditions which produced it. Firstly, the Fund was seen as complementary to the Empire Marketing Board, with a similar budget, so that the combined sum now available to assist various aspects of colonial development was much larger than anything which had been envisaged up to this point. Secondly, J. H. Thomas made it clear that more could be provided 'if the expenditure of this money can be justified'.[57] But thirdly, and by far the most important, the allocation was not conceived as the full amount of the capital to be spent in funding projects, but as a means of making it possible for colonies to raise much larger sums on the London capital market on terms which they would now be able to afford. It was assumed that the money would largely be used to meet interest payments on loans until capital expenditure became remunerative. It was on this basis that Hilton Young, author of the original Gairloch proposals, justified the fact that 'many of us on these benches put this Measure in the forefront of our campaign against unemployment',[58] and argued that it would make it possible to spend between £20 and £40 million,[59] the latter figure also being used by Thomas.[60] Thus the proposals for interest-free loans used to promote East African railways had been extended to a much larger range of projects and to the whole colonial Empire. The new Act also incorporated the East African Loan Act and the new Committee the functions of the East African Loan Committee, making it possible for the two schemes not yet authorized – the Zambesi bridge and the Tanganyika to Northern Rhodesia railway – to be considered on a new financial basis. The size of these two projects (which in present-day terms would involve tens of millions of pounds) gives a clear indication of the scale of the thinking involved. The Act also amended the Colonial Stock Act to bring Protectorates and Mandated Territories under its cover. The Colonial Development Advisory Committee (C.D.A.C.), which considered applications consisted, after Ernest Bevin's resignation in 1931, entirely of men with interest in business and experience of organizations connected with colonial development. All projects had to be initiated by the local administrations, except that the Committee was also allowed to consider applications which would be utilized by private enterprise, provided that the Government attempted to secure participation 'in any increase in values directly attributed to the advance'.[61]

The main reason for the lack of interest in the 1929 Act lies, in fact, not in its conception but in its implementation, and especially in the nature of the economic conditions which prevailed in its opening years. The measure had evolved during a period of rising economic activity when demand for raw materials was high and colonial revenues were correspondingly buoyant. These conditions made it possible for new works to be considered in many colonies even without direct assistance. But the onset of the Depression at the end of 1929 duplicated the conditions which led to the cutback in 1921–2, but this time in a much intensified form. Even the wealthiest colonies were immediately in economic difficulty, while the poorest were forced to come to the Treasury for direct financial assistance. All of them were forced to engage in massive programmes of retrenchment, which suppressed almost every tendency to think in terms of new projects, however tempting the terms on which the money could be made available. Although the Fund in fact only suffered one cut in its grant, of £250,000 in 1931, it only once reached 75 % of its allocation, and its overall impact was negligible in relation to what had been expected of it, as the following figures indicate:

TABLE VI

Operation of the Colonial Development Fund, 1929/30–1938/39 (£000s)

1 Year	2 Total Estimated cost of Projects Accepted	3 Expenditure in the United Kingdom	4 Free Capital Grant	5 Free Interest Grant	6 Direct Loan	7 Total 4–6	8 Actual Sums Issued	9 Col. 4 as a % of Col. 7
1929/30	5,629	2,288	173	609	588	1,370	—	12·6
1930/31	3,217	1,320	641	221	379	1,241	487	51·1
1931/32	380	139	165	—	16	181	701	91·1
1932/33	205	53	87	—	115	202	608	43·1
1933/34	2,203	1,099	186	276	321	783	371	23·7
1934/35	1,621	353	434	—	652	1,086	806	40·0
1935/36	1,203	259	542	—	433	975	740	55·6
1936/37	1,260	236	506	—	304	810	687	62·5
1937/38	931	158	493	—	288	781	700	63·1
1938/39	1,177	136	568	—	57	625	735	90·8
Total	17,826	6,041	3,795	1,106	3,153	8,054	5,835	47·0

Source: C.D.A.C., *Annual Reports.* Columns 2 to 7 are allocations; actual spending would have depended on contingencies. Since grants were made for a period of years further spending based on these allocations will have taken place after the end of the Fund. In its last report the Committee claimed that £8,875,000 had been spent or was already allocated, £5,672,000 in free grants, £3,203,000 in loans. Their running total includes adjustments not made in this table, so the final figures do not correspond exactly.

The C.D.A.C. at first certainly attempted to implement the Act in the spirit in which it had been brought forward. Urgent dispatches were sent to all colonial administrations asking for schemes to be submitted as soon as possible.[62] Schemes estimated at £8·8 million were approved within eighteen months, based upon £2·6 million worth of expenditure from the Fund, £829,000 of it in grants to cover interest on loans. But the pattern was only approximated again in the fifth year, never thereafter. The use of grants to cover interest ceased entirely, free capital grants became a larger and larger percentage of the whole, and the amount of direct spending in the United Kingdom decreased regularly. The C.D.A.C. initially expected local administrations to meet a considerable percentage of the cost of new schemes, and also refused to consider applications for recurrent expenditure. But the nature of the Depression ensured that this rule would 'result in a partial sterilization of the fund at a time when it is most needed'. They were therefore prepared to relax this principle 'as a temporary measure during the present period of economic and financial depression'.[63] Although the Zambesi bridge was in fact built during these years, the Tanganyika–Northern Rhodesia railway was indefinitely suspended after alternative routes had been surveyed and choices made.[64] Further, although the initial failure of the Fund can be attributed to the Depression, its continued failure in the latter years of the thirties suggested that the old easy assumptions about cumulatively increasing colonial expenditure based upon access to the open capital market with marginal contributions from British funds would not suffice.

Despite these limitations, however, the Fund did make some contribution to colonies with administrations active enough to make the attempt to exploit it. In East Africa the greatest use was made of it by Tanganyika, the worst hit by the Depression, the least by Uganda, which was accumulating large budgetary surpluses during most of the period. This was especially true once the worst effects of the Depression were over (Table VII).

Tanganyika went so far as to produce a 'comprehensive development programme for the Committee for road improvements, irrigation and topographical and hydrographical survey'.[65] But despite this the administration was very dissatisfied with the provision made for capital expenditure even in the latter part of the thirties.[66]

By the middle thirties demand had grown again, and since most of the Colonies had increased the volume of their exports to compensate for the fall in prices during the Depression, revenue increased fairly rapidly. But the traumatic effect of the Depression on attitudes was to take more than a decade to efface. Once budgets had been balanced British policy committed colonies to build up large surplus balances, to be invested in Britain in low-yielding assets to provide against the possibility of some future crisis. Since even the inadequate existing infrastructure had been allowed to run down during the preceding years the net result was a period of intensely conservative policies in the face of great needs and opportunities. In London pressure did begin to build up for a more expansionist policy in the second half of the decade. The J.E.A.B., probably less effectively connected with the Colonial Office during this period than it had been in the twenties, turned from a concern with financial and trading problems to those connected with the need for expansion. They began to call for a 'more active policy of development';[67] in 1937 they sent a delegation to

TABLE VII

Allocations to East Africa from the Colonial Development Fund
(£ooos)

Year	Kenya	Tanganyika	Uganda
1929/30	0	112	0
1930/31	67	81	18
1931/32	−14	63	0
1932/33	11	17	0
1933/34	0	13	−1
1934/35	117	126	2
1935/36	75	24	0
1936/37	25	94	1
1937/38	48	267	0
1938/39	25	40	0
1939/40	71	19	240
Total	425	856	260

Source: Abstracted from Table C, C.D.A.C., *Annual Report*, 1930/31–1939/40. Allocations only are indicated, not actual spending.

the Colonial Office to press for this, and subsequently produced a memorandum calling for a more vigorous attitude, more money and better planning of development.[68] At the same time, the new Parliament elected in 1935 produced Labour spokesmen, notably Creech Jones and Philip Noel Baker, who were not merely concerned with the defence of colonial labour, but also recognized the necessity to finance development. In the late thirties, in addition, the results of low commodity prices and deflationary policies had produced massive distress and social dislocation in the West Indies, leading to pressure in Parliament for action and to the appointment of the West India Royal Commission 1938–9, whose report was seemingly frank enough about conditions to require suppression. But their recommendations, which were published, included one for £1 million to be provided by Britain for the provision of social services and for development.[69] These pressures, together with the evident failure of the 1929 Act, led to the emergence of the 1940 Colonial Development and Welfare Act, which was no longer obsessed with the direct stimulation of British employment. Thinking was evidently now much more directly influenced by the Colonial Office view, which saw the returns to Britain from improved social and economic conditions in the Colonies taking the form of a long-term improvement in their trading position, from which the British economy was bound to benefit. The new Act provided £5·5 million a year, and imposed no such limits on expenditure on educational and social services as the earlier one had done.

NOTES

1. House of Commons, *Debates*, 22 iv 32, v. 264, c. 1787.
2. Cabinet Papers, GT 6887, meeting of 25 ii 19, p. 10.
3. *Ibid.*, p. 17.
4. *Ibid.*, pp. 4–5.
5. *Ibid.*, p. 6, cf. also pp. 2–3.
6. *Ibid.*, p. 7.
7. *Ibid.*, p. 9.
8. *Ibid.*, p. 9.
9. E.g. L. S. M. Amery, *Empire and prosperity*, London, Faber, 1931; *National and imperial economics*, Westminster, National Unionist Assoc., 1924.
10. Alfred, Lord Milner, 'Crown colonies', in *The nation and the Empire*, London, Constable, 1913, p. 468.
11. Cf. R. Oliver and J. D. Fage, *A short history of Africa*, Harmondsworth, Penguin Books, 1962, pp. 196–205.
12. *Final Report of the Committee on Commercial and Industrial Policy after the War*, Cmd. 9035 of 1918, p. 27, also W. K. Hancock, *Survey of British Commonwealth affairs*, vol. II, *Problems of economic policy*, London, O.U.P., 1940, pp. 94 ff.
13. Cf. *First Annual Report of the Colonial Research Committee*, Cmd. 1144 of 1921; *Report of the Committee on Research in the Colonies*, Cmd. 1472 of 1921.
14. *West Indies: Report of the Tropical Agriculture College Committee*, Cmd. 520 of 1920.
15. *Report . . . of the Empire Cotton Growing Committee*, Cmd. 523 of 1920; E.C.G.C., *Report of the Executive Committee*, 1922.
16. A. Redford and B. W. Clapp, *Manchester merchants and foreign trade*, vol. II, Manchester, U.P., 1956, pp. 220–1; Manchester Chamber, *Monthly Record*, 1920–4.
17. *The Empire Cotton Growing Review*, 1924– .
18. For descriptions cf. L. S. M. Amery, *My political life*, vol. II, London. Hutchinson, 1953–5, p. 346 and Hancock, *op. cit.* (note 12), pp. 201–3,

19. House of Commons, *Second Report of the Select Committee on Estimates*, H. of C. Paper no. 114, 1928, p. 152.
20. House of Commons, *Debates*, 19 x 21, v. 147, c. 79.
21. Details here and unless otherwise stated in this section from *The Times*, September and October 1921.
22. *The Times*, 23 September.
23. Discussions reported 3 October.
24. Cabinet Minutes, 76 (21), Appendix I, CP 3371.
25. *Ibid.*, Appendix I.
26. Cabinet Papers, CU 268.
27. Cabinet Minutes, 79 (21) 1, Treasury memo. CU 274.
28. Cabinet Papers, CP 3403.
29. Cabinet Minutes, 79 (21) 2.
30. Cabinet Papers, CP 3415.
31. Cabinet Minutes, 80 (21) 4.
32. House of Commons, *Debates*, 20 x 21, v. 147, c. 285.
33. House of Commons, *Debates*, 19 x 21, v. 147, c. 89.
34. House of Commons, *Debates*, 25 x 21, v. 147, c. 657.
35. *Third Report of the Committee on National Expenditure*, Cmd. 1589 of 1922, p. 9.
36. House of Commons, *Debates*, 16 vi 24, v. 174, c. 1732.
37. Cabinet Minutes, 90 (23), 8 ii 23.
38. Cabinet Minutes, 9 (23) 4, 14 ii 23.
39. Cabinet Minutes, 50 (23) 4, 23 x 23.
40. House of Commons, *Debates*, 10 iv 23, v. 162, c. 1102.
41. House of Commons, *Debates*, 25 ii 24, v. 170, c. 199.
42. *East Africa Commission*, p. 182.
43. Henn to Ormsby-Gore, 9 x 23 (Henn Papers).
44. *Memo. on Transport Development and Cotton Growing in East Africa*, Cmd. 2463 of 1925.
45. *Monthly Record*, July 1925, p. 207.
46. House of Commons, *Debates*, 7 xii 26, v. 200, c. 1991.
47. *Report of the East African Guaranteed Loan Committee*, Cmd. 2701 of 1926, p. 38. Schuster subsequently became a member of the Colonial Development Advisory Committee, which administered the 1929 Act.
48. Cf. Henn to Grigg, 15 ii 26, and Grigg to Henn, 30 iii 26, referring to a unanimous resolution by the Governors' Conference in support of the line.
49. *The Times*, 19 iv 29.
50. Cf. MacDonald, 24 v 29, cited in Conservative Party, *Gleanings and memoranda*, 1929, vol. I, p. 635; and Lloyd George, *ibid.*, p. 409.
51. Debated as follows: 12 vii 29; 15 vii 29, v. 230; 17 vii 29, v. 230; Supplementary Estimate, 24 ii 30, v. 235.
52. House of Lords, *Debates*, 23 vii 29, v. 75.
53. House of Commons, *Debates*, 26 vii 29, v. 230, c. 1574–5.
54. Passfield in the Lords, 23 vii 29, v. 75, c. 175.
55. Wilson to Grigg, 23 iii 30 (Altrincham Papers).
56. Colonial Development Advisory Committee, *Second interim report*, Cmd. 3876 of 1931, p. 5.
57. House of Commons, *Debates*, 12 vii 29, v. 229, c. 1302.
58. House of Commons, *Debates*, 12 vii 29, v. 229, c. 1282.

59. *Ibid.*, c. 1286.
60. *Ibid.*, c. 1259.
61. Colonial Development Act, 20 George 5, 1929, Ch. 5, p. 16.
62. Cf. C.D.A.C., *First interim report*, pp. 21–4.
63. C.D.A.C. *Second interim report*, p. 10.
64. For details cf. C. Gillman, 'A short history of the Tanganyikan railways', in *Tanganyika Notes and Records*, June 1942, no. 13, pp. 50–3; C. Hill, *Permanent way*, vol. II, p. 214.
65. C.D.A.C., *Sixth interim report*, p. 6; according to Sir George Schuster their schemes were generally better prepared than usual.
66. Interview with Sir Harold MacMichael, who attributed the work on the programme to Sir Philip Mitchell, then Chief Secretary.
67. J.E.A.B., *Annual Report*, 1936, p. 10.
68. *Ibid.*, 1937, pp. 28–9.
69. West India Royal Commission, *Recommendations*, Cmd. 6174 of 1940; also *ibid.*, *Statement of the action taken on the recommendations*, Cmd. 6656 of 1945.

5

Budgets and Markets

Since local production depended entirely upon the administration's ability to provide infrastructure and upon the terms on which producers were allowed to exchange their products, questions relating to financial policy and to control over markets were clearly crucial to the process of development. Decisions in this area directly and indirectly structured the whole pattern of economic change by determining its speed, its location and its impact upon social structure. It will be impossible to carry out a detailed analysis of these questions here, requiring as it does a full analysis of the pressures involved in formulating policy and in the effects stemming from its application. The rest of the chapter will merely look at the basic assumptions and factors which influenced this policy, and in particular at the impact on it of the economic crisis of the thirties. The material divides itself into three main areas – financial policy concerned with taxation and expenditure, tariff policies for the domestic market, and attempts to influence export markets through commodity restriction schemes.

FINANCIAL POLICY

Britain's central concern in this area was to ensure colonial self-sufficiency and balanced budgets. The first objective of any administration was to pay for all its services out of recurrent revenue; having once achieved this, to ensure that it maintained sufficient reserves to meet contingencies arising out of economic failures of any sort. Since revenue depended almost entirely upon the buoyancy of the export market for primary products, and since this was highly unstable, this commitment inevitably imposed the familiar restraints upon economic policy – deficit financing was virtually excluded and the stronger colonies were also forced to underutilize resources which had actually been accumulated. The previous chapter demonstrated how the nature of the British economic crisis of the twenties breached the principle of colonial self-sufficiency for some forms of capital expenditure. Despite many contemporary assumptions the actual expenditure on economic infrastructure was considerable up to the end of the twenties. In East Africa, almost 1,300 miles of new railway track were opened, with a corresponding expansion in rolling-stock, and five new deep-water berths were built in Mombasa between 1920 and 1932. But this liberalization in the field of capital was not matched for recurrent expenditure, and the previous chapter also attempted to show how quickly falls in world prices during recessions cut revenue and enforced a cutback in capital spending as well. The crisis of the early thirties was, of course, by far the most serious of these, neutralizing for half a generation all the positive effects, both in terms of ideas and of action, which the more favourable conditions of the twenties had induced. The negative conditions of the thirties are now most clearly remembered and the more positive effects of the earlier years almost entirely forgotten. The net effect of the policies and conditions of the whole period was therefore to create an essentially contradictory situation – an attempt on the one hand to stimulate a long-term process of colonial economic growth through the provision of the infrastructure for a rapid expansion in commodity production for export; a tendency on the other hand to respond to every short-run downturn in the market by retrenchment, which cut spending and hence reduced the overall level of economic activity. The situation would have been much worse had the expenditure of the twenties not created a good deal of spare capacity, especially in transport. This made it possible for production from favourably located groups, especially Africans around Lake Victoria producing cotton and coffee, to be expanded very rapidly despite very low prices and sharply reduced provision of administrative services. This increase in volume (more significant in Uganda and Tanganyika than in Kenya because peasant agriculture proved to be more resistant to low prices than did settler production) did not have an immediate effect upon revenue and the general level of economic activity because of the low prices in the Depression and the extreme financial conservatism which this produced. It did, however, create the basis for the rapid expansion in revenue and the gradual re-emergence of more expansionist attitudes during and after the Second World War.

Kenya and Uganda had both attained financial self-sufficiency by the end of the First World War; Tanganyika received British grants-in-aid to maintain services and repair war damage until

1925, when special assistance ended. Revenue was derived mainly from native hut or poll taxes and from customs duties. These two items produced from 60% to 80% of all revenue, with the former declining from about 50% of all revenue in 1920 to about 30% in the late 1930s. Customs duties were imposed for revenue purposes and were regarded as the main method of taxing the expatriate community; this group paid no income tax at all until the late thirties. Britain managed to impose such a tax in Kenya only in 1938, after withdrawing in the face of local opposition both in 1921 and in 1931. In Uganda an attempt to impose a similar tax was successfully resisted in 1931 and the financial position was thereafter so favourable that the attempt was not made again before the War. In Tanganyika a small non-native poll tax was imposed in 1931 as well as a levy on official salaries. But in general financial policy was made by people who assumed that taxation led Africans into paths of economic virtue by forcing them to produce for cash or work for wages, but that expatriates should pay as little as was decently possible in order to maximize their desire to settle or invest.

The Depression of the early twenties produced shortfalls in revenue in the three territories, but was quickly over. It was then followed by progressively rising revenues until 1929, while expenditure also expanded, but not quite as rapidly. The three territories therefore entered the Depression with surplus balances, which were sufficient to make up the initial deficits which occurred as soon as international commodity prices broke in response to the American and European collapse. The dominance of exports in the colonial economic structure rendered it particularly vulnerable to international price declines since the home market generated very little demand. Customs revenue, of course, responded immediately to any fall in commodity prices, while direct taxation was more stable but nevertheless became harder to collect in full. It was, in fact, only with the Depression that financial policy became a critical issue either locally or in British politics, thus exposing the nature of the assumptions which conditioned action in this field. The situation was rather different in each territory and they must therefore be dealt with separately.

The full extent of the crisis only became evident in 1931, more especially with the collapse of the Labour Government and its replacement by the so-called National Government. Their commitment to retrenchment extended beyond the British unemployed to colonies whose exports no one could now afford. By 1932 seven colonies were receiving grants-in-aid and Cunliffe-Lister, the new Secretary of State for the Colonies, was at pains to point out 'how truly it is in the interests of this country to see . . . that there are all possible economies practised in these colonial administrations.'[1] Balanced budgets were to be achieved by increasing taxation of the expatriate community – it was thought to be impossible to increase African taxation since virtually every able-bodied official and chief in the provincial services was already devoting most of his time to trying to collect existing taxes from a population which by and large found it impossible to earn enough to pay them – and more especially by retrenchment in existing services. Once budgets had been balanced all administrations were expected to build up large surplus balances to remove finally the need for British grants of any kind. These balances were subsequently to be invested in low-yielding British stocks and thus rendered totally unproductive. None of the East African territories fell into the weakest category, which had to come direct to the Treasury for assistance: they varied from Uganda, which only incurred small deficits in two years and was never in any difficulty at all after 1932, to Tanganyika, which to cover her deficits had to make drawings on certain loan funds which required special Parliamentary sanction and could therefore be said to have constituted aid of a kind. But despite these differences there is no evidence that the policy of retrenchment was implemented any more liberally in the strong colonies than in the weak ones – the commitment to solvency was made to take precedence over every other consideration, including any desire to maintain the level of economic activity and thereby speed up the return to a growth situation. The previous chapter has demonstrated how these conditions paralysed the Colonial Development Fund; they simply made it impossible for new development projects to be considered since markets could not be trusted and the pressure to cut costs was so very intense.[2]

After three years of budgetary surpluses Tanganyika recorded deficits on the combined railway and general accounts each year from 1929/30 to 1934. Total revenue on both accounts was roughly £14 million, the deficit £1·4 million, making recourse to Britain inevitable. A Treasury expert who was sent out in 1932 recommended a more differentiated tax system with more contribution from expatriates, an end to the various subsidies paid out by Tanganyikan consumers and producers to those in Kenya and Uganda resulting from the common services, an end to new developmental expenditure despite the fact that unexpended loan funds still existed, and stringent economies in recurrent expenditure.[3] Administrative staff were dismissed, schools closed and even road maintenance ceased, only being resumed again in 1936.[4] In Britain the formality of a grant-in-aid was avoided by making the territory raise a loan of £750,000 to refund money derived from revenue and spent on capital works during the previous years. The Commons passed the Act guaranteeing interest and repayment despite objections from both sides.[5] In 1935, when it appeared that a further deficit was inevitable, the Treasury agreed to remit £100,000 in interest charges until the position improved. But the economy campaign achieved its most immediate purpose by reducing expenditure on general account from £2·1 million in 1929 and 1930 to about £1·7 million between 1933 and 1935; the railway system also balanced its accounts by dismissing a third of its staff and cutting its operating costs by almost half over five years.[6] From a Treasury, though not from any other point of view the process could therefore be called a success – only £500,000 of the loan was required, and the remission of interest charges was also totally avoided. After 1935 the return to better conditions simply brought with it a commitment to build up a reserve fund of £1·25 million;[7] developmental expenditure began again only after 1935 and could be financed only from unexpended loan funds and grants from the Colonial Development Fund.

In Kenya questions of financial policy were complicated by the power of the settler lobby. Their presence raised two main problems. Their leaders had strong and grandiose ideas about the level of services appropriate for a community of white gentlemen who they felt were bringing civilization to darkest Africa; their ideas had been shared by the leading Governors of the twenties who had promoted a very expensive programme of public works. Secondly, the African community, too, paid taxes and required services, and, although most senior local officials had few doubts about the validity of settler claims by comparison with African, pressure from the humanitarian lobby in Britain was sufficient to ensure that the latter could not be entirely ignored. Thus, while financial policy up to 1930 was founded on the principle that Africans should pay taxes and Europeans receive services, the need for retrenchment made it desirable to reconsider this principle and at least increase the European contribution by a small amount. General revenues fell each year from 1929, when they were

£3,330,000, to 1933, when they were £3,120,000. Revenues declined more slowly, and losses were incurred each year from 1929 to 1934. The surplus balance, which had stood at £879,000 in 1928, was reduced to an apparent cash deficiency of £180,000 by 1934. The railway, financed from a separate account, incurred deficits totalling £650,000 in 1930 and 1931, although it had reserves from which these could be met. The position was worsened by the fact that the colony had raised £17,200,000 in loans between 1921 and 1933 on which charges amounted to just over £1 million per annum: £818,000 of this had to be met by the railways and £226,000 out of general revenue, much of it for the provision of public buildings considered by a visiting British official to be 'on a lavish scale considering the taxable capacity of the Colony'.[8] These loan charges were absolutely fixed, so that the problem of retrenchment was made that much more difficult. The railway was able to solve its problem through drastic reductions in staff and passenger services and to produce substantial surpluses from 1933.[9] But the continuing failure to balance the budget produced a series of local and British investigations designed to reduce revenue and increase taxation. The Joint Select Committee on Closer Union sitting in London in 1931 had recommended that the relative contributions to taxation and receipts from services going to the various racial groups be investigated. But Lord Moyne, commissioned to do this, found on arrival that he was also expected to play the role of financial adviser with regard to the financial crisis. His most notable recommendation was for an income tax; this was not surprisingly opposed by the settlers and an alternative set of proposals was agreed by the Secretary of State.[10] When these proved inadequate a number of local committees were set up to cut spending and find means of expanding production.[11] But the improvement was still insufficient and a further financial commissioner was sent out in 1936. He also recommended an income tax and further economies, although he was willing to consider a slightly more expansionist approach by recommending that the colony be allowed to borrow up to £100,000 per annum to tide itself over without too heavy an attack on services.[12] Income tax was at last imposed, although deficit financing from borrowing was not permitted. The return to higher international prices ended the crisis in the last years of the decade.

The Ugandan situation was very different. The rapid growth of the African-produced cotton crop after 1920 had provided it with a secure financial position. It also differed from Kenya in that it had no settler community in a position to make ambitious demands on services; the administration was therefore under much less direct pressure from the public since it did not have to meet the demands of an articulate and organized community with a very clear view of what was needed. In these circumstances decisions were determined primarily in relation to the bureaucracy's desire to secure a quiet and comfortable life. Services were allowed to expand very slowly and the territory had accumulated a surplus balance of £1·3 million by 1929, when total expenditure for the year was only £1·6 million. But a deficit of about a quarter of a million was incurred in 1930 and one of £52,000 in 1931, and these induced an immediate economy campaign which cut expenditure to an average of £1·3 million from 1932 to 1934. The budget produced surpluses each year from 1932 to 1938, with expenditure only regaining the 1929 level in 1936. By that year surplus balances stood at £1·7 million and were only £100,000 less than total revenue for the year. As late as 1934 Cunliffe-Lister reaffirmed this commitment to continued retrenchment when he stated that reserves were to be touched only in cases of 'greatest urgency' and that 'improved services, such as Agriculture, meant further taxation'.[13] An attempt to introduce an income tax to increase the expatriate contribution to revenue was also successfully resisted in 1931;[14] a return to some semblance of expansion occurred only in 1936 with a change in Governor and Secretary of State, when a five-year development plan of sorts was drawn up.[15]

The Depression also produced a crisis for the East African Currency Board, established in 1920 with the conversion of the rupee to the florin. The fall in world prices led to a considerable deficit on the balance of payments, most especially in Kenya where expatriate producers were much less able to resist the new conditions than peasant producers. As a result sterling assets held by the Board ran down very rapidly and the cover for East African currency fell to only 9·9% in 1932. The Board had to resort to short-term borrowing to meet its obligations, and in September 1931 was authorized to raise £1·5 million on the territorial accounts in London to 'ensure the conversion of East African currency at the existing parity'.[16] The loans were not raised but guaranteed the currency during the crisis. The cessation of large-scale development based on public and private spending, combined with reduced consumption, ended the overall balance of payments deficit, and reserves increased continuously, although it was only in 1950 that the Board achieved the 100% cover maintained by the West African Currency Board from 1926.[17]

This brief review of the effects of a very dreary area of policy simply reaffirms the short-sightedness of the financial response to the Depression, which affected the colonies much more seriously than the metropolis. The wide acceptance of the economic orthodoxy of the time is clearly demonstrated in S. H. Frankel's praise for the faint-hearted activities of the Uganda administration in its attempts to maintain its surplus balances whatever the cost in economic opportunities forgone.[18] It also demonstrates the importance of an aware and effectively-represented local community in resisting the worst excesses of policies advocated by the officials and the economists. Although we must criticize the use to which they were put, it is clear that the pressures brought to bear on the administration by the Kenya settlers ensured a much more intensive use of resources there than occurred in Uganda, where the African community was never in a position to insist that their own money be used to develop their own economy rather than that it should be lent out at low rates of interest to British borrowers. When the effects of these policies on recurrent spending are added to those produced on capital development, it is not difficult to understand why the thirties are regarded as an entirely barren period.

IMPERIAL PREFERENCE AND THE CONGO BASIN TREATIES

The Depression finally ended Britain's claim to international economic pre-eminence, the belief in her international competitiveness, and the commitment to free trade. But this only completed a process which had been going on for many years. The growing weakness of Britain's position had been recognized even before the War and produced the Imperial Preference movement in the Tory Party. This movement was originally led by Joseph Chamberlain; by the thirties its most powerful proponent had become Leo Amery, who felt that Britain would only be able to maintain her standards of living if she used her political and economic power in home and Empire markets to protect her manufacturers and workers.[19]

Protection at home and preferences in the Empire were inseparably connected. Protection would both open the home market to British manufacturers and also make it possible to give Empire exporters special privileges there. Thus it was argued that by linking the British economy to the overseas economies whose development had hitherto been most complementary to her own, both uninterrupted supplies of raw materials and soft markets for manufacturers could be guaranteed. Britain had traditionally provided both the Dominions and the Colonies with their main market; she exercised cultural hegemony over the former and political hegemony over the latter. The Imperialists felt it was high time that these assets were transferred into hard cash by using them as the basis for a closed trading system which would cut British manufacturers off from the merciless effects of un-regulated international competition.

Protection had already made considerable ground before the Depression, although it had not yet been accepted as a permanent element in economic policy. Certain duties had been imposed on some manufacturers during the War and maintained there-after, and the range had been increased by the Safeguarding of Industries Act in 1921. The Tories fought the 1923 election on protection but lost; the more favourable conditions from 1925 to 1929 made it possible to avoid the issue until the crisis. The first steps towards preferences had also been taken before 1929. The white Dominions had unilaterally granted Britain preferences in their markets at the end of the nineteenth century; Britain had also granted minor preferences to certain kinds of Empire produce, and these were extended by the 1921 Act.[20] But the British com-mitment to preference thereafter was limited to making the grant to the Empire Marketing Board already discussed. In June 1920 the British Government 'invited' the Colonies to grant preferences to goods of Empire origin and by 1922 twenty-six governments had done so, not altogether of their own free will.[21]

But the collapse of British trade and the major balance of pay-ments crisis which this produced[22] led to an almost immediate acceptance of the whole protectionist case. The National Govern-ment elected late in 1931 immediately set out to introduce pro-tection, the colonial economies being seen as an organic part of the proposed economic system. Cunliffe-Lister went to the Colonial Office, where he actively advocated a new policy which rejected equal access to colonial markets in favour of one committed to treating the Colonies as mere economic adjuncts to the British economy. Henceforth all developmental expenditure was to be 'related to some probable market in this country'[23] and Imperial policy based upon the need to get 'the best decision in the interests of British trade', and not deflected from this 'by any consideration of principle or whatever it may be'.[24] He arrived at the Colonial Office at the end of 1931, when he circularized Colonial Governors asking for information about preferences they would like to have and sought similar information from British firms interested in colonial trade. He made extensive use of advisers from the City in evolving his case and also strengthened the economic section of the Colonial Office to deal with the resulting information.

His case was apparently very well documented at the Imperial Conference which decided the question in Ottawa in 1932, and he was able to persuade the Dominions to give the same level of preference as the United Kingdom to most colonial products.[25] Despite the fact that international treaties made it impossible for the East African territories to reciprocate, the same benefits were extended to them in full. It is impossible to assess their effects with any accuracy, but Meyer argues that they benefited only 'to a minor extent from coffee and hard fibre preferences in the United Kingdom and South Africa',[26] and that it was possible that the Kenya maize industry may have benefited marginally as well.[27] Cunliffe-Lister summed up his interpretation of the changes in the Commons:

> I am not sure that it is realised enough what a standby that Colonial Trade has been in the difficult past years. . . . In 1924 only 6·8% of our export trade was done with the Colonial Empire. In 1931 that proportion had risen to over 10%, and that at a time when values were crashing in the Colonies and their purchasing power had been enormously diminished. That shows the value of that trade, and it emphasises . . . how very wide and valuable were the preferences which had for years past been given by those Colonies to this country. Since this House took its decision [on Imperial Preference] in February new preferences have been given. . . . The result is that nearly every Colony which has a tariff on manufactures and which is free to do so is at the moment giving a substantial preference to this country.[28]

Whatever the substantive impact of these preferences, they were certainly taken very seriously by the British trading and producing interests involved. The J.E.A.B. recorded its special appreciation of Cunliffe-Lister's work and 'of the satisfying results secured for the Colonial Empire at the Ottawa Conference, and for the East African Colonies in particular'.[29] A concerted effort to improve the position of East African sisal on the British market was initiated, in particular to persuade manufacturers and users to accept it as a substitute for other fibres. The British Empire Producers Organisation, a body representing British overseas plantation interests, the Rope, Twine and Netmakers' Federation, and the J.E.A.B. co-operated in an attempt to take advantage of the 10% preference provided by the new Act to increase British consumption. The Empire Marketing Board before its demise in 1932, the Imperial Economic Committee, and the Imperial Institute, were all drawn in to conduct scientific tests on its qualities and to help to promote it with potential users like the Navy.[30] These efforts must have had some effect, since Tanganyika's sisal exports to Britain went up from approximately 4,495 tons in 1931 to 20,742 tons in 1932.[31] No comparable campaigns appear to have been mounted for other crops in Britain, possibly because they were already strongly represented on the market.

From an East African point of view the preferences received in Empire markets represented a net gain, however limited their extent. But the preferences given by the Colonies to Britain in return were likely to represent a loss, especially where they enforced consumption of high-cost British products when cheaper sources of supply were also available. East Africa was, however, particularly fortunate in this regard, since Britain's freedom of action on trading policy in the area was limited by a series of international agreements. The region fell into the area of Africa covered by what were called the Congo Basin Treaties drawn up during the original partition of Africa and last revised and ratified in the Convention of St Germain-en-Laye in 1919 by Britain, Belgium, Japan and Portugal, and signed though not ratified by the U.S.A. and Italy as well.[32] These agreements guaranteed equality of access to the markets of the whole region for the participants, and these rights were reinforced for Tanganyika by the terms of the Mandate,[33] which also influenced policy in the rest of the region because of the existence of the customs union. In addition, British attitudes were likely to be influenced by the existence of the Anglo-French Convention of 1898, which extended equality of access to West African markets, since this made it possible for the French to retaliate against any breach of the agreement in the Congo Basin area.

During the twenties British manufacturers and merchants were happy enough with this situation because they were still able to compete successfully in the area and the reciprocal privileges accorded them in the rest of the zone offset the effects of competition in the British territories. Their position inside the latter was also reinforced by advantages of language and contacts, not to mention the Government's commitment to buy British, which was effectively realized through the work of the Crown Agents in London. But the Depression virtually ended new governmental buying, and it also coincided with a massive expansion of Japanese competition in cheap manufactures, especially in textiles, throughout the colonial Empire. Japanese production was aimed at the bottom end of the market and sold at prices which gave opportunities to consumers which British manufacturers had not previously been able to reach. This expansion in Japanese sales coincided with a rapid decrease in British exports and, although it seems evident that this was not exclusively caused by the competition, the fall was generally attributed entirely to its effects. It was soon widely assumed that Britain would only be able to maintain its position in equal competition in world markets by a drastic attack on living standards, and an immediate demand for preferential treatment in colonial markets emerged.[34] The substantive changes in trading patterns involved can be gathered from Tables VIII and IX.

The existence of the treaties was to preclude any change in the tariff structure during the thirties in East Africa, but a brief review of the attempts to modify it is nevertheless instructive. The primary mover in Britain was to be that citadel of free trade, the Manchester Chamber of Commerce. The connection between ideology and the conditions operating in the economic base in this central area of liberal theory is clearly demonstrated in their monthly record. In January 1925 they still felt that the question of Japanese competition in East Africa did 'not call for serious comment',[35] but by 1928 they already felt that 'Lancashire has yet to take active steps to stem the increasing trade of India and Japan, particularly in grey goods'.[36] By January 1929 the Chairman of the East Africa Section was sitting on a special committee set up to consider the problem of increasing foreign competition.[37] This concern also manifested itself in the Commons, where five or six questions a year came to be asked after 1926 with respect to the possibility of the Colonies' granting preferences to Britain, and especially to the obstacles which treaty obligations put in the way of action of this kind. The Congo Basin Treaties were due to be considered by signatories in 1929, and the J.E.A.B. set up a small sub-committee to consider the matter in 1927. A

TABLE VIII

British and Japanese Exports as a Percentage of Tanganyika's Imports

	1925	*1930*	*1931*	*1932*	*1933*	*1934*	*1935*	*1936*	*1937*	*1938*
Britain	64·5	42·3	36·4	30·4	29·1	27·6	29·0	27·2	24·3	26·9
Japan	7·2	6·7	10·7	16·4	21·4	22·3	22·0	23·3	23·8	17·2

Source: Abstracted from Tanganyika, *Annual Reports.*

TABLE IX

British and Japanese Cotton Textile Exports to Eastern Africa

	Quantity (million yards)			Distribution (%)		
Year	*Britain*	*Japan*	*Total*	*Britain*	*Japan*	*Others*
1929	23·6	32·6	109·4	21·6	29·8	48·6
1931	13·0	50·5	96·5	14·1	52·4	33·5
1933	11·7	78·2	104·0	11·3	75·2	13·5
1935	13·1	110·0	130·0	10·1	84·6	5·3
1936	10·5	122·4	140·1	7·5	87·3	5·2

Source: Hubbard, *op. cit.,* p. 389. Including Kenya, Uganda, Tanganyika, Nyasaland, and Zanzibar.

memorandum summarizing the position was drawn up in 1928 and agreed by the London, Liverpool and Manchester Chambers.[38] This came to no firm conclusions and merely recommended an official investigation of the situation. In 1930 British commercial opinion still felt that the advantages derived from rights in neighbouring colonial areas outweighed the disadvantages produced in their own areas,[39] a view which received official recognition at the Twelfth Congress of Chambers of Commerce of the British Empire.[40] As late as December 1931 the J.E.A.B. continued to advance this view, primarily because of the threat to British trade in French West Africa and the need to maintain the East African Customs Union.[41] But it had now become clear that the reciprocal advantages were not of much use since Britain could not compete effectively in these areas either – a small protected market now became infinitely preferable to a large open one in which British and Japanese commodities would have to compete on their merits. By March 1932 the Manchester Chamber was pressing the Board of Trade to secure freedom from treaty restraints in East Africa, and the London Chamber and the J.E.A.B. were also investigating the situation. By the middle of the year all the major interests were united in calling for preferences though also concerned to maintain the customs union.[42] Only the Liverpool Chamber expressed reservations because of fears that disturbance of the Treaties might harm British trade in the whole African zone.[43]

In East Africa itself the Uganda Chamber of Commerce, and the Association of Chambers of Commerce of Eastern Africa, which represented Kenyan and Tanganyikan commerce, accepted modification of the Treaties, although with a very strong proviso that this would be conditional on maintenance of the customs union.[44] These bodies were presumably dominated by British interests and did not represent either Japanese exporters or small retailers who handled the bulk of the African trade. The Mombasa Chamber, which represented many wholesalers supplying the interior, accepted the idea only with reluctance, expressing reservations about the likely effect of preferences upon official revenue, the customs union and the native trade.[45] The three Governors discussed the Treaties in April and concluded that 'it did not appear that any advantage would accrue to the East African Territories through abrogation of the Congo Basin Treaties.'[46]

Since the people likely to bear the cost of an abrogation of the Treaties were for the most part poor, uneducated and politically unrepresented Africans, the British Government could feel that the bulk of opinion favoured abrogation, an impression certainly confirmed by debate in Parliament, where many voices were raised to attack the Treaties, but few spoke in their defence. Cunliffe-Lister made his own position clear, saying: 'That day that [Britain] decides to renounce those Treaties, that day those Colonies will give a preference to this country.'[47] When he was asked whether he would consult the 'direct representatives of the adult population of the colonies likely to be affected', he replied 'No, Sir.'[48]

The matter was finally put into the hands of lawyers from the relevant British Ministries who had not made much progress by December, when the J.E.A.B. met Cunliffe-Lister.[49] The East African Governors considered the matter again in 1933 and, despite reservations about the possibility of merely shifting the trade from Japan to Italy or India, of adversely affecting revenue, and of creating 'a dear market for imported goods', they spent some time considering various means of providing 'some assistance to Manchester'.[50] In May 1934, after the breakdown of Anglo-Japanese trade talks, quotas were imposed on Japanese imports into West Africa which severely curtailed them there; similar measures were introduced into other parts of the colonial Empire and met considerable resistance from unofficial representatives where these had taken the opportunity to make their views known.[51] The Manchester Chamber took note of these objections but now propounded views which represented the world in very different terms than they had done ten years previously:

> We must give the unofficial minority [in the Colonies] the credit of supposing that they voted honestly with a view to the best interests of the Colony. I suppose the truth is that they have not been impressed with Lancashire's case, and have seen no reason why the native should suffer any interference in the supply of cheap goods in order to preserve the well-being of Lancashire. . . . [But] ultimately the welfare of all colonies depends upon their getting a good market for their produce, and in almost every case they find that market principally in England, or at any rate in the European countries with their high standard of living. If the Colonial territories . . . are going to buy their manufactured goods from countries which are incapable of consuming Colonial products in anything like the requisite volume, they will only render derelict the European markets on which they are in turn dependent.[52]

On the basis of this dubious exercise in ethics and economics many colonial populations were henceforth precluded from buying cheap Japanese products. In the event this was not of much use to Manchester, since the Japanese had created new markets which high-cost British producers could not maintain; the main beneficiaries of the new system were in all probability Indian and other Asian producers in the Empire who also benefited from the quota system and could produce successfully at the cheap end of the range.[53] The East African Treaty situation continued to be examined until October 1935 in the hopes of finding some means of circumventing the protection which they accorded local consumers, but with no success.[54] By this time the international situation had changed drastically. German, Japanese and Italian demands for colonies based on the desire to have access to free supplies of raw materials and export markets had made the whole issue a very delicate one. The possible surpluses which Lancashire might be able to squeeze out of the impoverished East African peasantry now seemed quite insignificant by comparison with the threat to world peace posed by the inequalities implicit in the nature of the international colonial system. In January 1936 J. H. Thomas told the J.E.A.B. that 'to raise at the present time the general question of a possible modification of the free trade provisions of the Treaties would be most inopportune, for reasons well known to everyone,'[55] and the issue was thereafter closed.

EXPORT CONTROLS: THE COMMODITY RESTRICTION SCHEMES

The attempt to control colonial imports was paralleled by some attempts to limit colonial exports and hence to stabilize raw material prices. With the exception of a brief period after the First World War British policy in this area was also one of free trade – few limits were imposed on production for export, and volume and prices were left to find their own level on the market. Immediately after the War, during the period still conditioned by attitudes induced by the wartime 'siege economy', Britain had attempted to impose preferential export duties on certain West African and Indian exports, and rubber producers had also attempted to limit output in order to maintain prices. Both these efforts failed and the British trading and producing interests involved soon found it necessary to have them discontinued.[56] But the Great Depression threatened many primary producers with extinction and the possibilities of limiting output were again actively considered.

The majority of East African crops were not affected by the new movement. Sisal producers put most of their effort into the attempt to expand the British market, described in the previous section. Coffee prices were a little more stable than the rest and suffered the major fall only after 1933.[57] Cotton was produced by hundreds of thousands of small peasant producers, who were not as vulnerable to falling prices as estate producers and were in any case very difficult to organize into any sort of control scheme. The crops which were affected were sugar and tea, which were only coming into production in the late twenties, and then on a relatively small scale. Despite the smallness of the operations involved, however, the cases shed some interesting light upon the effects of commodity restriction schemes upon new producers trying to break into existing markets.

Tea was introduced into East Africa on any scale only in the late twenties, but it was soon evident that the crop could be very profitably grown there. The most important producers were large-scale estates with British capital, although smaller-scale settler groups also became involved when it became evident that the crop provided wider margins than most alternatives. In February 1933 the major producers in India, Ceylon and the Dutch East Indies, who between them controlled 98% of the output, signed an agreement limiting production and exports in an effort to raise prices to profitable levels. Their participation was sufficient to control the market, but from their point of view it was very important that all other potential producing areas should also be drawn into the scheme. If they were not, East Africa's lower costs would make it possible for producers there to take advantage of the higher prices secured by the restriction scheme to expand production rapidly and take over a much larger share of the market. Because 'the well-being of a major Empire industry was at stake'[58] the International Tea Association, which represented the established producers, persuaded the Colonial Office to put pressure on East Africa to bring her local producers in. Cunliffe-Lister then asked the local administrations to take the matter up with the producers, and Colonel Walker, Secretary of the Governors' Conference, dealt with the producers while the Colonial Office acted as intermediary with the International Tea Committee.

These negotiations produced a formula in 1934 limiting extensions to some 6,000 acres over the next five years, 2,900 acres for Tanganyika, 2,000 for Uganda and 1,000 for Kenya. The International Tea Committee considered these 'extravagant' but accepted them because by June 1934 its 'overriding consideration was to get the East African Governments to sign as quickly as possible'.[59] Kenya appears to have accepted its low allocation because the Kenya Tea Association, which conducted the negotiations, was dominated by two large producers whose major interests were in Asia and thus had a personal concern with the success of the scheme.[60] But it met with considerable opposition from Tanganyika and Uganda, Sir Harold MacMichael stressing that it had inhibited a very promising line of development for small producers.[61] The scheme was negotiated afresh in 1938 when the International Tea Committee again opposed any extensions. But this time Kenya pressed hardest for extensions since a number of small settlers were actively involved and very dissatisfied with the 1934 allocation.[62] In Uganda the Uganda

Company was actively involved in trying to obtain extensions,[63] and Mitchell, the new Governor, was able to obtain concessions through personal intervention in London.[64] The final result of these negotiations was a further allocation for 1938 to 1943 of 1,450 acres for Uganda, 2,050 for Tanganyika and 2,500 for Kenya.[65]

From the British point of view the scheme was primarily designed to safeguard the position of British investors in the Asian plantation industry. The great importance of tea to the whole economy of Ceylon meant that the Colonial Office was far more concerned to safeguard the interests of the existing producers than to press for a more generous allocation to the embryonic East African industry, however important its considerable potential. This commitment is clearly manifested in the view put to the local governments in 1937 after the Tea Committee had opposed the entry of new growers in East Africa because this would cause dissatisfaction in the main producing countries:

> The Secretary of State, as was his predecessor in 1934, is impressed with these arguments and trusts that, particularly in view of the generous offer now made by the International Tea Committee, your Government will be prepared to waive its demand for an additional acreage for new entrants into the tea industry. He regards the maintenance of the scheme as of great importance to one of the major Empire industries, and would not feel able to support any proposal which might jeopardise its continuance.[66]

Although the scheme may have supported international prices and hence the margins of those producers who were able to obtain allocations, it certainly limited the entry of new growers, more especially, in McWilliam's view, the large and well-capitalized firms which might have been able to exploit East Africa's cost advantages on a large scale. While East Africa's position in the Empire inevitably drew her into the scheme and precluded expansion, other areas not so closely bound to British plantation interests, like the Belgian Congo and Portuguese East Africa, were able to expand rapidly outside the scheme.[67] East African interests were not represented on the Tea Committee until 1944, during the critical preceding years they had to allow themselves to be represented by the Colonial Office whose despatches often 'read as if they had been drafted by the International Tea Committee'.[68] It is therefore hardly surprising that their interests received less consideration than they might reasonably have expected.

Sugar restriction was less important in East Africa than tea, primarily because most of the producers were more concerned with the local than the international market and did not in any case have significant cost advantages there. Production began in Kenya and Uganda in the twenties, in Tanganyika in the thirties, and was entirely in the hands of large-scale estate growers able to afford the necessary crushing machinery. By 1931 the protected local market had been saturated and the major producers, with the exception of one Ugandan enterprise, formed an association to limit production to maintain prices. The final agreement involved the limitation of local supplies to keep up prices, excess production to be sold on the much less profitable international market.[69] The Uganda Government apparently brought pressure to bear on the recalcitrant Ugandan firm to bring it into line.[70] In 1933 the Governors' Conference accepted representations from producers for more control and forbade the import of additional sugar-crushing machinery with the exception of equipment for a Tanganyikan company already under way.[71] By 1935 an international restriction scheme had become possible,[72] and it was probable that the local market would be flooded when the new Tanganyikan capacity came into operation in 1936. From 1933 the local administration in Uganda had pressed for reduced prices and in 1935 these led to 'a marked increase in consumption'.[73] The international restriction scheme came into operation late in 1937 and under the International Sugar Agreement the British Government 'allocated an export quota of twenty-seven thousand tons of sugar to the East African territories per year'.[74] The producers were unable to agree on the division of the quota and so the Governments allocated 12,600 tons to Uganda, 9,300 to Kenya and 5,100 to Tanganyika.[75] The expansion of the local market through price cuts, together with the higher costs of East African producers, limited the effects of the scheme, and only the new Tanganyikan producer took up the whole of his quota.[76] The following year all colonial quotas were cut by 4·2% but Tanganyika retained the old allocation. The Director of Agriculture claimed that the company was satisfied with this but might want a larger quota in the future if it was to be able to reach full capacity.[77] In this case it therefore seems clear that the local producers did not suffer so directly from the effects of internationally imposed limitations on production; those who did were, rather, local consumers whose prices were maintained at artificially high levels and also potential new producers who might have wished to begin production. The latter possibility is probably not very important because profit margins would unlikely to have been high in a free market situation.

NOTES

1. House of Commons, *Debates*, 22 iv 32, v. 264, c. 1782.
2. Information from Sir Sydney Caine, then in the Economic Department, Colonial Office.
3. *Report on a financial mission to Tanganyika* (Armitage Smith Report), Cmd. 4182 of 1932.
4. Information from Mr Geoffrey Sawyer, then Colonial Secretary.
5. House of Commons, *Debates*, 14 iii 32, v. 263, c. 85.
6. Cf. M. F. Hill, *Permanent way*, vol. II, Nairobi, East African Railways and Harbours, 1957.
7. J.E.A.B., *Annual Report*, 1936, p. 11.
8. *Report of the Commission . . . on the Financial Position and System of Taxation in Kenya* (Pim Report), Col. 116, p. 22.
9. Cf. Hill, *op. cit.*, vol. I, 1949.
10. *Report of the Financial Commissioner . . . on Certain Questions in Kenya* (Moyne Report), Cmd. 4093 of 1932.
11. *The expenditure advisory committee*, 1933; *Select committee on economy*, 1934; *Economic development committee*, 1935.
12. *Op. cit.*, pp. 245–7.
13. *Uganda Herald*, 17 i 34.
14. K. Ingham, *The making of modern Uganda*, London, Allen & Unwin, 1958, pp. 205–8.
15. *Ibid.*, p. 210.
16. W. T. Newlyn and D. C. Rowan, *Money and Banking in British Colonial Africa*, Oxford, Clarendon Press, 1954, p. 59.
17. Cf. M. Perham, *Mining, commerce and finance in Nigeria*, London, Faber, 1946, ch. 4.
18. S. H. Frankel, *Capital investment in Africa*, London, O.U.P., 1938, pp. 273–5.
19. Cf. his statement cited above, p. 118.
20. Details from W. K. Hancock, *Survey of British Commonwealth affairs*, vol. II, part I, *Problems of economic policy*, pp. 138 ff.
21. *Ibid.*, pp. 125–6.
22. Cf. W. Ashworth, *An economic history of England, 1870–1939*, London, Methuen, 1960, p. 350.
23. House of Commons, *Debates*, 14 iii 32, v. 263, c. 102.
24. House of Commons, *Debates*, 1 vii 32, v. 267, c. 2211.
25. E.g. his autobiography, Lord Swinton, *I remember*, London, Hutchinson, 1948, p. 69.
26. P. Meyer, *Britain's colonies in world trade*, London, O.U.P., 1948, p. 126.
27. *Ibid.*, p. 92.
28. House of Commons, *Debates*, 22 iv 32, v. 264, c. 1787.
29. J.E.A.B., *Annual Report*, 1932, pp. 10–11 and p. 16.
30. *Ibid.*, cf. also E.M.B., *Marketing of sisal fibre*; E.M.B., *Sisal: a note on the attributes . . .*; E.M.B. 64, 1933; Imperial Economic Committee, *Hemp fibres*, 1932; Imperial Institute, *Admiralty test report*.

31. J.E.A.B., *Annual Report*, 1934, p. 11.
32. Details from a J.E.A.B. memorandum, *Annual Report*, 1928, pp. 20–8.
33. Cf. C. Leubuscher, *Tanganyika territory*, London, O.U.P., 1944, ch. IX.
34. For a discussion cf. Meyer, *op. cit.* (note 26), and G. E. Hubbard, *Eastern industrialisation and its effects on the West*, London, O.U.P., 1935.
35. Manchester Chamber of Commerce, *Monthly Review*, January 1925.
36. *Ibid.*, August 1928, p. 250.
37. *Annual Report*, 1929, p. xxxiii.
38. J.E.A.B., *Annual Report*, 1928, pp. 20–8.
39. Cf. J.E.A.B., *Minutes*, 5 iii 30; London Chamber of Commerce, *Annual Report*, 1930, p. 100; Manchester Chamber of Commerce, *Annual Report*, 1930, p. xxix.
40. J.E.A.B., *Annual Report*, 1930, p. 13.
41. J.E.A.B., *Minutes*, 18 xii 31; Memo. for Colonial Office Conference, 24 xi 31.
42. J.E.A.B., *Minutes*, 11 v 32.
43. J.E.A.B., *Minutes*, 24 xi 32.
44. J.E.A.B., *Minutes*, 7 vii 32; Memo. for Colonial Office, 24 xi 32.
45. Mombasa Chamber to J.E.A.B., 10 ix 32 (J.E.A.B. files).
46. *Proceedings of the Governors' Conference*, 1932, pp. 18–19.
47. House of Commons, *Debates*, 1 vii 32, v. 267, c. 2209.
48. *Ibid.*, 14 ii 33, v. 274, c. 830.
49. Minutes of the Colonial Office Conference, 8 xii 32 (J.E.A.B. files).
50. *Proceedings of the Governors' Conference*, February 1933, pp. 16–17.
51. Details in Meyer, *op. cit.*, Ch. 4; Commons announcement, 7 v 34, v. 289, c. 715–18.
52. *Monthly Review*, July 1934, pp. 204–5.
53. Meyer provides a careful documentation of the effects.
54. House of Commons, *Debates*, 1 v 34, v. 289, c. 162; 10 iv 35, v. 300, c. 1129; 9 xii 35, v. 307, c. 538; Board of Trade to J.E.A.B., 30 x 35; information from Sir Sydney Caine.
55. Colonial Office Conference, 21 i 36.
56. For details and an apologia cf. Hancock, *op. cit.* (note 20), pp. 113–22.
57. M. F. Hill, *Planters' progress*, Nairobi, Coffee Board of Kenya, 1956, pp. 83 ff.
58. M. McWilliam, *The East African tea industry, 1920 to 1950*, Oxford B.Phil. thesis, p. 51.
59. *Ibid.*, p. 55.
60. *Ibid.*, pp. 52–3.
61. Interview.
62. McWilliam, *op. cit.*, pp. 59–60.
63. Uganda Co., *Minutes of meetings of the Board of Directors*, 4 viii 37, 13 x 37, 10 xi 37. The J.E.A.B. decided not to intervene because of the inter-territorial differences on the issue. *Minutes*, 10 xi 37.
64. McWilliam, *op. cit.*, p. 65.
65. *Ibid.*, p. 64.
66. Walker to Tanganyika, 28 xii 37, in *ibid.*, p. 63.
67. *Ibid.*, p. 78.
68. *Ibid.*, p. 80.
69. Details from C. Ehrlich, 'The Uganda economy', in V. T. Harlow and E. M. Chilver, *History of East Africa*, vol. II, Oxford, Clarendon Press, 1965.

70. Dept. of Agriculture, *Annual Report*, 1934, p. 10.
71. Tanganyika Legislative Council, *Proceedings*, 12th Session, p. 183.
72. Uganda, Dept. of Agriculture, *Annual Report*, 1935, p. 12.
73. *Ibid.*
74. Tanganyika Legislative Council, *op. cit.*, p. 183.
75. *Ibid.*
76. *Ibid.*, p. 184.
77. *Ibid.*

PART III

Peasants against Settlers: Restructuring the Agricultural Economy

6

Kenya – Settlers Predominant

The Zambesi river now roughly divides white-dominated Africa from black. But this line by no means represents the full extent of the ambitions of the followers of Rhodes and Smuts; their vision (as they liked to call it) extended 'white civilization' from Cape Town to the Kenya Highlands. Looked at from their perspectives this ambition was not megalomania: it represented a natural desire to strengthen the exposed position of the existing centres of white dominance by creating allies for them in a potentially hostile continent. The success or failure of this vision, which was part of the larger Imperial vision then actively engaged in settling much of the underpopulated temperate world with Englishmen, depended upon the creation of an economically viable European community in East Africa. And since that region seemed to contain few mineral resources, this meant the creation of an agricultural system capable of maintaining a permanent white community large enough to be able to extend its control over every aspect of the life of the community. Since Africa was extensively populated before the arrival of the settlers, and since they required access to cheap labour in order to maintain their standards of living, this vision also required the subordination of African society to settler control.

Stripped of all its moralistic and pseudo-scientific encumbrances, this was the burden of the white man's task in Africa. In Southern Africa a sufficient number of men and controlled firepower could be brought together to ensure that African resistance to this subordination could be wiped out without soft-hearted quibbles about the number of dead or who had original title to the land. Once African resistance had been broken the settlers seized a sufficient quantity of their land to ensure that the survivors would have to work for wages; by so doing they transformed themselves immediately into capitalists and the African into a labourer 'incessantly [forced] to sell his labour power in order to live'.[1] But the settler system in the South was created gradually: there the white community built itself up in one area before sending or driving out groups of new colonists to open up new areas; whereas East Africa was appropriated whole by a metropolitan power which wanted to control the region but which did not have any clear notion in advance of what to do with it. This great area of territory, and more especially the large areas of temperate and well-watered land which it contained, presented to white ideologues like Smuts an enormous potential, but one which could only be realized if a large and committed group of European settlers could be persuaded to go out and bring it under their control. The area was not conquered first and administered after; it was brought under control, forcibly where necessary, not by groups of intending settlers like those who invaded the Orange Free State, Transvaal and Rhodesia, but by a metropolitan power which set up an administration and then had to look around for some means of making the place pay. Settlers did not come to East Africa by right of conquest as they did to the South; they came by permission of the administration and, as it proved, all but a few were eventually to leave when the permission expired. The settlers did not, therefore, control the area on their own terms, they had to negotiate terms with an administration which was not necessarily and inevitably convinced of their moral or economic indispensability. In the South the settlers simply seized the resources which they required to establish a way of life which approximated to their version of civilization. They did not necessarily bring with them a developed conception of what this new system required in the way of economic and social organization; they did not have to bother since their control over political power made it possible for them to do whatever seemed necessary by way of directing and exploiting the indigenous population. But in East Africa there were options. Not being irrevocably committed to settlement the administration and those they advised in London were having to make choices between the settler view and one which allocated a rather different role to the indigenous population. This fact made the whole situation very complex; it also vested the policy choices being made with a very special kind of significance.

The future of settlement in the region depended upon the ability to establish a viable community of white farmers in it. A settlement of this kind could survive only if a number of very specific conditions were met, conditions which would necessarily impinge directly upon the way of life of the whole society in the region. The State in the early twentieth century had the power to make the decisions which would make it possible for these conditions to be realized. The critical question for the region, and for much else, was whether the State would choose to do so. The rest of this section will be concerned to delineate these conditions and to consider the factors which determined the nature of the decisions taken by the administration with respect to them. The issue was raised in a very concrete way in all three territories and resulted in contrasting outcomes: Kenyan policy was very largely determined by the need to maintain the viability of settler agriculture, Ugandan by a primary commitment to peasants, while Tanganyikan decisions struck an uncertain balance between the two sectors. In this chapter the strengths and weaknesses of the settler position will be analysed in relation to Kenya, in the next, the position in the other two areas.

The viability of settler agriculture was determined by its relationship to two sets of social and economic conditions, those in the society from which the settlers were drawn and those in the society to which they were to go. The intending settler had to be both pushed from his original community and simultaneously attracted to the new by opportunities not available at home or in alternative areas open to him. Britain certainly produced a plentiful crop of settlers during the first half of this century; the activity was fashionable not only among the people actually seeking upward mobility and refuge from a stultifying class system; but also among those who dominated the class system and nevertheless regarded it as patriotic to encourage those lower down the scale to leave, assuming, probably correctly, that emigrants would find it easier to remain loyal to the British way of life abroad where they did not suffer from its more onerous consequences. But the problem for those concerned to advance settlement in East Africa was that the multitude of settlers was paralleled by a multitude of desirable opportunities – they could choose to go to any of a number of well-developed Dominions or the United States. To have any success in this market Kenya had therefore to offer something which a significant number of people would regard as preferable to anything available to them in the rest of the English-speaking world. Kenya could offer an attractive climate, open space and plenty of lions and elephants to shoot. All of this appealed very directly to a species of Englishman, of which Lord Delamere was a good example, brought up on the writing of Kipling and Haggard, and too undisciplined to find much satisfaction in the mainstream of English society. But a settlement had to be built on more than the romantic dreams of aristocratic misfits: it had to provide something substantial for ordinary people with a very clear view of the solid and secure opportunities available in places like Australia, New Zealand or South Africa. This apparently simple fact imposed severe constraints on the freedom of action of the settlement movement. It meant that success or failure would depend upon the ability to provide a sufficiency of the concrete resources required to provide a viable basis for an economic and social system capable of attracting and holding a permanent European community in a very competitive situation. Such people could not simply be dumped into the bush and told to get on with it; they expected to be provided with roads, railways, doctors, schools, clubs and all the other paraphernalia of the British way of life. And if they did not get them they could take themselves elsewhere.

To provide these facilities on an extensive scale required the establishment of a relatively highly evolved export-oriented economy, an economy which, given the conditions of the times, could only take fully evolved capitalist forms. The existing African agriculture was pre-capitalist in the sense that the bulk of production was for subsistence rather than for the market, and the means of production, notably land and labour, were not exchanged on the market for money. To bring peasants into the money economy did not necessitate the total transformation of this environment since it was only necessary to integrate some small part of their production into the new system, leaving the remainder to provide for a very wide range of subsistence needs. Hence the new peasant economies could be created more gradually since the range of new needs to be met from the monetary sector was limited to the requirements of producers who were only partly integrated into the new system. But the settler came out as fully developed capitalist man; he did not expect to build his own house and furniture, grow his own food, and make a large portion of his own clothing. He expected to produce for the market on a level which would enable him to purchase these necessities in a sufficiency which matched the expectations that he had brought with him. To achieve this sufficiency the employment of labour was an evident necessity – the local African population could not simply be swept into a corner, but had to be made to work for him. Any other solution would create insuperable problems by making white men work much harder than they were accustomed to do in other parts of Africa equally open to settlers, and by leaving the African population out of the range of the social control exerted by the necessity to find regular employment. And this necessity then raised in a very concrete way the nature of the local society as a problem for those who wished to see the new system of control superimposed upon it. For the new style to succeed, the African had to be made to enter the world of money as wage labourer rather than independent producer; for as long as he had an independent control over the means of production through his control over his own land the African peasant would not be forced to work for the settler but would continue to produce on his own account. And in this situation Marx's second conditions for capitalist production could not be met. For as long as the peasant had his land the capitalist could not expect to find 'labour-power in the market as a commodity', since the African would still be 'in the position to sell commodities in which his labour [was] incorporated', and would not therefore be obliged to sell his labour power itself.[2] Independent peasant production and capitalistic settler production therefore existed as sharply antagonistic modes, and any effective development of one necessarily precluded an equivalent development of the other in the same social universe.

The need to resolve this contradiction lay at the centre of the politics of agriculture in East Africa during the inter-war period. It has already been shown that colonialism required the establishment of an export-oriented productive system – to sustain the new system some part of the old subsistence production had to be diverted to the world market. The critical question which followed from this proposition was therefore whether this new cash-crop farming would be given over to settlers or kept in the hands of peasants, and this question could only be answered by those who controlled the allocation of the factors of production demanded by the new form of production. To be in a position to sell commodities on the market it would not be sufficient for Africans merely to be left in control of the resources which had sufficed for their economic system in the pre-colonial period. To break into the market certain things were required, notably access to transport, marketing facilities and technical information. To establish themselves, too, the settlers also required access to these resources as well as access to those already incorporated in the traditional economy in the form of land and labour. To succeed they had therefore not only to establish some kind of monopoly over the new economic infrastructure created by the colonial system, but also to be in a position to undermine the control which the

African systems had had over their own productive capacity. The political struggle in East Africa must therefore be analysed in relation to the competition for these critical agricultural resources. The key issues in inter-war Kenya did not have to do with the question of the franchise or with closer union – the subject-matter for most of the studies of the period conducted by colonial historians and retired Governors – they concerned the outcome of apparently technical arguments about the location of new railway lines, the structure of marketing systems, and the ability to grow particular cash crops. The constitutional conflict was very much the dependent variable in this context – those involved wished to guarantee their control over the State machinery in order to safeguard their ability to ensure economic decisions favourable to their particular needs. This being the case it seems to be plausible to argue that the most important aspects of the political economy of the period are to be sought in the battles which took place over points of economic policy, and it is to these that the greatest attention will be devoted.

During the latter years of the nineteenth century population in the highland regions of Kenya was drastically reduced by a combination of disease and warfare. Thus when the railway first came to be built across this land much of it appeared to be unoccupied – no one stopped to establish the fact that existing tribes still claimed rights of ownership over much of it, which they regarded as a natural outlet for increases in population. This apparently unoccupied land was also endowed with an attractive climate and romantic scenery, so that it immediately suggested the possibility of a new colony of settlement. Since the West African experiment in peasant production had also not yet fully justified itself, it could still be argued and quite legitimately believed that only large-scale estate agriculture based upon expatriate management would be capable of producing the export crops required to finance the new railway and the supporting administrative complex which went with it. Sir Charles Eliot, the first Governor, committed himself to this strategy, and a few hundred aspirants had arrived by the end of the first decade. Because of the commitment to settlement, they were given special consideration, they were soon drawn into the decision-making process and were allowed to intervene very directly in the formulation of policy. But this fact alone did not guarantee their success: in Uganda commitments to the development of an estate sector (admittedly less single-minded) were also made during the same period, but they were to come to almost nothing after the War. Experiments with African cash-crop farming were being undertaken in Kenya before the War, and this could have provided the basis for a different strategy had the settlers shown a real inability to function in the new environment. At the British end the commitment to settlement was strong but never overwhelming. While the settlers, with a good number of aristocrats, officers and gentlemen scattered among them, could expect much sympathy from their many relatives inside the traditional governing class, they also faced potential sources of opposition. The humanitarian lobby, with its strong missionary base, could be expected to support African claims on at least some issues, while commercial interests would not necessarily back settler claims if it was clear that peasant production would be more efficient and would leave a larger percentage of the final price of the crop in their hands than would the more sophisticated settler producers. Thus continuous battles were to be fought in both Kenyan and British politics over the allocation of the key resources, battles not really fully resolved until the early thirties, when a balance was struck which was to last until the Mau Mau emergency exposed its underlying instability in the fifties.

LAND AND SETTLER PARAMOUNTCY

To repeat, in the South the greater part of African land was confiscated by the settlers, the economically unproductive members of the population were herded into the small reserves set aside for them, and the able-bodied males were then forced by economic necessity to sell their labour to the settlers who had dispossessed them. In this sphere, as in many others, Kenya was not prepared to go so far. Conflicting pressures in Britain combined with the weakness of the settler group actually on the ground ensured that they did not get control over sufficient land to guarantee in and of itself that Africans would have to leave their own areas to work. The details of land policy in Kenya have been extensively treated in the literature[3] and need only to be summarized here. By the end of the War all the basic principles of the allocation had been established. It had been agreed that Europeans would have exclusive rights to control over an originally undisclosed amount of land in the Highlands in perpetuity. Neither Africans nor Asians would be permitted to hold land in the area and Europeans were allowed to hold it on 999-year leases. A large number of Africans in fact resided on parts of this land where they raised crops and grazed cattle; these individuals were regarded as squatters and their access depended on the grace and favour of the settler who owned the land. Before 1918 many of them were beginning to make payment for this access in cash and thereby virtually turning themselves into tenant farmers. But in order to stop this system from developing, and thereby threatening the inviolability of the settler domain, legislation was passed in 1918 laying down that payment could in future only be made in labour and not in cash, thereby turning the relationship from one of tenancy into one of serfdom overnight.[4] In 1934, after the expensive ritual of a British Commission, the European preserve was fixed at 16,700 square miles, including 3,950 square miles of forest reserve,[5] while the actual area alienated or available for alienation varied between $7\frac{1}{2}$ and $7\frac{3}{4}$ million acres (about 12,000 square miles) from the second half of the twenties.[6] This land probably constituted about 20% of the usable land in the territory; by 1937 some 48,000 square miles had been gazetted for African occupation, virtually all the productive land remaining, since the rest of the country was desert or semi-desert. The latter was for the use of a population estimated at about $3\frac{1}{4}$ million, more than half of them concentrated into the 8,856 square miles of the Kikuyu and Kavirondo districts.[7]

The obvious contrasts between these two allocations, intensified each year in the face of rapid growth of the population of the African districts, made land the central issue in local and British politics. But looked at more closely it is by no means clear that the land issue was the critical one in determining the outcome of the struggle. It is evident that the allocation of a large, consolidated and permanently alienated area of land was a prerequisite for the establishment of a settler community. Settlers needed long-term security since they were concerned with their children's and grandchildren's futures as well as their own. They needed sufficient space to make possible a large enough community to serve as the basis for the evolution of an integrated society capable of providing itself with a full range of social and economic services. They needed to keep out of this preserve people whose life styles they regarded as alien, especially those, like the local Asian community, potentially capable of performing the same function as themselves at a much lower price. They needed long-term title to their land because it was to serve as security for credit at the bank – most of them were permanently mortgaged, and anything which altered the market for land necessarily threatened their credit positions.

But the fact that settlement could not exist without privileged access to what was eventually to be called the scheduled areas, does not imply that an insufficient amount of land remained in the African sector to provide an adequate basis for the evolution of a cash-crop system which would enable them to meet all their monetary needs. The Chagga in north-eastern Tanganyika also lost much of their land to German settlers and lived a very crowded existence on Kilimanjaro. But their ability to produce Arabica coffee, a highly valued cash crop, made it possible for them to retain their economic autonomy despite the demands for labour emanating from the settler communities near by. While the language of African politics of the period was full of complaints about the scarcity of fertile land in the African sector, the Development Plan of 1966, with rather different objectives, pointed out that 'the former African areas contain 80% of Kenya's high potential agricultural land'.[8] This land would have been perfectly adequate to meet the local population's needs assuming, of course, that it was provided with all the other factors of production required for cash-crop farming. It was in fact the failure to provide these which consigned the African population to economic servitude on settler farms, a fact which only the most sophisticated of contemporary observers were able to grasp. In this area, as in many others, the technical complexity of the issues at stake made it impossible for many of those most directly involved to understand what was being done to them.

Before considering the details, one or two general points need to be stressed. The major cleavage in Kenyan agriculture was obviously that between estate and peasant agriculture, and it is this cleavage which will primarily concern us here. But a further cleavage also existed inside the estate sector, which is of analytical importance, most especially if the differences between the Tanganyikan and Kenyan patterns are to be understood. A clear distinction can also be made between what may be called settler and plantation agriculture, in ideal-type terms, between the kind of expatriate agriculture found in the white dominions and that found in the Asian colonies.[9] The distinction is more than one of scale: it concerns the whole social role of the individuals involved. Settlers went out permanently, intending to found a community, and therefore committed themselves wholly to their new country by changing nationality and becoming, if necessary, willing to fight and die to defend their new position. Settlers also tended to be small operators, hoping to achieve upward mobility because of the existence of underutilized resources and new opportunities in the new environment. Plantations, on the other hand, on the Asian model, were essentially operations, run not by 'permanent' settlers but by individuals whose only concern was with the economic return and who intended to return to the mother country on retirement or when their contract expired. They were more likely to be effectively capitalized and those who ran them were not likely to make as many demands for long-term social and political security as were settlers. Their children would be deliberately brought up in the old culture – preferably in the mother country itself – and would not be expected to follow their parents into a career in the colony. The direct demands of a plantation system upon the territory for services were therefore likely to be much smaller and its resistance to changes in economic and political policy less intense since much less was at stake.

The distinction is clearest with regard to the contrast between the position of the small-scale owner-occupier and that of the large plantation managed locally but owned and controlled in Britain by a well-capitalized company like Brooke Bond, with its extensive tea estates and British managers. In purely economic terms the small entrepreneur brought relatively little with him – a small amount of finance, some marginal managerial skills, in some cases a little largely irrelevant knowledge of British agriculture. Far from contributing a great deal to the new system, he had to be provided by it with resources before he could hope to become an effective producer – he had to be virtually given his capital in the form of land and then supplied with all the ancillary services required to make his farming system work. His permanent status also led him to demand access to a wide range of additional social overheads – education on an English standard, medical services, social clubs, sporting facilities, etc. It was the need to meet these demands on an adequate level which led the Kenya administration to invest in public works on the 'lavish' scale disclosed in the last chapter. But a plantation economy required a much smaller expatriate sector to manage it, and correspondingly smaller social overheads; more important, it was backed by adequate supplies of capital which in some cases made possible the development of crops – notably sisal, tea and sugar – which required expensive processing facilities, which would then have been very difficult to provide for small-scale peasant farmers. The latter, with their extensive experience of farming under local conditions, were obvious competitors with the small-scale settler sector, but their relationship with the large plantations was a much less directly antagonistic one. This distinction was blurred in Kenya because of the existence of a fair number of large-scale operators like Lord Delamere and Lord Francis Scott, who were settlers but at the same time in a position to operate on a plantation scale. They could therefore identify with all the social and political aspirations of the smaller settlers yet also had the resources to overcome at least some of the obstacles to the new forms of agricultural development themselves. Perhaps most important, their position enabled them to put all their very considerable political influence (including in Scott's case contacts in the Royal Family itself) behind settler claims which, for most of the white community, were based on a far more marginal ability to contribute as effective economic entrepreneurs.

Within this context the actual progress of settler agriculture can be gathered from the following tables.

TABLE X

Kenya: Main Agricultural Exports (000s)

	1920			1928			1938		
	Acreage	Quantity (cwt)	Value £	Acreage	Quantity (cwt)	Value £	Acreage	Quantity (cwt)	Value £
Coffee	60	66	201	84	212	1,120	94	342	768
Sisal	45	87	118	92	330	496	167	560	436
Maize and maize meal	141	293	101	216	1,005	355	113	1,301	289
Tea	0	0	0	6	0	0	14	84	501

TABLE XI

Kenya: Development of European Agriculture

	No. of occupiers	Area occupied (000 acres)	Area cultivated (000 acres)	%	No. of cattle (000s)	No. of sheep and goats (000s)
1920	1,183	3,157	176	5·58	138	104
1929	2,035	5,001	636	11·40	218	239
1934	2,027	5,138	556	10·82	256	255
1938	1,890	5,053	547	10·81	307	299

Source: Kenya, Agricultural Census.

These figures show very clearly that the major expansion occurred between 1920 and 1929; the settler community was not a viable economic or social unit by the end of the War, but ten years later the number of occupiers had almost doubled, the area cultivated had more than trebled and the value of exports had more than quadrupled. Further, the level achieved by 1929 was to mark a pre-Second World War peak – thereafter the number of occupiers declined as did the area under cultivation, although the value of output rose mainly because of a movement from less valuable crops like maize to more valuable ones like tea and coffee. This movement also tended to involve a move from small-scale settler production to large-scale plantation enterprise. The latter was dominant in tea and also sisal, the former in maize and other less important temperate-climate foodstuffs where East African producers had to face effective competition on world markets from other Dominion producers. In this respect the importance of coffee to the settler economy must be stressed – this was a valuable crop which, unlike tea and sisal, could be grown on a small scale without access to expensive processing facilities. It was to become the crop which rescued the smaller settlers who were unable to survive in temperate-climate production and it was also, precisely for this reason, the crop which induced the greatest degree of conflict with potential African growers who also had the resources to produce it on their own account. The course of this struggle will be set out in a subsequent section. It was the Depression, in fact, which exposed the weakness of the small expatriate producers operating on small margins. Despite various attempts to rescue them, many failed to survive into the late thirties, thereby intensifying the tendency to move from smaller to larger units of production.[10]

The small scale of settler agriculture before the First World War was paralleled by an equivalent contribution to export production. Africans produced at least 75% of all exports during this period, mainly in the form of hides and skins, maize and sesame seed, and were therefore responsible for generating the greater part of the colony's revenue and for supporting much of the administrative effort being largely devoted to the expansion of the small settlers, their direct competitors.

The general campaign in favour of the settler way of life must be considered within this context of economic marginality, a campaign whose most decisive battles were fought between 1920 and 1923 and which was to suffer significant setbacks thereafter but no major confrontations till the early fifties. The first step in their favour was taken immediately after the War with the Soldier Settlement Scheme, part of the wider attempt in Britain to fulfil commitments to returning heroes by finding them agricultural employment overseas. Sir Edward Northey, the first post-war Governor, a South African and a strong settler supporter, pressed it actively and successfully despite hesitations in the Colonial Office apparently stemming from fears about the adequacy of the labour supply. Amery told the Commons in February 1919 that there might be too little labour for 'a very large influx of settlers' and was dubious about the prospects of 'men without substantial capital'.[11] But it was finalized in March, and the first of the applicants arrived before the end of the year. It originally envisaged 257 farms of 160 acres to be given free and 1,053 covering almost 2,500,000 acres to be sold for 6s. 8d. to 13s. 4d. per acre. Applicants were required to have a minimum of £1,000, raised to £5,000 in 1920 when all of the difficulties involved had been recognized.[12] The only direct British assistance, of £80,000–£100,000, was given to a flax-growing scheme for disabled soldiers, which ended in total disaster.[13] The soldiers had no sooner begun work than they were faced with declining world prices at the end of 1920, and this, together with inexperience and the inadequacy of supporting services, rapidly ensured that the original ambitious targets would not be met. The terms of occupation had to be revised progressively – land prices were lowered by a third in November 1920, many farms revalued and mortgages allowed on land for which the first payments were still due. At the end of 1922 when first payments were due they were waived altogether.[14] The British Government itself even admitted that the scheme diverted a large percentage of the local administration's energy from the promotion of African production. By the end of 1925 it was claimed that only about 400 of the original farms 'were actually being worked, and in most cases by the original allottees'.[15] Despite these disasters it is very probable that the scheme did make a significant contribution to the settler position in the period immediately before they faced their greatest challenge. Even 400 new settlers constituted an important addition to the small numbers already there, while the fact that the bulk of them were officers and men of some means must have added to the community's contacts in Britain and especially in the Conservative Party. More especially it allowed a great deal of new land to be surveyed and opened up and thereby unalterably added to the white domain – 28,000 acres of it taken from the Nandi and 5,600 acres from the Lumbwa reserves.[16]

The crisis which lasted from 1921 to 1923 operated on both the economic and the political levels. Politically these years saw continuous conflict between European and Indian communities with respect to representation in the Legislative Council and to access to the White Highlands. The threat to settler predominance was at one point so intense that settlers were making plans to kidnap the Governor and virtually take over control.[17] But this threat on the political level, impossible for the British Government to ignore because of the influence of the India Office and the Indian connection, was merely the surface expression of a deeper economic crisis which threatened the white community's productive base and hence their ability to make a presentable claim to social and political predominance. Declining prices from late 1920 had faced many of them with ruin by 1921, and the Colony with a financial crisis. Milner and Amery, settler supporters with strong South African connections, had been replaced at the Colonial Office by Winston Churchill and Edward Wood (later Lord Halifax), who took a much less indulgent view of their weaknesses. The revaluation of the East African shilling in terms of sterling in 1920 had also raised their costs, and weakened both their export and their credit positions.[18] In 1922 Churchill ended the right of officials to vote according to their own judgement in the Legislative Council, cut the protective duties called for by the settler-dominated Economic and Finance Committee by 30% and recalled Northey at the end of June. In July Wood informed the Commons that Churchill was now 'in communication with the Governor in order to explore the possibilities of the development of native produce in Kenya', a clearly threatening statement for settler supporters despite the proviso that this need not 'prejudice the necessary labour where it is required for European settlements' since there was 'room for both'.[19] Ormsby-Gore, to be Wood's successor, claimed that settlement was on the verge of ruin, that Kenya should 'be regarded primarily as an African country', and that there should be 'restrictions of all kinds on non-African immigration'.[20] The British expatriate business community also appears to have added its support to the attack. Leggett, of the British East Africa Corporation and very influential with the Colonial Office, was always strongly opposed to their claims in favour of those of peasant production. Henn, of the

J.E.A.B., touring East Africa in 1922–3, claimed that one of Dalgety's* partners

> expressed the conviction of all the other business and banking men to whom I have spoken, that the real future of all these countries lies in the development of native production rather than white production.[21]

Sir Robert Coryndon, the new Governor, a disciple of Rhodes and 'South African born', was appointed from Uganda where he had just witnessed the failure of an attempt, which he had supported, to introduce plantation agriculture on a large scale.[22] Presumably assisted by some pressure from London and the business community, he nevertheless appears to have initially at least accepted the need to evolve independent African production. He told Henn in May 1923:

> I think you've rather neglected the great potentialities of native production on the future finance of Kenya – you do state this factor as to cotton in Uganda, but I hope to build up a big native production of maize particularly and other seeds in Kenya. The native has hitherto been regarded chiefly as a worker on European shambas and a payer of taxes – in Kenya at any rate he's never been considered hitherto either as a big and *cheap* producer of bulk crops and (when prosperous as a result) as a great and increasing contributor to customs revenue – and along quite proper and legitimate lines. This is a strong factor in my colonial policy. It will mean much to the native himself – better medical services and education being the chief needs.[23]

In 1923 the whole question of white settlement and its relationship with the other communities in Kenya was discussed in London in the context of the constitutional struggle over Indian rights. The new incumbents at the Colonial Office, the Duke of Devonshire and Ormsby-Gore, were even less sympathetically inclined than their predecessors and the prospects looked bleak. According to Huxley the settler delegation

> . . . heard disquieting rumours that the colony's future as a white man's country was likely to be prejudiced by the application of the so-called 'West-Coast policy' of which . . . Ormsby-Gore was a strong advocate.[24]

It was therefore in this context that the 1923 White Paper, *Indians in Kenya*, emerged, the document containing His Majesty's

* One of the major trading companies active in the Colony.

Government's 'considered opinion that the interests of the African natives must be paramount, and that if, and when, those interests and the interests of the immigrant races should conflict the former should prevail.'[25] But the advocates of settlement were apparently sufficiently persuasive to safeguard the really crucial items in their case. The empty assertions of the paramountcy declaration were offset by a very concrete undertaking that there would be 'no drastic action or reversal of measures already introduced, such as may have been contemplated in some quarters, the result of which might be to destroy or impair the existing interests of those who have already settled in Kenya.' Most notably, of course, this undertaking involved the maintenance of the inviolability of the Highlands, thereby safeguarding the market for settler land, and, incidentally, what must have been very large amounts of capital invested in it by the local British banks, which no doubt had something to say to H.M.G. before the final decision was made. The decision to maintain existing settler interests, in the light of the fundamental contradiction between their needs and those of the African population, necessarily meant that the commitment to African paramountcy must become null and void. To maintain settlement at the minimum level required to fulfil the conditions for its survival already set out, it was essential that settler interests rather than those of the African population became paramount. Despite hesitations and wavering induced by bad conscience, and more concretely by the poor performance of the chosen representatives of white civilization in this part of Africa, there can be little doubt that the British administration did in fact follow a policy which almost invariably allowed the interests of settlers to prevail at all the critical points where they conflicted with those of the African population.

But although they had conducted an adequate defence the settlers had not yet completely rescued their position. The tone of the declaration was still sufficiently ambiguous to ensure that they could be gradually dispensed with if they were to continue with their previous record of economic failure. The Labour Government in 1924 might have represented some sort of threat to their position, but Josiah Wedgwood, their main critic, was not given the Colonial Office, apparently 'under dictation from Liberal supporters of the new regime'.[26] Instead it went to J. H. Thomas, doubtless the worst Colonial Secretary of State this century, who made no noticeable attempt to understand any of the problems with which he had to deal and therefore invariably allowed matters to take the course already set for them. Presumably to find others to take his decisions for him, he attempted to set up all-party committees to discuss colonial questions,[27] and sent out the East Africa Commission in the middle of the year to investigate a wide range of political, social and economic problems. The Commission, although announced in response to a motion by Henn for an investigation of the possibilities of an East African federation,[28] can be seen as the outcome of long-standing pressure from moderate missionary and Conservative critics disturbed by the more brutal aspects of Kenyan policy.[29] Following the general commitment to the need for a consensus it contained representatives from the three parties – W. G. Ormsby-Gore as Chairman (a post originally offered to Sir Hugh Clifford[30]); Major A. G. Church for Labour, who had taken no part in the previous debates; and F. C. Linfield, a Liberal who had had some fairly critical things to say. The Commission was to exert a decisive influence on moderate British opinion in the settlers' favour, the visit coinciding as it did with a marked improvement in their economic fortunes resulting from the international upturn which was already well under way by the time of their arrival.

The party spent October and November in East Africa, and were treated to an elaborate public relations exercise by the leading settlers, travelling in Delamere's car and partaking liberally of unofficial hospitality.[31] The Chairman of the Convention of Associations, the settlers' caucus, personally attested to their good behaviour and receptivity to correct thoughts:

> The three Commissioners made themselves very popular in Kenya, and showed themselves genuinely anxious to get at the real truth of the matters they were out to investigate and to help us to solve our difficulties. I'm afraid I can't say the same of Calder [the Secretary] who appeared to have come with the preconceived ideas of the stereotyped Colonial Office hand and was extremely reluctant to admit that his views were capable of readjustment in consequence of the new light thrown upon many subjects by personal investigation.[32]

On their return Calder was removed from the East Africa desk at the Colonial Office for his 'unsympathetic manner',[33] and the three wise men produced a report which, with the exception of some reservations expressed by Linfield, could have been dictated to them by Delamere himself. They asserted that settler 'occupation has added greatly to the productivity of the country',[34] and most especially that the interests of the two major communities were complementary rather than contradictory. The argument assumed that there was no direct competition between the two sectors, but that settlement essentially brought resources with it which in effect contributed to the ability of the whole system to develop and thereby benefited the African as well. Most notably it was assumed, especially in subsequent debate, that settlement provided employment opportunities for Africans and at the same time enabled them to learn about advanced agricultural techniques which they would then be free to employ on their own land. The manifest inadequacy of these propositions needs no further attention, and Cameron subsequently made a probably very fair assessment of the quality of the data on which they were based when he said:

> The Commission came back with a mass of information which they had obtained anywhere and anyhow and, presumably overlooking the fact that the evidence on each question had not been fully ventilated and properly sifted, proceeded to make recommendations which are sometimes based on nothing more than Station gossip. I find myself constantly writing despatches on passages in the Report asking for information as to the evidence on which this or that sweeping statement is based.[35]

But a lack of firm data or of a valid understanding of the mechanics of the local situation did not stop the report from becoming the basis for the development of a comfortable consensus about Kenyan policy at the centre of British politics. According to Grigg:

> The unusual unanimity on African questions which characterised the Parliament from which I resigned in early 1925 was largely the work of that Commission, and so, broadly speaking, were most of the instructions given to me on my appointment as Governor.[36]

From now on the work of critics like Leys and McGregor Ross, despite their influence on the Left,[37] could be written off as that of 'extremists' and ignored. Until the evidence before the Joint Select Committee in 1931 stimulated another series of investigations as to the equity of the relationship between the two communities, the great middle ground had been captured by those committed to the settler interest, and policy during the absolutely critical years from 1925 to 1930 could effectively operationalize their primary aspirations.

This new-found faith in settlement should not, of course, be attributed too directly to a report which in fact merely supplied the rationalizations used to justify a system already being rescued from its economic crisis through the improvements in world prices. By the middle of 1924 Coryndon had already forgotten his faith in African production and reverted to the language of his earlier experiences in the South:

> Uganda and Tanganyika are capable of producing all the cotton Manchester can use, but those countries cannot give what *East Africa* needs – a central nerve ganglion – a power house – of exceptionally high class and capable Europeans to leaven, control, guide and encourage the immense dormant native energy. It is a fine, and a true conception of the real point, the 'ten thousand' whose mission it is to galvanise and control the ten million willing workers for whom they are trustees. Times and views have changed these last two years or so. The 'settlers' should not now be regarded as merely a turbulent wayward colony of wayward children, but a group of strong men very determined to maintain their duty to their race and colour, very sensible of their responsibilities to the native population, and always striving upwards.[38]

In London Thomas was succeeded by Amery, a long-time settler supporter, and by the now-converted Ormsby-Gore. On Coryndon's death Grigg was sent out, a former member of the Buxton Commission, which had given the Rhodesian settlers responsible government, and like his predecessor a long-time admirer of Rhodes. Unlike most colonial Governors he was not recruited from the Colonial Service but from the mainstream of British political life, and was on first-name terms with the leading Conservative Ministers and in direct touch with the King's Private Secretary. Once out there he quickly allowed his policy to be directly influenced by the settler representatives, whose impact on policy immediately became much stronger than 'the appearance of the constitution' suggested. In his own words:

> The unofficial members of the Executive Committee are in virtue of their office acquainted with all the aims, problems and difficulties of Government, and they have very properly recognised that the confidence reposed in them calls in turn for co-operation and the very best of their advice. They give these in all critical matters without reserve, and proportionate weight is given to their counsel.[39]

Between 1927, when the above words were drafted in an attempt to persuade London to give the settlers an unofficial majority, and 1930 every effort was made to consolidate and extend this growing influence. In 1927 the declaration of 1923 was considerably vitiated when the White Paper of that year recognized the settlers' right 'to share progressively in the responsibilities of government', and now assumed that 'their share in the trusteeship for the progress and welfare of the natives' must be developed if 'clashes of interest between [their] interests and those of the native populations are to be avoided'.[40] In 1929 a settler-dominated Agricultural Commission was appointed which called for a settler Minister of Agriculture and a Board of Agriculture with a settler chairman,[41] and Grigg accepted the latter recommendation though not the former.[42] By the end of the decade the composition of exports had been drastically changed: settlers were producing more than 80% of these, while the absolute value of African export earnings was not to recover to the 1925 peak until 1937. Since the whole economic position of the colony appeared to hang upon these export earnings the settler community could now claim indispensability and demand continued preferential treatment as a result.

During the Depression their position was again shaken – economic weakness once more being paralleled by threats to their political supremacy. Cultivated acreage began to decline after 1931, as did the number of occupiers. Faced with falling prices the temperate-climate foodstuff producers in particular found it very difficult to survive. They were given special financial assistance in 1930, but this could not be repeated because of the budgetary crisis already discussed. Maize acreages declined from 250,000 in 1929 to 93,000 in 1934, wheat acreages from 90,000 to 35,000 over the same period. But acreages of sisal, coffee and tea expanded and the value of output per acre had certainly increased by the end of the decade. During this period, whatever Grigg might have been saying in the House of Commons,[43] Kenya certainly ceased to be a colony for the small-scale temperate-climate foodstuff producer and became more heavily dominated by the larger units. On the political level they faced a change of Government in Britain, and Sydney Webb (Lord Passfield) at the Colonial Office was at least interested enough in his work to have some of Norman Leys's allegations about the colony investigated inside the Colonial Office.[44] In 1930 the principles of 1923, such as they were, were reasserted in two further White Papers, although these were again rewritten in 1931 when the Joint Select Committee on Closer Union concluded that:

> . . . the doctrine of paramountcy means no more than that the interests of the overwhelming majority of the population should not be subordinated to those of a minority belonging to another race, however important in itself.[45]

A little more concretely, Sir Joseph Byrne, the new Governor, showed himself much less receptive to settler claims than his three predecessors. The Board of Agriculture was reconstituted without its settler Chairman, the special financial assistance given to settler agriculture was withdrawn, and strenuous attempts were made to produce a balanced budget, in part by the introduction of income tax. Simultaneously, a renewed attempt was made to stimulate African agriculture. But by this time something much more drastic would have been required to unseat the settlers from their position of predominance. Their economic indispensability was now an article of faith, and although some pressure might be brought to bear on them from time to time, nothing could be done which might threaten the viability of the economic structure which had been so carefully created. They were not even made to pay income tax till 1938, and, with the scale of their activities contracting in the thirties, and a near monopoly of cash agriculture in their own hands, their ability to buy African labour rather than to have to compete with independent African producers on the market was no longer in doubt. Africans who needed a cash income, and all of them needed at least some cash with which to pay their taxes, had now to sell their labour power rather than commodities which they had produced themselves. As a result control over the surplus in the rural sector had moved decisively into settler hands, and with it long-term economic preponderance. This preponderance, it is true, was nowhere near as complete as the dominance established by their mature relatives in Southern Africa. The economic basis was always too limited, in large part because of the limits imposed upon expansion by the low prices of the thirties. But it was sufficiently developed to ensure that a violent confrontation with African opposition would be required before the basic presuppositions of the structure of the settler political economy could be re-examined and ultimately revised in favour of the group whose contribution to economic life had been so effectively crippled by the requirements of the expensive and ultimately very fragile imported plant grafted upon it.

This is by way of general introduction. But to understand the mechanics of the process which allowed settler agriculture to establish this dominance, it is necessary to look in more detail at the way in which the resources required for the creation of a viable export agriculture were allocated. Subsistence agriculture requires merely land and labour; export agriculture requires these and also transport facilities, markets, research and extension services, and a body of supporting social services, like medicine and education. For large-scale farming some form of credit is probably also essential, and this was certainly a significant factor in the evolution of white farming in Kenya. This is, however, an area where very little information was available to me, so it will not be covered here. In the rest of the chapter, therefore, the operation of policy with respect to the allocation of these critical factors of production will be considered, most especially with regard to the division between African and expatriate sectors. It will be shown how policy heavily concentrated allocations into the White Highlands, thereby increasing their capacity to produce for cash and bid for labour, and at the same time starved the African reserves, thereby reducing their ability to produce on their own account and forcing them into the labour market. This analysis makes it clear that the creation of capitalistic settler agriculture in Kenya was principally a function of official policy, and not in any way the outcome of the special capacities for tropical agriculture demonstrated by the new white community.

THE LABOUR SUPPLY

The analysis in the previous section attempted to demonstrate that the availability (and therefore the price) of labour was a function of the whole structure of economic policy in the agricultural sector. It depended essentially on the relative levels of capitalization of agriculture in the settler as opposed to the peasant sectors. A small portion of this capital was supplied by the individual proprietors in both sectors, but the greatest part had to be supplied (in the case of transport, research, extension and social services) or at least regulated (in the case of marketing and credit facilities) by the State. Once these resources had been effectively concentrated in one area or the other it would then become the primary area for cash-crop production and hence the main area for employment in the cash sector. If the settler sector became dominant this employment would take the form of wage labour, if the peasant sector it would take the form of independent cultivation for the market. In a fully developed capitalist system the actual use of state power for the direction of labour should be entirely unnecessary: once capital has been concentrated in the hands of a minority the corresponding inability of the majority to produce independently binds them to the owners 'by invisible threads' and ensures that they will always be available at a price which the latter can afford. But Kenya after the War was by no means a fully developed system and the embryo capitalists faced the greatest difficulty in recruiting labour in open competition with the peasant sector. In these circumstances they inevitably turned to the State, committed already to providing them with many of their other requirements, to put its coercive capacity more directly at their disposal and force labour out of the reserves and on to their farms. During the twenties their problem was complicated by the scale of the works, notably railway and road building, being carried on in the public sector. Farmers had therefore to compete for labour both with peasant agriculture and with the Public Works Department, and wages threatened to rise out of the range which many marginal farmers could afford. Their campaign had therefore a twofold objective – to ensure the maximum flow of labour out of the reserves and to keep wages in the public sector as low as possible.

The pressure to persuade the Administration to compel Africans to work on European farms had been considerable during the first years of settlement before the War.[46] During the War the Resident Natives Ordinance, already mentioned, was passed, effectively turning squatters into a cheap labour supply, and the Registration Ordinance of 1921 required Africans to carry a certificate of identification, primarily intended as a means of tracking down individuals who broke their contracts of employment and therefore became liable under the Masters and Servants Ordinance, the employers' charter.[47] The Kipande, as the certificate was called, was a major source of political dissatisfaction, was expensive to administer, and had no parallel in either Uganda or Tanganyika. The end of the War, when the influx of soldier settlers occurred after a period when the African population had suffered heavy casualties in the East African campaign, induced an acute labour shortage. Undercapitalized settler agriculture provided few incentives to draw voluntary labour from the peasant sector, so that coercion appeared to be the only alternative.[48]

In 1920 Milner allowed compulsion to be used to recruit labour for public works, being 'satisfied that the position justified the measure'.[49] The labour was to be limited to those who were not already in paid employment or who had not had three months' employment during the previous twelve, and was therefore clearly designed to reduce competition between settlers and public employers. The measure was reinforced by more direct activities on the settlers' behalf in the form of the labour circulars (the 'Northey circulars') published in 1919 and 1920 for the edification of District Officers in labour-supplying areas. That of October 1919 stated that it was 'the wish of the Government' that tribesmen should 'come out into the labour field', that District Officers should 'exercise every possible lawful influence' to this end, that women and children should be included when farms were near to reserves, that Chiefs and Elders should be induced to 'render all possible assistance on the foregoing lines' on pain of being reported to the Governor, and that if these methods did not suffice it might 'be necessary to bring in other and special methods to this end'.[50] Amery claimed that the document was not submitted to the Colonial Office for prior approval and that he had only received a copy in mid-February.[51] The Church immediately objected – the Bishop of Zanzibar condemned it out of hand,[52] although the Bishops of Uganda and Mombasa and the head of the Church of Scotland were more ambiguous; they accepted the need for some compulsion in the interests of 'economic development' but claimed that the methods laid down were open to grave abuse and were especially concerned about the references to women and children.[53] These vacillations made it possible for both the opponents and the supporters of the policy to use the Bishops' views to strengthen their position,[54] and it was in any event modified by a new Despatch in February. The new document informed District Officers that their task was to 'remind' natives to go out to work but not to become 'recruiters of labour' for particular employers; at the same time the persuasive value of the tax system was to be made more explicit:

> When unemployed young men are found in a Reserve enquiries should be made as to what they are doing and as to whether they have paid their Poll Tax. . . . No actual force can be employed to compel a man to go out to work, he can, however, be made to pay his tax.[55]

And no doubt to give added point to the lesson, the Hut and Poll Tax was raised from 10s. to 16s. three months later.

In Britain the circulars drew strong attack from the body of liberal opinion mobilized in the various sections of the humanitarian lobby. This being an area where the colonial practices clearly infringed liberal capitalist morality, it even drew some support from more paternalist spirits in the Conservative Party. The Aborigines Protection Society presented a strong memorial to the Secretary of State,[56] and J. H. Oldham mobilized the opposition of the Established Church, which culminated in dark talk of 'shambok and rope' in the House of Lords from the Archbishop of Canterbury[57] in a debate which saw considerable criticism from several other Establishment figures. The official response was initially to stall by claiming that the 'official copy' of the circular and the Governor's views were still being awaited,[58] an inadequate position since they were supposed to have arrived in June, eight months after publication and at least two months after Northey had been in London.[59] They were debated in the Commons, where Amery surpassed himself in a speech which claimed that they did not involve 'anything beyond advice or encouragement to work or discouragement to be idle', and that such measures were in the natives' best interests lest, like the Red Indians or certain Polynesian tribes, they die out for lack of interest in economic development.[60] In the Lords Milner merely promised that an amending circular was to be issued, but also felt that the policy was basically justified in order to draw Africans from their lives of 'idleness and vice' in the Reserves.[61] The subsequent circular issued in July made it clear that no pressure should be brought to bear on those cultivating their own crops and, after other minor concessions, nevertheless reiterated that 'it is in the interests of the natives themselves for the young men to become wage-earners and not to remain idle in the reserves'. Milner's subsequent despatch said again that there would be no compulsory labour for private purposes, but supported the local administration in virtually every detail of the policy laid down in the first circular.[62] The policy continued to be criticized in Parliament and outside both by the humanitarian establishment and by moderate Conservatives like Steel-Maitland and Cavendish Bentinck.[63]

The settlers' position also weakened in this area during the period of their economic decline in 1921–2. Churchill discussed the matter with Northey in 1921 and then issued a culminating despatch which was to guide all colonial labour policy in the following years. This specified that traditional compulsory labour in the Reserves was to continue (this included a great deal of service for the District Officials), that Officials and Chiefs should encourage 'habits of industry' in the Reserves, but that:

... beyond taking steps to place at the disposal of natives any information which they may possess as to where labour is required, and at the disposal of employers information as to sources of labour available for voluntary recruitment, the Government officers will in future take no part in recruiting labour for private employment.[64]

Further, compulsory labour was now to be used only 'when this is absolutely necessary for essential services', and an amendment was added to the 1920 ordinance requiring prior permission from the Secretary of State for this. While the original Ordinance was used to recruit 2,208 labourers between February and December 1920, the new powers were used only in 1925 when the railway building programme was at its height.[65] In addition, though probably mainly because of the political agitation organized by Harry Thuku, the Hut and Poll Tax was reduced to 12s., where it remained for the rest of the period. These limits on official involvement, although not complete, nevertheless did serve to take some of the load off the District Administration's shoulders – local officials could no longer be very directly pressurized from Nairobi into putting their considerable local influence at the disposal of the labour-recruitment effort for settlers. In this respect it was a victory for the humanitarian lobby although, looked at from the African point of view, it was little more than a victory in a defensive struggle. To make the new policies meaningful Africans would have had to be given far more direct access to the positive resources required to engage effectively in cash agriculture, and it was here that the efforts on their behalf were to prove much less successful, as the following sections will demonstrate. This particular victory was won because the radical fringe was able to win over the support of opinion from the middle ground of British politics – the Established Church, and liberal Tories – something which was not to occur again after the work of the Ormsby-Gore Commission and the settlement of the dispute over the Indian franchise. Effective limitation on the African sector's capacity to produce, combined with a limited use of compulsory labour, especially in the Reserves themselves, made it possible for settlers to find the labour they needed in the twenties, while in the thirties 'bands' of Africans were reported wandering the country 'looking for work',[66] a reserve army of the unemployed ready and available for work in the settler sector.

TAXATION AND SERVICES

The State's ability to create an economic infrastructure depends upon its capacity to extract a surplus from the population, and the way it invests that surplus determines the economic life-chances of the various actual or potential groups engaged in production. It is therefore necessary to ask questions about both the extractive and investment stages of the cycle, in simple terms to ask who pays and who receives, how much and for what purposes. I have already argued that the settler sector required a very costly level of services in order to meet the expectations created by the social origins of the community being established, and equally that in the early stages, and most especially up to the late twenties, they did not have resources at their own disposal at all adequate to provide such services either privately or through the mediation of the State. Since the African sector was the only other productive element in the colony, it therefore followed that the settler sector could only be capitalized in the first instance through a direct transfer of resources from the African to the settler sector. The doctrine of paramountcy, therefore, as practised in the Kenyan situation, demanded that Africans should be made to pay and Europeans to receive. Any other course would preclude the establishment of a viable new community of whites. But in addition to this indispensable function, the African involvement in the tax effort served a second and almost equally important purpose by creating in that population an urgent need for a cash income. According to a senior District Official:

> . . . I think that taxation has been imposed upon natives more with the intention of producing cheap manual labour than of conferring benefits on them.[67]

These conditions thus produced the basic assumption of colonial financial policy – that Africans should pay and Europeans receive – it being argued in addition, perhaps for the benefit of missionaries and the liberal press, that taxation of Europeans reduced their incentive to produce, while that on Africans forced them to engage in modern economic pursuits which would not otherwise have interested them. More seriously, however, the effects of a tax system of this kind could be expected actually to increase poverty and dependence in the native reserves by a net transfer of resources out of them – in this case by creating a system which forced a large percentage of the able-bodied men to go out to work in the public or private sector and simultaneously through low wages and high taxes supply that sector with the surplus used to build up its productive capacity. This particular aspect of development strategy therefore exhibited in a very pure form the tendency for development at one point in an economy to create underdevelopment in another.

From the settler point of view their need to maximize receipts and minimize payments required that they obtain institutional-ized access to the local financial machinery. The humanitarian opposition was aware of this general tendency, but hampered in attempts to identify and control it by the great difficulties in-volved in obtaining accurate and timely information, since here again the concrete effects of policy tended to be hidden in a mass of complex and often misleading figures. Once more the settlers scored their major successes during periods of boom. With prices rising revenue was buoyant and it was difficult to call for any major change in either revenue or expenditure – in this situation these tended to be largely determined by the nature of past allocations. But when revenue declined and new sources of funds had to be found it became possible for the whole question of the equity of the contributions of the two communities to be raised and the settlers threatened with an increase in their contributions.

Customs duties and the Native Hut and Poll Tax between them accounted for between 75% and 85% of tax revenue. Yields under the main headings were as follows:

TABLE XII

Kenya: Receipts from Main Heads of Taxation 1920–39 (£000s)
(four-year averages)

	1920–23	%	*1924–29*	%	*1930–34*	%	*1935–39*	%
Customs and Excise	337	36	788	48	672	42	850	47
Native Hut and Poll Tax	458	50	553	34	542	35	527	29
Other Taxation	128	14	285	18	358	23	433	24
Total	923	100	1,626	100	1,572	100	1,810	100

Source: *Report of the Commission . . . on the Financial Position . . . in Kenya*, (Pim Report) p. 260A for 1920–34; *Report of the Taxation Enquiry Committee, Kenya*, 1947, p. 66. Figures for 1920/21 are for twenty-one months and have been corrected to two years in calculating averages. Other taxation includes Non-Native Poll Tax, Petrol Tax (1922–39), Levy on Official Salaries (1932–37), Traders and Professional Licences, Income Tax (1937–39), and 'All other Sub-heads', the largest item. Payments for services excluded.

Accurate figures for the relative contributions of expatriate and African communities cannot be calculated because of the difficulty in breaking down the contributions to customs revenue. But Africans must have contributed nearly 70% in the first of the above periods, almost 50% in the second, slightly more in the third, and probably less than 40% in the fourth. A final point about the composition of these contributions also needs to be made. During the whole of the inter-war period settlers on the land constituted less than half of the total Kenyan white population, and a much smaller percentage of the total expatriate population. A great deal of the prosperity of the non-settler sector depended upon payment for administrative and commercial services provided to the other two territories in the region. These revenues in turn increased the local tax base, and made it that much easier for the expatriate community as a whole to finance a level of services which would not otherwise have been possible.

The nature of the assumptions informing taxation policy was clearly apparent during the first financial crisis, which lasted from 1921 to 1923. The fall in prices produced an almost immediate deficit and the Legislative Council raised the standard rate of Hut and Poll Tax to 16s. in May 1920. Since the tax, unlike taxation in Tanganyika, was payable on all the huts owned by any individual, actual average payments would be far in excess of this figure. A conservative estimate of the actual tax paid at the subsequent rate of 12s. was 15s. to 16s. per head.[68] Owing to pressure from the Secretary of State a land and an income tax were also introduced to raise a similar amount from the non-African communities.[69] But settler opposition stopped the former coming into effect and made the latter virtually impossible to collect. It was therefore repealed in 1922 and replaced by a number of duties on articles of mainly non-African consumption in May 1922. The protective duties on imported foodstuffs discussed in Chapter 3 were imposed at the same time – these would have the effect of actually reducing revenue and increasing the costs of local consumers for the benefit of the settler producers. The other duties interfered with the Customs Union and did not produce the necessary revenue so that a large deficit was recorded and a new tariff introduced after a Conference with Uganda representatives. The problem had also been intensified by the fact that the rise in direct African taxation combined with generally falling wages had led to the first serious attempts to organize colony-wide political opposition among Africans. This had culminated in the police killing some twenty-five demonstrators in Nairobi in March 1922 and the imprisonment of Harry Thuku, their leader. In England even the moderate critics objected to this,[70] and the rate was cut a month later to 12s. But the extent of this apparent victory is again severely diminished by an examination of the small print of the tariff settlement of 1923. This actually decreased a part of the settler's tax burden by retaining the old low rating on certain commodities required for industrial use and actually extending the free list of articles required for 'industrial and agricultural development'.[71] The protective tariff, which also served to shift resources from revenue to settler producers, was also retained. The standard rate was increased by 10% to 30% on certain luxuries and to 70% on most other articles. High specific duties were imposed on certain cheap articles, notably textiles, of mainly African consumption. Thus the resulting structure must have shifted much of the burden from the settler to the African and expatriate business and administrative communities. From a political point of view the new system also had the remarkable advantage of being invisible to the naked eye. The increase in the Hut Tax exposed the connection between the State and the African taxpayer in a very blatant form and produced immediate opposition; the increased customs duties had to be extracted by the local Asian trader in the form of increased prices. Hostility therefore tended to be directed against the Asian trader (always in East Africa a much maligned and much undervalued individual) and the political movement lost the focus around which it had been able to organize.

Settler participation in decision-making was especially detailed in this field. In 1920 the Secretary of State had accepted that the 'expenditure of public funds derived in Kenya should not be authorized without the sanction of the Council',[72] and in 1923 a Finance Committee, composed of three official and eleven unofficial members, was set up to scrutinize the budget in private before its final submission to the Council. Although the budget was drawn up by the administrators, this arrangement gave expatriate interests considerable influence over allocations within the general framework.[73] In 1926 a similarly constituted Select Committee on Estimates was set up to consider the annual and supplementary estimates before submission.[74] African representatives were given less adequate access; the Chief Native Commissioner himself was never consulted when the original estimates were drawn up, was not represented on the Finance Committee (although the nominated representative of African interests was), and only received his copy of the budget with the remainder of the unofficial members of the Council. His exclusion from this area of decision-making (and, indeed, from virtually all official responsibility during the Grigg era) may well have been connected with his overall assessment of its general tendency:

> I do think that the natives of the Colony have not had a fair deal in the matter of finances. They have been heavily taxed, and by no means an adequate return has been made to them in respect of that taxation.[75]

Between 1923 and 1929 rising revenues made any large new sources of taxation unnecessary, but two new sources were found. In 1924 Native District Councils were set up with power to raise local rates to finance their services (in Tanganyika they were financed by being allowed to retain a portion of the Poll Tax, although this was lower than in Kenya), and by 1931 twenty-four were raising from 1s. to 3s. a head to add to the already high tax burden. European local councils, set up in 1926 after the Feetham Report (yet another South African contribution to Kenyan policy), were financed by direct grants from central funds. In 1927 an additional education tax was imposed on expatriates – a further tax on wines and spirits, and a direct tax of 30s. for Europeans and 20s. for Asians. These taxes, however, failed to cover even the recurrent costs of expatriate education: there was, for example, a deficit of £28,000 in 1933.[76] No additional provision was made to cover the capital costs of the new schools, which amounted to £293,000 (of which only £56,000 went to Asians) over the period.[77] Criticism of this state of affairs was totally ineffective. Only Wedgwood in the Commons pointed out the regressive effects of the changes in the tariff structure.[78] The East Africa Commission suggested that non-Africans should pay a larger direct taxation including 'some form of income tax',[79] but this was ignored.

The actual contribution to African services returned to them from their large contribution to revenue during these years was as small as decency and the need to ensure the economic survival of the work-force would allow. In 1919 the Economic Commission itself described conditions in the reserves as:

> . . . notoriously bad. Subject to the few administrative officers the machinery of control consists of Government appointed Chiefs and spearmen whose authority rests on no sort of tribal sanction.[80]

The work of the Agriculture Department was extended into the reserves for the first time only in 1923,[81] and officials told Henn that all the veterinary services and almost all the medical services were expended on Europeans.[82] The stress on African production in that year did produce some improvements, but there were still only six agricultural officers in the reserves in 1925, and five full-time and two part-time veterinary officers.[83] Despite very great increases in revenue only three further agricultural officers were appointed before 1931.

During the second half of the twenties there was continuous criticism in Britain about the inadequacy of the return which Africans received for their taxation, but this did not have any noticeable effect during the Grigg–Amery régime. But the Depression and the change of government followed by the enquiry of the Joint Select Committee forced the settlers on to the defensive. In 1929 Kenya recorded its first deficit since 1923, the result of bad crops and locust infestations. In 1930 further locust attacks combined with the break in prices forced many small-scale maize and wheat farmers out of business. Production declined and with it customs revenue, which was not to recover till 1934. In 1930 the budgetary deficit was £197,000 and the railway deficit £83,000, but assistance totalling £286,000 was granted to the failing maize and wheat farmers in the form of credits, direct subsidies and the remission of railway rates and administrative charges.[84] During the late twenties there had been extended negotiations for the setting up of a Land Bank to provide soft credit to the settler sector, and this was finally done in 1931 with a capital of £240,000 raised from loan funds. This was increased to £500,000 in 1933, by which time it had issued £306,000 on terms comparable to those of the commercial banks, but to individuals no longer commercially creditworthy. These efforts on the settlers' behalf were complemented by greatly increased efforts in the reserves to ensure that the impoverished inhabitants continued to make their usual contribution to revenue. The official presence now manifested itself almost exclusively in the guise of the tax-gatherer. The Native Affairs Department recorded:

> Tax collection . . . has proved a real inconvenience to the tax-payers and a source of unending trouble to the District Commissioner and his assistants. In Nyanza Administrative Officers have been engaged for most of the year in tax collection which used to be completed in three months. In other provinces the work has only been less arduous in proportion to the size of the populations.[85]

Collections were in fact not significantly less than during the preceding years, so that a larger percentage of African income must have gone to the State. By 1934 impoverishment had advanced so far in South Nyanza Province that there was regular emigration to Tanganyika (estimated at 1,200 in 1934), which the D.C. attributed to the lower rates of taxation and court fees in force over the border and to the fact that cattle were seized and sold when money was not forthcoming.[86]

The crisis made a review of policy inevitable, and Passfield now drew on some of the criticism of the Kenya policy which had been ignored in the previous dispensation. He was directly approached by an active Labour back-bench group led by C. R. Buxton,[87] and supplied with a series of memoranda and minutes by the Party's Advisory Committee on Imperial Affairs, which included strong attacks on financial policy by Leys and by Archdeacon Owen from Kavirondo Province.[88] The Joint Select Committee in late 1930 heard both the supporters of settlement like Grigg defending the equity of the division, and opponents – Owen, Leggett and the Kenya African representatives – attacking it. The Chief Native Commissioner claimed:

> . . . from my experience of ten years . . . the very large bulk of the expenditure of the taxation derived from both native and other populations has been poured into that 6,000,000 acres [of European land], to the detriment of the remainder.[89]

The report of the Committee recommended an independent commission of enquiry into the position, and Lord Moyne, who as Lt.-Col. Guinness had made a strong attack on the Indians in Kenya and asserted that the interests of Europeans and Africans were complementary,[90] was sent out to complete this task. His report, not a radical document, was nevertheless moderately critical, arguing that the natives had 'long paid an ample contribution' towards revenue 'considering the services provided in return', whereas the settlers enjoyed 'all the amenities of civilization in return for a relatively light scale of contribution'.[91] He therefore recommended that no further income be derived from the African sector, and that an income tax be imposed on the expatriates, although this was evidently to be on a modest scale since there was 'fortunately . . . no reason for any such readjustment of the burden or benefit on this account as need interfere with the non-native standards of living.'[92] He also recommended the establishment of a special Native Betterment Fund to be taken out of the hands of the Governor and the settler-dominated committees in the Legislative Council and controlled by a committee predominantly representing natives' interests.[93]

The liberal Fabian rhetoric penetrated deep into the Colonial Office. The 1930 White Paper laid down that taxation should not be used to make Africans work, that it should be limited to capacity to pay without hardship (though this did not apparently stop District Officers from commandeering cows), and that Africans should get 'a fair return' for their payments.[94] Grigg learnt that the new Government took 'a rather different attitude towards native policy . . . from their predecessors',[95] but he went on with his special subventions to needy settlers nevertheless. An official minute was produced in the Colonial Office on the memoranda from Leys and Owen which claimed that Grigg's case on roads was adequate – a remarkable assertion in the light of the facts to be presented in the next section – and for the rest recommended yet more on-the-spot investigations with the possibility that Byrne, the new Governor, should prepare an annual statement, district by district, on revenue and expenditure. Leys's document he found not 'helpful' and at the end 'very wide of the mark'.[96] Thus armed with the full might of the liberal conscience Byrne went forth to rectify the balance. Soon after he arrived Cunliffe-Lister took over in the Colonial Office, which may well have blunted the edge of British resolve, although he was obsessed with the need to balance the budget and therefore also concerned that settlers should be made to make a larger contribution to revenue. From 1931 the special subventions to settler agriculture stopped and their influence on financial policy in the Legislative Council was reduced.[97] But this was the full extent of the victory. The Betterment Fund did not come into existence because of the financial stringency. The settlers responded to the demand for an income tax by a political agitation culminating in a deputation to London. Because the J.E.A.B. refused to oppose it they withdrew their support, which was only renewed after a visit to East Africa by the Chairman.[98] The doctrine of paramountcy was then applied again and the tax withdrawn in favour of an alternative set of less direct taxes which included increases on cheap imports for African consumption recommended to the Governors' Conference by Kenya on the grounds that they would both assist the revenue and decrease Japanese imports.[99] On the other hand, the need to expand production in the face of the collapse of small-scale settler farming did lead to an expansion of the Government's agricultural presence in the reserves, although this was matched by a cut in African medical and educational services. The number of Agricultural Officers there increased from nine to fourteen between 1931 and 1935, and four new Assistant Agricultural Officers were appointed despite cutbacks in other areas.[100]

Continued financial difficulties meant that Sir Alan Pim had to take up the question again in 1935, when his report also showed that Africans had not received an equitable return for their payments, and drew some very unfavourable comparisons with the situation in Uganda and Tanganyika in this regard.[101] This time the settlers could not stop a modest tax from going through, but they had to be given parity of unofficial representation on the Executive Council in exchange. In any event, the structure of economic policy over that of the preceding generation had effectively placed a near-monopoly of the agricultural resources of the colony in their hands, so they could now afford a larger contribution to revenue without fear that this might undermine their competitive position in their struggle with the peasant sector on the one hand and to obtain new settlers from abroad on the other.

TRANSPORT

Access to the railway determined the ability to produce for the export market. Transport costs constituted a high percentage of total costs, so that distance from the railway determined the potential profitability of land. The railway's costs per ton mile were also high because of the small amount of total traffic carried, the seasonality of demand and the nature of the traffic flow patterns, which necessitated many empty carriages running back from the coast at peak export periods. These costs determined the overall costs which the railway system imposed upon the community as a whole, a community, it will be remembered, which included the whole of Uganda and a large proportion of the most productive regions of Tanganyika. But the railway administration was free to allocate the burden imposed by these costs unevenly; it could and did require some users to subsidize others by a graduated rating structure. Thus the critical questions involved in this area of policy relate firstly to the actual location of transport facilities — railway lines and their associated feeder-road systems — secondly to the rating structure as it impinged on different classes of users. The issues involved are the more important when it is realized that investment in transport accounted for the great bulk of all the public capital investment in economic services during the period.

The original main line was built for strategic purposes and located without reference to the needs of particular groups of producers. Once built, however, it was assumed that the line could be made to pay only through settlement, and as a result 'the claims of development were held to require that Europeans should have the use of land in the immediate vicinity of the railway, even where such land was indisputably tribal territory.'[102] In addition, the rating policy established by 1919, already discussed in Chapter 3, heavily favoured the small-scale temperate-climate foodstuff producers, predominantly settlers, at the expense of consumers, especially African consumers, since cotton piece goods were placed in the highest class, and of the producers of higher-rated exports, notably cotton lint, coffee (till that time predominantly produced by peasants in Bukoba, Tanganyika), sisal, and subsequently tea. Far from settlement financing the railway, it was in fact African production which provided the railway with sufficient resources to make possible its use to subsidize the most inefficient sectors of settler agriculture. This point has been dealt with in more detail in Chapter 3 and will not be looked at here. This section will be mainly concerned with the equally large discrepancies in the capital development programmes as between the two sectors.

The branch-line programme, which took up a large percentage of the colony's developmental efforts between 1920 and 1932, was seen as an instrument for opening up the highlands to potential settlement and as little else. As a result, no rigorous economic surveys appear to have been made in advance, but the potential of often very sparsely settled areas was taken completely on trust. Of the 544 miles of line built after 1920, 397 passed through European areas, the remaining 147 through African areas.[103] Of the latter, a 61-mile section was part of the main-line extension to Uganda and was not 'undertaken in the interests of the Africans' [104] A further 42 miles formed part of the Thika branch-line extension, which could only reach the outer section of the European area by traversing the African lands between. Three other branch lines (Solai, Kitale and Thompson's Falls) passed exclusively through settled lands, and only one was built with African needs obviously in mind. The Butere line, built into the cotton-growing area of the south-west, was in fact originally planned during the early twenties when African production became briefly fashionable and was intended as part of the cotton-railway building programme projected for the cotton loan of 1924 discussed in Chapter 4.[105] But it was given low priority once settler control was re-established and it was in fact the last of the branches completed, the final track being laid in 1931.[106] Leggett told the Joint Select Committee that 'except in a very small degree on the Thika branch, and only in the most indirect possible way at all, can it be said that these [branch lines] affect natives at all'.[107] The African witnesses to the Joint Select Committee did not appear to be at all aware of the implications of the existing distribution, and merely requested that more godowns (i.e. storage sheds) be built since those which existed tended to be monopolized by European produce.[108]

This was also an area of policy where the European settlers gained great advantages from being fully conscious of all the technical and financial questions involved and from being able to obtain a dominant position on the critical decision-making body. Policy was decided by a Select Committee of the Legislative Council with an unofficial majority. According to Lord Francis Scott's testimony to the Joint Select Committee not even the 'town members' were on it so that the settlers were able to decide for themselves where new extensions were to be built.[109] His testimony also makes it clear that but for the Depression two further lines would have been built into European areas, since these were authorized in 1930.[110] The economic utility of these lines can be judged from the fact that total losses of £713,000 were estimated for 1926 to 1931, the calculation leaving out of account the whole of the capital costs involved, which must have been very high since total railway repayments amounted to more than £800,000 per annum in the thirties. The railway in fact stopped publishing these figures in the thirties because of the criticism which they aroused.

Allocations towards road building were made on a similarly inequitable basis. The actual amounts were much smaller, but the facilities were of great importance for anyone wishing to move a crop either to an urban market or to the railhead. Road building in the settled areas was made the responsibility of the European-controlled Rural District Councils, which were financed entirely by grants from central revenues. Roads in the reserves were mainly built and maintained from extra taxation in the form of cash and kind levied by the local Councils on their own populations. Their position was summarized accurately in 1938:

The roads in Native Reserves are maintained by small grants from Government funds and in most cases larger grants from Local Native Council Funds, but owing to the paucity of funds communal labour is still used to no little extent.[111]

The 1931 estimates, for example, allocated £37,827 to the European Councils; the Native District Councils spent on average £7,520 per annum from their own funds on roads from 1925 to 1938. Amery told the Commons that £50,850 was to be spent on roads in the settled areas, £32,550 in the African areas in 1929,[112] but Archdeacon Owen's memorandum to the Colonial Office in 1930 claimed that only £9,264 was spent on non-trunk roads in African areas, £44,968 on such roads in settled areas.[113]

As in other areas where technical issues were involved and access to accurate information before decisions were made was essential, the position of the humanitarian opposition in Britain was hopelessly weak. Leys and Ross had drawn attention to the importance of the transport issue, but despite regular Parliamentary questions and criticism, their supporters found it almost impossible to discover what was happening before money had been committed and building was under way. To give an example of the official capacity for evasion (a stronger word might be more appropriate), in December 1927 Ormsby-Gore claimed that he did not know the length of the Thompson's Falls branch, which ran through European land. Yet the previous month one of his officials displayed a truly remarkable knowledge of the location and details of lines. Writing about the attempt to clear the proposed loan with the Treasury, he said:

> It will help enormously with the Treasury if you can avoid any commitment on any outstanding point till we have squared them. I am thinking particularly of the Thompson's Falls railway, the Land and Agricultural Bank, and, now, the Nanyuki extension which I see from the Council Debates is being pressed by Kinealy. (I wonder if means have been found to avoid spoiling Mrs. Baine's view?)[114]

The question was discussed in detail by the Joint Select Committee, and another Commissioner was sent out to consider the equity of railway provisions. Gibb's work on the 'political' influences which characterized rating policy has been discussed; he had nothing to say about building, presumably because this was no longer a live issue. Moyne criticized the equity of rating policy, but, using an undisclosed calculation whose rationale is difficult to understand, concluded that branch lines had been 'fairly divided between all communities'.[115]

MARKETING FACILITIES

A brief look at the nature of state intervention in this area will serve to complete a record of the direct services placed at the disposal of the settler sector in their struggle to make themselves an effective economic force. Here the power of the local administration was confined to its ability to control the organization of the local market, since it could not, of course, influence conditions operating abroad. This imposed considerable limitations on its power, as the internal market for agricultural produce was largely confined to articles of consumption for the expatriate community, since Africans produced almost all their requirements from the subsistence sector. The only offsetting factor in this regard was the existence of the whole East African market, which explains the importance attached to this in the conflicts already described over the customs union and railway policy. The rest of this chapter will therefore be concerned with the way in which state power was used to exploit the internal market in order to create a basis for settler industries that would otherwise have been unable to compete with imports from more efficient overseas producers.

Perhaps the most important decision in this area was made in 1923, when the Tariff Amendment Ordinance introduced protective duties on a wide range of temperate-climate foodstuffs – wheat, wheat flour, butter, cheese, bacon, ham, timber, sugar, ghee, tea and beer.[116] Typically the decision emanated from a special committee on which the settlers had been given a formal majority, the Bowring Committee which made it being composed of two officials, one Indian and five settlers.[117] This protection, of course, involved a direct subsidy from the East African expatriate community as a whole to the settler sector; it equally involved an indirect subsidy from the African sector because they provided the economic base which sustained the administrative and commercial class in the areas of African production.

This measure was sufficient to ensure that the temperate-climate foodstuff producers would be able to survive the early twenties and by the end of the decade could supply the whole of the internal market in most of these commodities without difficulty. Two co-operative marketing organizations were set up by settler producers to handle both local and overseas sales, the Kenya Farmers' Association in 1919 to handle maize and wheat, and the Kenya Co-operative Creameries in 1925 to handle butter and milk. The protective tariff gave them higher prices on the internal market than the external; the decline in world prices after 1929 widened this differential and made the internal market a great deal more profitable than the external, provided that production for this market and competition for the crop could be regulated. Here too a good deal was done to assist the settler producers. In 1931 a Butter Levy Ordinance was passed which forced local consumers to pay a cess of 25 cents on every pound purchased, and this was then used to subsidize producers of export butter. The Kenya Farmers' Association was milling and marketing about 80% of the colony's wheat by 1930, and was responsible for all exports. When the world price fell in 1930 the Sale of Wheat Ordinance was introduced, which gave it the sole right to purchase and sell locally-produced wheat. This meant that local competition for the crop could not develop and force down the price on the local market to export levels. It was given power to import wheat with a remission of five-sixths of the import duty when local supplies were too small; its control over the supplies of wheat grain also enabled it to establish a virtual monopoly in wheat milling.

Butter and wheat were almost exclusively European-grown crops, so there was relatively little difficulty involved in regulating the supply to the local market since this was determined by what the single selling agent would take at the agreed price. But maize was a crop grown in both African and European sectors; much of it was devoted to subsistence, but a great deal of African maize entered the local market, where it was especially important in the diet of the agricultural labouring force. By 1930 the Kenya Farmers' Association was handling virtually all the exported maize and having to compete on the local market with local traders, a growing percentage of them Africans, who bought their supplies in the reserves. In this case it would have been impossible to stop African sales, both because of the enormous number of selling-points, and because it would have increased the costs of food supplies to the European farming sector as a whole. The Kenya Farmers' Association attempted to control the situation by itself buying in the reserves, but this merely intensified competition and caused their own prices to rise. In 1935, when the local market was threatened with 'collapse', the Legislative Council appropriated £12,500 to guarantee farmers a minimum return of Shs 4/50 per bag on everything sold on the export market;[118] the following year the Railway, that old friend of the settler maize grower, gave a temporary rebate of 5s. per ton on maize railed, and abolished branch-line charges and port surcharges.[119] But the Kenya Farmers' Association could not induce the Government to give it any further assistance and the position of the maize farmer therefore remained weak.

One final aspect of this question should be noted. In British colonies based on peasant production the whole developmental effort was generally devoted to export production. The resulting tendency for means of communication, marketing arrangements, and other elements in the infrastructure, to be totally geared in this direction is a common and justified criticism of the nature of the assumptions on which policy was based. But in East Africa, however limited and costly the experiment, the presence of the settlers did lead to a much higher degree of development of the local market, which was to play a much more positive role after the Second World War when it had expanded and industrialization developed. But for the effective economic nationalism of the settlers this would probably not have evolved to the level it did until very much later.

AFRICAN AGRICULTURE

The material advanced in the preceding sections largely explains the poor performance of the African farmer in the cash sector. But the steps actually taken in the reserves themselves to encourage or discourage this production must still be considered. In particular it will be necessary to look at the treatment of the individual crops which the reserves were capable of producing, and at the effects of official encouragement on them when conditions required that this be given. It will be remembered that African production tended to be encouraged during periods of low prices because of the failures of the settler sector and the corresponding need to increase exports and governmental revenue. The effects of this tendency can be seen in Table XIII, where it should be noted that the figures for the early thirties signified very large increases in production since prices were very low. The effects of the increase in attention tended to be felt only a year or two after the trough in prices because of the delay in organizing services, but the trend is clearly visible. The campaign of 1922–3 produced a very large expansion, the gross neglect from 1925 to 1930 produced virtual stagnation despite buoyant prices. The renewed pressure from 1931 ensured a steady expansion culminating in the peak in 1937. It was clearly the tragedy of Kenyan African peasant production that the efforts made to get it

TABLE XIII

Kenya: African Export Earnings, 1922–38 (£000s)

1922	180	1928	482	1934	301
1923	271	1929	543	1935	357
1924	480	1930	403	1936	472
1925	565	1931	222	1937	652
1926	471	1932	262	1938	488
1927	498	1933	365		

Source: Kenya, Agriculture Dept., *Annual Reports,* 1923–38. Estimates only, and not always internally consistent. The largest figure always preferred.

moving were always made during periods of low prices when the rewards to producers were correspondingly limited; there is little doubt that major expansions on Ugandan or Tanganyikan lines could have been produced if similar encouragement and financial backing had been available. This assertion applies to most of the crops grown in this sector, here attention will be confined to the two premier African-grown export crops of the region, cotton and coffee.

Although not as well-endowed as Uganda, Kenya undoubtedly contained large areas of land suitable for cotton production both on the coast and in the Nyanza Province around Lake Victoria.[120] But here production was obviously strongly influenced by policy and followed very closely the overall pattern of African production already discussed, as the following figures show:

TABLE XIV

Kenya: Cotton Exports, 1923–38 (bales of 400 lbs)

1923	1,200	1927	1,232	1931	783	1935	8,773
1924	1,653	1928	1,241	1932	1,744	1936	15,783
1925	2,250	1929	1,984	1933	4,276	1937	22,166
1926	2,046	1930	1,518	1934	6,749	1938	19,610

Source: Empire Cotton Growing Corporation, *Reports of the Administrative Council,* 1924–31.

On the official side virtually nothing was done about the crop till 1922; a favourable opportunity was thus missed, since prices were high because of disease in the American fields and the Ugandan industry was expanding rapidly. In 1922, however, the change in central policy led to a revival, agricultural supervisors were moved into the Nyanza region, ginneries set up with official assistance and large quantities of seed distributed.[121] Pressure was brought to bear on the population to increase production, the cotton railway (the Butere Line already discussed) was planned, and in 1925 an Empire Cotton Growing Corporation expert visited the area. But by the middle of 1924 Coryndon was already stating with 'neither shame nor anxiety' that 'Kenya will never produce very large cotton',[122] and the Empire Cotton Growing Corporation and subsequent British Cotton Growing Association experts found little promise because of competing labour demands, poor communications, and lack of research facilities in the reserves,[123] the reasons for which have already been fully explained. Henn himself subsequently commented on the existence of 'a white section in Kenya that have definitely opposed the policy of encouraging the Kavirondo to grow cotton'.[124] The situation was well summarized by Sir Edward Denham, Colonial Secretary under Grigg and a man whom the latter was constantly trying to get rid of, for reasons no doubt not unconnected with the sentiments expressed here:

> I did my best when last acting [Governor] to encourage [the activities of a certain cotton buyer] in Kavirondo and in fact hauled a District Commissioner – who has since retired – over the coals for not giving him the assistance I considered he deserved. I don't think there is so much to be made of cotton in that part of Kavirondo at the present time but that cotton can be grown and with success there is no doubt. . . . The Agriculture Department has never been as keen on cotton development as I think it might be. There are political considerations as you know, but I don't think these have been the determining factor – rather a lack of an equal and sufficient interest in Native agriculture.[125]

During the Depression official interest in the crop was renewed. The administration devoted much more energy to it both in Nyanza Province and on the Coast, and considerable pressure was brought to bear to induce people to grow it. In 1932 Kenya featured in the Annual Report of the Empire Cotton Growing Corporation for the first time since 1925; in 1935 the Corporation was asked for assistance, an expert spent some time there and they indicated a willingness to provide assistance; by 1938 they were discussing the need for a local research station. The growth in output during the decade was very vigorous, but had, of course, to start from a very low base and to struggle against the effects of low prices. The contribution which the crop could have made to regions involved was clearly considerable when the relative prosperity existing over the border in Uganda is considered.

But the losses to the African sector from official neglect of cotton are probably very small when compared with the effects of their deliberate opposition to the growth of African coffee. Cotton is a relatively labour-intensive crop and the returns per acre and unit of labour are very much smaller than is the case for coffee. This means that it can make a very significant contribution to the economy of communities where land is scarce, and, indeed to those at some distance from transport facilities, because of its high value to weight ratio. Further, it was well known that very large areas of the reserves, especially in Kikuyuland, were very suitable for the production of the highest quality coffee, and it was, in fact, virtually the only suitable crop for areas between 5,000 and 6,000 feet.[126] But despite these facts and all the rhetoric about paramountcy, the Kenya Government intervened decisively in the twenties to stop Africans from growing the crop, and in the thirties only allowed derisory acreages to be cultivated in some of the most remote agricultural areas of the colony. The reasons for the policy are clear – the settler sector strongly opposed the development of an African industry and, according to the well-established principles of Kenyan administration, when the interests of European and African conflicted those of the former were allowed to prevail. The evolution of policy in this area provides an illuminating insight into both the attitudes and the structures which determined colonial policy in the period.

Opposition to African coffee-growing stemmed from the deepest fears and prejudices of the settler community. Since there were few economies of scale to be secured in coffee growing – indeed if anything there were diseconomies because of the difficulties of organizing and supervising labour – African growers could compete on more or less equal terms with settlers. If they were allowed to do this they would be able to produce commodities on their own account and would refuse to enter the market as labourers, and this would necessarily 'strike at the roots of the settler economy'.[127] But in addition European coffee farmers also opposed it because they believed that African cultivation would be poor and give rise to disease, that the quality would be inferior, which would reduce the reputation and the price for all Kenya coffee, and that once it was possible for Africans to be in legal possession of raw coffee thefts from European plantations would increase.[128] The question of African growing was at issue during most of the period considered here, but it fell into two distinct parts. During the twenties the settlers were assured of administrative support, and of strong and largely effective official discouragement of African growing. Instead they directed their attention to Tanganyika where the Chagga, now one of the most advanced African communities in the region because of their access to the crop, were being allowed to cultivate Arabica coffee on the boundary of an area of European settlement and also showed a disconcerting ability to produce a crop which achieved higher prices on the London market than their settler neighbours. In the thirties, on the other hand, experiments with African coffee were begun in Kenya itself and attention had to be shifted to having these either stopped or stringently limited.

During the twenties African political organizations in Kenya – the Kikuyu Central Association and the North Kavirondo Taxpayers Welfare Association – both pressed for permission for Africans to grow the crop.[129] In 1927 at least three farmers were cultivating coffee in Nyanza (no law ever existed to stop them doing so) and two were persuaded to destroy their plants.[130] In 1929 the Acting Chief Native Commissioner felt that they would not 'be able for long to persuade natives not to grow profitable crops if they have a right do do so'.[131] But these objections were limited and easily overcome since Grigg supported the policy[132] and Alex Holm, the Director of Agriculture (and another South African) would have liked a 'definite prohibition'.[133] But immediately across the border the Chagga were growing the crop in close proximity to the European coffee industry. The crop expanded dramatically with official encouragement in the early twenties,[134] and the obvious discrepancy between conditions there and in Kenya quickly led to awkward questions being asked in Britain.[135] In 1924 settlers on both sides of the border pressed to have the whole Kilimanjaro region transferred to Kenya.[136] The possibility was never seriously considered, however, and the danger continued because even the Ormsby-Gore Commission was only prepared to argue that the prohibition in Kenya be maintained for the present and until 'far more data regarding the results of experiments now being undertaken in the Kilimanjaro and Bugishu [Uganda] areas are forthcoming'.[137] In London the J.E.A.B. intervened in 1925 on the settlers' behalf, trying to have Africans on Kilimanjaro dissuaded from growing the crop until the Governors had instituted enquiries into the matter.[138] In

July 1926 they went so far as to submit a strong memorandum to the Colonial Office, which concluded:

It is submitted that from whatever point of view the matter is regarded, the cultivation of coffee by natives is neither in the interests of Europeans nor of natives themselves. The present position is not at all satisfactory to European cultivators with the result that the introduction of fresh capital into the industry is being withheld.[139]

But in reply Ormsby-Gore claimed that the cultivation of Arabica (i.e. the higher-valued coffee) in the Kilimanjaro area was 'a specific problem', that native growing of the crop should be confined to Kilimanjaro and to Mt Elgon in Uganda, but also:

In view of the danger of the dissemination of disease in Kenya there was no intention of introducing the growing of coffee by natives in that Colony.[140]

This was a significant advance on the recommendation in his own report, and the matter could be allowed to rest there.

But in 1929 the report of the Hilton Young Commission called for an enquiry into the situation, pointing out the discrepancies between the treatment of Africans in Kenya and its two neighbours.[141] The policy was extensively discussed before the Joint Select Committee and condemned by all but those with vested interests in its continuance, and the report itself called for 'an early and sympathetic consideration by the Kenya Government of the natives' representations' on, among other things, 'the cultivation . . . of coffee and other export crops'.[142] This, co-inciding with a general move towards African production, led to the first experimental plantings in 1933. These occurred in very remote areas where there could be no possibility of contamination of settler crops, and were on such a small scale that only 160 acres of Arabica and 106 of Robusta (the lower-quality crop) existed by 1938.[143]

But even this amount of freedom was sufficient to induce a strong reaction from the settlers and their allies. In 1932 the coffee planters had advocated the 'indefinite postponement of a step so utterly unwise';[144] and in the Commons Conservative backbenchers were mobilized to question its wisdom.[145] A representative of the coffee planters was then commissioned to describe to the Secretary of State 'the present critical situation of the coffee industry', and the extent to which this was 'aggravated by the present policy of the Government in encouraging the natives to grow coffee'.[146] In July 1933 the Kenya Coffee Board was assured by the Kenya Government that it intended to proceed 'very slowly . . . and to adopt no measures which could in any way endanger [the European coffee] industry'.[147] In September, Gare, the Kenya representative, interviewed leading figures in London, including the Coffee Trade Association, M.P.s, the Under-Secretary of State and a senior Colonial Office official, and the J.E.A.B.[148] In November he saw Cunliffe-Lister accompanied by a representative of the Coffee Trade Association. Here he was given the following apparently definite assurance:

> Sir Philip said that it would not be politic to prohibit native growing as the public generally would declare this to be an injustice to the native races.
> We pointed out that we were not asking for prohibition but that the Government should not encourage native growing owing to the evils it would result in as much for the native as for the white man.
> Sir Philip assured us of his determination that whatever native planting was allowed it should do no harm to white settlers' shambas* and that the experimental plantations should not be extended unless their working results had been satisfactory.
> Sir Philip agreed that if we found that our complaints were not being faithfully transmitted to him by Nairobi he would receive representations through the medium of the Coffee Trade Association of London.[149]

The experiments were not stopped, but limited to such an extent that they constituted no serious threat to the European industry and equally contributed virtually nothing to the attempt to establish a viable peasant agriculture in reserves already affected by population pressure and provided with only the most rudimentary transport services. The settlers were still not entirely satisfied with the fact that even this amount of freedom should be allowed to African enterprise,[150] but the victory was clearly theirs.

*   *   *

This concludes the account of the Kenya settlers, an account which has tended to stress the strength of their bargaining position within the Kenyan economy. Although it is clear that this does not exaggerate their ability to control resources in competition with Africans, it should not be allowed to create an impression of undue strength. Kenya was always the weakest of the areas of European settlement proper in sub-Saharan Africa, and even with the

* Farm or holding.

support which it was able to extract from other sectors and territories it was never able to build up an economic base which would make it independent of support from London. This was in part a function of its inability to attract settlers even on the Southern Rhodesian scale, an inability much affected by the shortage of mineral resources and the limitations of its attempts at industrialization. It was also a function of its isolation from the other centres of settlement which might have rallied to its support in times of emergency. It may also have derived from the accompanying political weakness of the settler sector, which was never able to gain direct control over the bureaucracy and army as the Rhodesians did, and thus had to depend on support from Britain when the crisis came in the early fifties. It could also be argued that the presence of the humanitarian opposition in Britain, weak though it was, did have some limiting effects upon the tendency for the African sector to be put totally at the disposal of the European during crisis periods. No doubt this opposition did have some effect in mitigating the worst efforts of the settlers with regard to labour policy in the early twenties and to tax policy in the early thirties. But the importance of this factor was probably very small and virtually negligible in most of the critical areas of policy – land, transport, marketing and African cash-crop cultivation. The real weaknesses of the settler position derived from the fact that they had very little positive to offer in real economic terms – they were essentially parasites upon the Kenyan economy and therefore found it very difficult, even with heavy state assistance, to accumulate the resources required to make their position a tenable one. The British opposition should not be congratulated upon its efforts in holding the settlers at bay, but asked to explain its inability to limit the obvious success of so weak and incompetent a force. Certainly this particular piece of colonial history contributes little to British claims to have exercised an imperial trust.

NOTES

1. K. Marx, *Capital*, London, Allen & Unwin, 1946 reprint, p. 59.
2. *Ibid.*, p. 147.
3. M. R. Dilley, *British policy in Kenya colony*, New York, Nelson, 1937, pp. 248–71; R. L. Buell, *The native problem in Africa*, New York, Macmillan, 1928, pp. 298–328; L. Mair, *Native policies in Africa*, London, Routledge, 1936, pp. 79–89; E. Huxley and M. Perham, *Race and politics in Kenya*, London, Faber, 1944, pp. 42–82.
4. C. Wrigley makes this point in 'Kenya: the patterns of economic life, 1902–1945', *in* V. T. Harlow and E. M. Chilver, *op. cit.*

5. *Report of the Kenya Land Commission* (The Carter Commission), Cmd. 4556 of 1934, p. 491.
6. Figures in Kenya, *Agricultural census*, 1928–38.
7. Figures in Kenya, *Blue book*, 1938, p. 560; *Kenya Land Commission*, p. 350.
8. Kenya, *Development plan*, 1966–70, p. 125.
9. This point is again well made in Wrigley, *op. cit.* (note 4).
10. Cultivated acreage per occupier did not increase proportionately because of the movement from extensive temperate-climate foodstuff production to intensive sub-tropical crops like tea and coffee.
11. House of Commons, *Debates*, 17 ii 19, v. 112, c. 596.
12. House of Commons, *Debates*, 14 xii 20, v. 136, c. 227.
13. Cf. Leggett's evidence to the Joint Select Committee on Closer Union, vol. III, p. 51.
14. By Ordinance no. 29 of 1922.
15. House of Commons, *Debates*, 23 xi 25, v. 188, c. 895.
16. House of Commons, *Debates*, 8 xii 22, v. 159, c. 2209–12.
17. Their antics are described in the literature cited in note 3 above.
18. Cf. Newlyn and Rowan, *op. cit.*, pp. 57–8; House of Commons, *Debates*, March to June 1921 and esp. 26 iv 20, v. 128, c. 896 ff., 911–13.
19. House of Commons, *Debates*, 4 vii 22, v. 156, c. 230.
20. *Ibid.*, c. 254–5.
21. Sir Sydney Henn, *Notebook of a trip to East Africa*, 1922–3, entry dated 25 iii 23, similar comments dated 25 i 23 (Henn Papers).
22. Cf. R. C. Pratt, 'Administration and politics in Uganda', in V. T. Harlow and E. M. Chilver, *op. cit.*
23. Coryndon to Henn, 2 v 23 (Henn Papers).
24. E. Huxley, *White Man's Country*, vol. II, London, Macmillan, 1935, pp. 155–6.
25. Cmd. 1922 of 1923.
26. Henn to Coryndon, 11 ii 24 (Henn Papers).
27. The Southborough and Islington Committees, cf. House of Commons, *Debates*, 23 vi 24, v. 175, c. 70–1; 30 vi 24, v. 175, c. 931.
28. House of Commons, *Debates*, 8 iv 24, v. 172, c. 351 ff.
29. Cf. R. Oliver, *The missionary factor in East Africa*, London, Longmans, 1952, pp. 252–3; House of Commons, *Debates*, 14 vii 21, v. 144, c. 1571, 1585, 1592.
30. Henn to Coryndon, 25 viii 24 (Henn Papers).
31. Huxley, *op. cit.*, pp. 190, 191 and interview with Major E. A. T. Dutton, Private Secretary to the Governor.
32. Archer to Henn, 24 xii 24 (Henn Papers).
33. Henn to Archer, 6 iii 25 (Henn Papers).
34. *Report of the East Africa Commission*, Cmd. 2387 of 1924, p. 149.
35. Cameron to Oldham, 8 xi 25 (Oldham Papers); cf., also, Cameron to Oldham, 1 vi 25 (Oldham Papers).
36. Lord Altrincham, *Kenya's opportunity*, London, Faber, 1955, p. 34.
37. Discussed above, p. 60.
38. Coryndon to Henn, 5 v 24 (Henn Papers).
39. Sir James Grigg, *Imperial policy in East Africa*, Confidential Memorandum for the Conference of Governors, London, 1927, p. 30 (Walker Papers).
40. *Future policy in regard to Eastern Africa*, Cmd. 2904 of 1927.
41. Kenya, *Report of the Agricultural Commission*, 1929, pp. 2–5.

42. G. Bennett, *Kenya, a political history*, London, O.U.P., 1964, p. 89.

43. Cf. references given in note 45 to Chapter 1 above.

44. Cf. Passfield Papers, London School of Economics.

45. Joint Select Committee, vol. I, p. 31.

46. Dilley, *op. cit.*, pp. 213–38; W. McGregor Ross, *Kenya from within*, London, Allen & Unwin, 1927, pp. 145–66.

47. Discussed in N. Leys, *A last chance in Kenya*, London, Hogarth Press, 1931.

48. Settler views in this and other fields are extensively set out in the report of the local *Economic commission*, 1919.

49. *Despatch . . . relating to native labour . . .*, Cmd. 873 of 1920, p. 3.

50. Cited in *Despatch, op. cit.*, pp. 6–7.

51. House of Commons, *Debates*, 23 ii 20, v. 125, c. 1688.

52. Cf. McGregor Ross, *op. cit.*, pp. 106–7.

53. *Despatch, op. cit.*, pp. 8–11.

54. Huxley, Amery and Milner on the one hand, Wedgwood and Cavendish Bentinck, a Tory M.P., on the other.

55. *Despatch, op. cit.*, p. 12.

56. Cited in Dilley, *op. cit.*, p. 226.

57. House of Lords, *Debates*, 14 vii 20, v. 41, c. 136.

58. House of Commons, *Debates*, 26 ii 20, v. 125, c. 1891.

59. He left for London for an operation late in 1919 (Huxley, *op. cit.*, p. 69), and was there in April (House of Commons, *Debates*, 26 iv 20, v. 128, c. 954).

60. House of Commons, *Debates*, 26 iv 20, v. 128, c. 955.

61. House of Lords, *Debates*, 14 vii 20, v. 41, c. 155.

62. *Despatch, op. cit.*, pp. 3–7.

63. House of Commons, *Debates*, 14 vii 21, v. 144, c. 1566–9 and c. 1590–1.

64. Cmd. 1509 of 1921.

65. Cf. Cmd. 2464 of 1925.

66. Kenya, Native Affairs Department, *Annual Report*, 1931, p. 97.

67. Provincial Commissioner Nyanza to Chief Native Commissioner, 30 xii 25 (Nyanza Province Archives, 62/11, 30 xii 25). Thanks to John Lonsdale for material from this source.

68. Chief Native Commissioner's confidential evidence to the Joint Select Committee (Passfield Papers).

69. Cf. on this issue esp. Dilley, *op. cit.*, pp. 92–5; McGregor Ross, *op. cit.*, pp. 154–62; *Report of the Commission . . . on the financial position . . . in Kenya* (Pim Report), pp. 29–33.

70. House of Lords, *Debates*, 10 v 22, v. 50, c. 354 ff.; House of Commons, *Debates*, 9 iii 21, v. 139, c. 479; 14 vii 21, v. 144, c. 1570; 4 vii 22, v. 156, c. 248–50.

71. *Report of the Commission . . . on the financial position . . . in Kenya* (Pim Report) p. 30.

72. Dilley, *op. cit.*, p. 89.

73. *Ibid.*

74. Kenya Legislative Council, *Debates*, 1926, vol. I, p. 50.

75. Confidential evidence to the Joint Select Committee (Passfield Papers).

76. *Report of the Commission . . . on the financial position . . . in Kenya* (Pim Report), p. 167.

77. *Ibid.*, p. 163.

78. House of Commons, *Debates*, 4 vii 22, v. 156, c. 458–60.
79. *Op. cit.*, p. 175.
80. Kenya, *Report of the economic commission*, 1919, p. 19.
81. H. Fearn, *An African economy*, London, O.U.P., 1961, p. 68.
82. Notebook, *op. cit.*, 16 iii 23.
83. Native Affairs Department, *Annual Report*, 1925, pp. 42–7.
84. Kenya, *Annual Report*, 1930, p. 7.
85. Native Affairs Dept., *Annual Report*, 1932, p. 2.
86. D.C. South Kavirondo to P.C. Nyanza, 12 xii 34, Administrative archives, 37/1/2: 32A.
87. Correspondence with Passfield in the Passfield Papers.
88. Confidential memoranda, no. 44, 68A, 74, 82, 84 (Passfield Papers).
89. Confidential evidence, Joint Select Committee (Passfield Papers).
90. House of Commons, *Debates*, 4 vii 21, v. 156, c. 277 ff.
91. Cmd. 4093 of 1932, pp. 26–7.
92. *Ibid.*, p. 27.
93. *Ibid.*, p. 38.
94. Cmd. 3573 of 1930, p. 14.
95. Wilson (Permanent Secretary, Colonial Office) to Grigg, 1 v 30 (Altrincham Papers).
96. Colonial Office memorandum, 2 xii 30 (Passfield Papers).
97. Bennett, *op. cit.*, pp. 79–86.
98. J.E.A.B., *Annual Report*, 1932, 1933.
99. *Proceedings of the Governors' Conference*, February 1933, pp. 16–17.
100. *Report of the Commission . . . on the financial position . . . in Kenya* (Pim Report), pp. 136–7.
101. *Ibid.*, pp. 106–8.
102. Wrigley, *op. cit.*, pp. 227–8.
103. The clearest picture can be obtained from the endpapers map in the *Report of the Kenya Land Commission, op. cit.*
104. Fearn, *op. cit.*, p. 155.
105. Cf. House of Commons, *Debates*, 25 ii 24, v. 170, c. 191; Kenya Legislative Council, *Debate*, 1927, vol. II, pp. 627–32.
106. Kenya, *Railway Report*, 1931, p. 36.
107. Joint Select Committee, *op. cit.*, vol. II, qu. 3660.
108. *Ibid.*, qu. 4060.
109. *Ibid.*, qu. 7329, 7330.
110. *Ibid.*, qu. 7325.
111. Native Affairs Department, *Annual Report*, 1938, p. 75.
112. House of Commons, *Debates*, 5 vi 28, v. 218, c. 26–7.
113. Memo. no. 84 (Passfield Papers).
114. Bottomly to Grigg, 23 xi 27 (Altrincham Papers).
115. *Op. cit.*, p. 17.
116. Cf. Wrigley, *op. cit.*, p. 236.
117. G. Bennett, 'Settlers and politics in Kenya', V. T. Harlow and E. M. Chilver, *op. cit.*, vol. II, pp. 296–7.
118. Kenya Agriculture Dept., *Annual Report*, 1936, pt. I, pp. 8–9.
119. *Ibid.*, 1937, p. 13.
120. S. Milligan, *Inspection note on the Kenya cotton crop in November and December 1935*, pp. 1, 10, 12.

121. Kenya, *Annual Report*, 1923, p. 16.
122. Coryndon to Henn, 5 v 24 (Henn Papers).
123. E.C.G.C., *Report of the administrative council*, 1925, p. 8; W. H. Himbury, *Diary notes of a tour through Kenya* . . . , 1926, pp. 32, 39, 44–5.
124. Henn to Denham, 22 x 28 (Henn Papers).
125. Denham to Henn, 16 xii 28 (Henn Papers).
126. Cf. Kenya, Native Affairs Department, *Annual Report*, 1932, p. 94; Huxley, *op. cit.* (note 24), p. 289; Leggett, evidence to Joint Select Committee, vol. II, qu. 3551; and J. W. Rowe, *The world's coffee*, London, H.M.S.O., 1963, Ch. V for an outline of the explosive development of African coffee once official discouragement was withdrawn.
127. Wrigley, *op. cit.* (note 4), p. 246.
128. Cf. Kenya, *Report of the Agricultural Commission*, 1929, pp. 34–5.
129. Cf. Bennett, *Colonial history of Kenya*, p. 64; P.C. Nyanza to Chief Native Commissioner, 9 xi 27 (Provincial archives, 3807/3/10 (7)).
130. *Ibid.*
131. Memo. to Hilton Young Commission, Central Archives, file 1/14/1, 12 iv 29.
132. Joint Select Committee, vol. II, qu. 970–5.
133. Acting Chief Native Commissioner to P.C. Nyanza, 21 iii 29, 3807/3/10 (20).
134. Discussed in Chapter 7.
135. House of Commons, *Debates*, 7 v 23, v. 163, c. 1899; 4 vi 24, v. 174, c. 1272; 23 vi 24, v. 175, c. 27.
136. J.E.A.B., Minutes, 3 ix 24.
137. East Africa Commission, *op. cit.*, p. 36.
138. J.E.A.B., Minutes, 4 xi 25 citing letter to C.O.
139. Memo. presented at conference with the C.O., 20 vii 26 (J.E.A.B. files).
140. Conference Minutes, 20 vii 26; also Cranworth to Mellersh 3 viii 26 (J.E.A.B. files).
141. *Op. cit.*, pp. 62–3.
142. Report, vol. I, p. 44.
143. For details see reports of the Departments of Native Affairs and Agriculture.
144. Cited in Wrigley, *op. cit.*, p. 245.
145. House of Commons, *Debates*, 1 vii 32, v. 267, c. 2163; 8 xi 33, v. 281, c. 164–6; and for the conditions of the concession, 6 xii 33, v. 283, c. 1632–3.
146. Gare to J.E.A.B., 22 ix 33 (J.E.A.B. files).
147. Minutes of a meeting, 18 vii 33 (J.E.A.B. files).
148. Gare to J.E.A.B., 22 ix 33 (J.E.A.B. files).
149. Minutes of interview, 2 xi 33 (J.E.A.B. files).
150. Archer to Henn, 8 iv 34 (Henn Papers).

7

Uganda and Tanganyika – Peasants Predominant

We must now consider the two territories in the region where peasant interests were to remain paramount and where the basis for the cash economy was to be created by transferring a part of the subsistence to the cash sector but leaving the greater part of the pre-colonial system of production and social control unchanged in the short term at least. In both of these cases the decision to allow the peasantry the greater part of the developmental resources was not an automatic one. In Uganda a great deal of conflict developed both in the administration and in the economic sphere itself between the proponents of large-scale plantation agriculture and supporters of peasant production, and it was by no means certain until 1923 that the latter would win the almost total predominance which they were to enjoy thereafter. In Tanganyika, indeed, superficial observers might have assumed that development was quite capable of following the Kenyan path until the depression of the thirties, since the plantation and even the small-scale settler sector made an important contribution to production and one which could have been expected to grow provided the appropriate infrastructure – notably a railway into the south-western highlands – could be created. But in Tanganyika the commitment laid down in the 1923 White Paper on Kenya was in fact put into effect – planters and peasantry existed side by side, but the interests of the latter were preferred when they conflicted with the former. The result, as I will attempt to show in the rest of this chapter, was to make it impossible for settlement to grow except in certain narrow and restricted spheres on the basis of plantation rather than settler enterprise. The material in the last chapter indicated the difficulties involved in creating an even marginally successful settler sector in Kenya in competition with the potential for peasant production inside the territory and with other export-oriented settler economies in the rest of the world. It suggested that given the conditions of the time peasant development was far easier and, if the word can be used, more 'natural' than the creation of a settler economy. The latter required massive administrative and economic injections on behalf of an economic structure which found it very difficult to compete effectively on world markets. The African peasantry, on the other hand, requiring very little in the way of capital and being prepared to work long hours for small returns, provided a valid base on which to establish and maintain the modest administrative and commercial superstructure which British colonialism imposed. Once the fundamental decision had been taken to prefer this system, policy tended to operate in a relatively untroubled environment – the intense conflicts which characterized the whole process of change in Kenya were eliminated and the administration was brought under very little direct pressure from groups either inside or outside the territory. This was true of both areas, although more so of Uganda than Tanganyika since the settler presence was better developed in Tanganyika.

UGANDA: PEASANTS DOMINANT

The Uganda case can be disposed of very quickly, more especially since this aspect of its development has been extensively described elsewhere.[1] Southern and Eastern Uganda, and notably the Kingdom of Buganda, were densely populated and effectively administered before the British arrival.[2] Buganda in particular had, during the nineteenth century, been able to extend its empire in part on the basis of its ability to maintain positive trading links with the outside world. Its relationship with the colonial power was therefore a relatively equal one, its terms enshrined in the Buganda Agreement which ensured that the territory would be a Protectorate rather than a Colony proper. Too much should not, however, be made of these constitutional details. As with all other British acquisitions, Uganda had to be made to earn its keep by producing agricultural exports. Once the railhead reached Kisumu on Lake Victoria the development of a steamer service opened up the hinterland to cash production. In 1902 the British Cotton Growing Association embarked on a campaign to encourage cotton growing in the Empire and its experts visited Uganda and persuaded the administration to attempt to establish the crop among the peasant farmers close enough to the transport system to grow it commercially. They also established the British East Africa Corporation, as an independent commercial operation, to establish processing and marketing facilities for the crop –

the firm of which Humphrey Leggett was to become chairman. This firm, together with the Uganda Company[3] (which was originally started by missionaries eager to encourage a 'legitimate trade' in the area and which operated in the same way), were therefore committed from the beginning to the encouragement of peasant production. The effective Baganda system of local administration also made it possible for a good road system to be established in the cotton-growing districts which connected them with the lake steamer service. In addition a railway was constructed before the War connecting Lake Victoria to the Victoria Nile at Namasagali, thus opening up a considerable area in the north of Busoga and in southern Teso to cotton growing as well. Thus by the end of the War Ugandan peasants in the south-centre and in the east were well established as cash-crop producers, production having reached 47,000 bales of 400 lb by 1919.

But this development was paralleled by active efforts emanating from certain sectors of the administration to establish an important plantation sector as well. No obstacles were placed in the way of prospective estate operations, but conditions were not favourable till 1906, when world rubber prices were very high and it seemed that rubber could be successfully cultivated in Uganda. Several estates were established from 1906 and acreage continued to increase until 1919.[4] After 1910 a rise in the world price of coffee induced a new expansion in settlement, taking the number of estates from twenty cultivating about 2,000 acres in 1911 to 135 cultivating 21,675 acres in 1915. During these years land was not a limiting factor on settlement. The Mabira Forest Rubber Company was given a lease of 100 square miles, and although the Government could not alienate land to settlers in Buganda they were free to purchase it freehold until 1916 and thereafter in leasehold. Between 1911 and 1921 a local committee chaired by Sir Morris Carter, Chief Justice in Uganda (and in 1934 of the 'neutral' Kenya Land Commission), investigated the availability of land for settlement in the four major districts where climatic conditions and potential availability of transport made expatriate agriculture possible. It concluded that no less than 80% of the available land in these areas could be alienated without damaging the interests of the indigenous populations.[5] By 1920 200 estates covered 126,000 acres, of which 36,000 were under cultivation. Although this figure was small by comparison with Kenya, it included a much larger percentage of 'the more intensely cultivated and valuable crops' than did non-African agriculture in

Kenya at this stage.[6] Before and during the War it was the Colonial Office which had restrained the local government's desire to give way to the demands of the more active proponents of settlement led by Carter.[7] But between 1919 and 1921 the sympathy in London for settlement reached its peak and in 1921 the Carter land recommendations, rejected in 1915, were accepted by Churchill at the Colonial Office.[8] This decision followed the work of a local Development Commission, which produced what was 'a planter's charter' which read 'like a caricature of the prejudices of white men in Africa',[9] and was complemented by a decision to set up a local Legislative Council which heavily represented expatriate and especially European interests.[10] Perhaps most important, between 1909 and 1922, compulsory labour was extensively used for public works, thus much reducing the competition for labour and therefore the price for the plantation sector.[11]

But all these concessions in the planters' favour operated in an environment in which a considerable commitment of resources had already been made to the peasant sector and in which the contribution which this sector made to revenue and trade was too important to allow it to be undermined as it was in Kenya. From the end of 1920 the planters' position was weakened by the same factors as those which affected Kenya – the revaluation of the local currency in 1920, and the fall in world prices at the end of that year. This was intensified in their case by the importance in their system of rubber, which collapsed totally, and by the fact that they discovered that Arabica coffee grown in the lower-lying areas where most of the plantations were located required very special cultivation, was otherwise susceptible to disease, and did not produce the highest quality crop. Further, their relative lack of political control at the centre, combined with the fact that Ugandan planters were unable to exploit the railway system and subsequently the customs union as the Kenyans were, limited their ability to have sufficient resources diverted in their direction to see them through the crisis. Settler weakness at this point was complemented by peasant strength, because the American cotton fields were infested with boll weevils in 1920 and the raw cotton price remained very high until 1925.* African production had always received considerable support in the Department of Agriculture and among the Provincial Administration and the effects of the crisis of the early twenties was to confirm their con-

* Cf. Ch. IV pp. 121–3 above.

fidence in the economic viability of the African peasant and the vulnerability of the whole estate sector. This attitude in Uganda was complemented in London by the influence of the textile industry and the campaign for Empire-grown cotton – Ugandan peasant producers were no doubt effectively spoken for at the Colonial Office by Humphrey Leggett, backed by the British East Africa Corporation and the London Chamber of Commerce. The Empire Cotton Growing Corporation took up Uganda as a major sphere of activity and devoted a considerable percentage of its resources to promoting the crop there after 1923. The cumulative effect of all of these events was to move official interest decisively away from the estate sector to the peasantry, and the acreage under plantation crops fell from 37,800 in 1920 to 31,700 in 1925. African cotton production, on the other hand, increased from 36,500 bales in 1919/20 to 196,000 in 1925, making it without any question the main base for the whole economic and administrative system. After 1923 this fact became accepted at all levels and the pattern of allocation of resources decisively favoured peasant production thereafter.

TANGANYIKA: PEASANTS PREDOMINANT

For the white visionaries of Africa Tanganyika was an area of crucial importance, representing as it did the means of connecting the Kenyan outpost with the stronger areas of settlement in the deep south. For Delamere:

> Tanganyika was the weak link in the chain of white settlement that he, following Rhodes and Smuts, wanted to see securely fastened down Africa's highland backbone from Lake Victoria to Rhodesia.[12]

Despite large areas where settled agriculture was not possible, Tanganyika contained a great deal of high land around the Kilimanjaro and Usambara Highlands in the north-east and in the south-western highlands around Iringa and Tukuyu close to the Northern Rhodesian border. The Germans had alienated almost two million acres, and nothing in the Mandate precluded further transfers of land or, for that matter, an active settlement policy on Kenyan lines.[13] But despite a much greater economic presence than developed in Uganda, the attempt to create a viable white farming community securely committed to the British Empire had clearly failed by the end of the thirties. By 1938 the European community numbered only 9,345; of these 4,054 were

British and 3,205 were Germans whose loyalty to the British system was questionable. In the same year British settlers controlled 788,000 acres of land, Germans 476,000 and Asians (against whom no Kenya-style discrimination was practised) 280,000. Unlike in Kenya, these landholdings were not heavily concentrated around the capital and provided with good communications, but were scattered across the country and were particularly isolated from Dar es Salaam and each other. Their contribution to the export economy was always significant, but never became overwhelming, as the following very approximate figures suggest:

TABLE XV

Tanganyika: Source of Agricultural Exports, 1923–37 (%)

	1923	*1925*	*1927*	*1929*	*1931*	*1933*	*1935*	*1937*
African	61	55	48	45	42	49	49	44
Sisal	25	26	40	45	49	40	40	50
Other Non-African	14	19	12	10	9	11	11	6

Source: Tanganyika, *Annual Reports*, and Department of Agriculture, *Annual Reports*, 1923–31. Cf. also Armitage Smith's estimate of African production worth £13,900,000 and non-African production worth £11,300,000 between 1921 and 1931. *Report . . . on a financial mission to Tanganyika*, Cmd. 4093 of 1932, p. 9.

Mineral production, accounting for 25% of all exports by the end of the thirties, was controlled by expatriates, but Africans would have supplied the local market for low-cost foodstuffs, thus expanding their share of total cash agricultural production to 50% or more. The figures again bring out their resilience in adverse market conditions, since their share of exports rose dramatically during the first half of the thirties. The overwhelming importance of sisal in the estate sector also points to a further significant difference between the Tanganyikan and the Kenyan patterns. Sisal required heavy capital outlays, was largely grown in dry areas not generally regarded as suitable for permanent settlement by Europeans, and was therefore conducted on plantation rather than small-scale settler lines.[14] A great deal of the capital involved came from abroad, although during the thirties when prices were very low some of this was taken over by local Asian entrepreneurs. The industry did not, in fact, make very heavy demands on the centre for assistance of the kind required to set up the small-scale temperate-climate foodstuff producers of Kenya, and its needs did not therefore create the kinds of political conflicts between non-African and African development which characterized that country during these years. During the twenties an attempt was made to set up this kind of small-scale development in Tanganyika, but its lack of success can be assessed from the limited contribution which all other expatriate activities were able to make to agricultural exports.

The reasons for this failure must again be looked for in the deployment of economic resources between expatriate and African sectors as well as in relation to the position of the Tanganyikan settlers in the international economy. With reference to the latter, it is evident that Tanganyika was in an even more precarious position than Kenya. It was 1925 before war damage was effectively repaired and the new administration fully established. This meant that little could be done to encourage settlement before that date, so that the whole effort had to be virtually confined to the years between 1925 and 1929 when market conditions were favourable. Equally important, the existence of the common market meant that Tanganyikan temperate-climate foodstuff producers had to compete on equal terms with their much better established northern neighbours[15] as well as with other producers on the world market. This fact virtually ruled out the possibility of an effective Tanganyikan industry in this sector and limited small-scale settlers to areas which could grow coffee, and subsequently tea. But equally important, these economic disadvantages were paralleled by an official policy commitment to African production which only partially recognized the legitimacy of the expatriate sector and which therefore tended to concentrate productive resources in the former rather than the latter.

From this point of view the critical decisions were taken during the twenties under the régimes of Sir Horace Byatt and Sir Donald Cameron. Both came in with experience of areas dominated by African production, Byatt from Somaliland and Cameron from Nigeria, where he had been strongly influenced by the Indirect Rule paternalism of Lugard and Clifford. Of the two Byatt was if anything the most single-mindedly committed to African development. Henn claimed that he 'realised (quite rightly) that the future of the country depended chiefly on native production', and carried this 'obsession' to the point of refusing either to see representative of 'the plantation industry' or to visit their estates.[16] His Administrative Officers shared this view, resolving at a conference in 1924 that the further encouragement of

non-African production should be opposed.[17] Legislation was enacted without discussion, and a Development Committee set up in
1924 was composed only of senior officials.[18] Agricultural Officers
were concentrated in African rather than European areas and attention concentrated on cotton growing. In 1925 it was admitted
that assistance to European coffee growers had been very limited,[19]
and in 1928 that little had been done for sisal. Local whites
strongly resented this treatment, northern settlers petitioned for
transfer to Kenya,[20] and unofficial representatives used the first
session of the Legislative Council set up under Cameron to air
their grievances.[21] Their feelings were especially strong with
regard to African coffee-growing and regulations relating to native
labour. The Chagga on Kilimanjaro were actively encouraged
after 1921 to grow Arabica coffee, sometimes in close proximity to
European plantations, by Dundas, the local District Commissioner.[22] This led to the request for secession, and to a request
to the J.E.A.B. to intervene on their behalf.[23] But Byatt refused to
give way and the J.E.A.B. to act, so that nothing was done when
the African industry was in its infancy and it might have been
possible to limit its spread. In 1924 local planters attempted to get
the administration to change the terms of a labour contract from
six months' to 180 days' labour, since the former did not meet the
needs of employers who were recruiting labour from considerable
distances. On this occasion the J.E.A.B. did take the matter up
with the Colonial Office, where they held a meeting with Byatt
himself in attendance. The latter stated that 'the first duty of the
Government was to the native', and that they should not be
absent from their homes long enough 'to be torn from their tribal
organizations'. He felt that they should be offered a 'bonus for
regular work' if planters wished to hold them, and the Colonial
Office official refused to accept a suggestion that the Government
should supervise recruitment,[24] a very different attitude from that
displayed in the north. During this period the major transport
development was the decision to build a line from Tabora to
Mwanza on Lake Victoria, to traverse an area of exclusively
African production.

Cameron's attitudes were not nearly so simple or clear-cut as
those of Byatt. Conditions were now favourable for settlement since
prices were high, restrictions on German landholdings had been
lifted in 1925, and the Kenya settlers had begun to take an
interest in the territory, especially in the development of the
south-western highlands. The arrival of the first Germans in the

second half of 1925 also led to an increased interest in London in the stimulation of British settlement – this being an important factor in the J.E.A.B.'s interest in the area. Cameron himself, although predominantly concerned with African interests, nevertheless accepted that expatriate enterprise could make a valid contribution to development provided certain conditions could be met. He quite consciously made the distinction between effectively-capitalized plantation industry operating in areas and crops which Africans could not yet finance and small-scale settlement. He was therefore prepared to encourage 'certain kinds of agricultural processes which European enterprise and capital can undertake but which are beyond the capacity of the African tribesman and will be . . . for a long time to come.'[25] He was not, however, prepared to support small-scale settlement or to allow any resources to be diverted from African production in order to make development of this kind possible. His attitude was thus completely opposed to that of Grigg, who was far more concerned with small-scale settlement because of the social and political advantages which he felt the creation of a community of this kind would produce. Cameron's attitude to expatriate production was complemented by an attitude to African development which placed political development, to be firmly based upon the evolution of indigenous forms, higher up the order of priorities than economic change. The indirect rule system was to give Africans 'a place in the political structure' and provide them with institutions which would ultimately allow them to 'stand by themselves as a part of the community'.[26] Writing to Oldham he said:

> I dislike and am somewhat alarmed by the present day attitude (reflected all through the [Ormsby-Gore] Report and, indeed, from every quarter) of regarding the native from the standpoint of what he can produce. I regard him from the standpoint of what we can and ought to do for him whether he can produce immediately or not. You cannot attempt to force him to produce as do the Belgians. You have got to teach him and develop him and the process is slow. The frankly material point of view from which the native is regarded at the moment is, to me, disappointing and disquieting.[27]

His policy, particularly during the opening years, was therefore characterized by a willingness to consider the demands of expatriate interests more sympathetically than his predecessors, but at the same time to attempt to initiate a programme of action designed to strengthen and, if need be, to create anew, effective 'indigenous' political structures at the local level.

With regard to settlement, Delamere in Kenya formed a company in May 1925 to promote this in Tanganyika with the princely capital of £6,000.[28] He organized a conference of such people from Kenya, Tanganyika, Nyasaland and Northern Rhodesia, which met in south-western Tanganyika in October that year. This passed resolutions calling for a more active policy to promote settlement there and especially for the extension of a railway into the area, which were then put to the Governors' Conference in January and 'formally endorsed'.[29] In London the J.E.A.B. accepted that the interests of the Tanganyikan settlers be taken care of by the three representatives of the Convention of Associations until they were more numerous,[30] and began to take an active interest in promotion towards the end of 1926. Soon after his arrival Cameron set up the Legislative Council, to which representatives of the various expatriate communities were nominated, and increased the speed of land alienation, opening up new areas in the north-east and making land available in the south-west for the first time. At this point he was reported to be on very friendly terms with Delamere,[31] but his policy was being held back by reservations in the Colonial Office.[32] In 1928 it was allowed to continue, and he appointed a Land Development Survey which was to work until 1933, determining all the areas where scarcity of population made it possible for settlement to take place. Towards the end of 1926 the J.E.A.B., in association with the Royal Colonial Institute and the London Chamber of Commerce, had taken the question up in response to their belief that the Germans were subsidizing settlement and trade as part of a programme designed to regain control.[33] Questions were asked in the Commons about the extent of German penetration, and it was decided that a Tanganyika Land Settlement Organization be set up on the general lines of the South African 1820 Memorial Settlers' Association.[34] A scheme to acquire a grant of 100,000 acres of land to be divided up was formulated and discussed with Cameron at the Colonial Office in February 1929. Here Cameron defended his land policy, and it was agreed that settlers would have to be men of means since Cameron claimed that otherwise money would have to be found to provide amenities for them which would require subsidies 'guaranteed by the Imperial Government'[35] – hardly the solution adopted in Kenya, where the African taxpayer was made to perform this function. But this scheme, along with serious hopes of evolving an effective settler presence in the area, disappeared with the Depression the following year, although it was probably the basis for the Chesham settlement scheme started in 1936.[36]

But these concessions took place within very narrow limits, limits which effectively precluded an evolution which would restrict the African contribution to the cash economy to wage labour. The Land Survey adopted very stringent standards, accepting that the existence of more than two African families per square mile precluded alienation,[37] while fairly stringent provisions were also adopted with regard to the occupation of land to preclude speculation.[38] The labour supply was apparently not a major problem for effective plantation operators during the period, since improved administration and health services made it possible to increase recruitment from remote districts, particularly in the south. The maximum contract period was increased from six to twelve months, and in 1926 Administrative officers received a circular which, if anything, favoured wage labour rather than peasant production.[39] But the use of the tax system to force labour out was strongly rejected, and the work of the Labour Department, founded in 1926, was not, as in Kenya, essentially concerned to keep Africans bound to their contracts, but to inspect conditions on private and public undertakings and to assist travellers on the major labour routes.[40] But most important, the encouragement of African cash production in the regions close to the main transport routes, and the reinvestment of the greater part of African taxation in African areas, tended to keep the price of labour high. Labour was available, but had to be recruited from great distances in areas too far from transportation for the local population to enter the export market independently; this, combined with pressure to maintain standards of housing and conditions, must have limited the ability of undercapitalized operators to acquire and maintain their labour force.

The predisposition towards African production can be traced in other areas as well during these years. Transport investment continued, on balance, to favour African rather than European production, with the bulk of railway building going into the former areas, although with a slight tendency for road building to favour the latter. The extension from Tabora on the main line was completed all the way to Mwanza on Lake Victoria, a total of 236 miles, which was to provide the basis for a large expansion in cotton production from the thirties onwards. A ninety-three-mile branch from Manyoni, also on the main line to Kinyangiri (subsequently torn up as uneconomic), was built to stimulate peasant production. To balance this the Northern Line was extended 54·5 miles from Moshi to Arusha, a predominantly settler area. In terms of capital development, the railway programme accounted for £3,592,000, on roads for only £323,000, under the East African Guaranteed Loan.[41] In this area, in fact, most controversy surrounded the proposal to extend the Central Line to the south-west and ultimately to connect it with the Northern Rhodesian system. Three possible routes were surveyed, one favouring settlement, one African production and the third a compromise between the two.[42] Cameron's final recommendation strongly favoured the African area, despite the fact that this would disappoint the Iringa settlers and those who had 'formed extravagant ideas with regard to the Southern Highlands'.[43] The debate, in any event, turned out to be academic, since the project was shelved after the Depression and only effectively reactivated in the sixties in very different circumstances.

With regard to finance, the tax structure was much more directly biased in favour of Africans than that in Kenya. Twenty-five per cent of the Poll Tax was retained by African Local Councils, which used this to provide local health, educational, and transport services.[44] Tariff policy was gradually integrated with that of Kenya and Uganda until the full customs union was created in 1927.[45] The provision of central services, heavily biased in the direction of stimulating peasant production under Byatt, was modified in the settlers' favour, but not fundamentally changed. In agriculture the first Agricultural Officers were appointed to assist settler production in both the north and the south-west, while four primarily expatriate-oriented projects were proposed for Colonial Development Fund assistance. But these changes occurred during a period of rapidly rising income when departmental expenditure increased from £30,273 in 1925/6, to £90,744, and the number of European staff from 25 in 1926 to 56 in 1930. The Department still claimed that it was doing virtually nothing for the sisal industry and in 1930/1 that £38,474 of its expenditure went into the African sector, £22,436 was indivisible, and only £3,053 went directly to the non-African sector.[46] Again, when prices failed efforts were made to secure special help for estate agriculture both in London and in Dar es Salaam. But on sisal the Colonial Office stated that 'there was no possibility of Government entertaining any question of subsidy at all';[47] while Symes, Cameron's successor, claimed that the failure to give assistance was because they 'could not afford to subsidise any one branch of agriculture or class of cultivators at the expense of the rest'.[48] Research facilities were established for coffee and sisal through the Colonial Development Fund, but taxation was also increased through the Non-Native Poll Tax Ordinance, despite strong unofficial opposition.

During Cameron's period his concern with political rather than economic change in the African areas led to a concentration of effort on the evolution of viable local government structures rather than on a massive expansion in cash-crop production. But this priority nevertheless required that Africans have firm rights to land and an equitable share of the revenue and economic services provided by the centre. With regard to land rights Cameron evidently felt that the territory was firmly committed to a policy of African paramountcy since he could write to Oldham in 1928:

> ... if I left Tanganyika tomorrow and my successor endeavoured to alienate land to non-native use which political officers considered should not be alienated there would be sufficient strength in the Administrative Service to prevent a Governor from transgressing in this manner.[49]

And the whole thrust of his policy with regard to taxation and services tended to increase the ability of local councils to provide the social and economic infrastructure necessary for development. His policy received strong support from the Tanganyikan African representatives to the Joint Select Committee, who also strongly criticized the land policies in Kenya and Uganda.[50] He had strong links with the humanitarian lobby in England, and this group rarely raised Tanganyikan issues in Parliament, presumably because they approved of his overall approach. The Colonial Office, too, must have approved of what he was doing since it allowed him a completely free hand in evolving the indirect rule system.[51] This stress on infrastructure, and the relatively cautious attitude adopted to the need to stimulate actual cash-crop production, may have been partially responsible for the relatively slow growth in African exports during this period, which, it will be recalled, fell as an absolute proportion of all exports. Cotton production stagnated, 25,212 bales being produced in 1925 and only 20,556 in 1930. During these years the work of the Empire Cotton Growing Corporation was suspended in the territory because of a failure to agree on policy with the two Governors. Probably equally responsible for the low production, however, was the diversion of manpower to extensive railway and road building in Lake Province, the main cotton-growing area, and the low prices prevailing on the world market from 1926. The latter were said to have led many growers to have left cotton unpicked in 1927 and to have limited acreages in 1928.[52]

Coffee, the other main African cash crop, remained a political issue. No questions were ever raised about African production of Robusta coffee in Bukoba on the western shore of Lake Victoria, which grew steadily until 1935. But Arabica production on Kilimanjaro remained at issue and the administration showed some willingness to tighten up on African growers. By 1925 it had decided that growing should be discouraged rather than encouraged, because the crop was a precarious one and growers depended upon it too much; further, that they would probably not be able to implement the regulations which would soon have to be introduced to limit disease.[53] The J.E.A.B., at the request of Kenya and Kilimanjaro settlers, continued to press the Colonial Office for limitations in 1926 and 1927. In 1926 Ormsby-Gore told them that '7,000 natives were cultivating 1,250,000 trees', that they were well supervised and that 'the Colonial Office were not justified in stopping this flourishing native trade'.[54] In September that year Cameron announced that he wished to 'discourage natives from growing coffee', but that he could not prohibit it and that where they wished to do so they should be assisted in growing it properly.[55] The following July he attended the J.E.A.B. Conference where Henn claimed that natives were growing coffee close to European estates and 'urged that the natives be definitely prohibited from growing Arabica coffee'. But Cameron claimed that any such legislation would be 'objectionable as it would be class legislation', that he wished to discourage further planting but that government had unquestionably to assist growers once they had started. He also believed that prohibition at Moshi would produce 'a movement to boycott native labour on white estates'. He did, however, accept a final resolution as follows:

> That the growing by natives of Arabica coffee in East Africa shall be confined as far as possible to the areas where it is already being grown and that any extensions be discouraged excepting in areas where no European coffee estates exist.[56]

Despite doubts Ormsby-Gore agreed to forward the discussion to the relevant local governments.[56] In June 1928 a Coffee Ordinance was passed requiring the registration of all plantations and coffee dealers, and empowering the Agricultural Department to inspect all plantations.[57] Subsequent regulations permitted strong action against diseased estates. One cannot establish how far this conservatism actually limited the extension of the crop into potential new areas – it must certainly have stopped the Agriculture Department from following a forward policy and may have slowed down extension to the more remote centres. On the other hand there is no sign that it limited the production of the established areas – African production of Arabica increased steadily, being 75 tons in 1925, 801 in 1930 and 1,595 (the effect of planting in 1928–31) in 1934.[58] Certainly nothing remotely approaching the attitudes so dominant in this field in Kenya was ever allowed to prevail at any point in Tanganyika.

Once more the Depression effectively ended the prospects of an economically viable expatriate sector on the land. Symes felt that the inability to extend any financial assistance to this sector meant that they could not anticipate any 'important expansion of settlement' until 'world conditions were more favourable'.[59] Without the railway, the south-west could never support anything other than large and specialized plantations, while the possibility that the territory might be transferred to Germany inhibited growth after 1936. At the same time African producers were demonstrating their usual resistance to economic depression, and all the administration's energies were devoted to persuading them to produce enough to offset falling prices and restore the territory's financial viability. Armitage-Smith strongly supported this view,[60] and after 1932 a 'grow more crops' campaign was initiated by the Agriculture Department, designed to increase African production.[61] The new conditions led to pressures from the centre of a kind of which Cameron would certainly not have approved. Local Chiefs, on whom the carefully nurtured Native Administrative system depended, were now expected to mobilize efforts to meet new agricultural targets, and this undermined their local standing. But whatever its effects upon the legitimacy of what were in any case very dubiously 'traditional' structures, the campaign certainly led to sharp increases in production, no doubt much assisted by the investment in administrative and economic infrastructure of the previous six years. African coffee production continued to expand and cotton now re-established itself. The Empire Cotton Growing Corporation was brought back into the territory, and production increased threefold, averaging 60,000 bales during the four years 1936–9.

What remained at the end of the decade, therefore, was an estate sector overwhelmingly based upon sisal with small-scale European farming on the Dominion model almost nowhere in evidence. Politically this community was divided and unable to exert any decisive pressure upon the administration either in Dar es Salaam or in London. The scale of sisal production tended to conceal the full implications of the economic base which had in fact already been created in the peasant sector; this, while suffering from all the disadvantages of colonial primary production, nevertheless provided a viable defence against distortions on the Kenyan pattern, which would have turned the African worker into an agricultural proletarian dependent on wages for cash and on his own small-holding for subsistence for his family, and for himself when too old to work. This pattern explains the inability of the expatriate community in the forties and fifties to exert any decisive impact upon the process of political change, and the very limited effect of their replacement in the agricultural sector after independence.

NOTES

1. Notably C. Wrigley, *Crops and wealth in Uganda*, Kampala, E.A.I.S.R. 1959; C. Ehrlich, 'The Uganda economy, 1903–1945' and R. C. Pratt, 'Administration and politics in Uganda, 1919–1945', both in V. T. Harlow & E. M. Chilver, *History of East Africa*, vol. II, Oxford, Clarendon Press, 1965.
2. Cf. R. Oliver (ed.), *History of East Africa*, vol. I, London, O.U.P., 1963.
3. Cf. C. Ehrlich, *The Uganda Company Ltd.*, Kampala, Uganda Co., 1953, for the official history.
4. C. Ehrlich, 'The Uganda economy', *op. cit.*, pp. 413, 432.
5. Discussed in Pratt, *op. cit.*, p. 477.
6. Wrigley, *op. cit.*, pp. 33–4.
7. Pratt, *op. cit.*, pp. 477 ff.
8. *Ibid.*, p. 481.
9. Ehrlich, *op. cit.*, p. 424.
10. Its composition and the nature of its influence are set out in G. Engholm, *Immigrant influences upon the development of policy in . . . Uganda, 1900–1952*, London Ph.D., 1967.
11. Cf. P. G. Powesland, *Economic policy and labour*, Kampala, E.A.I.S.R., 1957, pp. 18 ff.
12. E. Huxley, *White man's country*, *op. cit.*, p. 207.
13. B. T. Chidzero, *Tanganyika and international trusteeship*, London, O.U.P., 1961, pp. 357–62 for the terms of the Mandate.
14. Cf. K. Stahl, *The metropolitan organisation of British Colonial Trade*, London, Faber, 1951, pp. 180, 205, 257 ff., and Tanganyika, *Report of the Tanganyika Railway Commission*, 1930, p. 6.

15. Cf. Cameron's contributions to the 1930 Governors' Conference, *Proceedings*, *op. cit.*
16. Henn to Bottomley, 23 xi 24 (J.E.A.B. files).
17. Cf. Buell, *op. cit.*, vol. I, p. 491.
18. *Agricultural Report*, 1925–6, p. 3.
19. *Ibid.*, 1928–9, p. 3.
20. Discussed above, pp. 248–9.
21. *Proceedings*, 1st Session, 1926, p. 32.
22. Cf. Sir Charles Dundas, *African crossroads*, London, Macmillan, 1955, pp. 117–28.
23. J.E.A.B., Minutes, 3 ix 24.
24. J.E.A.B., Colonial Office Conference Minutes, 17 vi 24.
25. Sir D. Cameron, *My Tanganyika service*, London, Allen & Unwin, 1939, p. 39.
26. Tanganyika, Native Administration memoranda, *Principles of Native Administration*, pp. 2 and 3.
27. Cameron to Oldham, 26 vii 25 (Oldham Papers).
28. Huxley, *op. cit.* (note 12), pp. 207–8.
29. *Ibid.*, pp. 205–6.
30. J.E.A.B., Minutes, 6 i 26.
31. Cf. Cameron, *op. cit.*, pp. 37–8, 40–1; Huxley, *op. cit.*, p. 321.
32. Cameron to Grigg, 28 xii 25 (Altrincham Papers).
33. J.E.A.B., Minutes, 6 x 26, 6 iv 27, 4 v 27.
34. J.E.A.B., Minutes, 4 vii 28.
35. Conference Minutes, 27 ii 29.
36. Cf. C. Leubuscher, *Tanganyika territory*, London, O.U.P., 1944, pp. 33–6, 45.
37. *Reports of the Land Development Survey*, 1st to 5th, 1928–33.
38. Tanganyika, *Ordinances*, 1926, Appendix, pp. 16–18, 1927, pp. 90–100.
39. Cited in Buell, *op. cit.*, p. 553.
40. Cf. L. Mair, *Native policies in Africa*, pp. 143–50; and Tanganyika, *Report upon Labour in the Tanganyika Territory*, 1926, p. 15.
41. Tanganyika, *Annual Report*, 1931, pp. 37–8.
42. Cf. C. Gillman, 'A short history of the Tanganyika railways', *Tanganyika Notes and Records*, June 1942, no. 13, pp. 50–3; Tanganyika, *Report of the Railway Commission*, 1930; Hill, *op. cit.*, vol. II, p. 214.
43. Legislative Council, 5th Session, p. 1, & pp. 7–8.
44. Cf. *Report of the Commission ... on the Financial Position ... in Kenya* (Pim Report), pp. 106–8.
45. T. A. Kennedy, 'The East African Customs Union', in *Makerere Journal*, vol. 3, 1959.
46. Dept. of Agriculture, *Annual Report*, 1930, p. 2.
47. Report on a delegation to the Colonial Office, J.E.A.B., Minutes, 13 vii 31.
48. Legislative Council, 7th Session, p. 6.
49. Cameron to Oldham, 24 iii 28 (Oldham Papers).
50. Joint Select Committee, vol. II, qu. 4807/7.
51. Information from Mr Geoffrey Sayer, formerly Colonial Secretary, Tanganyika.
52. Empire Cotton Growing Corporation, *Report of the Advisory Council*, 1927 and 1928.
53. Buell, *op. cit.*, p. 494; *Annual Report*, 1925, p. 53.

54. Conference Minutes, 20 i 26.
55. Buell, *ibid.*
56. Conference Minutes, 13 vii 27.
57. *Ordinances*, 1928, pp. 112–17.
58. Agriculture, *Annual Reports.*
59. Legislative Council, 7th Session, p. 7.
60. Report, *op. cit.*, p. 9.
61. Agriculture, *Annual Report*, 1933, p. 15, and information derived from local records by Dr Ralph Austen.

PART IV

Secondary Economic Structures

8

Processing and Marketing – Oligopoly in Uganda

The material already presented gives some indication of the facilities created by the colonial system for the expansion of the agricultural export economy. Whatever its motivation, it can be argued that colonialism achieved this objective relatively efficiently in many parts of tropical Africa, and, where settlers were excluded, relatively equitably as well. Indeed, the whole case of the apologists for Britain's African record depends upon their achievements in the peasant-based systems, of which Uganda is a good example. Cranford Pratt's assessment is typical of a broad spectrum of this kind of opinion:

> Without a doubt the fact that African peasant agriculture was proving economically superior to foreign-owned plantations greatly increased the influence and strength of these [welfare-oriented] values. But this economic fact reinforced the values rather than created them. The trusteeship concern for the security, the development, and the welfare of Africans was no mere rationalization of an economic necessity. It was a strongly held conviction that was itself an important determinant of policy in Uganda.[1]

This view, which is often, as in this case, associated with some criticism of the limited provision made for educational and political development for the indigenous populations, is valid only when the process of change is considered from the perspectives of an essentially colonialist framework. These perspectives, outlined in the first three chapters, were simply concerned with the creation of the basis for primary export production; they were not concerned to facilitate the structural change needed to move on to higher levels of economic activity requiring the rapid expansion in the internal circulation of commodities and the introduction of progressively more complex forms of production and exchange. These attitudes, of course, perfectly explain the almost total absence of industrialization in most African economies at independence and also the failure to develop effective internal entrepreneurial classes and expanding markets for agricultural and fabricated commodities. But explanations which attribute this failure to the attitudes of the decision-makers are hardly sufficient; what is required is a detailed analysis of the mechanics of the processes involved. It is necessary to look at those areas of the economy where progress towards more complex and evolved forms of activity could have been expected to begin and to understand both the way in which policy tended to inhibit this change and the nature of the forces responsible for the decisions actually taken. This final section will thus attempt to do this, looking in this chapter at the organization of processing and marketing and in the next at the regulation of secondary industry.

The creation of facilities for processing and marketing cash crops was, like the provision of other infrastructure services already discussed, dictated by the requirements of the agricultural export economy. But whereas the changes introduced into the lives of producers by the decision to introduce cash crops into an otherwise subsistence-based system had relatively little impact upon life-style and outlook in the short run at least, actual involvement in the secondary services associated with marketing, processing, and ultimately exporting the crop meant a movement into a very different sphere of operations and one likely to make a very large difference both to the outlook and to the life chances of the individuals involved. Thus the organization of these secondary economic activities was of the greatest possible importance for the future development of the economy – to the extent that these made it possible for members of the indigenous population to move out of purely agricultural activities into trade they would also make it possible for individuals or groups to acquire the attitudes, skills and capital required for a subsequent move into processing and ultimately into simple manufacturing as well. Any tendency, on the other hand, to inhibit the freedom to move into this sector and appropriate some part of the surpluses which it generated would be likely to destroy the only avenue likely to be open to Africans to move out of an environment bounded by almost exclusively 'traditional' values and modes of operation into one which provided open-ended opportunities for upward mobility.

But this material is not only important because of its implications for structural change of this kind, it is also important for an understanding of the working of the agricultural economy itself. The organization of marketing and processing has a direct and significant impact upon the distribution of the income derived from cash-crop production. This income can be distributed in vastly different ways as between the various groups involved in the productive process, of which the farmers, the traders and processers, and the administration, are the most obvious. For our purposes here the main question will relate to the relative returns allocated to farmers and the commercial interests, an allocation which depended very directly upon the nature of the organization of the marketing system and hence upon the power of the state responsible for its regulation. The interests of farmers and merchants are complementary on one level – both depend for their success on the existence of a large and valuable crop – but antagonistic on the other, since each will attempt to maximize their share of the fixed income which the crop fetches on the world market. Our concern must therefore be with the extent to which the organization of the system tended to promote an efficient and low-cost commercial organization which maximized the returns to the growers, or, on the other hand, encouraged inefficiency or exploitation by failing to impose effective restraints upon the individuals and firms involved. And this problem, too, is more complex than it looks, because the actual interests involved were by no means homogeneous. Marketing required that many thousands of small parcels of produce be bought from small growers widely distributed and badly connected to commercial centres. Processing demanded that these be brought together in large enough amounts to justify quite sizeable investments in plant, while the firms which handled the crop on the world market required extended lines of credit and international contacts and information.

During the early phase of the processes to be described here the crop was bought from the grower by middlemen who were either the direct agents of the processer or, very often, independent entrepreneurs who sold to the highest bidder. Once processing facilities had expanded to provide for the requirements of the crop the possibility of competition between operators became a reality, and conflict of a very antagonistic kind could be expected to develop between them. This competition could be expected to take the form of a willingness by the processer to increase the price paid for unprocessed produce, a price likely to be paid in the first instance to the middleman or agent. But since it required very little investment to become a middleman – a bicycle and sufficient cash to pay for the first hundred pounds of produce would suffice – this was likely to be a very competitive field as well, and the grower could be expected to profit by being able to hold out for a larger share of the price. Thus the interests of high-cost processers stood in antagonistic contradiction to those of low-cost processers and to the middleman system in general, since the competition engendered by both could be expected in the long term to raise the price for their supplies of raw produce to levels which they could not afford to pay and remain in business. For them free competition meant death. For low-cost processers, on the other hand, the situation was more ambivalent. Under free competition they would have to pay high prices for their raw materials but they could expect continually increasing supplies because of their ability to force their competitors out. In the long term they might also expect to see competition reduced as a result of their success, although the possibility of new entrants would probably still serve to restrain gross exploitation of this situation. On the other hand, they could also benefit from a system which eliminated competition in the interests of the high-cost operators provided that they were allowed to stay in business on the same terms. In this case they would do less business but would expect very high profit margins, which would at least partially compensate for the limits imposed upon their right to compete.

This latter situation would, of course, be very much against the interests of a shadowy, but not by any means unreal, interest, namely that of the potential processers – those groups which might wish to enter the industry once they had accumulated the capital and the connections. Such groups, of which the African Co-operative Societies were ultimately to become the most powerful representatives, might expect to be able to move into an industry characterized by free competition provided that they had access to capital (and capital assets might be relatively cheap where numbers of high-cost producers were being forced out of business); they would, of course, be totally excluded from a system which confined access to those already established in the field. The middlemen and the growers, on the other hand, could be expected to benefit most from a system of free competition since this would give them maximum room within which to manoeuvre. Any tendency to limit the freedom of processers to compete among each other for supplies would reduce the middleman's ability to play one off against the other; this fact would in turn limit the producer's ability to extract optimum terms from the middleman.

Further, and with reference to the earlier discussion of the effects of the organization of this sector upon economic mobility, any limits upon the opportunities of middlemen were necessarily limits upon potentialities for upward mobility among the indigenous population, since it was at this level that they could expect to make their first beginnings. Any tendency to increase the costs of becoming a middleman – by reducing his sphere of action or increasing his costs through licences, special regulations and so on – would invariably have the greatest effect upon the poorest sector of that class where the bulk of the African operators would be likely to be found. Further, any tendency to limit competition among processers would inevitably increase the value of the assets of those already in business and correspondingly increase the costs of new entrants attempting to set themselves up. Since the early entrants were invariably expatriates – initially Europeans and subsequently Asians – this, too, could be expected to inhibit the upward mobility of potential African entrepreneurs.

This chapter will confine itself almost exclusively to the organization of the cotton industry in Uganda because this demonstrates very clearly the dominating forces and the outcomes of the colonial political process in this area of economic policy. The case shows the limits and the effects of colonialist paternalism in the name of 'trusteeship', a trusteeship which drew some of its inspiration from a concern for the welfare of Africans, but a great deal more from a concern for the welfare of established, high-cost British and to a lesser degree Asian capitalists. But this story could be repeated for virtually every significant crop and every colony and it is therefore more than an account of an isolated phenomenon.[2] The impact of the kind of thinking manifested in this field made itself felt across the whole of tropical Africa and has had incalculable effects upon the development of entrepreneurship and the accumulation of indigenous sources of capital. It is to the effects of central policies in this sphere, more than any other, that the failures of indigenous entrepreneurship are to be attributed, not to the prevalence of supposedly 'traditional' beliefs and practices inhibiting the emergence of 'achievement orientation' and private accumulation. In the rest of the chapter the Ugandan cotton industry will therefore be considered in some detail and brief reference will then be made to similar experiences in other sectors and colonies.

During the initial stages of cotton development in Uganda the primary problem facing the administration was to induce private enterprise to establish processing facilities in new areas and thereby enable growers to find a market for their crop. This function tended to be performed by British companies whose interests were not exclusively commercial – the Uganda Company had its origins in missionary initiatives, and the British East Africa Corporation and the British Cotton Growing Association itself derived theirs from the British concern to stimulate cotton growing in the Empire. To encourage the establishment of ginnery facilities in remote areas the Government laid down that in up-country areas there would be buying centres at which the ginner had the sole buying rights, and further, that no other buying post would be set up within a five-mile radius. At the same time, after 1913 central marketing places were set up where buying was to be conducted under official supervision although limits were not imposed upon the numbers of buyers who could take part. This system operated across the Eastern Province but was not extended to Buganda, which was still the most important growing area. But the rapid expansion in the crop which began to gather momentum towards the end of the War, combined with a shift in external markets from Britain to India, led to a rapid growth in the provision of ginning facilities and an expansion in the scale of Asian participation both in processing and in buying. The number of ginneries expanded from nineteen in 1916 to 155 in 1925, of which more than 100 were owned by Asians. Some of these belonged to large Indian firms with considerable assets in India itself, like Narandas Rajaram & Co.; a great many others belonged to small operators who may well have originally made their money out of operating as middlemen. The three main British firms owned thirty-two ginneries at this point and their position was strongly threatened by this intrusion of entre-preneurs prepared to accept low incomes and to work long hours in order to fight their way into the industry. British costs and standards of efficiency were determined by conditions in the metropolis: managers had to have British levels of pay and inducements which included regular home leaves and facilities for boarding their children at expensive public schools; they were necessarily 'unable or unwilling to accept living standards which could be endured by their Indian rivals'.[3] The intensity of the contradiction between the interests of these two groups was heightened by the fact that this growth in the provision of facilities far exceeded the growth in the crop itself. The fact that fixed costs made up so large a proportion of total costs meant that profits depended very heavily on throughput. Any failure to acquire sufficient raw material to process would immediately threaten the viability of the enterprise, whereas the costs of expanding output would be low and the corresponding rewards very high. The existence of surplus capacity therefore meant that someone would have to suffer: the political question to be answered during the twenties and early thirties was, who was this going to be?

By the start of the 1920s the dimensions of the problem had already become evident. There was already more ginnery capacity than cotton, and itinerant middlemen travelled from grower to grower in Baganda bargaining for supplies, and in turn sold to the ginner prepared to pay the highest price for raw cotton. In the Eastern Province the controlled markets reduced this freedom somewhat, but they did not change the basis of the system, so that the less efficient firms had now to look around for some means of limiting competition if they were going to be able to stay in business. In 1919, when Liverpool prices had shown signs of falling, the Uganda Company had still been able to form a cartel with the two other major British companies in the field:

> for co-operation and control of prices, so far as this could be secured in districts where the Companies might be competitors in buying cotton.[4]

A similar arrangement was attempted at the end of 1920, when prices again showed signs of falling, but on this occasion the local administration entered the field and bought directly since it feared that a shortage of buyers might lead farmers to leave cotton unpicked.[5] The administration had its supplies ginned by the British East Africa Corporation and 'an Indian firm', and this led the Uganda Company and the Uganda Cotton and Buying Company to protest to the Colonial Office.[6] But by 1921 the growth in facilities ruled out the possibility of combinations between the British firms alone; the problem was now how to stop new entrants in the field and how to limit competition between those who were already established. These two tasks, essentially political because they could only be carried out with the backing of the State, were to be achieved by 1933–4 and were thereby to produce a settlement which determined the shape of the industry, with minor modifications, until Independence.

Most of the actors involved in this particular conflict have already been specified – the ginners large and small, the Asian and African middlemen and buyers, the African growers. All of them were competing for access to the administration which had in its power to determine the conditions under which they would be allowed to operate on the market; but for this enterprise they had been equipped with vastly unequal weapons.

The large British ginning firms, although weaklings in the field of direct economic competition, were undoubtedly armed most effectively in the political sphere. Their British directors had direct access to the Colonial Office – Humphrey Leggett of the British East Africa Corporation was, as has already been said, the favoured adviser there in the early years of the twenties. Cotton interests were also represented on the Joint East Africa Board, but the firms themselves were in any event prestigious enough to be able to command direct access to the Colonial Office whenever they felt the need. And in Uganda the local managers of these firms were always among the most influential members of the local unofficial community and prominently represented on the Legislative Council.[7] The small ginners, on the other hand, and especially the Asians with limited capital working on a family basis, were unrepresented in London and much less closely connected to the authorities in Uganda, where in any event informal contacts between officials and high-status European unofficial persons were strong and exerted a powerful influence on policy. Ginners in Uganda were organized through the Uganda Cotton Ginners' Association, subsequently the Uganda Cotton Association, which tended to be dominated by the larger firms, both British and Indian, the British representatives being used to conduct negotiations with the administration.[8]

The middlemen, however, were certainly least effectively equipped for the political struggle. They were for the most part small-scale operators, often semi-literate and with limited command of English. Their work kept them out in the field while matters of high policy were being decided in the capital and they had low status in genteel society; hardly one of them can have crossed the doorstep of the Kampala or the Entebbe Clubs during the whole period. They had no connections in London, and indeed the interests which they represented would have seemed so insignificant that none of their Indian connections would have been of any use to them there. Further, the prevailing prejudice against traders and more especially against small traders among British administrators and humanitarian interests in general meant that the latter could not be expected to come to their rescue when they were threatened. The relationship between middleman and peasant, although probably in the long term a positive one for the peasant, was also characterized by a good deal of hostility, thus making it difficult for those who thought of themselves as representing African interests to take up the middleman's case.

African interests, again, were not represented at the centre with anything like the force and directness of those of the large ginners, but they had a good deal more leverage in this situation than the middlemen. Their primary resource was the fact that the whole political and economic superstructure depended upon their willingness to produce a cash crop, whereas they did not depend on this crop for anything more than marginal requirements – to pay taxes, buy clothes and other consumer goods. Since they could provide their subsistence needs from the non-cash sector they could afford to limit production if the rewards became too small. The administration could not afford to see this happen since its own income depended on the scale of export production, so it could never afford entirely to neglect the interests of the growers in its attempts to regulate the way their cotton was handled.

The administration operated in this struggle as much more than a neutral referee. On one level its primary responsibility was to create and maintain the legal and administrative framework within which commercial activity could take place, and hence to adjudicate between the competing private interests. But the struggle was not part of a game with clearly demarcated rules which could be applied impartially; for individual participants it was essentially an attempt to persuade the authorities to recognize and apply rules which would give them decisive advantages against their opponents, and the Government's attitudes to them therefore decisively affected the outcome. Taking into account the preceding analysis of the resources at the disposal of these participants, this meant that the struggle was an inherently unequal one – given the colonial political situation ginners, middlemen and farmers did not confront each other as equals but on terms of inequality determined by the degree to which the Government approved or disapproved of their activities and orientations. And this tendency to partiality was necessarily strengthened by the fact that the administration had direct interests of its own to further through its manipulation of the marketing system. Since cotton produced some 80% of its revenue the success of the crop determined the scale of the resources which it would have at its disposal: any decline in the value of the cotton crop was immediately reflected in a decline in official income, and once this reached what seemed to be critical levels, as in 1929–30, things could become very uncomfortable indeed. This insecurity was intensified by the fact that officials took a very low view of the economic intelligence of the average grower. It was, indeed, true that almost all of them were new to production for the world market (although not, of course, to production for internal 'traditional' markets), and many myths circulated about the supposed irrationality of peasant responses to economic incentives. They believed that African farmers would be unable to grasp the principles of modern agriculture and needed to be forced to adopt proper practices to avoid disease and ensure quality; also that any sharp reduction in price might lead them to withdraw from cash-crop production altogether. The Hilton Young Commission expressed the prevailing prejudice very exactly:

> Government intervention in trade is, of course, in some respects dangerous, but when a population of primitive natives is encouraged by the Government to grow crops for export an abnormal situation is created, and the Government cannot escape responsibility in the matter.[9]

This responsibility was largely delegated to the Department of Agriculture, which was imbued with this overall paternalism and expressed it in ways strongly influenced by its own pattern of recruitment and organization. The Department was made up almost exclusively of agriculturalists trained in scientific and technical matters but having little or no knowledge of economic or commercial issues, let alone those concerned with politics. This was strongly reinforced by the technical rather than commercial orientation of the Empire Cotton Growing Corporation, which exerted a great deal of direct influence in Uganda after 1923. These commitments led to an obsession with quality control, which they felt could only be safeguarded through a system of carefully regulated marketing which would make it impossible for low-grade cotton to find a buyer. They were therefore much more concerned to see that only high-grade cotton was able to secure a reasonable price than that the peasant received the highest possible rate of return for his efforts. These attitudes necessarily made the agricultural service the enemy of the itinerant middleman and of any system of unregulated competition. Their commercial naïveté led agriculturalists to ignore completely the advantages to the grower resulting from competition and to favour instead a controlled marketing system based upon the larger firms, which could be relied on to behave 'responsibly' with regard to questions of proper storage, quality and so on. This naïveté also led them to take the protestations of these firms at face value and to assume that they would return the advantages which they derived from controlled marketing to the peasant in the form of higher prices rather than to their managers and shareholders in the form of higher salaries and dividends. In this they were to be sadly mistaken.

The first stage of the struggle over marketing concerned the right to enter the ginning industry. Cotton rules introduced in 1918 had required that all ginneries be licensed, and by the middle of 1919 the Government had announced that where a district in the Eastern Province was adequately covered 'fresh applications for sites . . . will ordinarily be refused'.[10] But the Government still appeared to be more concerned to ensure adequate buying facilities than to protect the interests of established capital. By the end of 1921 competition for cotton was so strong that the Uganda Company complained of excessive prices to growers,[11] yet the following year the administration began to allow buying posts within the five-mile limit despite past undertakings that the ginner would be given a clear field.[12] Their Chairman complained to the Colonial Office, where he found the officials helpful but the Uganda Director of Agriculture not.[13] The Empire Cotton Growing Corporation and the British Cotton Growing Association were also unable to get action,[14] and in June 1923 the Uganda Company refused to consider a new ginnery site because of Indian and Japanese competition.[15] But these pressures were not entirely fruitless. Sir Geoffrey Archer, the new Governor, arrived in 1923, a man whose favourite occupation was shooting,[16] 'whose favourite approach to major problems was to hold a confidential round-table conference',[17] and who had been carefully briefed by the Chairman of the Uganda Company at a lunch attended by a Colonial Office official before his departure.[18] In August the ginners met to decide policy but were divided,[19] 'certain ginners', presumably the high-cost operators, were evidently now trying to persuade the administration to restrict buying.[20] At a conference in September the Director of Agriculture talked of bringing 'the cotton grower, and the actual cotton ginner as far as possible into direct contact', and suggested further limitations on markets and buying in the Eastern Province and the introduction of that system into Buganda[21] — all this, of course, would mean the end of the middleman and much reduced competition. The *Herald* (which was controlled by planting groups which had 'an interest in the sale and purchase of pirate ginneries'[22]) believed that ginners were asking for monopoly, and it published correspondence from Africans making clear their opposition to any change in the existing system.[23] In London the Uganda Company, the British Cotton Growing Association and the Empire Cotton Growing Corporation were involved in correspondence with the Colonial Office,[24] which was apparently sympathetic but unable to take action until the Governor had reported.[25]

In April 1924 a new policy was announced which established the basis for a major concession to the established firms. Using language which paid no regard to normal English usage, the policy statement declared that the Government intended to maintain 'free competition for the purchase of seed cotton', and simultaneously to prevent 'as far as possible, any excess of buying facilities in districts where free competition was already secured'. Although the Government had no intention of reducing 'middlemen's activities' nor of regulating prices, it confirmed the decision to extend the Eastern Province system over the whole country and to maintain the prohibition on competition within the five-mile radius around ginneries. It intended to pursue free competition by maintaining 'close Government control of the Cotton Industry . . . in the interests of all concerned', and set up a Cotton Control Board to advise the Governor on 'the position and number of central markets [and] applications for the erection of new ginneries'. And to ensure that the ginners should be made effective judges in their own cause three of the four official members of this body were ginners, and the fourth was the Kabaka of Buganda, who was expected to represent the growers.[26] According to Ehrlich, a middleman was added only after strong representations and despite the opposition of the big ginners,[27] although Engholm appears to deny this.[28] The decision to stop new building was found to be inadequate in law and the Government was unable to stop all new ginnery applications going through although it certainly did its best – the Cotton Board in fact turned down 210 applications at one meeting in 1925 alone.[29] The existence of various loopholes made it possible for new ginneries to be built until 1927, when power was finally taken to stop this altogether, with the closing tally at 197.[30]

The decision to stop further ginnery building represented an important victory for established capital since it ensured that the crop would now have to be shared out between those already in the field, and newcomers could not hope to exploit new areas of production by setting up facilities on the spot. It necessarily increased the capital value of existing assets since anyone who wished to move into the field would now have to pay not only for the physical assets but also for the licence to operate. But it did not by any means meet the needs of the weaker members of the community since capacity now exceeded production by so much that a great deal of room for competition remained. Between 1926 and 1931 world cotton prices and average cotton production declined sharply so that competition was intensified and the margin available to ginners was also cut. This situation could only be met by complete regulation of the market – all the ginners, collectively, could only stay in business by increasing their share of the ultimate selling price, and this could be achieved only by eliminating the share going to the middleman and reducing that going to the grower as well. In 1924 the Government was not prepared to assist in this process or to allow it to occur unofficially – the Uganda Company, for example, agreed that they would be unable to form a combination to prevent the 'inflation of prices' since the Government would step in again, as it had done in 1920, 'and offer inducements for the erection of further ginneries'.[31] But this attitude was to change decisively during the following decade as pressures for controlling the market increased both in Britain and East Africa.

In 1924 the Ormsby-Gore Commission had come out in favour of established capital – it opposed the 'excessive competition' resulting from the activities of middlemen in Buganda, it favoured the extension of ginnery licences only to firms able both to buy and to gin cotton, and it strongly opposed any 'free trade in ginneries' on the ground that 'too many ginneries would be erected and that persons would be attracted to this branch of the industry who have not sufficient capital to undertake it properly'.[32] In 1925 the report of a visiting expert from the Empire Cotton Growing Corporation said much the same thing, and this was reiterated to the Chief Secretary and Governor by the General Manager of the British Cotton Growing Association, who noted that the latter 'was pleased he had our support in this'.[33] Both the E.C.G.C. and the B.C.G.A. formally reiterated their demand for control,[34] while the Hilton Young Commission, also briefed by the Uganda Company before departure,[35] also supported official control and the then current growth of unofficial combination among ginners, provided that it was 'subjected to strict control by the Government, so as to ensure the grower gets a fair price'.[36] These views gained increasing support from the Department of Agriculture, which felt that pressure to buy too quickly had neutralized the Government's attempts to improve quality, and that the excessive number of ginneries was keeping ginning costs too high.[37] These beliefs were much strengthened by a change in control in March 1929, when Simpson, whose attitudes were ambiguous in this area, was replaced as Director by J. D. Tothill, whose support for the large ginners was much more whole-hearted.[38]

As official attitudes gradually became more favourable the big firms were able to make attempts to control the market more effectively. At the end of 1926 the Uganda Company again explored the possibility of establishing a buying combine, but this made no progress because of the intense competition then prevailing.[39] The following year, however, when they had to pay much higher prices for cotton in the unregulated Buganda and Western Provinces than in the 'efficiently' controlled Eastern Province, they opened negotiations to establish a buying combination in Buganda. The extent of the difference made by the nature of the buying system can be estimated from the fact that with 17s. their bank-even price, the Company paid growers an average of 11s. per cwt in the Eastern Province, more than 17s. in Buganda and 18s. in the Western Province.[40] The scheme was discussed with Gowers, the Governor, whose attitudes were apparently also more favourable to the ginners than those of his Director of Agriculture.[41] With his support a combination called the Buganda Seed Cotton Buying Association (B.S.C.B.A.) was established in November 1927, whose avowed intention was to 'eliminate buying competition between ginners and to eliminate intermediary buyers or middlemen'.[42] In public Gowers claimed that his support had only been given after he had been assured that the intention was not to lower prices to growers, but to raise them through more efficient organization as a result of the elimination of 'unrestricted and rather wild competition'.[43] In fact the work of the Association, hardly surprisingly, led to a reduction in prices in Buganda even in relation to those of the Eastern Province. The Department of Agriculture itself actually estimated that the growers in Buganda received £136,000 less for their crop than they would have done 'under normal competition'.[44] Gowers was fully aware of this fact since writing in the privacy of an official despatch six months before the public statement cited above he admitted that 'the direct result of these combinations was a deliberate depression of price'.[45]

The establishment of the B.S.C.B.A. led to an attempt by middlemen to create an organization to defend their interests, and to an intensification of African opposition to combinations,[46] some of which may well have been expressed in what the Government most feared, a reduction in planting. In West Nile, a recently opened area, cotton acreage fell from 8,000 to 100 after the activities of a buying association,[47] while in Buganda they expanded from 107,000 acres in 1923 to 197,500 in 1925, but then remained more or less constant around that figure until rapid expansion began again in 1931.[48] But despite fears of this kind Gowers was not prepared to return to open competition; instead he felt that the danger of reducing the price to the grower below the level at which it would be worth his while to cultivate could be overcome by 'the fixing of a minimum price by the Government'.[49] To consider this and the other questions raised by the new situation a local Commission was appointed, chaired once again by Chief Justice Sir William Morris Carter, whose work on behalf of special interests on the Uganda and Kenya Land Commissions has been noted in the preceding chapters.

Their deliberations, based upon evidence from officials, ginners, growers and middlemen, produced what could most accurately be described as the inefficient ginners' charter. It recommended the reorganization of the industry through the extension of combinations of ginners across the whole country, with membership to be legally enforced in any area where 80% of those involved agreed. It wanted the complete elimination of the middlemen and a reduction in the number of ginneries to increase efficiency; but whereas it advocated the establishment of a compensation fund to which Government, ginners and growers (sic) would contribute to ease the passing of redundant ginners, it made no such suggestions with respect to the middlemen, whose whole livelihood was to be destroyed. Its one concession to non-ginning interests was the recommendation that there be a fixed minimum price for cotton, but it also accepted that this be based on the need to allow the high-cost ginners to stay in business.[50]

The report now introduced a phase when the Government was definitely prepared to support reorganization through the basis of officially-assisted associations, but was still committed to a

minimum price and was not yet prepared to offer official 'legislative and financial assistance in the reorganizations suggested'.[51]
The growers, not unexpectedly, remained strongly opposed to the
whole direction which policy now seemed to be taking, and active
efforts were made to bring their feelings to the notice of the
Governor and the Secretary of State.[52] (It was to be of great
significance to future political development, in fact, that whereas
in Kenya articulate African opposition to colonialism was roused
through the effects of settler penetration on the land, in Uganda
it was initiated through the struggle against marketing and
processing monopolies.) The middlemen's position, needless to
say, was totally hostile to the report and its modifications, although
little notice appears to have been taken of their views. But at this
stage the ginners' position was ambiguous, and this delayed a final
resolution of the problem. The ginners in 1929 were not yet certain
that they would need much governmental assistance to secure
oligopoly and were sensitive to any possibility that this might in
any event only be forthcoming on terms which would not be
sufficiently attractive. The Carter Commission had been set up
not just in response to their needs, but also in an attempt to meet
the demands imposed by the need to keep African producers
active. They took the 'very greatest exception' to the Commission's criticism of prices paid to growers, and totally rejected
enforced redundancy of any kind even with compensation.[53] What
they did want was government action to stop the free movement
of cotton out of controlled areas into those where even limited
competition still existed. Simpson, in particular, had refused to
prevent Buganda growers from taking their cotton for sale to the
Eastern Province in order to avoid the controls exerted by the
B.S.C.B.A.[54] The ginners were prepared to accept the principle of
the minimum price, but they asserted that the provision made in
the report for their costs and profits in calculating this was much
too low. Their pressure was backed by active efforts in London by
the main firms organized by the Uganda Company.[55] The firms
could afford to take a strong line at the end of 1929 because the
Buganda operators had managed to maintain their profits at the
expense of middlemen and growers through the B.S.C.B.A., and
it was assumed that a similar organization would be set up in the
Eastern and Western Provinces as well without official assistance.
Most firms could therefore look forward to monopolistically
maintained prices through combination while the freeze on new
ginnery building ensured that newcomers would not be allowed

to break the ring. The Governor for his part accepted their position, stating that he did not wish to force 'reorganization or reforms on an entirely unwilling community', and that he was prepared to see 'little or no legislative intervention', 'provided the natives can be satisfied that their interests are being safeguarded by an entirely impartial body'.[56] The solution, to last only till 1933, was worked out at a conference in October whose 'impartiality' was guaranteed by its composition — it represented only members of the Cotton Associations, the Chamber of Commerce and the Government; African and middlemen's representatives were excluded.[57] Here the Governor stated that he thought combination should be made compulsory provided the ginners undertook to gin at 'a fair price'.[58] This view was not enforced. The idea of enforced redundancy was dropped (with it went any claim that the reorganization would actually rationalize the provision of facilities), and the principle of a minimum price was accepted, although again not legally enforced. But again, presumably with the need for 'impartiality' in mind, the ginners' belief that this should be lower than originally anticipated to allow them higher costs and profits was accepted, as well as the truly remarkable recommendation that its level should be fixed by a board consisting of four ginners and three officials. This Board produced recommendations which allowed 50% increases in management and inspection charges, higher travelling and transport costs, higher banking charges, and profits of 6 cents on a total cost of 39 cents.[59] Without providing legislative backing, this ginners' committee was set up to advise on minimum prices during the following season on 'an experimental basis'. The administration's total inability to understand the nature of the forces which it was dealing with (prejudiced observers might argue its complete cynicism over the matter) was indicated by the Chief Secretary's preface to the new table of costs in which he noted that if past prices were calculated on the basis of the figures which it contained it could be shown that 'ginners made heavy losses in years which are known to have been good years from their point of view'. But as was usual when colonial administrations were dealing with the demands of rapacious private interests, it was assumed that their behaviour could be improved by moral exhortation. He therefore asserted that the value of the exercise would be demonstrated by the extent to which the average price paid could 'exceed the minimum', and that this would also be a test of the effectiveness of the rationalization of the industry (i.e.

the elimination of competition), which should both 'maintain the price to the producer, while reducing the working expenses of the manufacturer'.[60] To back up this whole system of ginner-dominated marketing the Colonial Office was sounding out the Liverpool and London Chambers of Commerce on local proposals for legislatively-regulated buying, which the two Chambers were prepared to support.[61]

But the contingencies which made it possible for the ginners to envisage the maintenance of their own cartel system with no more than moral support from the Government for a price which guaranteed them all both comfortable costs and high profits ceased to operate in 1930. The crop was very small, owing to a combination of poor weather, disease and possibly a failure to plant because of hostility to buying associations. World prices were also very low, so that everyone's margins were cut. Faced with the prospect of drastically reduced throughput the new association failed to materialize in the Eastern Province, while the B.S.C.B.A. collapsed and competitive buying forced prices up from Shs. 12·50 to Shs. 20 per cwt.[62] The big companies made heavy losses and something clearly had to be done if they were to be kept in being. Between 1931 and 1933 competition for the crop continued, being intensified by growing use of lorry transport, which made it possible for middlemen to expand their sphere of operations both as buyers and as sellers. The gravity of the position can be assessed from the fact that the Uganda Company made losses in each of these years, a grand total of £62,000 on all of its operations, cotton ginning being the most important.[63] There is no reason to believe the other British companies fared any better, since the Uganda Company was the only one of them to increase its scale of operation over the whole period: the remainder all cut back very sharply.[64] Increased competition led the high-cost firms to press for regulation, increased use of motor transport intensified the Department of Agriculture's fears about the spread of disease and the possibility of a decline in quality.

These two pressures, arising out of the context of the official and unofficial discussion and action of the previous decade, culminated in the passage of the Cotton Zone Ordinance in 1933, which brought the Government even more directly into the marketing system to regulate competition on behalf of the ginning industry. The Ordinance divided the territory into fourteen zones from which raw cotton could not be removed for processing or sale, and laid down that all lorries to be used for carrying cotton would require a special licence. Although this was not included in the legislation, the Ordinance was intended by the Government to 'eliminate unnecessary competition among ginners',[65] and, once it was passed, official assistance was given to them to establish buying combinations in all the new zones.[66] The prohibition on the movement of cotton necessarily made these combinations far easier to sustain than had been the case in the past, and the moral pressure from the Government in their favour helped to maintain them for the rest of the period. These changes inevitably weakened the position of the middlemen, but the Ordinance worsened their position even further by laying down that a maximum charge be imposed by ginners when they ginned cotton on behalf of middlemen or growers. This was fixed at 10 cents per bale, although the middlemen claimed that they had previously only had to pay between $3\frac{1}{2}$ and 7 cents.[67] The ginners, in turn, agreed to insist on enforcing this 'maximum ginning charge', and, in order to discourage even this being allowed, to have 75% of it distributed 'among members [of the combinations]'.[68] The interests of the growers were supposedly safeguarded by the maintenance of a minimum price. The value of this exercise to them, of course, depended on the pressure which was brought on high-cost ginners in setting it. But in the hands of an administration committed to a policy designed to safeguard the position of established capital,[69] it became a means of ensuring that the price to the grower be kept low enough to ensure that everyone stay in business. The colonial system never allowed any commitment to competitive market theory to interfere with its desire to assist its friends — what was established here, as in many other areas, was a controlled system designed to safeguard those who had already invested their capital and to exclude newcomers who might interfere with their profits by introducing more efficient or aggressive methods. Far from being set in accordance with some notion of economic efficiency, the price which ginners would be made to pay was to be determined by a committee consisting of the Director of Agriculture and two ginners, which did not publish the basis on which it made its calculations.[70] After 1934 Africans were admitted to its deliberations as observers, but the whole question was so technical that apparently they could not 'understand the committee's work'.[71] The whole system seems to have been designed collaboratively by the large ginners which dominated the Uganda Cotton Association and the Department of Agriculture, with the results fully justifying the President of the U.C.A.'s claim:

During the past year, the Government has shown more willingness than ever to consult the Association on matters of importance before introducing Legislation and this co-operative spirit, which we heartily welcome, is nowhere shown more clearly than in the amendments which have been introduced into the Cotton Ordinance.[72]

The new system, therefore, imposed official restraints upon the free movement of cotton, officially encouraged (though not enforced) combinations among ginners (or 'pools') to control the prices paid to growers and to eliminate competition between themselves, placed official restraints upon the activities of middlemen which were strengthened by the ginners' hostility, and fixed minimum prices to growers to ensure that they did not reach levels so low as to discourage them from continuing production. During the rest of the thirties the crop expanded very rapidly, mainly as a result of strong official pressure imposed directly on the growers. The pool system worked with varying degrees of effectiveness in different parts of the country. Competition still had a tendency to break out between firms, but the degree of control exerted by the Government was apparently sufficient to keep the established firms in business. One may be certain that without it many more would have failed. Writing to Ponsonby of the J.E.A.B. and Uganda Company in 1939 about the effects of State intervention, Mitchell, the Governor, claimed quite rightly that 'the industry as at present constituted has only survived by not being left alone'.[73] Very fundamental changes had therefore been introduced into the system with which the twenties had been opened, changes which were to determine the organization of the post-war period, when the ginners were given an even more favourable deal. It remains to consider its impact upon each of the main groups involved in the economic system, and its general implications for further economic development in the light of the considerations set out at the start of the chapter.

For the Department of Agriculture and the ginners the system was an almost unqualified success. The limits on the movement of cotton made it easier to enforce quality standards and to control the distribution of seed and the spread of disease. The ginners, too, could now look forward to a much more secure and profitable life – high-cost ginners could hope to stay in business, low-cost operators to make super-profits. In 1934 the Uganda Company made a profit of £10,000 in the Eastern Province where a pool operated, but lost £1,200 in the Western Province (including Buganda) where 'competition was as fierce as ever and we had to pay an uneconomic price to get cotton'. Total Company losses were reduced from £16,000 in 1932/3 to £3,000 in 1933/4 and the manager hoped that the cotton legislation, which had 'greatly helped' the formation of the pools, would 'become permanent'.[74] The 1936 results were even more gratifying since the Company was able to declare an overall profit of £8,491, its first for eleven years. A special vote of thanks should have been accorded to the Government by the shareholders, since cotton had realized a profit of £21,263, 'largely due to increased buying and consequently lower costs, but more especially to the smooth working of the Pools'.[75] Cotton profits were £16,917 and £5,466 in the next two years, total profits £12,973 and £5,462.[76] But for the Government's efforts the Company would certainly have made losses during these years; had it not done so one can hardly see how it could have escaped bankruptcy after the losses of the previous decade. Thus far from contributing capital to Uganda from the outside during this period, this private company at least was provided with the profits required to stay in business through governmental intervention at the expense of both grower and middleman. Whatever the talk about the 'rationalization' of the industry, nothing at all was done to make it more efficient. Carter's suggestions for planned redundancy of surplus ginneries were rejected by a Committee of Enquiry in 1936, hardly surprisingly since this was largely representative of ginning interests.[77] A further Commission in 1938 called for such action in that year, but this led to pressures from England calling on the Government to leave the industry alone,[78] and nothing materialized till the post-war period.

For the middlemen, on the other hand, the new system meant gradual strangulation. The effects of the pool system combined with the enforcement of the maximum buying charge was to restrict their freedom of action to the point where their margins were entirely eroded. Officialdom had always regarded them with something close to aversion – the Director of Agriculture for example told the 1936 Committee that their activities were now redundant,[79] while the 1938 Commission noted that there were only forty-four independent operators left handling 2·7% of the crop,[80] and that 'no useful purpose would be served by their re-entry'.[81] What emerged to take their place was a more or less covert system of buying agents or 'touts' who worked for the ginners on a commission basis. With competition greatly reduced the grower had much less choice between competing outlets and it therefore became easier for the ginners' agents to give short weight without redress. 'Cheating' of growers, which undoubtedly was on a large scale, therefore became much easier, and this as much as anything else brought the whole system into disrepute with them and gave a major impetus to the co-operative movement in the post-war period.[82] Much more important, the elimination of the middleman system ended the possibility of Africans' penetrating the higher levels of the industry as independent operators. Many of them undoubtedly continued to operate as touts, but this was a role which tied them to the ginner and ensured that they would be unable to set themselves up in opposition to established expatriate enterprise. Further, governmental intervention had the effect of imposing an artificially high price on the acquisition of ginning facilities, for the reasons already discussed. The maintenance of guaranteed profits through the officially-supported pool system further inflated the price and correspondingly reduced the opportunities for upward mobility into the industry from below. Only one serious attempt was made by Africans to break into the closed circle during the period and this failed totally. In 1930 a group of Baganda arranged to buy themselves into a partnership with the Uganda Company. They committed themselves just before the breakdown of the Buganda Seed Cotton Buying Association, which was partly caused by the Uganda Company's decision to accept them. The arrangement was based upon the assumption that the Uganda Company would continue to provide the administrative structure for the new owners, and this, in turn, implied that they would have to retain the Company's cost structure, which made it uncompetitive with Asian firms in the free market. The collapse of the B.S.C.B.A. soon after the arrangement had been finalized introduced a period of intense competition, the new owners made heavy losses, and the venture collapsed with the Company having to attempt to extract what the Baganda owed to it through the courts.[83] Given the controls exerted over the industry the only way in which Africans could hope to move upward was by buying themselves into established firms in this way, and this was something that the most successful firms would never have considered at a price which any Africans could hope to afford. But had the Government allowed unsuccessful firms to go out of business new operators would have been able to take over their assets at knock-down prices and attempt to operate on a low cost basis. No doubt many would have failed, but at least there would have been some chance that some might have succeeded. As it was Africans were never able to begin to operate in this kind of way on a private enterprise basis and, as a result, the pressure to Africanize the processing sector was led by African co-operative rather than private enterprise when it did arise – a result which could hardly have been foreseen in the thirties, when the 1938 Commission still considered that they did not merit any special assistance.[84]

While a large part of the ginners' newly discovered profitability was secured at the expense of the middlemen, the remainder appears to have been derived from the growers. They, of course, could never be made entirely redundant, but they could be paid less provided that the administration put its best efforts behind campaigns to increase production – something which the ginners never tired of pressing for. Ginning output increased rapidly during the thirties as the crop virtually doubled, reaching a record figure of 418,000 bales in 1938. Throughput therefore increased, thereby reducing ginning costs. Although still low, world prices improved somewhat, this too making it possible for ginners to return a larger margin to the grower. Had the administration's assumption that increased 'rationalization' would lead ginners to return a larger percentage of the final price to the growers in the form of higher prices rather than to their owners in the form of higher profits been valid, there should have been a marked improvement in the growers' lot during these years. But according to Ramchandani the average Liverpool price increased by four shillings per 100 lb lint in the five years 1934–8 over the previous four, while the average payment to growers declined by 1·27 shillings per 100 lb raw cotton.[85] The profits cited by the Uganda Company earlier, which were probably a good deal less than those of many of their more efficient competitors, indicate very clearly who had won the political battle of the previous two decades. 'The trusteeship concern for the security, the development, and the welfare of Africans'[86] does not appear to have characterized the administration in this area of policy, where strongly entrenched and effectively organized British financial interests were able to take full advantage of their strength and the naïveté of many of its officials to secure special privileges at the expense of the other sectors of the industry.

For Uganda this case was the most important during the inter-war period, but it merely exemplified the attitudes which were to characterize policy in many other areas. Engholm's carefully documented study clearly shows this process at work in one sector after another, with political power being used to buttress insecure economic interests and thus limit competition and the prospects of new entrants.[87] Perhaps the most important of these cases were the controls introduced over coffee curing and marketing which limited the field to the larger firms; and, perhaps the most glaring case, that of groundnuts where A. Baumann and Company were given an exclusive buying licence through the Native Produce Marketing Ordinance, leading to the elimination of all the smaller competitors and almost certainly reducing the incentive to farmers to produce a potentially promising crop for the market.

Similar attitudes towards restrictionism and central control in the interests of established organizations prevailed in the other two territories. In Tanganyika it was illegal after 1921 to build new ginneries within a ten-mile radius of existing ones; in 1933 a zoning system similar to that in Uganda was introduced, the building of new ginneries prohibited and minimum prices to growers established.[88] In 1932 marketing legislation was enacted which made it possible to establish controlled markets and give exclusive trading licences to particular organizations. In this case the system was used to protect the interests of co-operatives as well as the private sector – Arabica coffee produced in Kilimanjaro region was handled by the Kilimanjaro Native Planters' Association, set up with administrative assistance in 1924. This became the Kilimanjaro Native Co-operative Union in 1932 and it was given a monopoly of coffee-buying in the region in 1937. A tobacco co-operative was given similar buying rights in Songea District in 1935. These events in Tanganyika were to point to the future in a very important respect since the African response to the limits imposed on them by the controlled marketing system was to establish co-operative organizations and eventually to use political power to eliminate the established private operators.

In Kenya the evolution of agricultural marketing and processing was heavily influenced by the presence of settler interests, and again by the disposition towards the use of central political authority to create monopolistic or oligopolistic systems. The role of the State in supporting the settlers' co-operative buying and processing agencies in temperate-climate foodstuffs – the Kenya Farmers' Association and the Kenya Co-operative Creameries – has already been discussed in Chapter 6. African cotton was controlled by regulations introduced after 1923 which limited new building and the purchase of raw cotton to the ginners and their agents. The Marketing of Native Produce Ordinance was passed in 1935 along the general lines of those passed already in the other two territories. This provided for the establishment of controlled marketing centres, the licensing of traders and the right to allocate companies exclusive buying rights for a given crop in a particular area. As in Uganda and Tanganyika it was strongly opposed by Asian trading interests, but imposed nevertheless. By the Second World War, for example, maize, legumes and sesame seed were controlled throughout the Coast, Nyanza and the Central Provinces, and the British American Tobacco Company had been given an exclusive buying licence for tobacco in the main producing areas.

These similarities can only be understood within the ideological and structural context of British colonialism at this period, the context briefly described in the first three chapters. The final outcome in economic terms was a control system based upon the State bureaucracy on the one hand and the large capitalist firm on the other. The paternalism of the bureaucracy combined with the economic self-interest of the large firm to create a system in which central power was used to guarantee the comfortable survival of the latter in exchange for the provision of various facilities – buying, selling and processing of one kind or another. Reliance upon these firms guaranteed stability and security; it ensured that the African grower would be confronted by agencies run in accordance with the same bureaucratic principles as the administration itself. It eliminated the activities of small operators who operated on competitive principles and in accordance with a code of behaviour which bureaucratic paternalism abhorred and which also undermined the profitability of the large expatriate firms. Equally important, any willingness to allow an unregulated system based upon small operators to flourish would inevitably have created openings for Africans to move out of their traditional agricultural pursuits and to become full members of the modern economic community. Should they have done this they would equally inevitably have moved out of the control of traditional authority and hence of the indirect rule system on which so much depended. This would have exposed the basic contradictions implicit in that system – if Africans moved out in sufficient numbers, if they were able to accumulate capital and establish an independent economic base, then the structure of assumptions which sustained the whole colonial system would be brought into question. This system required that Africans be allowed to develop so far and no further; the limits imposed upon their participation in non-agricultural sectors of the economy can be seen as an almost instinctive administrative reflex stimulated by the recognition of this fact. In this regard it is not necessary to be able to establish whether the new system was imposed simply in response to the avowedly self-interested pressures of capitalist interests, or out of some sincerely held desire to protect the peasants from the exploitative activities of 'unscrupulous middlemen'. The evidence to which I have had access on this point is incomplete – it simply leads to the unremarkable conclusion that both of these pressures were present and that some of the administrators higher up the system (for example Gowers and Mitchell in Uganda) were aware of the advantages which the system gave to the less efficient processers, but probably accepted that this was not too large a price to pay for the political and social advantages which the whole colonial scene derived from their presence. But this debate about motives is much less important than the debate about the ultimate implications of their actual behaviour upon the long-term developmental process:

> the many individual wills active in history for the most part produce results quite other than those intended – often quite the opposite; *their motives, therefore, in relation to the total result are likewise of only secondary importance.*[89]

The case studied here was no exception – a system introduced to rationalize a system of control and to eliminate competition and exploitation simply changed its nature and produced in the forties and fifties the material base on which the movement of nationalist protest in Uganda was to arise. This was essentially based upon grievances related to the whole system of agricultural marketing and control, which played a major part in producing the riots of 1949 and the political and economic agitation which later resulted in the formation of the Uganda National Congress by Ignatius Musazi.[90] Had a less restrictive system been allowed to develop the forms taken by subsequent political and economic movements would undoubtedly have been very different.

NOTES

1. R. C. Pratt, 'Administration and politics in Uganda', *op. cit.*, pp. 482–3.
2. Cf. for example W. K. Hancock's sophisticated account of marketing in West Africa in *Survey of British Commonwealth affairs*, vol. II, *Problems of economic policy*, London, O.U.P., 1940, vol. II, pp. 203 ff. Even this, however, is dominated by paternalist attitudes and based upon the supposed indispensability of the large British firm: cf. esp. p. 223.

3. C. Ehrlich, *The marketing of cotton in Uganda*, London Ph.D. thesis, 1958, p. 173.
4. Uganda Company, Minutes of meetings of Board of Directors, 22 i 19.
5. *Ibid.*, 1 xii 20, 15 xii 20; Dept. of Agriculture, *Annual Report*, 1920, p. 7; 1921, p. 7.
6. Uganda Company, Minutes, 1 vi 21, 22 vi 21, 26 vii 21, 7 ix 21.
7. For its composition cf. G. Engholm, *Immigrant influences upon . . . policy in . . . Uganda, 1900–1952*, London Ph.D. thesis, 1967, pp. 65, 214; this also contains a useful account of the evolution of policy in this area, pp. 74–87, 200–6.
8. Information from Mr Ramchandari of Delhi University, who had access to Cotton Association papers.
9. *Report of the Commission on Closer Union . . . in Eastern and Central Africa, op. cit.*, p. 61.
10. Uganda, *Government Gazette*, 1919, p. 256.
11. Minutes, 5 x 21.
12. *Ibid.*, 21 vi 22.
13. *Ibid.*, 5 vii 22, 19 vii 22.
14. Conference at the Colonial Office, cited in Uganda Company, Minutes, 6 ix 22; refusal noted 3 i 23.
15. Minutes, 19 vi 23.
16. Sir G. Archer, *Personal and historical memoirs of an East African administrator*, Edinburgh, Oliver and Boyd, 1963.
17. G. F. Engholm, *Immigrant influences on the development of policy in . . . Uganda . . . .* Ph.D. thesis, London, 1967, p. 445.
18. Minutes, 17 i 23.
19. *Uganda Herald*, 31 viii 23.
20. *Ibid.*, 7 ix 23.
21. *Ibid.*, 14 ix 23.
22. Engholm, *op. cit.*, p. 80.
23. *Uganda Herald*, 28 ix 23, 9 v 23 (letter from Young Baganda Association), 23 v 24.
24. Uganda Company, Minutes, 5 ix 23, 19 ix 23, 27 xi 23, 18 xii 23.
25. *Ibid.*, 2 x 23.
26. Uganda, *Cotton policy*, 1924.
27. *Op. cit.*, p. 170.
28. *Op. cit.*, p. 83.
29. Governor to Legislative Council, *Government Gazette*, 1929, p. 458.
30. For details, Engholm, *op. cit.*, pp. 78–81.
31. Uganda Company, Minutes, 21 x 24.
32. *East Africa Commission*, p. 144.
33. W. H. Himbury, *Diary notes [of a tour of] Kenya, Uganda, and Tanganyika*, 1926, p. 59, also p. 108.
34. Annual Reports, cited in Ehrlich, *op. cit.* (note 3), pp. 193, 194.
35. Uganda Company, Minutes, 20 xii 27.
36. Report, *op. cit.*, p. 61.
37. Cf. *Annual Reports*, 1925–7.
38. Engholm, *op. cit.*, pp. 84–6; Ehrlich, 'The Uganda economy', in *Oxford History of East Africa, op. cit.*, pp. 456–7.
39. Uganda Company, Minutes, 16 xi 26.

40. Uganda Company, Minutes, 1 iii 27, 6 iv 27, 18 v 27, 3 iv 27.
41. Engholm, *op. cit.*, p. 84.
42. Ehrlich, *op. cit.* (note 3), p. 187.
43. Speech to Legislative Council, 5 ix 29 (*Uganda Gazette*, 1929, p. 455).
44. Cited in Ehrlich, 'The Uganda economy', *op. cit.*, *History of East Africa*, p. 446.
45. Despatch no. 102, 22 iii 29; E.A.S.M.P. no. H. 51, Min. 9, cited in R. R. Ramchandani, *Asians' role in the cotton industry of Uganda*, Makerere College, Faculty of Agriculture, R.D.R. 20, 1966 (mimeo).
46. Ehrlich, *op. cit.*, p. 447; *Uganda Herald*, 8 ii 29; Dept. of Agriculture, *Annual Report*, 1928, p. 8.
47. Ehrlich, *ibid.*, p. 447.
48. Figures from Dept. of Agriculture, *Annual Reports*.
49. Speech to Legislative Council, *op. cit.*, p. 456.
50. Uganda, *Report of the Commission of Enquiry into the Cotton Industry of Uganda*, 1929. With regard to the question of the basis for fixing legitimate ginning costs cf. also Gowers' speech, *op. cit.*, p. 459.
51. *Government Gazette*, 1929, pp. 352–3.
52. Ehrlich, 'The Uganda economy', p. 450.
53. Unless otherwise stated, all statements from *Joint memorandum by the Uganda Cotton Association and the Buganda Seed Cotton Buying Association on the Report of the Commission of Enquiry into the Cotton Industry in Uganda*.
54. Engholm, *op. cit.*, pp. 84–5.
55. Uganda Company, Minutes, August and October, 1929.
56. Speech, *op. cit.*, p. 457.
57. Composition in Engholm, *op. cit.* (note 17), p. 87.
58. Details from *Uganda Herald*, 1 xi 29.
59. Figures from *Cotton Commission Report*, pp. 51–2 and *Supplement to the Report of the Cotton Commission*, 1929, pp. 6–7.
60. *Supplement to the Report of the Cotton Commission*, *op. cit.*, p. 1.
61. Colonial Office to London Chamber of Commerce, 1 v 30; Liverpool Chamber to London Chamber, 20 v 30 (J.E.A.B. files).
62. Ehrlich, 'The Uganda economy', *op. cit.*, p. 451.
63. Uganda Company, *Annual Report of the Directors*, 1930/1–1932/3 (Uganda Company Papers).
64. Uganda Company holdings increased from ten to fourteen ginneries, the five other firms declined from twenty-five to nine between 1925 and 1939.
65. Governor's statement, *Uganda Herald*, 16 v 34.
66. Dept. of Agriculture, *Annual Report*, 1933, p. 8.
67. Uganda, *Report of the Cotton Committee*, 1936, pp. 11–12.
68. Uganda Company, *Annual Report of the Managing Director*, 31 x 1938 (Uganda Company Papers).
69. For an elaborate defence of this position, cf. Hancock, *op. cit.* (note 2), p. 223.
70. *Report of the Cotton Committee*, 1936, p. 4.
71. Ehrlich, *The marketing of cotton*, p. 251.
72. President's Annual Report, cited in *Uganda Herald*, 1 xi 33.
73. Mitchell to Ponsonby, 3 viii 39 (J.E.A.B. files).
74. *Annual Report of the Managing Director*, 31 x 1934 (Uganda Co. Papers).
75. *Ibid.*, 31 x 36.

76. *Ibid.*, 31 viii 37, 31 viii 38.
77. *Op. cit.*, pp. 5, 14.
78. *Report of the Uganda Cotton Commission*, pp. 67–75; and Mitchell to Ponsonby, *op. cit.*, 3 viii 39 (J.E.A.B. files).
79. *Op. cit.*, p. 19.
80. *Op. cit.*, pp. 52–4.
81. *Ibid.*, p. 77.
82. Cf. E. A. Brett, 'Problems of co-operative development in Uganda', in R. Apthorpe, *Rural co-operatives and planned change in Africa*, Geneva, United Nations Research Institute for Social Development, 1970.
83. Details from Ehrlich, *The marketing of cotton*, pp. 260–2; Uganda Company Minutes, 8 i 30, 14 iii 30; *Uganda Herald*, 4 iv 30, 11 iv 30.
84. *Op. cit.*, pp. 78–9.
85. *Op. cit.*
86. Pratt, *op. cit.*, p. 482.
87. *Op. cit.*, esp. pp. 180–200.
88. J.E.A.B. records in 1932 and 1933 show very clearly the close links between representatives of the British firms and the Colonial Office in the formulation of this decision.
89. F. Engels, *Feuerbach and the end of classical German philosophy*, cited in G. Lukacs, *History and class consciousness*, p. 47. (Emphasis in the original.)
90. Cf. Engholm, *op. cit.*, pp. 410 ff.

9

Colonial Non-industrialization

The substantive section of this study now concludes with an examination of the relationship between the colonial system and the evolution of an indigenous industrial sector. Leaving aside the forms which such industrialization should take, it can nevertheless be argued that the success of a developmental effort can be measured in relation to its tendency to introduce long-term structural change in the direction of more complex and productive economic processes. In this respect it can be argued that the colonial tendency to create (at least in the region studied here) a new export-oriented primary producing sector was in itself a progressive step, in that this linked the producer to a more complex economic system and made possible a further development not possible before – the point (among others) made for example by Marx in his work on India, as well as by the whole historical tradition of apologists for the colonial system of which Hancock in the British school is probably still the most sophisticated representative. But this study has argued that the colonial system, while opening up this range of opportunities in African countries – and doing it in the East African case with a great deal of restraint, honesty and good-will absent in many other places – imposed requirements on the situation which made it impossible for this process of development to advance beyond a certain very limited point. Once the initial structural change from subsistence to cash production had been made, subsequent change tended to become purely quantitative, leading to an ever-widening extension of the area of cash-crop production, but to no significant changes in agricultural techno-logy, nor to the evolution of productive sectors not directly related to the extension of the primary exporting economy. On the most general level this fact, concretely manifested in the insignificant degrees of industrialization existing in the tropical African eco-nomics at independence, is explicable in terms of the interests and orientations which dominated colonial economic policy. But a statement at this level of generality is clearly inadequate, since it leaves unanswered the question whether secondary industry could possibly have developed in Africa during the colonial period (some have argued that the local market was too narrow), and secondly, gives no insight into the forms which the small amounts of industrialization which were allowed to develop actually assumed. In this regard, again, the use of the East African case is also a useful one, since it did, for special reasons not repeated in other parts of tropical Africa, begin to evolve a secondary industrial sector by the end of the thirties which was to provide the basis for a not insignificant post-war development in Kenya in particular. It therefore provides us with an arena in which to examine the dynamic factors which operated inside the colonial political process to inhibit some kinds of change and initiate others.

The East Africa of the twenties and the thirties did not provide the basis for an immediate industrial revolution – the internal market was limited to the cash income generated by a highly unproductive primary-export economy. Further, the fact that the surplus generated by this economy was largely controlled by the colonial bureaucracy committed to the maintenance of traditional values and structures through the indirect rule system, and by the large and generally expatriate marketing and processing firms, ensured that the capital required for an effective rural animation programme, which would revolutionize the agricultural base and lead to economic diversification, would not be forthcoming. But even within these limitations it cannot be argued that there was no base for industrialization in these countries at all. By the end of the 1920s the extension of the monetary economy was certainly wide enough to permit simple import substitution in articles of mass consumption – cotton textiles, boots and shoes, matches, etc. Secondly, there was no intrinsic reason why colonial industrialization should be determined exclusively by the potentialities of the internal market. Although the social and technological underdevelopment of these areas would have made it impossible for them to produce sophisticated products for the world market they probably had certain cost advantages for the production of lower-quality products requiring labour-intensive techniques. Most especially, they should have been well placed to submit their own raw products to increasingly complex levels of processing before export – by moving, in other words, from the export of raw materials to that of semi-manufactures like yarn and baler twine. Although the full details of this story would require access to documentation which was not available to me, sufficient evidence was available to give some indication of the general tendency of the various groups involved and of the outcome of their activities. I will first attempt to document the negative elements in the situation – which were certainly predominant during the whole period – and thereafter to describe and account for the positive initiatives which were allowed to develop.

On the general level it is easy to show that the outcome of the British desire for the evolution of colonial economies complementary to her own was a strong lack of interest in direct official action to stimulate industrialization – necessarily a key factor in the situation when the central role of direct State intervention in the economy during this period is taken into account. The work of the developmental agencies set up in the twenties reflected this attitude very exactly. The Empire Marketing Board gave no assistance to manufacturing and specifically limited itself to the 'marketing of Empire food and raw materials'.[1] The Colonial Development Advisory Committee placed no such limit on its actions but virtually ignored this sector. By March 1939 it had allocated just under £8 million, of which £151,000 was for industrial projects. Of this latter amount, however, only £23,000 or 0·3% of the total allocations had ever been spent:[2] £16,000 of this went to a meat processing plant for Tanganyika which had been set up to provide a market for surplus African stock endangering the fertility of the region.[3] It therefore bore no relation to any desire to encourage industrialization for its own sake. A further £6,747 of the £23,000 was accounted for by a sisal fibre-softening plant in Kenya which was characterized by special conditions to be discussed shortly. In the twenties and early thirties these negative attitudes were completely dominant in the colonial establishment, since the East African market was still dominated by British manufacturing exports and the import–export trade by British firms which survived by exchanging primary exports for British finished products. Conservative interests supported the development of this 'complementary' rather than 'competitive' economic system for the reasons already given. Humanitarian interests also tended to support this restrictive attitude out of a wholly sentimental desire to shelter African populations from the rigours of an industrial revolution and a more hard-headed desire to avoid the development of low-wage competition. At the risk of repetition it is worth quoting two clear statements of these positions which tended to characterize official policy in the metropolis throughout the period. Talking of the importance of developing the Colonies Cunliffe-Lister said in 1925:

> I am perfectly certain that it is most important to-day that those in this country who have money should invest that money not only where it may be that orders will be placed at once, but where it will mean bringing in trade which in the future will mean a complementary and not a conflicting trade. . . . Last year for example, or quite recently, the people of Uganda took from us between six thousand and seven thousand bicycles in six months. When Uganda is producing that cotton which in the long run Uganda will be able to produce, we shall not only be selling bicycles to them but Morris cars; therefore in the administration and development of these Colonies the duty of Administration and the interests of British industry march hand in hand.[4]

And Josiah Wedgwood on the other hand, spokesman for the humanitarian interests, could only put forward as an alternative the need to keep the African out of the modern economic process altogether:

> I think that the Government might even now see what can be done, with the help of Lancashire, to stop this drift towards using the black man as labourer. That is at the bottom of the whole business. Ultimately it may be that to pursue this policy will mean that you kill out the black race. . . . It is a frightful responsibility to try to impose a form of civilization which suits us best upon a savage people. Leave them alone, give them freedom, cease to try to press them into the labour market, whether by driving them off the land or by taxation.[5]

The effects of these attitudes are likely to be mainly invisible since potential entrepreneurs must have been made fully conscious of the lack of support which any attempts to break into this sector in the Colonies would be likely to receive. But it is possible to show something of the working of this policy with regard to the destruction of two potentially significant enterprises in Tanganyika, the first relating to a match factory intended to produce for the home market, the second to a sisal-twine industry hoping to produce for export.

In May 1928 Sir Humphrey Leggett told the J.E.A.B.:

> . . . that information had been received that Japanese interests were establishing a factory for the manufacture of matches in the Tanga district, which might result in the diminution of the public revenues of Uganda, Kenya and Tanganyika of £30,000 derived from existing import duties, and he suggested that the Colonial Office

should be recommended to institute a countervailing excise duty. It was agreed that Sir Humphrey Leggett should write to Mr. Amery on the subject and thereafter the Chairman would take an opportunity of following up the matter with the Colonial Office.[6]

Three months later Leggett reported that he had informed the Colonial Office and they:

> . . . had immediately cabled out these facts to the Tanganyika Government who it is hoped, will take action to protect their revenues. He pointed out that schemes of this sort might have serious results if carried out in the East African territories.[7]

The Company was informed in June of the Government's intention to impose an excise duty on local production which would be sufficient to cancel out completely the protective effects of the existing import revenue duty.[8] The decision was unanimously opposed by the unofficial members of the Legislative Council, whose leader said:

> If we are to accept it as a hard and fast principle that no industry can be allowed to establish itself without having to pay the full cost of Customs protection as it exists in this country today, we can never hope to establish local industry in this country, and what will our position be in the future if this is allowed to happen?[9]

In its defence the Government cited the need to safeguard the revenue, although this was hardly adequate since Kenya had already protected beer and cigarette manufacture by increasing the import tariff at the same time as it imposed an excise duty on local production for revenue purposes. It also claimed, apparently in all seriousness, that the decision had been motivated by the fact that British manufacturers had exported £350 worth of matches to Tanganyika in the first quarter of the year, and that the firm 'did not come to the Government first and ascertain what the attitude of the Government would be in the event of their establishing an industry'.[10] Presumably entrepreneurs wishing to follow this example would now realize both that official permission would be necessary before they could go into business, and that it would be refused. The match factory failed and the Government claimed that its costs were so high that it would not have been able to compete with imports either with or without an excise duty.[11]

The second case is even more significant because of the much greater potential implicit in colonial exports of simple processed commodities than in import substitution. Presumably in response to the very difficult market situation for sisal in the early thirties a group of sisal interests set up three factories to manufacture binder twine for export. Here they seemed to be in a strong position since the Imperial Preference system was supposed to guarantee them free access to the British and other Commonwealth markets. Production expanded very rapidly from 15,252 cwt in 1934 to 46,493 cwt in 1936.[12] In 1934 500 tons of twine were exported to Britain, and the Rope, Twine and Netmakers' Federation immediately approached the Colonial Office and threatened 'to put an end to the whole sisal agreement' recently negotiated which increased the minimum Empire content of binder twine imported to Britain from 25% to 50% to enable it to qualify for a 15% Empire preference.[13] Cunliffe-Lister fully supported the British manufacturers' position. After stressing the importance of the agreement on Empire content to East African producers he said:

> It is obviously an essential interest of the sisal producers to retain a market in the United Kingdom which will be not only secure but expanding. The retention of such a market would, however, manifestly be jeopardised if the manufacturers in this country, who had undertaken to co-operate with the sisal producers were to be exposed to severe competition in the United Kingdom market by sisal manufactures produced in a sisal producing country. Consequently I came to the conclusion that, in the interests of the sisal producers themselves, there was no alternative but to inform the Tanganyika Cordage Company that, failing an agreement between them and the federation, I should not be able to oppose the imposition of a prohibitive duty on binder twine imported to this country from the Colonial Dependencies.[14]

This despite the fact that a government spokesman subsequently admitted with reference to the possibilities of low-wage imports from the Empire:

> ... the Import Duties Act and the Ottawa Agreements Act have laid down the general principle that goods grown, produced or manufactured within the Empire should enter the United Kingdom free of customs duties.[15]

The Secretary of State had made the position on this perfectly clear in a letter to the Cordage Company:

> The [prohibitive] duty would, of course, be confined to Colonial products and would not be applicable to imports from the Dominions. You will appreciate that it would be most unfortunate if a precedent for imposing duties on this basis were created.[16]

The Tanganyikan company was therefore forced to negotiate with the Federation and the ultimate agreement laid down that it could export as much as it wished to Britain but only after consulting the Federation 'in regard to the question of the price at which its products . . . shall be marketed'.[17] *The Times*, writing before the publication of the facts, then claimed:

> Thus a commercial question has been happily settled in a commercial way without the intervention of other parties. Consequently no more is likely to be heard of the extraordinary suggestion that prohibitive duties should be imposed to exclude from this country binder twine manufactured in Tanganyika.[18]

Very little was in fact heard of the actual official confirmation of this suggestion in the Commons, since *The Times* at least made no comment on the final revelations, even omitting them from its summary of Parliamentary proceedings.

Having been thus forced to give up its price competitiveness the new industry did not survive for long. Production fell to 10,527 cwt in 1937 and ceased altogether in 1938. The Government attributed the failure to 'the tariffs imposed in manufacturing countries on the finished product (cordage), tariffs from which the raw material (sisal) is usually exempt'.[19] This decision stimulated some opposition in Britain, presumably because the new factories were set up by British capital, Conrad Walsh, the moving figure behind the venture, being also the chairman of the sisal producers' committee which had negotiated the agreement on Empire content, and a member of the Joint East Africa Board. After the official revelations in the Commons a number of questions were asked attempting to elicit a clear policy statement on the question of the development of colonial manufacturing industry. Cunliffe-Lister now denied that 'all goods manufactured by native labour within the Colonial Empire' would be debarred from Britain, but stressed that 'the great interest of the Colonies is to secure markets for their primary products', and underlined the importance of 'complementary' preferences covering primary exports to Britain and British manufactured exports to the Colonies. He concluded:

> It is only in comparatively few cases that a conflict of interest arises; and in such cases I hope that the realization of the importance of the general policy will lead to satisfactory agreements as in the case [of the Cordage Company].[20]

He further claimed that this view 'covers any case',[21] and reaffirmed the position three weeks later on being asked to clarify because of the 'great uncertainty' in the minds of primary producers.[22] The position was further developed in the debate on the estimates in 1935 by Sir William MacLean, a man who had been closely associated with Cunliffe-Lister at the Colonial Office when he was preparing the case for colonial products at Ottawa and producing the Economic Survey of the Colonial Empire. Discussing colonial industrialization he said:

> This has become a problem in our trade relations with the Dominions, but fortunately it has not yet become a Colonial problem, although there has been some discussion of it.

Accepting the fact that some industry was being set up in the Colonies he continued:

> The suggestion, however, that the Colonies should actively promote industrialization is quite another matter, and requires special consideration, because it has serious limitations. It is obvious that manufacturing countries like ours could not afford to provide free or assured markets for manufactured goods in direct competition with their own. All questions of starting new industries in the Colonies must, therefore, be examined on their merits, and with due regard to the welfare of the Colony as a whole and as a primary producer.[23]

Ultimately a factory making sisal bags was set up in Kenya, but this produced only for the local market and did not raise any of these problems. But this case and the general statements made after it presumably marked the end for the immediate future of any attempt to build up local processing industries directed towards external markets. It might also be noted that the Empire Economic Union, great proponents of the economic unity of the Empire, of which Amery, Grigg and MacLean were members, was recommending protection in Britain against cheap colonial imports by 1935.[24]

At the British end the interests of British manufacturers facing potential colonial competition therefore had a direct and negative impact upon the possibilities of establishing colonial industrialization. At the local end the administration's overriding need to keep the African population anchored in the agricultural–traditional system also had a direct impact upon their view of the situation. This view came out very clearly at the Governors' Conference in 1935, when they had to consider a proposal being made to set up a blanket factory in Uganda.[25] The general question of industrialization was discussed and the Governors of both Uganda and Tanganyika were opposed to it. The former stated:

So far as Uganda was concerned he could state definitely that it was of greater importance to preserve the agricultural population and therefore he did not favour any idea of industrialization. He held the view quite apart from the fact that if industrial undertakings were started in East Africa a certain loss of revenue through the falling off of customs duties might accrue to Uganda.

MacMichael of Tanganyika agreed 'generally with the views of Uganda', but preferred 'not to formulate too rigid principles', and then quoted the views of the Secretary of State in a despatch of 4 December when he had said:

> ... that it was undesirable to accelerate the industrialization of East Africa which must, for many years to come, remain a country of primary produce.

Only the Acting Governor of Kenya disagreed, because the special problems of agricultural overcrowding there made him believe that 'if certain industrial undertakings could be started it would be of great assistance', although only 'provided [any factory] was able to look after itself and did not require undue protection'. Their final resolution nevertheless effectively re-iterated the Ugandan position:

> THE CONFERENCE, while not wishing to bind itself to a rigid adherence to any stated principles,
>
> Agreed generally with the views put forward by the Government of Uganda that the establishment of a local industry which is unlikely within a short period of time to be able to bear an excise duty approximately equal to the Customs duty on the imported article should not be encouraged unless it can be shown that the establishment of the industry
>
> (i) will permit of agricultural production which could not be undertaken for purposes of export alone; or
>
> (ii) will give profitable agricultural employment to so large a number of the local population that the resultant prosperity is likely to make a substantial contribution to economic welfare; or
>
> (iii) will, by the development of the local market, without undue exploitation of the local consumer produce a substantial exportable surplus.

They further agreed that 'the blanket factory scheme did not present any special features justifying special treatment'.

British policy at the highest level was therefore very unsympathetic to the possibilities of colonial industrialization during the inter-war period. But the mere fact that the issue had to be taken up and debated makes it clear that there were interests with some resources actively pursuing a more positive position. To understand both the tendencies which officialdom was attempting to resist and the source of the positive initiatives which were to become much more important in the forties and fifties it is now necessary to look more closely at the origins and timing of these forward tendencies. At no point was any official attempt made formally to forbid private attempts to establish manufacturing industries: the effects of policy made themselves felt in the failure to give any direct assistance to such activities or, as in the cases examined here, to place financial pressures upon them which they could not hope to withstand. For as long as the balance of political forces favoured British manufacturing interests on the one hand and the paternalist administration on the other, there was no likelihood that the developmental process would move beyond the primary exporting stage. But there were interests which did stand to benefit from change of this kind which were also politically articulate at both the local and the metropolitan levels, which need to be considered in more detail now.

The previous section has already shown how prevailing attitudes in Uganda and Tanganyika tended to discourage forms of economic change which might lead the African population off the land into secondary and tertiary economic activities. In both cases this did not have anything to do with any commitment to governmental non-intervention in economic matters, since both governments fully accepted the need to intervene actively where private enterprise did not appear to be able to act or where it required assistance of one sort or another. In this field the Government did actually intervene directly in both territories to assist in setting up processing industries which seemed to them to be likely to contribute to desirable agricultural policies in the manner indicated in the Conference resolution quoted above. In Uganda a cigarette factory was set up in Jinja in 1928 by the British American Tobacco Company. This followed the establishment of the crop in Bunyoro the previous year, with the Government undertaking the 'actual purchase of the crop'[26] for the Company, which itself was ultimately to become directly involved in supervision of the growers and buying the crop as well. By 1938 cigarette exports, mainly to the rest of East Africa, were valued at £42,974.[27] By 1938 Tanganyika was employing only 480 people on a range of processing activities which included brick and beer production, meat canning, a vulcanizing factory and a tannery. There the administration took over a salt factory from the Germans, which they ran directly till 1925, when they entered into a partnership with a firm in Zanzibar which acquired 49% of the capital and provided the management.[28] The Government also encouraged a group of private investors to set up a meat factory at Mwanza on Lake Victoria to provide a market for surplus African stock which was endangering the fertility of the area.[29] The company was given a monopoly and a guaranteed return of 10% on their capital over five years. After closing in 1930 it was reopened with the Colonial Development Fund loan already mentioned, and after unsuccessfully attempting to find an export market, closed again in 1935. At all times it was justified:

> . . . not as a commercial proposition but as a most valuable experi-
> mental plant in relation to the problem of overstocking and utiliz-
> ation of cattle products.[30]

The situation was very different in Kenya, where attitudes were far more positive. The difference can be attributed directly to the presence there of the settler community, with its strong political position and its commitment to a limited form of economic nationalism, as well as to the destabilizing effects of the settler economy upon the local society. The settlers, although initially an exclusively agricultural community, accepted the need to indus-trialize partly in order to provide more secure markets for local agricultural products, partly out of a desire to see a viable modern economic system established on the lines of the others already under way in the white Dominions. Equally important, their presence had the effect of breaking down the self-sufficiency of the African economic systems much more rapidly than did the peasant systems based on indirect rule. In the Kenyan case this had become evident by the mid-thirties (as the intervention of the Acting Governor at the Conference cited above indicates), taking the form of apparent rural impoverishment through over-crowding and worklessness. In such circumstances the adminis-tration was able to jettison any hopes of saving 'traditional man' from the demoralizing effects of factory labour much more rapidly than was the case in the peasant economies. The effects of these tendencies can be seen in the development of policy over the whole period.

The financial crisis of the early twenties produced the first assertion of the need to move beyond a simple agricultural system. The Customs Tariff Committee and the Economic and Finance

Committee, both dominated by unofficial persons, recommended a policy of protection which, while mainly directed towards assisting temperate-climate foodstuff producers, was intended to be applied to processing and manufacturing industry as well. Whereas the Governors of the other two territories considered the tariff exclusively as a revenue-producing instrument, the Customs Tariff Committee strongly affirmed the need to use it as an instrument of economic policy:

> When a local industry has to compete with supplies from other countries where the industry is well established it starts at a disadvantage as its costs of production and manufacture are likely to exceed those in the older country until such time as the new industry gets firmly established.[31]

The principle of protection was reaffirmed by the Kenya Tariff Committee in 1929[32] and formed the basis of the approach both of the Kenya Governor and the Kenya settlers to the question at the Governors' Conference in 1930.[33] During the twenties a number of processing industries were set up with official assistance. Wheat-milling benefited directly from the temperate-climate food-stuff tariffs and protective railway rates already discussed. A beer factory was set up before 1923 with the assistance of a protective duty of 2s. per gallon. In order to contribute to the revenue an excise tax of 20s. for 36 gallons was imposed, which therefore left a substantial margin of protection. In 1931 the import duty was increased to 3s. and the Government could claim that 'an entirely adequate protection is maintained in all the territories'.[34] In 1931 an Ordinance was passed giving the Government power to give a sisal bag factory a monopoly position in the home market to establish a new industry and assist local producers badly hit by falling world prices. On the unofficial side this received strong support because it was 'of the greatest importance to the welfare of this country that we should have as many industries instituted here as possible'.[35] Similar action was taken in 1935 to guarantee a monopoly position to anyone willing to invest in 'the coir fibre industry',[36] while an increase in excise duty on cigarette manufactures in that year was also accompanied by 'a margin of protection . . . quite ample to allow it both to develop in the field in which it is already established and to expand to new areas'.[37] The Economic Development Committee in 1935 devoted almost all its attention to agriculture, but nevertheless recommended the establishment of a Standing Board of

Economic Development which would, among other things, 'study the possibilities of secondary industries' and publish the results.[38] In 1937 a meat-canning factory was started in one of the reserves by a commercial firm after repeated government efforts for more than a decade, but this was the outcome of the same attitudes as characterized the Tanganyikan enterprise.

These commitments at the official level in Kenya were supported by the changes which the settler economy induced in the social and economic circumstances of African life. The tendency to proletarianize the African population analysed in Chapter 6 necessarily created a potential labour force for the factory system as well – one which would be available very cheaply and which would already have been forced to accept the discipline of wage labour under the capitalist system. Further, Kenya devoted the greater part of the money which it did spend on education to industrial rather than clerical training. Between 1913 and 1924 technical schools were opened in Machakos, the Coast Province, Masai Reserve and at Kabete near Nairobi. The presence of the workshops for the Kenya–Uganda railway in Nairobi also played a significant role in this respect since it provided industrial employment and ran a Training School for its own artisans. This, combined with the development of Kenya as the commercial and professional centre of the region, provided the basis for the development of an industrial system there which was already under way by the end of the thirties, and was to benefit directly from the shortage of manufactures during the War and by the more positive attitudes to colonial industrialization thereafter. These factors decisively influenced the location of manufacturing facilities in East Africa, where the existence of the common market ensured that Kenyan commodities would have no difficulty in reaching consumers over the whole region. The effects of this were already evident by the late thirties, as evidenced in the figures of Tanganyika's internal trade provided in Table V in Chapter 3.

To conclude this chapter it is necessary to document the changes in the attitudes of those sections of British capital directly involved in East Africa itself. The earlier section indicated that British manufacturing exporters were certainly opposed to the emergence of competitive industries in the colonies, and that these attitudes had a direct and important impact upon official attitudes in London and at the local level. But the case of the Tanganyika Cordage Company has already indicated that these attitudes did not characterize the whole of British capital, since plantation interests at least were prepared to move into processing when faced with declining demand for their crop. In the later years of the thirties these pressures spread to the Joint East Africa Board, both from local interests concerned to be given more opportunities to move into more complex forms of production, and from British trading firms which now found it much more difficult to retain their share of the local market because of the Japanese competition which had taken over in a number of the cheaper sectors. Since British manufacturers could no longer hope to export directly the most useful option was now to establish local processing facilities which would be able to claim the market from inside some sort of protective barrier.

In April 1936 the whole question of industrialization was raised as the result of suggestions made in a letter from the Kenya Farmers' Association. At this point, despite some opposition because of possibilities of competition with British goods, the general view was favourable.[39] In June sympathy was again expressed 'provided such industries were organized in conjunction with industry in this country', and the Kenya Farmers' Association was recommended to contact the East African Section of the London Chamber of Commerce.[40] The following year the Association stressed the need for a decision from the Colonial Office, which was taking a very negative position, as the Managing Director of Smith MacKenzie, one of the leading import–export firms, pointed out the year after:

Mr. Jenkins considered that the Colonial Office should make a statement of their policy with regard to industrial development in East Africa, and suggested that enquiries should be made to find out what particular industries were not looked upon with favour by the Colonial Office. There were several different industries which could be worked successfully in East Africa, and the products of these industries sold locally in East Africa. He himself had been concerned in two or three schemes within recent years which had not been followed up when it was discovered that the Colonial Office did not regard them favourably. The Government appeared to object to the native becoming an industrial worker, in spite of the benefits of high wages and good conditions, although there was evidently no objection to so-called home industries. With regard to one scheme the first argument put forward against it was that it would compete with a similar industry in England. When it was pointed out that East Africa imported from England only 2% of part of the commodity in question, and the remaining 98% from foreign countries, a new argument had to be produced. It was that the revenue of the

Kenya and Uganda railway would suffer. He could find no grounds for that contention. No request for a monopoly, subsidy, or protective duties had been made.[41]

In the discussion various reasons for official opposition were considered and it was claimed that 'there was no law by which the Colonial Office could prohibit industries', to which Jenkins replied: '. . . there were indirect methods of making industries unattractive, of which manipulation of rates on a state owned railway was one.' After the case of the Cordage Company had been cited by Wigglesworth, representative of a large sisal company, the Board decided to take the matter up with the Colonial Office. In April Jenkins felt that the Government's opposition was weakening,[42] and in May it was claimed that opinion in England on secondary industry in the Dominions 'was now altering for the better', and that:

> The British manufacturer would not suffer, though neither they nor the Colonial Office realized it. It was time for a change of policy on the question.[43]

By 1939 the Board had resolved to take a strong line in a delegation to the Colonial Office:

> The Board will press for a clear policy based on a recognition of the fact that East Africa cannot develop solely as an agricultural country, and that the future of native agriculture itself depends on many of the inhabitants from crowded areas finding different work. They will press at the same time for care in avoiding the creation of slums in townships.[44]

The wording is clearly reminiscent of the statements made by the Kenyan Acting Governor in 1935, and the prime beneficiary of this commitment was to be the industrial centre in Nairobi. Presumably the ability to exclude Japanese competition from British West Africa in 1934, combined with the much stronger influence of indirect rule to inspire paternalism, inhibited the emergence of similar attitudes there until very much later.

Finally, it is perhaps worth noting that the emergence of British firms committed to establishing manufacturing facilities inside the East African market, combined with the negative effects of policy in agricultural processing and marketing upon the emergence of indigenous entrepreneurship, was likely to ensure that the industrialization process would be heavily dependent upon the importation of expatriate capital and skills when it did get under way. In Kenya the industrial base was heavily dependent on the large British and Indian companies already involved in processing and trade and there has been a tendency since that time to rely on these and similar companies to keep the process going. In Uganda a strong official commitment to increased industrialization was to emerge in the early fifties, especially under Sir Andrew Cohen's Governorship. But in this case the attitudes of the earlier period continued to exert their influence. These produced the Uganda Development Corporation which was very successful in narrow economic terms, but nevertheless a highly bureaucratized answer to the problem of transferring modern technology to an under-developed environment, and one which did very little to stimulate indigenous entrepreneurship or to evolve truly autonomous solutions to the problem of raising the level of local economic activity.

NOTES

1. *Second Report of the Select Committee on Estimates,* House of Commons, Cmd. 114 of 1928, p. 134.
2. Abstracted from Colonial Development Advisory Committee, *Annual Reports,* Appendix 'A'.
3. *Annual Report,* 1926, p. 55.
4. House of Commons, *Debates,* 6 vii 25, v. 186, c. 81–2.
5. House of Commons, *Debates,* 27 vii 25, v. 187, c. 155.
6. J.E.A.B., Minutes, 2 v 28.
7. *Ibid.,* 1 vii 28.
8. Decision cited in Legislative Council, *Proceedings,* 2nd Session, pt. II, p. 90.
9. *Ibid.*
10. *Ibid.,* p. 93.
11. *Annual Report,* 1928, p. 25.
12. *Annual Reports.*
13. Correspondence cited, House of Commons, *Debates,* 25 vii 35, v. 304, c. 2055; J.E.A.B., *Annual Report,* 1932, p. 16 for details of the agreement.
14. House of Commons, *Debates,* 15 xi 34, v. 293, c. 2167–8.
15. House of Commons, *Debates,* 30 i 35, v. 297, c. 331.
16. House of Commons, *Debates,* 25 vii 35, v. 304, c. 2055.
17. *The Times,* 31 x 34.
18. *Ibid.*
19. *Annual Report,* 1937, p. 72.
20. House of Commons, *Debates,* 14 xi 34, v. 293, c. 1945.
21. *Ibid.*
22. House of Commons, *Debates,* 5 xii 34, v. 295, c. 1559.
23. House of Commons, *Debates,* 25 vii 35, v. 304, c. 2115.
24. Empire Economic Union, *Future fiscal policy,* 1935, pp. 44, 60.
25. *Proceedings,* April 1935, pp. 6–7.
26. Dept. of Agriculture, *Annual Report,* 1928, p. 17.
27. J. D. Tothill, *Agriculture in Uganda,* London, O.U.P., 1940, p. 401.

28. Sir D. Cameron, *My Tanganyika service, op. cit.,* pp. 138–40.
29. *Annual Report,* 1926, p. 55.
30. Governor to Secretary of State, 18 x 34, Tanganyika Archives, Secretariat Minute Papers, 12452, vol. III.
31. Cited by the Director of Agriculture, Legislative Council, *Debates,* 1925, 1st Session, vol. II, p. 981.
32. *Op. cit.,* pp. 3–6.
33. *Proceedings,* January 1930.
34. Legislative Council, *Debates,* 1931, p. 693.
35. *Ibid.,* 1932, p. 362.
36. *Ibid.,* 1935, p. 49.
37. *Ibid.,* p. 40.
38. *Op. cit.,* p. 142.
39. Minutes, 2 iv 36 referring to K.F.A. letter dated 18 ii 36.
40. Minutes, 9 vi 37.
41. Minutes, 11 ii 38.
42. Minutes, 8 iv 38.
43. Minutes, 11 v 38.
44. *Draft agenda for the Colonial Office (July),* 1939 (J.E.A.B. files).

Conclusions

Colonialism, Underdevelopment and Class Formation in East Africa

The Introduction suggested the existence of three major theoretical positions with respect to the impact of contact with the West upon social change in the Third World. The older tradition of Imperial history and the more recent literature in the behavioural social sciences assumes that the relationship has produced essentially beneficial results since contact has tended to diffuse the values and techniques required for 'modernization' to backward and isolated societies which would otherwise have found it much more difficult to obtain access to them. At the other extreme a view is now gaining strength which assumes that contact is essentially exploitative, that an increase in such contact can only increase servitude and that a process of genuine development will only be possible when Third World societies can cut the connections which tie them to the dominant Western powers altogether. Between these two extremes lies the classical Marxist position which argues that the impact of the relationship is profoundly ambivalent; that it tends on the one hand to create exploitation and subjugation while on the other it produces new forces in colonial societies which will be capable of overthrowing external dominance and of using the positive achievements of the developed world as a basis for the elimination of their own backwardness and subordination. It should now be possible to illuminate this debate by looking more closely at the substantive issues resolved through the colonial political process in East Africa in the inter-war period. Before doing this, however, it is necessary to make a number of preliminary points about the nature of the political–economic relations which characterized the colonial system as an entity.

Colonial society was linked with the outside world through the system of international capitalism, whose political and economic centres were located in the most advanced parts of Europe, the United States and, a little belatedly, Japan. By the end of the First World War virtually all the societies of the non-Western world had been drawn into relations of dependence upon these centres, and this had in turn restructured their own societies to produce relations which were both 'pre-capitalist relations; [and] also capitalist relations'.[1] But although dominated by this international capitalist context, the process of internal development was necessarily very different from that which had produced the original capitalist revolution in the dominant centres. Capitalism had evolved organically in the areas of origin, but it was injected into the colonial world from the outside and, where necessary, imposed upon unwilling populations there at the point of a gun. The process of organic evolution, for example in Britain, produced an indigenous capitalist class which was securely rooted in the social structure and culture and which, whatever its limits, had necessarily to rely upon internal sources of support to legitimate and defend its claims to social predominance. The dominance of this class in European society was subjected to intense opposition both from the old feudal order and from the emergent working class, but its claims to represent at least one significant tendency within the national culture could never be entirely rejected. But external dominance in the Third World meant that the commanding heights of the new economy and administration were occupied by expatriate groups from the beginning; expatriate groups, moreover, with access to resources derived from their metropolitan base which were far in excess of anything which indigenous groups could hope to acquire in the short run. The crucial question for the long-term development of the society as a whole therefore relates to the effect of their dominance upon the emergence of indigenous social formations which might be capable of replacing them and establishing an autonomous base for the exercise of political and economic power.

Whatever the differences between them, the dominant expatriate groups in the colonial political economy derived their ability to exploit East African resources from the power of the colonial state on the one hand and the inability of members of the indigenous society to compete with them on the other. These two factors were closely related to each other. Where indigenous classes had already acquired skills and capital the power of the State could be used to destroy this to allow expatriate interests full play – the destruction of India's textile industry in the nineteenth century is perhaps the most notorious example of this kind, but by no means the only one. Where, on the other hand, pre-colonial society was relatively undeveloped – and this was very much the case in the East African interior – skilled personnel would have to be imported in the first instance to man the administrative, educational and economic institutions required to integrate the region into the international system of exchange. The undeveloped nature of existing social structures was, of course, used by the expatriate groups to justify their claim to these positions of power and privilege and is still used by implication to justify the culonial record by academic apologists. But what is really critical in the context of the debate about development is not whether the initial situation justified the dominance of external groups, but whether the system of dominance established during this period would tend to perpetuate itself or to produce indigenous groups capable of replacing it and establishing a genuine independence. And here the role of the colonial state was clearly crucial – because it determined access to resources it also exercised a very direct influence over the prospects for development of the indigenous population.

This assertion immediately raises the question of the relationship between the State and the social forces generated by the creation of the new system of colonial production. Classical economic theory assumes that production will be regulated by market forces and, more especially, that an optimum allocation of factors of production will derive from an international market system which places no 'artificial' barriers in its way. This theory separates economic from political factors and makes it possible for much of current theory to ignore the real nature of the connections between the two spheres. The assumption that the 'market' has ever operated independently of political and social structures in allocating resources has never been true except in the most limited sense. In the colonial sphere it is even more misleading because of the direct and extensive role played by the State in the economy from the beginnings of colonial production. The new system of production must be described as at least partially capitalistic because it was mainly controlled by private individuals and directed to the market. But access to the productive resources which determined success or failure on the market was directly controlled by the State. The State, in turn, was not an independent force but directly dependent on the balance of social forces in the system which it notionally controlled, and most especially upon the dominant economic forces in the metropolitan country and their local representatives. The colonial state can therefore be viewed as the managing agent of the dominant private interests in the capitalist system, with a vested interest in maintaining their dominance inside colonial society. If this is true – and I would argue that the concrete cases reviewed in the body of the text do substantiate this position – it is possible to argue that the dominant forces in the colonial system were bound to use their power to limit the access of indigenous groups to resources required for autonomous development and hence to perpetuate the underdeveloped nature of their condition.

One crucial difference between the nature of capitalism in the advanced countries and the Third World therefore lay in the dominance of essentially external social forces over local development; a second lay in the impact of the capitalist system as a whole upon the indigenous social structure. The organic evolution of capitalism in western Europe eventually subjected the whole society to its laws, thereby creating a structure in which capital was concentrated into relatively few hands, the bulk of the population being without independent means of support and therefore forced to sell their labour on the market. For the labourer in this situation, freedom, such as it is, resides in the right to spatial mobility and to sell his labour to the highest bidder; for the capitalist it lies in the right to produce whatever he can sell within very broad limits imposed by the law. The development of this system took many generations and involved the elimination of pre-capitalist forms of social organization which were based upon different principles and whose existence hampered the full development of the capitalist system. By the end of the nineteenth century this process had been effectively completed in the leading capitalist countries, but it had hardly begun in East Africa, where the external world had hitherto exploited the population through the slave trade without changing the basic structure of production and political organization very significantly. The period of direct colonial control accelerated the tendencies drawing African production into the international economy and introduced capitalist structures into the indigenous economies. But these structures existed as islands within a sea characterized by pre-capitalist forms of organization. From a developmental perspective the crucial question raised by this situation concerns the relationship between these capitalist and pre-capitalist structures. In particular it relates to the extent to which the presence of the new capitalist structures tends to draw the whole of the indigenous society into its ambit, thereby reproducing the classical confrontation of wage labour and capital in the developed world or, on the other hand, tends to create a dualistic situation in which islands of capitalist modernity continue to co-exist with great seas of pre-capitalist traditionalism more or less indefinitely.

This question, too, is directly related to the broader debate about the nature of the developmental process set out at the start of this chapter. The behavioural theorists assume that this dualism exists and that there is a necessary tendency for the values and skills existing in the modern sector to be diffused outwards into the traditional sector, although they feel that this process can be retarded because of the strength of the opposition to these values stemming from the hold which traditional values exert over the population. A. G. Frank, the Latin American theorist, at the other extreme, totally rejects dualism, claiming that the whole of Third World society has been fully drawn into the international capitalist system but that the so-called traditional sectors are simply those which have to be kept in subordination to the dominant metropolitan centres in order to make it possible for the surplus to continue to be extracted from them.[2] The interpretation derived more directly from classical Marxism, clearly argued by Ernesto Laclau in a recent article, accepts Frank's assertion that the traditional sector is an organic part of the overall system of capitalist exploitation, but asserts that he is incorrect in arguing that this sector is characterized by essentially capitalistic relations.[3] In his view the capitalist system created a situation in underdeveloped countries where the capitalist centres co-existed with pre-capitalist or feudal structures, and that the former could more effectively extract profits from the latter because of their essentially feudal and servile nature. This therefore suggests an organic connection between the two sectors but not one which necessarily leads to the progressive development of the less by the more advanced. On the contrary he argues that:

> ... servile exploitation was accentuated and consolidated by the very tendency of entrepreneurs – presumably 'modern' in type – to maximise profits; the apparent lack of communication between the two sectors herewith disappears. In such cases we can affirm that the modernity of one sector is a function of the backwardness of the other, and that therefore no policy is revolutionary which poses as the 'left wing' of the 'modernizing sector'.[4]

The debate between these three positions is no mere academic matter since fundamental questions of political strategy for the future hinge upon the way in which they are resolved.

It is now possible to examine the substantive material presented in the text in relation to the issues raised in this wider debate. Our general problem is to assess the impact of the colonial presence upon indigenous society. To do this it is first necessary to break this presence down into its component parts and to look at each of these separately. Thereafter it will be possible to present some general hypotheses about the overall impact by examining some of the longer-term consequences of the whole process upon post-colonial African society. For analytical purposes four main categories can be identified within the colonial political economy – primary producers almost entirely located in agriculture;[5] processers and traders who handled their products; the metropolitan export industries with access to colonial markets; and the colonial administrative and political apparatus responsible for managing the whole operation. Their combined influence was so extensive that little will remain to be said once its effects have been examined in any detail.

i. *The Agricultural Sector*

Colonialism required the creation of an export sector in the local economy, and this in turn required the evolution of a rural class with the resources required to sell some part of its production on the international market. In fact the growth in production of this kind in East Africa during the period under review was very considerable in terms of quantity (although not necessarily in terms of value because of the effects of the Depression of the thirties), as the following figures demonstrate:

TABLE XVI

East African Agricultural Exports (three-year averages)

	Sisal (000 tons)		Cotton (000 bales)		Coffee (000 cwt)	
	1923–5	*1936–8*	*1923–5*	*1936–8*	*1923–5*	*1936–8*
Kenya	12	31	2	19	145	353
Uganda	—	1	138	359	37	256
Tanganyika	17	91	17	58	102	263

Source: Colonial Annual Reports.

The rapidity of this growth can be largely attributed to the relatively favourable terms on which the British authorities provided the infrastructure services which sustained it – in this respect East Africa certainly benefited considerably from its association with what was still the wealthiest of the European colonial powers. The positive contribution of this growth to the future development of the region must not be undervalued, however fundamental the criticisms to be made about other aspects of the colonial impact. The productive capacity represented by these exports (which were to rise rapidly in value during and after the Second World War) is, however limited, the foundation on which future economic change will have to be based.

But any analysis which confined itself to the examination of growth rates would be likely to obscure more than it revealed; these, as was argued in the Introduction, have to be examined in relation to the changes in the structure of production, distribution and political control which such growth induces and which is then influenced by them in turn. The crucial structural issue in agricultural development in East Africa related to the mode of production and in particular whether this was based upon settlement, plantations or the peasantry – this choice in turn determined the evolution of rural social structure and political control since each strategy involved sharply differing processes of class formation. The study attempted to demonstrate how the settler strategy required a process of capital accumulation in that sector based upon a net transfer of capital and of labour to it from the peasant sector. This process, which can perhaps best be viewed in terms of Marx's analysis of primitive accumulation,[6] produced a rural structure based upon large-scale expatriate capital employing African wage-labour in the settler sector, and was combined with the continued existence of subsistence-based pre-capitalist production in the African reserves, which served to maintain and reproduce the reserve army of agricultural workers when they were not required in the capitalist sector itself. The plantation structure which co-existed with this in Kenya and was the leading expatriate sector in Tanganyika, required very little capital from the peasant sector, but depended upon the availability of cheap labour which in turn depended on the inability of farmers in certain areas to produce directly for the world market because of poor infrastructure services. It too, therefore, produced a structure based on large-scale capital, African wage labour and a subsistence sector disconnected from the market. The peasant strategy, on the other hand, was based upon small-scale production mainly dependent on family labour with subsistence production co-existing with production for the market. In Laclau's sense this therefore also represents the maintenance of a pre-capitalist mode of production, but one involving a much lower degree of servility than those which continued to exist in the subsistence areas which served as labour reservoirs for plantation or settler-based systems. Further, although this study necessarily treated peasant society as an undifferentiated entity (a tendency shared by those who still consider African society to be 'classless'), it is evident that access to the market and to the resources which it provides makes a process of capital accumulation inside peasant society possible and, some would argue, must inevitably over the long term produce inequalities in access to capital which will lead to the development of a landed and a landless class, and hence to the evolution of a capitalist structure in the classical sense.[7] The limitations of the material presented in this study make it impossible to take this line of argument any further here, although something more will be said about the implications of the peasant structure for the subsequent process of political development. What the material does do, however, is to make it possible to look in more detail at the implications of plantation and settler strategies in this regard, a question of primary importance for the nationalist struggle in both Kenya and Tanganyika.

Plantation development was justified by its proponents for crops which required large-scale processing facilities. The fact that these could not be found locally was thought to legitimate expatriate control, provided (at least in the view of the more enlightened proponents like Donald Cameron) that all this initial capital was in fact brought in from the outside and not extracted from the African population. But the assumption that plantation development was cost-free from the point of view of the local population must be looked at in the wider context of its sources of labour and of its effects upon the development of the areas from which this labour was drawn. In East Africa plantations depended upon the failure to open up these areas, since an extension of cash crops there would have reduced the supply of labour or increased its price to a level which only the most efficient producers could have paid. The situation thus strongly reinforces Myint's general conclusion that 'the existence of an indigenous subsistence agricultural sector seems to have worked, at least in the transitional stage, for the *lowering* of the wage in mines and plantations'; and further, 'that the colonial powers have been able to maintain low wages in the mines and plantations by neglecting and impoverishing the subsistence agricultural sector'.[8] The whole effect, much reinforced by the strength of the political representation given to plantation interests both locally and in London, would therefore be cumulatively to strengthen regional inequalities and hence the development of a system of dualism involving 'servile exploitation'. The system, based as it was upon expatriate capital, also probably made a small contribution to the stimulation of more advanced forms of economic production in other sectors of the economy, as was the case with the more mature plantation systems of India and South-East Asia.[9] This was therefore a classic example of a situation where high initial returns on relatively cheap forms of investment tended to generate powerful obstacles in the long term to an effective developmental process.

All these negative effects of plantation development were much intensified in the case of settler development. The predominance of plantations in Tanganyika only extended to a limited range of crops and regions and did not preclude the emergence of a dynamic process of peasant development in a number of areas. In Kenya settler dominance virtually excluded peasant development, it required a net transfer of resources from the African to the European sector, and it required that the former sector be reduced to an underdeveloped labour reservoir for the latter. The most reactionary aspect of the settler strategy stemmed from the fact that they contributed virtually nothing to the development of the exchange economy which existing peasant producers could not provide as well or better. This fact, combined with their demand for the style of life of the English gentry, meant that the whole force of the State had to be brought to bear in order to extract the resources from the local population which were required to maintain their position. The negative effects of this strategy have been extensively documented in earlier chapters; what must still be considered here is the nature of its effect upon African politics.

The development of the settler sector depended directly and heavily upon the support of the colonial state. While Africans in the remote regions of Tanganyika who were forced to walk 300 miles or more to work on the plantations could not be expected to realize that this was the outcome of particular aspects of colonial policy, those in Kenya subjected to the Kipande system, land alienation, and a prohibition on cash-crop production, could not avoid making this connection. They learnt very quickly that their poverty and dependence was the direct result of the relationship between the settlers and the colonial state. This fact also forced them to realize that liberation could not be derived simply from an involvement in 'tribal' politics at the local level, but would require a movement which could direct pressure against the colonial centre where all the crucial decisions were taken. Further, European politics were based upon the need to maintain their racial monopoly over the key developmental resources; they could allow neither Africans nor Asians access to their privileged domain in the White Highlands. This monopoly meant that Africans could not hope for upward economic and other forms of mobility on an individual basis – they would be excluded because they were African and could therefore only hope to progress within the broader context of the African community as a whole. For the African élite as well as the masses, therefore, nationalism was an imperative.

African nationalism was to emerge as a political force throughout colonial Africa after the Second World War, but the conditions from which it arose differed sharply. It invariably required the existence of a small Western-educated élite within the African population capable of organizing a national movement which could deal with the colonial authorities on their own terms.[10] It also required the support of large sections of the rural population, which would only be forthcoming where they could be shown that their interests had come into direct conflict with the policies of the colonial state. In the peasant-dominated areas of Uganda and Tanganyika this conflict did not arise out of policies related to control over agricultural production because the peasant strategy tended, if anything, to increase the resources going into the African sector rather than to diminish them. In these cases opposition was to arise out of issues derived from processing and marketing, to be discussed in the next section, which took much longer to mature. But the creation of settler dominance drew large sections of the rural population directly into anti-colonial struggle from the earliest stages of the evolution of the cash economy, a fact which explains the relatively early emergence of nationalism in Kenya, its violence and its ability to mobilize wide strata of the population, notably in the areas most directly affected by the settler presence. But the effects of this situation went even further than this. The dependent subsistence sector had to be administered, and this was only possible, as the right-wing Indirect Rule theorists like Smuts and Grigg recognized, through the maintenance of the authority of 'traditional' institutions like the chieftainship. African agents had to be found to man these institutions – chiefs, headmen, clerks and so on – and these were rewarded with superior access to the benefits of the colonial world. They were then expected to maintain the authority of the colonial system in the reserves and were assumed by officialdom to represent the interests of the African population as a whole. They became dependent indigenous structures in the sense defined in the Introduction and their position was necessarily to bring them into opposition with the emerging nationalist forces, which were challenging the colonial structure that gave them their privileges.[11] This tendency also emerged in areas of peasant development – for example in the Lake Region of Tanganyika[12] – but it was far more intense in Kenya because of the much greater exploitativeness of the system as a whole. Thus the conflicts engendered by the system were not confined to those which existed between Africans and Europeans, but were also developed inside the African community itself – as was to emerge very clearly during the Mau Mau movement, when the loyalists were a prime target for attack.

ii. *Trading and Processing*

Colonial policy throughout East Africa was concerned to destroy free competition between middlemen and processers for raw materials, in order to increase control over growers and maintain the profitability of high-cost expatriate operators. This was done by creating a system of controlled marketing which gave these expatriate processers a monopolistic relationship to their sources of supply. In Kenya settler produce was largely controlled through producer-dominated co-operatives, but elsewhere this occurred through British and, increasingly, Asian private firms. This system effectively eliminated an autonomous middleman sector and replaced local middlemen as intermediaries between grower and processer by agents directly dependent on the latter. As a result growers received a lower price for their crop, Africans lost the opportunity to become middlemen themselves and thereby to become capitalist traders in their own right, and a larger percentage of the surplus could be funnelled out of the country than would have been possible otherwise. What, then, were the wider political implications of these decisions, which at the time appeared to be essentially technical in nature?

Although Africans were given every encouragement to become

peasant producers in Uganda and Tanganyika, the existence of this expatriate monopoly in marketing and processing effectively excluded them from any but the most servile positions – as labourers, buying agents, etc. – in the latter sector. This, again, was the direct result of the intervention of the colonial state at the behest of the dominant expatriate interests, and its effect once more was to block the development of a fully capitalist system in order to create a structure of servile dependency which would maximize monopoly profits. The overall result was to freeze relationships in the rural sector into a rigid hierarchy with European and Asian processers at the top, their Asian (and to a limited degree African) agents in the middle, and the great mass of the peasantry consigned irrevocably to the bottom. It is important to emphasize that the failure of Africans to move upwards did not stem in any way from any of the attributes supposedly associated with 'traditional values' – indeed, the full power of the colonial state had to be brought in to eliminate small Asian and African middlemen who were competing only too effectively on the market where the opportunities existed. Their failure stemmed directly from the limits imposed on the free operation of the market system by the State and can therefore only be understood in a context which takes into account the factors which determined the operation of that State.

While the commitment to settlement was the factor which took the State into the centre of African politics in Kenya, it can be argued that it was the commitment to the expatriate processers which very largely achieved this end in Tanganyika and Uganda. Africans protested actively about the creation of the monopoly when this occurred. Faced with its success they began to organize co-operative societies – led, so far as one can see, by individuals who might in other circumstances have become independent middlemen – which would provide them with some limited defences against exploitation. These societies provided Africans with almost their only organized base in the rural areas, and the limits which the nature of the colonial marketing system imposed upon their further development provided the issue around which the élite and masses could be united in opposition to the colonial state. This was very clear in Ugandan politics in the forties, when the riots of 1949 were directly related to marketing and pricing policies, and where the Uganda Farmers' Union (also known as the Federation of Uganda African Farmers) began as an attempt to fight the expatriate monopoly and ended as the Uganda

National Congress, committed to the elimination of the colonial state. In Sukumaland in Tanganyika political contact between town and countryside also 'came first through the co-operatives' for the same reasons.[13]

These facts thus determined in large measure the issues around which the African opposition would develop; they also ensured that a strong element in the nationalist movement would derive from a co-operative rather than a capitalist economic base. Little research has gone into the class composition of the early nationalist movements, although it seems likely that this did contain small-scale African trading as well as clerical and co-operative components. But the weakness of the purely 'capitalistic' element in the movement was to be of great significance for the future when, it probably gave the leadership much more freedom of action in relation to the evolution of ideological positions with a socialist component. It was in this sense that African society could be realistically described as 'classless', since the nature of the colonial presence had precluded the development of an authentic capitalist revolution in the rural sector and, by so doing, created a situation which inhibited long-term structural change in social and economic relationships.

iii. *Metropolitan Exporters*

The needs of British manufacturing industry created the dynamic which determined the speed and the structure of colonial development by establishing a market for raw materials and supplies of manufactured consumer goods. Africans could be quickly persuaded to enter this exchange process both as producers and consumers; what was more difficult was to provide them with sufficient purchasing power to make a visible impact upon the demand for British products in a world in which more and more people were questioning their reliance on traditional British sources of supply. British exporters therefore had to press for policies which would expand local markets by increasing exports of raw materials and, if necessary, by excluding competition from alternative sources of supply. Here it is now necessary to consider the implications of their demands in three areas of policy – the aid programme, tariffs and colonial industrialization.

The crisis of unemployment in British engineering and textiles in the twenties produced the aid programme which culminated in the 1929 Colonial Development Act. The major impact of this was felt in colonial railway-building, with many hundreds of miles completed in East Africa between 1921 and 1932. This programme was initiated as a result of British rather than local pressures – it was always simply assumed that transport was the primary need in local development and that railways were the most efficient means to provide this. If it could be shown that this was in fact the case in East Africa after the twenties there would be no need to criticize it simply because it was also of direct assistance to British textile and steel producers. But it is in fact very doubtful that this was the best way to spend the enormous sums which were provided as a result of these pressures.

There is no doubt that the original railways built into the East African interior were of fundamental importance in opening it up to production for the world market. But grave doubt attached to the benefits to be derived from the subsequent expansion. O'Connor's carefully documented study concluded that the lines serving Uganda 'appear to have been of progressively decreasing importance in terms of their impact on the country',[14] and that those built in the twenties 'had very much less effect on economic development, for although they immediately handled a large volume of traffic, much of this was merely diverted from the Lake services'.[15] His assessment of the contribution in Tanganyika is not much brighter.[16] There one may also note that the ninety-three-mile extension to Kinyangiri was torn up before the Second World War as uneconomic, the Tabora Mwanza Line was never an economic proposition because the Kenya–Uganda Line took most of the traffic from the Lake region, and the Moshi–Arusha extension was intended for settler development which never became really significant. In Kenya the branch lines were almost exclusively built to service the settler sector (which O'Connor claims would hardly have hoped to survive the Depression 'if they had not been served by the various branches');[17] as a result they were heavily underutilized and never justified their costs in purely economic terms.

When one comes to set these limited achievements against the direct and indirect costs which they imposed on the local populations the picture becomes even darker. The Kenya–Uganda Railways spent some £16·5 million on capital investment between 1921 and 1933; thereafter it had to meet interest and capital repayments of well over £800,000 each year. By 1932 Tanganyika's railway debt was £5·8 million out of a total debt of £8·9 million, and repayments amounted to £310,000 per annum or more than 13% of the total expenditure of administration and railways combined. These costs can be compared with expenditures in Kenya in 1934 of £170,000 on education, £125,000 on agriculture and £198,000 on medical services; and with £81,000 on education, £105,000 on agriculture and veterinary services and £194,000 on medical services in Tanganyika in 1935. Less directly, the commitment to capital-intensive technology implied by the choice of railways rather than roads (Kenya spent only between £60,000 and £80,000 per annum on these throughout the thirties) meant that development had to be concentrated into a limited number of regions. As a result the areas around the railway could be intensively developed, while those more than a few score miles away had to be starved of resources because of the drain imposed by the costs of the capital-intensive sector. Looked at in this light the argument then used that 'scarce resources' made it impossible to open up remote areas of the country falls into perspective. These resources were not scarce because of a lack of availability of capital; they were scarce because the capital was only forthcoming on terms determined by metropolitan interests, who benefited from the use of the capital-intensive technology which provided employment to British workers, rather than the labour-intensive technology which might have been used to provide a territory-wide programme of rural animation based on local road-building, agricultural extension and research. This, too, tended to intensify the nature of the dualism in the economy, concentrating development in a small number of regions and leaving the rest in a pre-capitalist situation where they could be effectively exploited as low-cost labour reservoirs for the developed regions fortunate enough to have access to the railways and other economic infrastructure.

British exporters were also directly affected by the nature of both internal and external colonial tariff policies. With respect to the former the interests of British traders and, to a lesser degree, direct exporters, were strongly committed to the extension and maintenance of the East African customs union. This was no doubt important in relation to the extension of the internal market, but the power of Kenyan settler interests ensured that they would largely monopolize its benefits with respect to agricultural production, while the strength of the Kenyan urban centres together with a more favourable attitude among policy-makers made it possible for them to monopolize the advantages with respect to industrialization as well. This latter fact in particular was to become a major source of conflict within the region in the post-war period and was to make it very difficult for the same degree of economic co-ordination to be maintained after Independence.

With regard to the external tariff British interests initially accepted the principle of non-discrimination in favour of British goods because they assumed that they were strong enough not to require special assistance and hoped that the same principle would be adopted by other colonial powers elsewhere. But the expansion of Japanese competition in textiles in the late twenties and early thirties reversed this situation and led to demands for discriminatory preferences in favour of British high-cost producers. The existence of international treaty obligations protected East African consumers against discrimination of this kind, although those in most of the rest of the colonial Empire were not so fortunate.

British exporters therefore attempted to exclude external competition through tariffs; they initially attempted to pre-empt the development of internal competition by discouraging colonial industrialization. But in this case the change in the international trading situation produced changes in policy which were perhaps more favourable to local interests. While British products dominated the local market British opposition to local industrialization was complete. Once the market had been lost to the Japanese, and the attempt to obtain preferential treatment had failed, British firms became interested in recapturing the market by setting up production inside the protection afforded by the revenue tariff and the high costs of transport to East Africa's inland centres. Their needs, combined with pressures from the settler minority, had begun to bear fruit in Kenya in the late thirties, and the process of industrialization was to be intensified by the effects of the War and the more positive policies adopted thereafter. As a result a small but not insignificant industrial centre had been established there by the end of the colonial period, a partial contradiction of the alleged tendency for colonialism to inhibit all developments of this kind in the interests of metropolitan manufacturing centres.

This investigation therefore shows that any simple association of colonialism with anti-industrialization will not suffice. On the other hand it also raises some questions about the limitations imposed upon a programme of this kind by the dominance of metropolitan interests in the decision-making process. East Africa was protected from the full effects of this dominance by international treaties – the Mandate in Tanganyika and the Congo Basin Treaties over the whole region – which stopped the metropolitan power from excluding competition as it did in West Africa. It would be useful to know whether the lower rate of industrialization exhibited by the West African economies – despite larger internal markets – can be attributed to the fact that British exporters were able to maintain a foothold there for longer than they were in East Africa because of the protection afforded by the introduction of quotas on Japanese imports in 1934. But what is if anything more important is the fact that industrialization, when it did come, was not begun in order to create opportunities for local entrepreneurship, but as a means of protecting British capital from low-cost Japanese competition. The previous section has shown how African entrepreneurship was stifled by the effects of marketing and processing policies; this failure to provide them with opportunities to accumulate capital, combined with the commitment to British firms, meant that the industrialization process would have to occur through the importation of capital-intensive technology managed by expatriates and controlled from abroad. This then laid the foundation for future dependence on the multi-national corporation for the capital and skills required for further industrialization; it also produced the massive structural imbalances now visible throughout the East African economies which have resulted from the low capacity of this technology to provide non-agricultural employment. An alternative strategy based upon the attempt to establish small-scale industry using technology which could be managed by members of the indigenous population would probably have taken longer to mature, but would not have had the negative effects so clearly visible in the present situation. This situation can therefore again be shown to have intensified dependency and the dualism based upon the juxtaposition of an advanced and highly profitable expatriate sector with an indigenous social structure for which most of the potential channels of upward mobility had been blocked.

Finally in this section it is worth digressing slightly to say something about the contribution of the Colonies to development in Britain itself. The active interest taken by government in colonial development in the twenties contradicts in some measure the popular view that interventionism in the interests of full employment only began with the triumph of Keynesianism in the latter part of the thirties. Government was prepared to intervene in this way, especially under Lloyd George during the Coalition period, and direct intervention was not confined to the colonial projects examined here. Yet it is equally true that the prejudices of the Establishment limited this activity very severely in Britain itself, although there was less opposition to public works in the Colonies, where *laissez-faire* doctrine was of less importance to the dominant interests. In fact it can be argued that the existence of the Empire made it possible for the English ruling class to avoid confronting the real nature of the crisis before them during these years. Many of the most active and articulate Tories – like Amery and the whole Imperial Preference movement – believed that their problems could be solved by expanding the complementary trade within the Empire through the programme of preferences and colonial development. They therefore used their considerable energies to promote essentially defensive strategies, which involved using Britain's international power to buy her the privileges which would make it possible to shield her manufacturers from the full effects of their growing lack of competitiveness on a world market increasingly dominated by the United States, Germany and Japan. The limited success of these Imperialist policies bought British exporters a few more years of competitiveness in protected markets and hence absolved some of them from the need to make the structural changes at home required to meet this international competition on equal terms. The resulting maintenance of archaic economic structures within British industry then served to make the gap even more difficult to bridge when the imperial crutches finally disintegrated in the fifties and sixties.

iv. *The Colonial Administration*

The colonial administration, standing at the point of intersection of the political pressures emanating from British society on the one hand and local society on the other, was expected to manage the whole system although not to run it. With certain limited exceptions, the means of production and distribution were controlled by private interests whose position had therefore to be taken into account when policies were decided. Government could make choices between the options presented by the conflicts between the needs of private groups, but could never free itself from its fundamental dependence on the capitalist system itself. Its influence, which must not be underestimated for this reason, was therefore confined to the choice between alternative strategies for capitalist development, which it could exercise by providing one group of entrepreneurs with opportunities to operate as against another – settlers rather than peasants, processers rather than middlemen, importers rather than domestic producers, and so on. The outcome of these choices was clearly critical for the long-term evolution of the social system, and the basis on which they were made as well as their long-term implications must therefore be looked at with care. Further, the administration in East Africa was accorded great social status and provided a high percentage of the opportunities of employment at all levels in the non-agricultural sector. Its impact on the evolution of social attitudes and on social change inside the local population was therefore also to be crucial. In this section it will be necessary to look at the implications of its attitudes and structure upon the evolution of African social and political organization, and upon the general development of the exchange economy.

Colonial administration constantly operated within an unresolvable contradiction – on the one hand the demands of the cash economy required that Africans be drawn out of their old routines and systems of social organization; on the other, they could only be effectively kept in order provided traditional habits of deference were maintained. Change was both essential and dangerous. The population had to be persuaded to ask for more but not for too much more; to produce for the market but to allow it to be regulated by forces entirely outside their control. Lugard and his followers knew full well that the colonial situation inevitably produced 'a disintegrating effect on tribal authority and institutions',[18] and that any attempt to draw African society fully into the new system would, by so doing, require 'complete political repression, or concession to political agitators, a class which has never failed to be created by a system of direct rule, of some western form of self-government'.[19] This led both the peasant and the settler theorists to advocate the maintenance of traditionalism institutionalized in the Indirect Rule system. This tendency was, of course, fully compatible with the maintenance of the dualistic development described earlier in this section – if Africans could be persuaded to limit their incursions into the new world to growing a few stands of cotton or coffee or to working for wages for a few months of the year, it would mean that they could both retain their loyalty to the local authority structure and provide the resources required to keep the settlers, processers and traders in business. On the other hand, if they moved out of these lowly roles and acquired the mobility and resources derived from economic entrepreneurship they would threaten not only the profits of expatriate enterprise, but also the authority of the traditionalistic systems of rule to which they were subjected on the local level. More will be said about the limits of this strategy in the concluding section; here it will suffice to note that its contradictions not only operated on the economic plane but in the sphere of administrative organization as well. While Indirect Rule assumed that 'traditional' authorities were to develop independently of central political authority they had necessarily to operate within the broad context of the colonial value-system, more especially in the areas most strongly affected by the growth of the cash economy. This meant that the authority of the chief had, in the last resort, to be subordinated to that of the District Commissioner, and he therefore ceased to depend on his standing with his own people, to whom he was now only nominally responsible. Thus, as Austen puts it:

> conscious expressions of dedication to Indirect Rule are consistently accompanied by the strengthening of the bureaucratic apparatus which denies the possibility of autonomous local development . . . the more colonial native policy, the less African tribal politics.[20]

While Indirect Rule theory tried to freeze African systems of social and political organization, or at least to delay their integration into the structures which determined events at the centre, the presence of the administrative apparatus itself created a new élite which was superimposed upon the whole of indigenous society, and yet derived its values and its life-style from its metropolitan base. From an administrative point of view, therefore, dualism consisted of the juxtaposition of the colonial control structure, against its access to the full apparatus of Western bureaucratic theory, with a 'traditional' structure which still operated at much lower levels of technical competence, and which was in any event directly dependent on the advanced sector for its authority and its methods of operation.[21] But, as in the case of the economy, this dualism did not imply separation – the two systems were functionally linked to each other, with the underdevelopment of the traditional sector a prerequisite for the maintenance of the superiority of the modern. But this separation could never be complete. The central administration was monopolized at the decision-making end by Europeans, but lower-level positions in the executive and clerical grades were filled either by Asians or, as the educational system developed, Africans in increasing numbers. Because of the limitations imposed on African mobility in the economic sector this class of literate clerks was to occupy a very prominent position in the evolving structure of African society. They became a part of the 'modern' sector and were able to learn at least some of its techniques of organization and control; they were probably better placed in this regard than the chiefs, whose positions were so completely confined within the bounds of local society. Further, the racial division of labour within the administration prevented their upward mobility beyond the lowest level and thereby ensured that their loyalty to the colonial system would be less than complete. Although it is probably that many of these actually in employment would limit their opposition because of the constraints which their superiors could impose upon them, this did not stop members of the group from playing a leading role in the formation of pressure groups and parties. Perhaps more important, the need to educate a class of clerks and technical assistants of one sort or another led to the expansion of the educational system, and this was ultimately to produce people who chose not to go into administrative service, but into nationalist politics instead.[22]

Finally, there is little doubt that the bureaucratic theory introduced into East Africa by the administrative class strongly reinforced the tendency to favour large-scale monopolistic forms of organization, which emanated from the dominant expatriate economic groups. Two theories of economic organization confronted each other during the early colonial period. Classical liberal theory supported the evolution of a system of essentially unregulated competition which would have provided small entrepreneurs with the opportunity to operate freely, subject only to the constraints derived from the economic power disposed of by the large operators. In East Africa the social base for small-scale entrepreneurship was initially the Asian business community, but Africans were also beginning to move into this sphere by the twenties. On the other hand, an essentially bureaucratic approach to problems of economic organization saw competition as 'wasteful' and assumed that these problems could be solved through the application of 'rational' techniques to organizations which occupied monopoly positions. It attributed great virtue to size, assumed that only large organizations could provide efficient and modern services, and considered that the abuses deriving from monopoly power could be controlled through the supervision of the State, which it was thought could be relied on not to favour any particular party. The social base for this view was, of course, the large expatriate enterprise, where it served to justify the claims of settlers, processers and, subsequently, industrialists, to monopoly privileges. The bureaucracy, with its ideological roots in the Weberian tradition of scientific administration, and its social identification with the expatriate business and agricultural class, strongly supported this latter position; the more so because of its dislike of the Asian trading class, which it suspected of dishonesty, and of its desire to stop Africans from moving out of their traditional pursuits into the modern sphere. The end result was a tendency to intervene to substitute centralized bureaucratic controls for free competition on the market in virtually every sphere of economic life.[23]

This tendency has exerted a powerful influence over the subsequent evolution of the East African economy, which is still heavily influenced by its commitment to bureaucratic forms of centralized organization and hostility to the development of small-scale entrepreneurship through free access to the market. It began with the need to shelter expatriate capital from the small-scale competition of Asian or African entrepreneurs; it thereby created a structure in which almost the only channels of upward mobility were through these large-scale organizations which depended so directly upon administrative support. This meant that Africans, once they reached the point where they could move out of the agricultural sector, could only think of doing so by moving into these organizations, since the opportunities for entrepreneurship at levels which they could manage without assistance from the State had been so severely limited. The educational system, in its turn, was evolved to train Africans for these bureaucratic roles rather than for entrepreneurial ones by stressing academic rather than practical training which would have improved skills in agriculture, business and small-scale manufacturing. And the continued strength of this tendency, strongly reinforced by the continued dominance of the Western powers and the multi-national corporation, serves to perpetuate reliance on imported and capital-intensive technology and forms of organization. Instead of developing a strong entrepreneurial base in marketing, processing and manufacturing and thereby providing the basis for an organic growth of an indigenous capitalist class and a level of technology adapted to local circumstances, it ensured the dominance of imported capital and skills and hence continued dependence on the outside world. In this sense the bureaucracy was a primary agent in the creation of the contemporary state of underdevelopment in East Africa.

v. *The Dynamics of Dualistic Development*

It remains, at the risk of some repetition, to attempt an overall assessment of the impact of the colonial revolution upon the long-term evolution of East African society by relating the concrete material presented earlier to the wider theoretical debate about the nature of the developmental process. This material shows very clearly how colonialism accelerated the integration of African society into the system of international exchange dominated by the leading capitalist powers. It also shows how this system provided these societies with the infrastructure required for the simplest forms of export production and hence with a base for continued exchange with other sections of that system. But what are open to great differences of interpretation are the long-term developmental implications of this process from which diffusionist and differing brands of Marxist theory draw very different conclusions. Having presented my own version of the facts, it is now necessary for me to locate my own position in this larger debate.

It seems to me to be incontrovertible that Britain provided East Africa with the infrastructure for its initial step into the international economy on very favourable terms. A great deal in the way of transport and administrative overheads was given free, while subsequent administration was provided relatively economically and with an exceptional absence of the extortion and physical violence so characteristic of the colonial situation in many other places and periods. From this point of view the cases reviewed here present colonialism in its most favourable light. This should serve to protect my position from accusations of partiality and, equally, to strengthen all the criticisms to which the material nevertheless gives rise.

Although colonialism induced a rapid expansion of the cash economy in East Africa, it has also left behind an economy characterized by continuing and perhaps intensifying structural imbalances, massive and growing inequalities, apparently irreducible dependence on external sources of technological innovation, and a tendency towards political authoritarianism and instability.[24] These problems exist in differing degrees in each of the three countries, but none are qualitatively better off than the others, and few observers would predict a trouble-free progress towards something near to modernization for any of them. The origins of this situation have to be sought in the nature of the economic strategy imposed upon the region by the choices made by the dominant power groups which controlled it during the colonial period. This power structure required that primary production for the export market be started and it therefore imported the resources required to get this under way very quickly. In agriculture expatriate enterprise was able to monopolize a large percentage of the resources so created in some areas through the introduction of the plantation or settler systems; in many others African peasants were able to use them to raise their own level well above that which had existed before. Outside the agricultural sector, however, the expatriate monopoly was virtually complete, and the complementary nature of the needs of the British administration and those of the large firms made it possible for a powerful ideological consensus to develop which ensured that the full power of the State would be utilized to maintain this monopoly. The humanitarian groups in Britain were able to limit the worst excesses of exploitation in Kenya, but they showed no real understanding of the fundamental issues involved and were therefore totally incapable of influencing the total situation in any meaningful way. The effect of this monopoly, as we have seen, was to limit African mobility out of the most menial positions and hence to preclude the evolution of an entrepreneurial class of the classic capitalist kind. And the absence of this class in turn meant that the surplus would continue to be monopolized by these expatriate interests and therefore that the indigenous society would display that 'weak impulse to modernization'[25] displayed by so many post-colonial societies.

If this argument is accepted the optimistic diffusionist theories about development must be set aside. It suggests instead that the interests of many of the dominant expatriate groups in the Third World conflict very directly with the evolution of autonomous indigenous forces capable of lifting their societies out of their conditions of underdevelopment. Taken to its logical conclusion it leads instead to Frank's assertion that underdevelopment is the product of contact with the international capitalist system, and that it will only be overcome when the linkages created during the colonial period are broken off entirely. But while this material certainly contradicts the theorists who assume that development could follow a simple intensification of the contacts between the developed and the underdeveloped regions, it also seems to contradict some crucial assumptions in the latter position.

In the first place, it is clear that African society was only partially integrated into the capitalist system. In this respect Laclau is correct in pointing out that the creation of relations of servile dependency do not constitute the evolution of the capitalist system proper, but only a bastardized version of it. This in turn implies that the class basis for a socialistic opposition to that system in the form of an urban or even a rural proletariat will not have been fully developed through the colonial process. Instead we have the development of a system characterized by capitalist modes of production in a limited number of areas taken over by expatriate enterprise. These dominated the market economy, but the persistence of peasant production in this sector limited the accumulation of capital and emergence of an authentic working class even here. This cash sector then co-existed with an essentially pre-capitalist subsistence sector, which provided it with a source of labour during periods of such limited expansion as was to occur, and served as a refuge from unemployment when it was not required. This fact therefore implies that the classical capitalistic revolution had hardly begun to work itself out and that no genuine basis had been created for a socialist revolution of the kind that Frank assumes to be possible for Latin America.

A second problem of the far left position is the difficulty which it has in explaining the emergence of those elements in local society which did come forward in the post-war period to organize the nationalist movement. If colonialism simply extracted resources from the periphery and contributed nothing to the development of indigenous political structures it is highly unlikely that any local elements would ever be able to organize any form of resistance to it. But as Marx showed, the imperial presence performed a double function – its exploitation broke down local structures, but its needs also required the evolution of new classes in indigenous society capable of eventually creating the nationalism which would ultimately come to question this external dominance. Previous sections have pointed to the areas where such development was possible even within the constraints of British policy in East Africa. The development of peasant production produced the resources required to sustain an educational system and to produce a small but nevertheless critically important group with primary, secondary and even tertiary education by the forties and fifties. Clerical employment in the administration, the educational system itself, and private business, justified these investments and also produced some of the skills required for political organization. Despite the limits of the system, some opportunities for petty trade did exist for Africans; perhaps more significantly, the limits on trade led to the emergence in many areas of African co-operatives, which served to provide a pool of organizational experience which could subsequently be transferred to nationalistic purposes. In the urban sector the prevailing Fabian assumptions about the treatment of colonial labour combined with an essentially capital-intensive approach to development created a labour aristocracy which was allowed to evolve a trade-union structure which served the same functions as the co-operatives did in the countryside. From all these groups emerged an African élite, the direct product of the changes induced by the colonial system, and capable of exercising at least some of the skills required for political organization in the modern sector. And whatever the limits of this élite resulting from the weak articulation of the African entrepreneurial class, its continued existence and evolution depended upon the maintenance of at least some of the link with the outside world.

Further, the classic colonial system created not only the group which was to be responsible for the organization of the movement which led to its replacement, but also for the popular hostility to its presence which enabled the élite to mobilize a wide range of the population behind nationalist demands in the more advanced regions. We have seen how this process differed in the peasant as opposed to the settler areas, but the end result was not altogether dissimilar. Again it is important to note that the evolution of opposition was a function of contact with colonialism and not of distance from its effects, since mobilization was most intense in the most developed cash-crop-producing areas and hardly occurred at all in the areas out of touch with the cash economy which connected the colonial periphery with the metropolitan centre. This, too, leads us to a view which is rather different from Frank's and much closer to classical Marxist assumptions about the dialectical nature of the evolution of opposition movements through direct exposure to the contradictions created by processes of capitalistic exploitation.

On the other hand, what has already been said about the weak development of the capitalist system in the colonial context and most especially about its tendency to lock large sectors of the indigenous society into conditions of pre-capitalistic dependence is of great importance in explaining the relative weakness of the nationalist response when it did occur. In this respect Frank and Frantz Fanon[26] are certainly right to point to the limited nature of the demands made by the national bourgeois class, and their inability in the post-colonial situation to provide an effective basis for an autonomous rather than a neo-colonial developmental strategy. This suggests that although Marx's general assumptions about the necessary connection between colonial exploitation and the ultimate emergence of a regenerated local society are basically correct, the obstacles to the full realization of this local potential are much larger than he assumed. While colonialism necessarily broke down traditional structures, it was also capable of using its very considerable resources to inhibit the emergence of alternative forces capable of challenging its fundamental dominance, particularly in the economic and cultural spheres. Further, the contemporary substitution of various forms of indirect control for the classical colonial system continues to impose powerful limitations on the effective development of Third World society.

This study has considered some of the factors which have made this possible; it also implies that only profound changes in social and political structures will make it possible to initiate a self-sustaining growth process. Thus, while some aspects of Frank's analysis must be rejected, those parts of it which relate to the need to change the present basis on which exchanges take place between the developed and the underdeveloped areas must be fully accepted. What is required is not a process involving total separation, but one in which indigenous social forces are able to create a political basis which is strong enough to enable them to change the terms on which these cumulatively unequal exchanges now take place. The establishment of new systems of government based upon the nationalist movements of the forties and fifties was a necessary step in this direction, but the weakness of their social and economic base has limited the changes which they have been able to induce in the structure of the colonial political economy. The contemporary East African governments have adopted increasingly divergent strategies in order to attempt to solve this problem; all of them face great difficulties and, in all probability, the intensification of internal conflict as they do so. There is no point in attempting to predict the outcome of these efforts, or to look in detail at their differences, since this would take us too far afield. What this does suggest, however, is that the process of social differentiation inside these societies will have to proceed much further before an effective base will emerge for a popularly based and genuinely radical attack upon the problems which now beset them. This study has attempted to look at the events which served to create the framework within which this struggle is to take place and thereby to improve our understanding of how it should be conducted. More specific prescriptions with respect to contemporary strategies must depend upon a closer examination of the dynamics of the contemporary situation.

NOTES

1. R. Pares, 'The economic factor in the history of the Empire', *Econ. Hist. Review*, vol. VII, 2, May 1937, p. 144.
2. A. G. Frank, 'Dialectic not dual society', in *Latin America, Underdevelopment or Revolution*, New York, Monthly Review, 1969.
3. E. Laclau, 'Feudalism and capitalism in Latin America', *New Left Review*, 67, May–June 1971.
4. *Ibid.*, p. 31.
5. I am excluding mining since its total contribution in East Africa was relatively limited.
6. K. Marx, *Capital*, vol. I, part VIII, London, Allen & Unwin, 1958.
7. For an interesting attempt to examine the long-term implications of this process in Kenya cf. C. T. Leys, 'Politics in Kenya: the development of peasant society', *British Journal of Political Science*, vol. I, no. 3, 1971.
8. H. Myint, *Economic theory and the underdeveloped countries*, New York, O.U.P., 1971, p. 155.
9. G. Myrdal, *Asian drama*, London, Allen Lane, 1968, vol. I, pp. 447–53.
10. Cf. K. Post, *The new states of West Africa*, Harmondsworth, Penguin Books, 1964; T. L. Hodgkin, *Nationalism in colonial Africa*, London, Muller, 1956,
11. J. Nottingham and Carl G. Rosberg, *The myth of Mau Mau*, New York, Praeger, 1966, esp. p. 85.
12. R. Austen, *Northwestern Tanzania under German and British rule, op. cit.*; A. Maguire, *Towards Uhuru in Tanzania*, Cambridge, U.P., 1969.
13. Maguire, *op. cit.*, p. 82.
14. A. M. O'Connor, *Railways and development in Uganda*, Nairobi, O.U.P., 1965, p. 47.
15. *Ibid.*, p. 49.
16. *Ibid.*, pp. 139–40.
17. *Ibid.*, p. 149.
18. Lord Lugard, *The dual mandate in British Tropical Africa, op. cit.*, p. 215.
19. Tanganyika, *Native administration memoranda*, no. 1, 1930, p. 5.
20. R. A. Austen, *Northwestern Tanzania under German and British rule, op. cit.*, p. 254.
21. For an excellent examination of this problem, cf. L. A. Fallers, *Bantu bureaucracy*, Chicago, Univ. of Chicago Press, 1965.
22. On East Africa cf. Nottingham and Rosberg, *op. cit.*; R. A. Austen, 'Notes on the pre-history of TANU', *Makerere Journal*, no. 9 (March 1964); for a

good study of a West African case, J. S. Coleman, *Nigeria, background to nationalism*, Berkeley, Univ. of Calif. Press, 1958.

23. This tendency in East Africa is perhaps best examined by Cyril Ehrlich, especially in *The marketing of cotton in Uganda, 1900–1950*, London Ph.D. thesis, 1958, and 'Some social and economic implications of paternalism in Uganda', in *Journal of African history*, vol. IV, 1963.

24. For an examination of the Kenyan case cf. C. T. Leys, 'Politics in Kenya: the development of peasant society', *British Journal of Political Science*, vol. 1, no. 3, 1971.

25. Barrington Moore's phrase, *Social origins of dictatorship and democracy*, Boston, Beacon Press, 1966, p. xiii.

26. In *The wretched of the earth*, Harmondsworth, Penguin Books, 1967, chapter 3.

Bibliography

I. *Unpublished Sources*

Correspondence of Lord Altrincham, Governor of Kenya, 1925–30 (Private Collection).

Correspondence and Notebooks of Sir Sydney Henn, Chairman of the Joint East Africa Board (Private Collection).

Diary Notes [of a tour through] *Kenya, Uganda and Tanganyika, 1926*, by W. H. Himbury of the British Cotton Growing Association (Makerere College Library).

Joint East Africa Board:
  Minutes of Meetings, 1923–39.
  Minutes of Conferences with the Colonial Office, 1923–38.
  Correspondence and Memoranda (J.E.A.B. files).

Kenya, Nyanza Provincial Archives (selected references provided by Dr John Lonsdale).

Correspondence of Dr J. H. Oldham, Secretary of the International Missionary Council (consulted in the Library of Nuffield College, Oxford).

Tanganyika, Secretariat Minute Papers (selected references provided by Dr Ralph Austin).

Uganda Chamber of Commerce, *Minutes of Meetings*, 1919–38 (Makerere Library).

Uganda Company Limited:
  Minutes of Meetings of the Board of Directors, 1919–39.
  Annual Report of the Managing Director, 1934–9 (Makerere College Library).

Correspondence and papers of Col. C. W. G. Walker, Secretary to the Governors' Conference, 1926–36 (Private Collection).

Papers and Correspondence of Lord Passfield (Sydney Webb), Secretary of State for the Colonies 1929–31 (Private Collection, London School of Economics).

United Kingdom, *Cabinet Minutes and Cabinet Papers*, 1919–27.

II. *Official Publications*

(a) *United Kingdom*

Final Report of the Committee on Commercial and Industrial Policy after the War, Cd. 9035 of 1918.

Report to the Board of Trade of the Empire Cotton Growing Committee, Cmd. 523 of 1920.

West Indies, *Report of the Tropical Agriculture College Committee*, Cmd. 562 of 1920.

Despatch . . . relating to native labour in Kenya Colony, Cmd. 873 of 1920 (Milner Despatch).

First Annual Report of the Colonial Research Committee, for the period ended 31st December, 1920, Cmd. 1144 of 1921.

Report of the Committee on Research in the Colonies, appointed by the Secretary of State for the Colonies, Cmd. 1472 of 1921.

Despatch to . . . the Government of the Kenya Colony and Protectorate relating to Native Labour, Cmd. 1509 of 1921.

Report on the Railway Systems of Kenya, Uganda and Tanganyika, by F. D. Hammond, 1921.

Committee on National Expenditure, *Third Report*, Cmd. 1589 of 1922 (Geddes Committee).

Indians in Kenya, Cmd. 1922 of 1923.

Private Enterprise in British Tropical Africa, Cmd. 2016 of 1924.

Report of the East Africa Commission, Cmd. 2387 of 1924 (the Ormsby-Gore Commission).

Committee on Industry and Trade, *Memorandum on Transport Development and Cotton Growing in East Africa*, Cmd. 2463 of 1925.

Kenya, *Compulsory Labour for Government Purposes*, Cmd. 2464 of 1925.

Kenya, *Correspondence with the Government of Kenya relating to an exchange of land with Lord Delamere*, Cmd. 2500 of 1925.

Kenya, *Tours in the Native Reserves and Native Development in Kenya*, Cmd. 2573 of 1926.

Report of the East African Guaranteed Loan Committee, Cmd. 2701 of 1926 (Schuster Committee).

Imperial Shipping Committee, *Report on the Control and Working of Mombasa (Kilindini) Harbour, Kenya Colony*, Cmd. 2713 of 1926.

Empire Marketing Board, *Note on the Work of the Board* (Annual), 1926/27–1931/32.

—— *A Year's Progress* (Annual), 1927–33.

Future Policy in Regard to Eastern Africa, Cmd. 2904 of 1927.

Second Report of the Select Committee on Estimates, House of Commons, Cmd. 114 of 1928.

Report of the Commission on Closer Union of the Dependencies in Eastern and Central Africa, Cmd. 3234 of 1929.

A Summary of the Progress and Development of the Colonial Empire from November 1924 to November 1928, Cmd. 3268 of 1928–9.

Committee on Industry and Trade, *Final Report*, Cmd. 3282 of 1929.

—— Minutes of Evidence.

Report of Sir Samuel Wilson . . . on his visit to East Africa, Cmd. 3378 of 1929.

Second Report of the East African Guaranteed Loan Committee, Cmd. 3494 of 1930.

Colonial Development Advisory Committee Reports, Cmd. 3540 of 1930; 3876 of 1931; 4079 of 1932; 4316 of 1933; 4634 of 1934; 4916 of 1935; 5202 of 1936; 5537 of 1937; 5789 of 1938; 6062 of 1939; 6298 of 1941.

Memorandum on Native Policy in East Africa, Cmd. 3573 of 1930.

Statement of Conclusions of His Majesty's Government in the United Kingdom as regards Closer Union in East Africa, Cmd. 3574 of 1930.

Papers relating to the question of the Closer Union of Kenya, Uganda, and the Tanganyika Territory, Col. no. 57, 1931.

Memorandum on the measures proposed by His Majesty's Government to secure reductions in National Expenditure, Cmd. 3952 of 1931.

Joint Select Committee on Closer Union in East Africa:

Vol. I. *Report*, House of Lords 184 of 1931.

Vol. II. *Minutes of Evidence*, House of Lords 29 of 1930.

Vol. III. *Appendices*, House of Lords 29 of 1930.

Report by the Financial Commissioner (Lord Moyne) on certain Questions in Kenya, Cmd. 4093 of 1932.
Report by Sir Sydney Armitage-Smith . . . on a Financial Mission to Tanganyika, Cmd. 4182 of 1932.
Report by Mr Roger Gibb on Railway Rates and Finances in Kenya, Uganda, and Tanganyika Territory, Cmd. 4235 of 1932.
Imperial Economic Committee, *Hemp Fibres*, 24th Report, 1932.
Empire Marketing Board, *Sisal*, E.M.B. no. 64, 1933.
Report of the Kenya Land Commission, Cmd. 4556 of 1934 (Carter Commission).
Kenya Land Commission Report: Summary of Conclusions reached by His Majesty's Government, Cmd. 4580 of 1934.
Report of the Commission appointed to enquire into and report on the financial position and system of taxation of Kenya, Col. no. 116 of 1936 (Pim Report).
Higher Education in East Africa, *Report of the Commission*, Col. no. 142 of 1937.
Statement of Policy on Colonial Development and Welfare, Cmd. 6175 of 1940.
Colonial Office, *The Processing of Colonial Raw Materials; a study in location*, by Charlotte Leubuscher, 1951.
House of Commons, *Hansard*, 1919–39.
House of Lords, *Hansard*, 1919–39.
The Colonial Office List, 1919–39.

(b) *Local*

(i) *East Africa*
Proceedings of the Conference of East African Governors, 1930–6.
East African Transport Policy Board, *Report on Co-ordination of Transport in Kenya, Uganda and the Tanganyika Territory*, by Sir H. Osborne Mance, 1937.

(ii) *Kenya*
Annual Report, 1919–38.
Department of Agriculture, *Annual Reports, 1919–38.*
—— *Agricultural Census, 1924–30.*
Blue Book, 1919–38.
Legislative Council, *Debates, 1923–38.*
Native Affairs Department, *Annual Reports, 1919–38.*
Ordinances, 1919–38.
Railways, *Annual Reports, 1919–38.*
Report of the Economic Commission, 1919.
Report of the Port Commission of Enquiry, 1926.
Report of the Agricultural Commission, 1929.
Report of the Kenya Tariff Committee, 1929.
Report of the Expenditure Advisory Committee, 1933.
Report of the Select Committee on Economy, 1934.
Report of the Economic Development Committee, 1935.

(iii) *Tanganyika*
Annual Reports, 1921–38.
Department of Agriculture, *Annual Reports, 1926–38.*
Government Gazette, 1926–38.
Ordinances, 1922–38.

Legislative Council, *Proceedings, 1926–38.*
Report . . . upon Labour in the Tanganyika Territory, with a covering Despatch from the Governor, 1926.
Report of the Tanganyika Railway Commission, 1930.
Native Administration Memoranda: Principles of Native Administration, 2nd ed., 1930.
Report of the Committee . . . on . . . the supply and welfare of Native Labour, 1938.

(iv) *Uganda*

Annual Reports, 1919–38.
Department of Agriculture, *Annual Reports, 1919–38.*
Blue Book, 1919–38.
Government Gazette, 1919–38.
Legislative Council, *Summary of Proceedings, 1921–38.*
Report of the Commission of Enquiry into the Cotton Industry of Uganda, 1929 (Carter Commission).
Report of the Cotton Committee, 1936.
Report of the Uganda Cotton Commission, 1938.

III. *Publications of Private Bodies*

Chamber of Shipping, *Annual Reports, 1919–39.*
Conservative Party, *Gleanings and Memoranda, 1919–33.*
—— *Politics in Review, 1934–9.*
Empire Economic Union, *A plan of action, 1932.*
—— *Report dealing with tariffs and treaties, most favoured nation clause – duties* vs. *quotas, 1933.*
—— *Future fiscal policy, 1935.*
—— *Further considerations on economic policy, 1936.*
—— *The fiscal situation today, 1937.*
Empire Industries Association, *Memorandum for . . . the Imperial Economic Conference at Ottawa,* by H. Page Croft (n.d.).
Empire Cotton Growing Corporation, *Report of the Executive Committee, 1922, 1924.*
—— *Report of the Annual General Meeting, 1922, 1923.*
—— *Report of the Administrative Council, 1923–39.*
—— *The Extension of Cotton Cultivation in Tanganyika Territory,* by Hastings Horne, 1922.
—— *Report of the Cotton Growing Industry in Uganda, Kenya and the Mwanza district of Tanganyika,* by C. N. French, 1925.
—— *Inspection note on the Kenya Cotton Crop in November and December 1935,* by S. Milligan, 1936.
Federation of British Industries, *Annual Reports, 1918–19, 1921–2.*
—— *Resources of the Empire,* 10 vols., 1924.
—— *Industry and the Nation, 1931.*
—— *Industry and the Empire, 1931.*
—— *Report on Empire Monetary and Financial Policy,* with the Empire Economic Union, 1931.
—— 'Principles of an Industrial Tariff', in *A plan of action,* by the Empire Economic Union (q.v.).
—— *British Commercial Policy, 1934.*
—— *A new British Financial Policy: Industry's Plan, 1932.*
—— *Survey of Britain's recent Commercial Policy, 1935.*

Joint East Africa Board (J.E.A.B.), *Annual Reports, 1924–39.*
—— *Mandates,* 1936.
London Chamber of Commerce, *Annual Reports of the Council,* 1919–39.
—— *Memorandum adopted at a Joint Meeting . . . for submission to the Private Enter-prise Committee (Colonial Office),* 1923.
Liverpool Chamber of Commerce, *Monthly Journal,* 1919–25.
Manchester Chamber of Commerce, *Monthly Journal,* 1919–39.
—— *Annual Reports,* 1919–39.
Uganda Herald, 1919–38.

IV. *Secondary Sources*
Aaronovitch, S. and K., *Crisis in Kenya,* London, Lawrence & Wishart, 1947.
Altrincham, Lord, *Kenya's opportunity,* London, Faber, 1955.
Amery, L. S. M., *National and imperial economics,* Westminster, National Unionist Assoc., 1924.
—— *Empire and prosperity,* London, Faber, 1931.
—— *My political life,* vols. II and III, London, Hutchinson, 1953–5.
Archer, Sir G., *Personal and historical memoir of an East African administrator,* Edin-burgh, Oliver and Boyd, 1963.
Ashworth, W., *An economic history of England, 1870–1939,* London, Methuen, 1960.
Austen, R. A., *Northwestern Tanzania under German and British rule,* New Haven, Yale U.P., 1968.
—— 'Towards a pre-history of TANU', in *Makerere Journal,* no. 9 (March 1964).
Bates, M., *Tanganyika under British administration,* Ph.D. thesis, Oxford Univer-sity, 1957.
Bennett, G., 'The development of political organisations in Kenya', in *Political studies,* v. (2), June 1957.
—— *Kenya, a political history,* London, O.U.P., 1964.
—— 'Settlers and politics in Kenya', in Harlow, V. T. and Chilver, E. M., *History of East Africa,* vol. II (q.v.).
Bourdillon, Sir B., *The future of the colonial empire,* London, S.C.M. Press, 1945.
Buell, R. L., *The native problem in Africa,* 2 vols., New York, Macmillan, 1928.
Bullock, A. L., *The life and times of Ernest Bevin,* vol. 1, London, Heinemann, 1960.
Cameron, Sir Donald, *My Tanganyika service and some Nigeria,* London, Allen & Unwin, 1939.
Carter, F. V., *Education in Uganda,* Ph.D. thesis, London University, 1967.
Chidzero, B. T., *Tanganyika and international trusteeship,* London, O.U.P., 1961.
Croft, H. P., *My life and strife,* London, Hutchinson, 1948.
Cunliffe-Lister, Sir Philip, *see* Swinton, Lord.
Dilley, M. R., *British policy in Kenya colony,* New York, Nelson, 1937.
Dundas, Sir C., *African crossroads,* London, Macmillan, 1955.
Eden, Sir A., Lord Avon, *The Eden Memoirs; facing the Dictators,* London, Cassell, 1960.
Ehrlich, C., *The Uganda Company Limited,* Kampala, Uganda Company, 1953.
—— *The marketing of cotton in Uganda, 1900–1950,* Ph.D. thesis, London Univer-sity, 1958.
—— 'Some social and economic implications of paternalism in Uganda', in *Journal of African history,* vol. IV, 1963.

—— 'The Uganda economy, 1903–1945', in Harlow, V. T. and Chilver, E. M., *History of East Africa*, vol. II (q.v.).

Fage, J. D. and Oliver, R., *A short history of Africa*, Harmondsworth, Penguin Books, 1962.

Fearn, H., *An African economy*, London, O.U.P., 1961.

Ford, V. C. R., *The trade of Lake Victoria*, Kampala, E.A.I.S.R., 1955.

Frankel, S. H., *Capital investment in Africa*, London, O.U.P., 1938.

Furse, Sir R., *Aucuparius: recollections of a recruiting officer*, London, O.U.P., 1962.

Gillman, C., 'A short history of the Tanganyika Railways', in *Tanganyika Notes and Records*, 1942.

Grigg, Sir Edward, *see* Altrincham, Lord.

Hailey, W. M., *An African survey*, Revised 1956. London, O.U.P., 1957.

Hancock, W. K., *Survey of British Commonwealth affairs*, vol. I, *Problems of nationality*, London, O.U.P., 1937.

—— *Survey of British Commonwealth affairs*, vol. II, *Problems of economic policy*, London, O.U.P., 1940.

—— *Wealth of colonies*, Cambridge, U.P., 1950.

Harlow, V. T. and Chilver, E. M., [*Oxford*] *history of East Africa*, vol. II, Oxford, Clarendon Press, 1965.

Heussler, R., *Yesterday's rulers: the making of the British Colonial Service*, Syracuse, U.P., 1963.

Hill, M. F., *Permanent way*, vol. I, *The story of the Kenya and Uganda Railway*, Nairobi, East African Railways and Harbours, 1949.

—— *Permanent way*, vol. II, *The story of the Tanganyika Railways*, Nairobi, E.A.R. & H., 1957.

Hobson, J. A., *Imperialism: a study*, 1902, London, Allen & Unwin, 1902.

Hubbard, G. E., *Eastern industrialisation and its effects on the West*, London, O.U.P., 1935.

Huxley, E., *White man's country*, vol. II, 1914–31, London, Macmillan, 1935.

Huxley, E. and Perham, M., *Race and politics in Kenya*, London, Faber, 1944.

Huxley, J., *African view*, London, Chatto and Windus, 1931.

Ilersic, A. R. and Liddle, P. F., *Parliament of commerce; the story of the Association of British Chambers of Commerce*, London, A. of B.C. of C., 1960.

Ingham, K., *The making of modern Uganda*, London, Allen & Unwin, 1958.

Karimi, S. K., *Changing political institutions in East Africa*, M.A. thesis, London University, 1960.

Kennedy, T. A., 'The East African Customs Union', in *Makerere Journal*, no. 3, 1959.

Kenyatta, J., *Facing Mount Kenya*, London, Secker and Warburg, 1938.

Koebner, R., 'The concept of Economic Imperialism', in *Econ. Hist Review*, vol. II, 1949.

Leubuscher, C., *Tanganyika territory: a study of economic policy under mandate*, London, O.U.P., 1944.

Leys, N., *Kenya*, London, Hogarth Press, 1924.

—— *A last chance in Kenya*, London, Hogarth Press, 1931.

Lugard, Sir F. D., *The dual mandate in British tropical Africa*, Edinburgh, Blackwood, 1922.

McGregor Ross, W., *see* Ross, W. McGregor.

McWilliam, M., *The East African Tea Industry, 1920 to 1950*, B.Phil. thesis, Oxford University, 1957.

Maguire, G. A., *Towards Uhuru in Tanzania*, Cambridge, U.P., 1969.

Mair, L., *An African people in the twentieth century*, London, Routledge, 1934.

—— *Native policies in Africa*, London, Routledge, 1936.

Meyer, P., *Britain's colonies in world trade*, London, O.U.P., 1948.

Milner, Lord, 'Crown colonies', in *The Nation and the Empire*, London, Constable, 1913.

Mitchell, Sir Philip, *African afterthoughts*, London, Hutchinson, 1954.

Newlyn, W. T. and Rowan, D. C., *Money and banking in British Colonial Africa*, Oxford, Clarendon Press, 1954.

O'Connor, A. M., *Railways and development in Uganda*, Nairobi, O.U.P., 1965.

Ormsby-Gore, W. G. M., *The development of our Empire in the Tropics*, Nottingham, no pub., 1927.

—— *Developments and opportunities in the Colonial Empire*, London, no pub., 1929.

Oliver, R., *The missionary factor in East Africa*, London, Longmans, 1952.

Oxford History of East Africa, see Harlow, V. T. and Chilver, E. M., [*Oxford*] *history of East Africa*.

Pares, R., 'The economic factors in the history of the Empire', in *Econ. Hist. Review*, 2nd series, VII, 1937.

Perham, M., *Lugard: the years of authority, 1895–1945*, London, Collins, 1960.

—— *The Colonial Reckoning*, London, Collins, 1961.

—— *Mining, commerce and finance in Nigeria*, London, Faber, 1946.

Powesland, P. G., *Economic policy and labour*, Kampala, E.A.I.S.R., 1957.

Pratt, R. C., 'Administration and politics in Uganda, 1919–1945', in Harlow, V. T. and Chilver, E. M., *History of East Africa*, vol. II (q.v.).

Ramchandani, R. R., *Asians' role in the cotton industry of Uganda*, Paper given to the Rural Development Research Programme, Makerere, 1965 (mimeo).

Redford, A. and Clapp, B. W., *Manchester merchants and foreign trade*, vol. II, 1850–1939, Manchester, U.P., 1956.

Robinson, K., *The dilemmas of trusteeship*, London, O.U.P., 1965.

Robinson, R. and Gallagher, J., *Africa and the Victorians*, London, Macmillan, 1961.

Ross, W. McGregor, *Kenya from within*, London, Allen & Unwin, 1927.

Royal Institute of International Affairs, *The Colonial Problem*, London, O.U.P., 1937.

Rowe, J. W., *The world's coffee*, H.M.S.O., 1963.

Smuts, J. C., *Africa and some world problems*, Oxford, Clarendon Press, 1930.

Stahl, K., *The Metropolitan Organisation of British Colonial Trade*, London, Faber, 1951.

Swinton, Lord, formerly Sir Philip Cunliffe-Lister, formerly Sir Philip Lloyd-Graeme, *I remember*, London, Hutchinson, 1948.

Thomas, H. B. and Scott, R., *Uganda*, London, O.U.P., 1935.

Tothill, J. D., *Agriculture in Uganda*, London, O.U.P., 1940.

Wrigley, C., *Crops and wealth in Uganda*, Kampala, E.A.I.S.R., 1959.

—— 'Kenya: the patterns of economic life, 1902–1945', in Harlow, V. T. and Chilver, E. M., *History of East Africa*, vol. II (q.v.).

Index